American Power and Policy

Edited by

Robert Leeson

First published 2009 by
PALGRAVE MACMILLAN

Palgrave Macmillan in the UK is an imprint of Macmillan Publishers Limited,
registered in England, company number 785998, of Houndmills, Basingstoke,
Hampshire RG21 6XS.

Palgrave Macmillan in the US is a division of St Martin's Press LLC,
175 Fifth Avenue, New York, NY 10010.

Palgrave Macmillan is the global academic imprint of the above companies
and has companies and representatives throughout the world.

Palgrave® and Macmillan® are registered trademarks in the United States,
the United Kingdom, Europe and other countries.

ISBN-13: 978–1–4039–4956–1   hardback

This book is printed on paper suitable for recycling and made from fully
managed and sustained forest sources. Logging, pulping and manufacturing
processes are expected to conform to the environmental regulations of the
country of origin.

A catalogue record for this book is available from the British Library.

A catalog record for this book is available from the Library of Congress.

10   9   8   7   6   5   4   3   2   1
18   17   16   15   14   13   12   11   10   09

Printed and bound in Great Britain by
CPI Antony Rowe, Chippenham and Eastbourne

Contents

Notes on Contributors   vii

1. Introduction   1
    Robert Leeson

2. American in the Shadows: Harry Dexter White
    and the Design of the International Monetary Fund   6
    James M. Boughton

3. Building up a Multilateral Strategy for the United States:
    Alvin Hansen, Jacob Viner, and the Council on
    Foreign Relations (1939–45)   24
    Sebastiano Nerozzi

4. A Hands-off Central Banker? Marriner S. Eccles and
    the Federal Reserve, 1934–51   69
    Matías Vernengo

5. The Great Inflation of the 1970s: Evidence from
    the Archives   91
    John Lodewijks and Robert Leeson

6. An Archival Case Study: Revisiting *The Life and
    Political Economy of Lauchlin Currie*   105
    Roger J. Sandilands

7. New Evidence on Allyn Young's Style and Influence
    as a Teacher   134
    Roger J. Sandilands

8. A Scholar in Action in Interwar America: John H. Williams
    on Trade Theory and Bretton Woods   180
    Pier Francesco Asso and Luca Fiorito

9. Shaping Monetary Constitutions for Developing
    Countries: Some Archival Evidence on the
    Bloomfield Missions to South Korea (1949–50)   243
    Michele Alacevich and Pier Francesco Asso

Name Index   267
Subject Index   274

Notes on Contributors

Michele Alacevich
Research Fellow
Department on Politics, Law and Society
University of Palermo
michele.alacevich@unipa.it

Pier Francesco Asso
Professor of History of Economics
University of Palermo
Department of European Studies and International Integration (DEMS)
pfasso@unipa.it

James M. Boughton
Historian
Development and Review Department
International Monetary Fund.
JBOUGHTON@imf.org

Luca Fiorito
Associate Professor of History of Economic Thought
University of Palermo
Department on Politics, Law and Society
lucafiorito@sciepol.unipa.it

Robert Leeson
Visiting Fellow
Hoover Institution
Stanford University
Adjunct Professor of Economics
Notre Dame Australia University
r.leeson@stanford.edu

John Lodewijks
Professor of Economics and Head of School
University of Western Sydney
j.lodewijks@uws.edu.au

Sebastiano Nerozzi
Researcher
University of Palermo
Department on Politics, Law and Society
Sebastiano.nerozzi@tele2.it

Roger J. Sandilands
Professor of Economics
University of Strathclyde
r.j.sandilands@strath.ac.uk

Matías Vernengo
Assistant Professor of Economics
University of Utah
vernengo@economics.utah.edu

1
Introduction

Robert Leeson

Having examined the structure of influence within the Keynesian and anti-Keynesian traditions (volumes 1 and 2 in the series Archival Insights into the Evolution of Economics), this volume focuses more directly on economists and the policy process. In the twentieth century, the United States replaced the United Kingdom as the center of both academic economics and the international economy. In the process, the position of the United States with regard to multinational bodies was transformed: from declining to be involved (League of Nations, 1920) to collaborative construction (Bretton Woods, 1944) to all the arrogance and anxieties of sole superpower status.

The chapters below highlight aspects of a multi-layered structure of influence within the policy process. They are primarily concerned with the nine economists associated with the birth of the International Monetary Fund (IMF) and the expanding influence (and independence) of the Federal Reserve System: Harry Dexter White, Lauchlin Currie, Alvin Hansen, Jacob Viner, Marriner Eccles, Arthur Okun, Allyn Abbott Young, John H. Williams and Arthur Bloomfield.

The first six will be familiar to many non-economists. White's plan underpinned the IMF; Currie was the first professional economist to work as a presidential adviser in the White House (a forerunner to the post-war position of chair of the President's Council of Economic Advisers, CEA). Hansen and Viner (presidents of the American Economic Association, Hansen in 1938 and Viner in 1939) were influential leaders of competing schools (Keynesian and Chicago, respectively). Eccles, the son of a rags-to-riches Mormon polygamist, was chair of the Fed (1935–48) during the period of the first stage of its (institutional) independence from the Treasury. Okun (after whom the 'Okun gap' – the gap between full employment output and actual output – was named) was chair of President Johnson's CEA.

The final three are less well known amongst non-economists, but were influential nonetheless. Young was important primarily for the influence he exerted over his students; Williams and Bloomfield were influential economists at the New York Fed (Williams was vice president and research director, and Bloomfield was chief economist of the Balance of Payments Division and then senior economist).

Hansen (the 'American Keynes') 'recruited' Keynesians via his Harvard Fiscal Policy Seminar (run jointly with John H. Williams); Viner 'recruited' students to the increasingly anti-Keynesian Chicago School via his University of Chicago price theory course. Viner, White, Currie and Williams were part of a remarkable group of policy-focused international economists who had been supervised at Harvard by Frank Taussig. In the depths of the Great Depression three of these 'Harvard boys' (White, Currie and P.T. Ellsworth) wrote a paper advocating deficit spending to combat the Depression. This paper, which remained unpublished for 70 years, undermines Milton Friedman's assertion about the uniqueness of the Chicago oral tradition. In his Harvard PhD thesis, Currie also blamed the Fed for the severity of the Great Depression (decades before Friedman and Anna Schwartz). Williams also advanced a similar thesis around the same time.

The deliberations about post-Second World War reconstruction reflected the new mid-century power structure. In Chapter 2, James M. Boughton, the official historian of the IMF, analyzes the competing forces that struggled for influence at the birth of that institution. At Bretton Woods in 1944, White and the Americans dominated; John Maynard Keynes and the British were unable to prevail.

In 1934, Viner recruited White and Currie to President Roosevelt's Treasury. (White was, successively, chief of the newly created Division of Monetary Research, head of International Economic Policy and finally assistant secretary). President Truman appointed White the first US executive director of the IMF in January 1946. But White abruptly left this position in June 1947 after suffering two heart attacks. White and Currie were accused of being Soviet agents. On 13 August 1948, White testified before Richard Nixon and a hostile House Un-American Activities Committee. Three days later he died of a further heart attack.

During the Second World War, it was by no means certain that the United States would accept or embrace the new post-war position implied by the Bretton Woods agreement. In 'Building up a Multilateral Strategy for the United States' Sebastiano Nerozzi (Chapter 3) explores the process by which Viner and Hansen shaped America's strategy for the post-war economic order.

At the end of the twentieth century, two related traumas (the inflation of the 1970s and the disinflationary costs of the 1980s) created a constituency for inflation targeting and central bank independence. In New Zealand, Canada, Australia, Britain, the countries of the European Union and elsewhere, economists successfully sought to insulate monetary policy from overt political influences. Previously, monetary policy had tended to produce a political business cycle rather than macroeconomic stability.

The Federal Reserve System was created in 1913, in the teeth of significant opposition. Eccles (and Currie, his personal assistant) drafted the 1935 Banking Act which created the current structure of the Fed; Eccles was the first chairman of the Board of Governors of the Fed. However, 4 March 1951 is regarded as the Fed's true 'Independence Day' (Hetzel and Leach, 2001).

The process by which the Fed gained control of monetary policy is as worthy of scrutiny as that other Declaration of Independence, 175 years before. Roosevelt appointed Eccles chair of the Fed: the expectation was that he would be effectively assistant secretary of the Treasury for monetary affairs. Matías Vernengo (Chapter 4) examines Eccles's contributions to the struggles over Fed independence.

Eccles played a pivotal role in the Keynesian policy revolution; he was an advocate of fiscal expansion and 'orderly' interest rates (virtually fixed at a low level). Accommodating monetary policy – 'the peg' – facilitated the policy of cheap Treasury borrowings by keeping debt-servicing expenses low. Cheap money facilitated the recovery of the 1930s and the financing of the war; but inflation began to emerge as a serious post-war issue. Eccles's concerns about inflation led him to propose tax increases: in 1948 President Truman declined to re-appoint him as Fed chair, appointing instead Thomas McCabe.

The Cold War, and the Korean War (1950–53) in particular, enabled Truman to associate the monetary policy peg with patriotism and its abandonment with 'what Mr. Stalin wants' (Hetzel and Leach, 2001, p. 40). Truman was confronted with both an independent and recalcitrant General Douglas MacArthur in Korea and a Fed in Washington increasingly determined to exercise monetary independence. Almost simultaneously, Truman fired General MacArthur and replaced McCabe with William McChesney Martin. But Martin negotiated the 4 March 1951 'accord' between the Treasury and the Fed and revealed himself to be more independently minded than Truman had anticipated. The modern Fed was born.

President Nixon replaced Martin with Arthur Burns as Fed chair. During Burns's tenure (1970–78), the consumer price index rose by over 72 percent. American political and military power appeared to be waning as stagflation undermined her economic power. The Old Keynesian-fiscalist school was associated with this 'national malaise' and yielded influence to Friedman and the Chicago School as a consequence. Gregory N. Mankiw (George W. Bush's CEA chair 2002–05) attributes this loss of influence to a Keynesian complacency about inflation. Yet Burns and the Fed controlled monetary policy: neither Keynesians nor monetarists were responsible for these outcomes.

Some Old Keynesians saw benefits from inflation (in terms of supposedly lower unemployment) – others did not. For example, John Lodewijks and Robert Leeson (Chapter 5) examine the contributions of President Johnson's CEA chair, Arthur Okun in this respect. The archival evidence illuminates Okun's position: in 1975 he wrote to John Hicks that 'Among American Keynesians, I have been nearly alone in regarding the inflation problem as real rather than as merely a figment of imagination or money illusion among the unsophisticated masses.'

Roger Sandilands (Chapter 6) examines the career of the acknowledged leader of the 'spending wing' of the New Deal, Lauchlin Currie. In 1939, Roosevelt 'poached' Currie from the Fed and in 1941 put him in charge of the Chinese component of America's Lend-Lease program (a program designed to keep Nationalist China from falling to Japan). After 1949, Currie was one of the many 'China hands' who were blamed for 'losing' China to the Communists. As a PhD student at Harvard, Currie had been strongly influenced by Allyn Abbott Young, and in Chapter 7 Roger Sandilands examines Young's pervasive influence on this generation of economists.

Pier Francesco Asso and Luca Fiorito (Chapter 8) analyze Williams's contributions to post-war reconstruction. In cooperation with the Taussig group in the Roosevelt administration, Williams advocated the establishment of a tripartite exchange rate stability agreement with France and Great Britain. This evolved into the 'key currency' idea which initially competed with the Keynes and the White Bretton Woods Plans. The US Treasury and the Federal Reserve attempted to prevent Williams from criticizing White's plan. At the request of Treasury secretary Henry Morganthau, Fed chair Eccles asked the Fed's Board of Governor's to dismiss Williams because 'his part time job [as vice president and research director] left him free to make public statements'.

In 'Shaping Monetary Constitutions for Developing Countries' Michele Alacevich and Pier Francesco Asso (Chapter 9) describe one of the Federal Reserve's missions to advise various third world countries about their monetary constitutions: that of Bloomfield in South Korea (1949–50). After graduating from Chicago, Bloomfield was a research economist at the New York Fed (where Williams was his mentor). He co-authored the Act establishing the Bank of Korea in a situation of extreme political and economic instability: the slide towards civil war (June 1950).

These chapters illustrate an important proposition: the subterranean world of economics and public policy provides numerous insights into the process by which our subject is constructed and our influence disseminated. Unpublished archival evidence illuminates this subterranean world. The market for influence is as worthy of attention as the other markets that economists have traditionally examined.

Reference

Hetzel, R. and R. Leach, 2001, 'The Treasury-Fed Accord: a New Narrative Account,' *Federal Reserve Bank of Richmond Economic Quarterly*, 87(1)(Winter): 33–55.

2
American in the Shadows: Harry Dexter White and the Design of the International Monetary Fund

James M. Boughton

The charter for the International Monetary Fund (IMF) was drawn up in stages, starting in 1941 and culminating in an international conference held at Bretton Woods, New Hampshire, in July 1944. The discussions and the drafting were led by John Maynard Keynes, the head of the British delegation at Bretton Woods, and by Harry Dexter White, the principal member of the US delegation. Keynes's role in the process is well established through his published writing, his collected correspondence, and numerous memoirs and biographies.[1] White's role, in contrast, has long been obscured by the fragmentary state of his own documentation and by the fact that he was the leader of a team of US Treasury economists rather than a clearly dominant actor. To isolate his personal contribution requires delving into archival records with some diligence.

Establishing White's contribution to the design of the IMF is important for at least three reasons. First, without a full understanding of White's role, it is impossible to properly assess that of Keynes. Since Keynes – easily the most famous and iconic economist of the twentieth century – continues to be the subject of endless analysis and controversy, simply regarding White as an input to Keynesiana is sufficient reason to undertake the task. Second, the IMF has become the leading international financial institution in the world and a major object of scrutiny and controversy. An understanding of the intellectual and political origins of the institution is essential for a fair and accurate assessment of its role and history. Third, White himself is a far more important figure in the history of economic thought than is generally recognized. Since the design of the IMF was his greatest practical contribution, it is worth taking the trouble to trace the steps that he took.

2.1 Harry Dexter White

White's contributions as an economist are obscure because he spent almost all of his professional life either in the US Treasury or in the IMF. Moreover, that career was short – just 13 years from his arrival at the Treasury in 1934 to his premature retirement from the IMF in 1947 – owing to a late start in his education and to his life being cut short by ill-health. White was born in Boston in 1892 to Jewish immigrant parents from what was then the Lithuanian region of the Russian empire. As a young man, Harry White (he would add 'Dexter' as a middle name only later) worked in one of the family hardware stores and then served in the US Army during the Great War. Only then did he devote himself to higher education. He graduated from Stanford University in 1924 and then went to Harvard for graduate studies in economics. By the time he completed his PhD at Harvard, he was 38 years old. On the strength of his outstanding record as a student – his dissertation won the university's David Wells Prize and was published by Harvard University Press (White, 1933) – he was able to stay at Harvard as an instructor in the economics department for another year, after which he accepted a position as associate professor at Lawrence College in Wisconsin.

The critical moment in Harry White's career came soon thereafter, in 1934, when Jacob Viner asked White to work for him at the Treasury in Washington. The initial offer was for a three-month project analyzing the effects of the January 1934 increase in the dollar price of gold. That job segued into a permanent position as an economist in the Division of Research and Statistics, which was headed by George C. Haas. White quickly progressed up the bureaucratic ladder, eventually becoming assistant secretary (then the chief policy position under the secretary) of the Treasury. After the IMF agreement was ratified at the end of 1945, President Harry S. Truman named White to be the first US executive director at the Fund. White's health then deteriorated rapidly, and he resigned just over a year later, after suffering a heart attack while on an IMF mission with Robert Triffin and other staff in Ecuador. He then worked intermittently as a consultant on central banking and monetary policy issues, mainly for the Mexican central bank, until his death from a third heart attack in 1948.[2]

As this biographical sketch suggests, Harry Dexter White's canon of publications was quite small. Aside from his dissertation, he contributed to the third edition of Frank Taussig's classic book on tariffs and trade protection (Taussig, 1931), wrote a review essay on Haberler and Ohlin for the *Quarterly Journal of Economics* (White, 1934), and wrote three articles on currency stabilization and the IMF (White, 1943, 1945, and 1947).[3] Only his dissertation gives any inkling of his economic philosophy (see Flanders, 1990, pp. 236–41), and it was written before White really developed as an economist. Consequently, to understand the extent to which his thinking was innovative and ahead of the mainstream of the profession, and what he contributed to the evolution of economic institutions, one must turn to the archives.[4]

2.2   The archives

The best-known and most readily accessible archive on White is the collection of Harry Dexter White papers in the Seeley G. Mudd Manuscript Library at Princeton University.[5] This collection of 13 boxes of documents written from 1930 to 1948 was donated to Princeton by White's widow, Anne Terry White. It comprises the papers that were in his possession when he died. It is therefore neither a comprehensive nor a systematic introduction to White's writings, but it does serve as a useful introduction by suggesting what he probably felt was worth saving. For example, it includes a paper that he and fellow students Lauchlin Currie and P.T. Ellsworth prepared (but never published) while studying at Harvard in 1932, advocating a policy of deficit spending to combat the Depression. As Laidler and Sandilands (2002) have shown, the paper is prescient in arguing for a comprehensive package of expansionary monetary and fiscal policies as a way of maintaining macroeconomic stability.

A second and more systematic archive of White's papers is in the US National Archives at College Park, Maryland.[6] This collection comprises 21 boxes, the first 13 of which are a chronological file maintained by White's secretarial staff at the Treasury from 1934 to 1946. The materials include memoranda and other internal papers drafted by White or his staff, most of which were sent to the Secretary of the Treasury, Henry Morgenthau, Jr. The last eight boxes contain related staff memoranda and records of meetings in which White participated at the Treasury. As a record of White's thinking about economic policy, however, the key materials are in the first two boxes, which cover 1934–39. In March 1938, White was promoted to chief of the newly created Division of Monetary Research. From that date on, most of the memoranda produced in the division were drafted initially by his staff. White normally approved and signed the documents before sending them to the secretary, and in many cases he redrafted them to some extent, but only the final documents have been preserved. White's own contribution therefore cannot be isolated. Before he became division chief, White was often the original author, and his own thinking emerges more clearly.

The third archive for this purpose is the Institutional Repository of the International Monetary Fund in Washington, DC.[7] This archive, which has been open for public use since 1994, includes materials pertaining to the preparatory work for the Bretton Woods conference, ratification of the Articles of Agreement by the United States and other original member states, and the work of the IMF thereafter. Some of this material – notably two drafts of White's plan and two of Keynes's plan for the IMF – was published as a supplementary volume in Keith Horsefield's (1969) history of the origins and early years of the IMF. Some items, however, including a 1948 scheme that White drew up to rectify the inadequacy of funding for the IMF,[8] remain unpublished.

2.3 The design of the IMF

What can we learn from these archives about White's contributions to the original design of the IMF? That design[9] included several features that either were new to the international financial system or that restored practices that had been lost or diminished since the start of the Great War in 1914:

- International trade was to be based on a gold exchange standard, with exchange rates to be fixed in relation to gold and with stocks of gold to be held by governments or central banks as monetary reserves.
- The US dollar was to be the de facto core currency in the system. From the outset, official holdings of dollars would serve as a second form of monetary reserves, the dollar would be the primary vehicle for settling international payments, and most states would determine the par values of their currencies in relation to the dollar rather than in relation to the equivalent gold content of the dollar. Over time, other currencies would become strong enough to supplement dollars for these purposes.
- Exchange rates were to be 'fixed but adjustable,' with large changes in rates being acceptable only to correct a 'fundamental disequilibrium' in international payments. The IMF was to be the arbiter of whether such a correction was appropriate, although its powers to sanction member states for unapproved changes were limited.
- The IMF was to serve as a central repository for a portion of each member state's gold and foreign exchange (mainly US dollar) reserves,

with the amount to be deposited based on a quota formula linked to the country's output and international trade.

- To help member states cope with disequilibria that were less than fundamental, the IMF was to stand prepared to make this pool of resources temporarily available to any member that needed funds to finance a deficit in current payments, in amounts that were limited in relation to the member's quota, subject to interest charges and other fees. Although these transactions were the exact financial equivalent of loans, they were legally distinct from loans in that there was no loan contract. Instead, the borrower would 'purchase' foreign exchange from the IMF in exchange for its own currency and then later 'repurchase' its currency with the foreign exchange.

Each of these features had a specified purpose aimed at helping promote the growth of international trade and the stability of international payments. The overall aim was to restore multilateral trade and payments and open competition after a long era of disruptions characterized by autarky, bilateral arrangements, and mercantilism. In broad perspective, these goals were widely shared during the Second World War among economists and officials in all of the leading allied countries. The detailed strategy, however, involving questions of sequencing and timing, affected vital national interests and raised serious controversies.

In 'fighting for Britain,' to adopt Robert Skidelsky's phrase, Keynes was seeking to create an institution that would provide maximum financing automatically in support of a British economic recovery from the devastation of the war. At the same time, he was seeking to delay the dismantling of the Commonwealth's preferential trading system and the release of blocked sterling balances held in countries within the sterling currency area. White and his American colleagues were aiming for a more rapid move to a fully open multilateral trading system and for more limited and controlled access to financing of payments deficits (see Boughton, 2004).

The fact that White won virtually all of his key battles with Keynes over the design of the IMF obviously reflects the vastly stronger economic position of the United States at the close of the war. Nonetheless, the shape and strength of White's arguments were not just a product of his time and place. They also reflected his personal development as an economist both at Harvard and in the Treasury (Boughton, 2002). To understand the effects of that development on the IMF agreements, one must turn to the archives.

(a) The role of gold in the system

The Princeton archive includes two lengthy studies by White on the role of gold in the US and international monetary systems. The first, prepared in the space of a few months in 1934, is a 450-page treatise on the benefits for the US economy of adhering to the gold standard, conditional upon a willingness to adjust the price of gold in 'periods of stress.'[10] Written at a time when economists generally divided into advocates of a strict gold standard with fixed rates of exchange between currencies and those who favored fiat systems and managed rates, this essay – which was never circulated outside the Treasury – pointed toward an innovative middle road. Although the mechanics of this approach were still vague, it at least prefigured the 'fixed but adjustable' gold exchange standard that was a centerpiece of the IMF design that emerged from Bretton Woods a decade later.[11]

White returned to this topic in the early 1940s, at the same time as he was developing his detailed plan for the IMF. Over the space of some four years, apparently writing in his spare time, White produced a manuscript of around 300 pages that he called 'The Future of Gold.' The manuscript at Princeton is the only known version, but it is not a finished draft, and there is no way of knowing whether White ever intended to publish it. It fleshes out his earlier ideas on a state-contingent monetary policy based flexibly on gold, and it might have been influential had White not abandoned it in 1944.[12]

While the Princeton archives are valuable principally for uncovering the development of White's views on the role of gold and the adjustable peg, the National Archives offer a trove of information on various aspects of the design of the IMF. These include the necessity for broad international agreements as a replacement for the bilateral diplomacy of the 1930s, the possibility of extending credit to countries without engaging in formal loan contracts, and the necessity for capital controls as a backup plan for limiting the inherent instability of an open multilateral trading system.

(b) The necessity of multilateral agreements

The last general attempt at multilateral cooperation on international finance before the Second World War was the World Economic Conference, held in London in 1933. That effort broke down over disputes on how comprehensive an agreement was needed (Clarke, 1973). After that failure, the most notable cooperative effort was the Tripartite Agreement between the United States, the United Kingdom, and France in September 1936. Although that agreement probably prevented the devaluation of the French franc from leading to a spiral of compensating devaluations by Britain and other countries, it did not engender a lasting framework for further cooperation. That gap was not filled until the establishment of the IMF at the end of the war. What role did White play in advancing this agenda?

White's entry into international financial diplomacy came on his first overseas trip, when the US Treasury sent him to London in May 1935 for meetings with British Treasury officials. This trip was precipitated by concerns that the British were about to allow the pound sterling to depreciate markedly. White's analysis indicated that the prevailing rate of $4.86 was not overvalued, and he and his colleagues were worried that a depreciation would overshoot and put substantial pressure on US exporters. In meetings with Keynes and other Treasury officials, White argued for stabilizing the pound in the range of $4.60 to $4.70, which he thought would be sustainable and not seriously problematic for the United States. He apparently did not make a strong impression, and although the pound did not depreciate as the Americans had feared, the episode probably helped convince White that bilateral negotiation on financial policy was not terribly effective.[13]

In the months following White's trip to London, he began looking for ways to minimize the potential fallout on the US economy if the pound did drop sharply in value. This led him to conclude that the key was to develop close trade linkages with as many other countries as possible and, in particular, to convince those countries to peg the values of their currencies to the dollar. In a long note to George Haas, the division chief, in October 1935, White argued that this strategy would generate a virtuous cycle of stability and growth:

> Though it doesn't matter very much whether New York or London does the most foreign acceptance business, it is important to have as many currencies as possible linked to the dollar rather than to sterling, if the rate between dollars and sterling is not fixed. The more currencies tied to the dollar (i.e., exchange rates fixed to the dollar), the less power will British authorities have to influence American monetary policy. The more international business a country does, the more likely will it be to attract other currencies in its orbit of influence, and the more currencies it attracts the greater will be its international business.[14]

As the immediate danger of a sterling depreciation seemed to pass, White shifted his attention to the French franc. Although the value of the franc was of relatively minor concern to Washington by itself, a devaluation could trigger a response by Britain, for whom trade with France was much more important. In May 1936, when France was one of just four countries still adhering to the gold standard, White began urging the Treasury to develop a contingency plan if France should devalue the increasingly overvalued franc. 'The crux of the matter,' he wrote to Morgenthau, 'is the behavior of sterling.' Moreover, the way to avert the threat, in White's view, was to present a united Anglo-American front. To that end, the Treasury staff was considering a proposal to help the Bank of England build up its official reserves by allowing it to buy gold in the US market.[15] If Britain had a large enough reserve to defend its currency, then the two Anglophone countries together could convince the French that devaluing would lead to retaliatory measures. As White put it, 'France would hardly dare now to devalue to a lower level than that which both the United States and England indicated was the maximum they would permit without taking steps to defend their respective currencies.'[16] After some hesitation, however, White realized that permitting England to buy gold in the US market would do little to reduce pressure on exchange markets, and he recommended against it.[17]

By late June, 1936, events proved White's view to be correct, as the newly elected French government under Léon Blum stated publicly that it was prepared to devalue only if it could be assured that other major countries would maintain their parities. That led to negotiations between the US, British, and French treasuries and thus to the Tripartite Agreement three months later. Morgenthau himself played the key role in negotiating the agreement, but White served as a consistent advocate within the Treasury for finding a multilateral, cooperative solution to the perceived misalignment of the three major currencies.[18]

White's multilateralism had a strong influence on the design of the IMF. The seeds of a multilateral stabilization fund may be found in a series of US Treasury memoranda in December 1937. Several Latin American countries, notably Cuba and Mexico, were having difficulty servicing their substantial debts to US and other bondholders. That problem was not new – much of Mexico's external debt had been in default since 1914 – but the drift toward a new war in Europe was making the consequences more severe as the debtors began to look to the Axis countries – Germany, Italy, and Japan – for financial assistance. To counter that influence, Morgenthau developed a proposal for the US government to help Latin America restructure its external debts. Since direct interference in bond markets was impracticable, White steered the secretary toward an alternative plan to provide direct financial assistance by purchasing silver and thus maintaining a stable price for this key export and (in Cuba) the monetary base.[19]

Six months later, White expanded this silver-purchase proposal into a plan to establish an Inter-American Silver Bank. By this time, the United States had accumulated a large stock of silver bullion that was in danger of dropping in value because no country in Latin America other than Cuba was on a silver standard.[20] By propping up the price, the administration could serve both its own narrow interests and the interests of other silver-producing countries throughout the region.

Although this particular idea was not pursued further, it resurfaced less than two years later as a proposal to establish an Inter-American Bank, without the link to silver. White was one of the principal drafters (along with his counterpart at the State Department, Assistant Secretary Adolph Berle) of a plan for an institution that would have combined many of the functions that eventually accrued to the IMF and the World Bank. The plan was approved at an international conference in Havana, Cuba, in February 1940 under the chairmanship of US Under Secretary of State Sumner Welles, but a sufficient number of Latin American republics failed to ratify it, and the treaty died a quiet death.[21]

(c)   Loans that are not loans

White acted quietly throughout the late 1930s to convert the Exchange Stabilization Fund (ESF) from a fund to stabilize the gold value of the US dollar into a fund to help stabilize the dollar more directly against other currencies, including those of Latin American and other developing countries. The ESF had been established by Congress in January 1934 as a component of the Gold Reserve Act that devalued the dollar in relation to gold. Using a stock of earmarked gold, the Treasury was authorized to intervene in foreign exchange markets to stabilize the price of gold. The following year, White suggested that the discretion accorded to the Secretary of the Treasury by the Act provided an opportunity to use the ESF more broadly to further US international financial interests. 'In fact, one may go further and say that any earnest attempt to carry out the intent of Section 10(a) [of the Gold Reserve Act] would involve occasional operations in domestic and foreign security and money markets, as well as operations directly on the exchange market.'[22]

Within two months of White's proposal, the Treasury began using the ESF to enter into repurchase agreements with developing countries, beginning with Mexico in January 1936. Using silver as collateral, the Mexican government exchanged pesos for dollars for a specified period, to be repurchased at the same exchange rate plus an interest charge. The dollars for this operation were obtained by the Treasury from the ESF.[23] That operation was kept secret, but in July 1937 the Treasury entered into two similar agreements, one with Brazil (secured by gold) and one with China (secured by silver). In November 1938, White proposed generalizing this practice, primarily to provide financial assistance to Brazil and other Latin American countries.[24] Although Morgenthau was skeptical,[25] White kept raising the idea in specific cases, including for Chile in 1940 and Liberia in 1942.[26]

The Liberian case serves as an informative example of how White balanced his advocacy of US national interests with his concern for the broader implications of US policy actions. In 1939, the Firestone Tire Company – which controlled the production and export of natural rubber in Liberia – proposed to pay its employees there with US rather than the British coins that were then in general circulation. When the US State Department asked the Treasury for an opinion, White responded that he had no objection. Then in 1942, the State Department proposed to extend this plan by providing large amounts of US coins to the Liberian government and thus further to drive British coins out of circulation. White opposed this scheme on the grounds that it would bring trivial benefits to the United States and would risk greatly offending the British. After two months of debate, however, he devised a compromise under which the Treasury would use the ESF to buy up to £250,000 ($1 million) in coins from the Liberian government and then either issue the British coins to US troops stationed in Northern Ireland or sell them to the UK Treasury.[27] Eventually a $2 million ESF credit was extended to Liberia on a stand-by basis. It was not drawn upon, but in 1943 the Liberian government made the US dollar legal tender.[28]

As Bordo and Schwartz (2001) have shown, the expanded use of the ESF for repurchase arrangements became the inspiration and prototype for the White plan for the IMF in 1942. The Keynes plan for an international currency union (the competing scheme for creating a multilateral stabilization fund) envisaged that each participating state would be assigned a quota in terms of an international currency unit ('bancor') and would be entitled to draw overdrafts against that quota. It thus was derived from the structure of the British banking system and provided a fairly straightforward process for lending to participants. The White plan, drawn up independently around the same time, also envisaged assigning each participating state a quota, but in this scheme the participant (or member) would *deposit* a portion of the quota in its own currency and the rest in gold. Members would then draw on the pool of resources by exchanging more of their own currency for the foreign exchange (that is, US dollar) equivalent. As in the ESF arrangements of the 1930s, there would be no loan contract and thus no formal creditor-debtor relationship between the provider of the dollars (the ESF or the IMF) and the recipient country. Economically, the transaction amounted to a loan that would have to be repaid with interest.

White's experience with ESF lending also convinced him that the IMF should not extend credits automatically. His initial plan of April 1942 suggested that the Fund should respond to requests from borrowing countries by first making a careful independent assessment of the policy changes that the country should make to correct the underlying causes of its balance of payments problem. Only if the country was prepared to make those policy changes would the IMF approve the request. Keynes objected to this idea and argued in favor of automatic lending to any country with a balance of payments 'need,' subject to ex post policy conditions only if the borrower failed to take appropriate measures on its own and was unable to repay the loan on time.[29] White eventually agreed to go along with Keynes on this issue. The final Articles of Agreement did not provide explicitly for policy conditions on IMF lending, and it was only in the 1950s that the executive board introduced the conditional lending that gradually became standard practice.

(d)   The 'intelligent control' of capital flows

Another central feature of the IMF is the provision in Article VI of the charter that encourages member countries to impose controls on capital flows. If a country faces a balance of payments deficit on account of a large and sustained outflow of capital – as opposed to a deficit in the current account – the Fund is enjoined from lending for the purpose of financing such a deficit, and it is empowered to require the country to impose controls as a precondition for borrowing. In practice, this provision has never been invoked. Starting in 1956, when the United Kingdom asked to borrow from the Fund to cope with a speculative outflow during the Suez crisis, the IMF has justified such lending as necessary to prevent a capital deficit from spilling over into the current account (Boughton, 2001). In the 1940s, however, when private-sector cross-border capital flows were of limited scope and importance, the current and capital accounts of the balance of payments were much more clearly separated.

The strong pro-control wording in Article VI owes more to Keynes than to White. Keynes drew a clear line between good capital flows – those that financed trade or real investment – and those that were speculative or volatile or that promoted capital flight. His February 1942 plan for the Fund cited the encouragement of international cooperation in the formulation of capital controls as an important and general advantage of the proposed institution (Horsefield, 1969, p. 13). In contrast, the more nuanced practice regarding capital flows has been more in line with White's thinking, as revealed both by his original plan for the Fund and his earlier work at the US Treasury.

Although White's view of capital controls evolved over time, his considered opinion was that controls were a necessary evil that should be used with discretion so as to avoid discouraging useful flows. As he concluded in his PhD dissertation on the French international accounts, 'some measure of the intelligent control of the volume and direction of foreign investments is desirable' (White, 1933, pp. 311–12). That same year, he wrote to his thesis adviser, Frank Taussig, that he was exploring the idea that the best way for the United States to reap the benefits of international trade while protecting itself from external shocks was through 'centralized control over foreign exchanges and trade' (Rees, 1973, p. 39). Once he joined the Treasury staff a year later, he toned down this enthusiasm considerably, arguing in 1934 that capital controls should normally be unnecessary but should be kept actively in reserve to be used in case of a speculative attack.[30]

By 1935, the United States was facing massive gold inflows from Europe and elsewhere, and these flows were thought to be creating problems for domestic monetary stability. White drafted a memorandum to Morgenthau in which he attributed the bulk of the inflow to speculation, safe-haven demand, and a normal return of gold that had been moved out of the country in the two years prior to the January 1934 devaluation. Although White did not regard this inflow as a major problem, he did offer suggestions for controlling it, either by taxing foreign purchases of US securities or by finding some more direct means of control that would avoid the 'derangements that might be caused by sudden withdrawals of gold by foreigners.'[31] Three years later, when the French balance of payments was continuing to worsen in spite of the continuing weakness of the franc, White again advocated controls as the preferred solution, but only because the alternatives – further devaluation or import controls – were even less desirable. The 'imposition of exchange controls over noncommercial transactions … seems to us now, as it has in the past, to be the best of the bad choices,' he wrote to Morgenthau.[32]

This view of capital controls as 'the best of the bad choices' was manifest in White's plan for the IMF. As a general principle, White suggested that all of the Allies should be eligible to become members of the Fund, provided that they agreed to 'abandon … all restrictions and controls over foreign exchange transactions with member countries, *except with the approval of the Fund'* (emphasis added). After setting out the rationale for the completely free movement of capital, he noted that there were 'times when it is in the best economic interests of a country to impose restrictions on movements of capital, and on movements of goods. ... The task before us is not to prohibit instruments of control but to develop those [controls that] will be most effective in obtaining the objectives of world-wide sustained prosperity' (Horsefield, 1969, pp. 63–4).

2.4   Concluding observations

The overarching message from the archival evidence is that Harry Dexter White played a dominant role in the design of the IMF, not only because he was in a prominent position in a powerful Treasury, but also because he had shown himself to be an innovative, flexibly responsive, and forward-looking economic thinker. Many of the ideas that he set out in internal memoranda were half-formed and badly in need of refinement, and his own thinking tended to shift and evolve in response to feedback from colleagues and others. Nonetheless, this responsiveness also enabled him to develop fresh solutions that – more often than not – ultimately carried the day.

White's role has long been underestimated and misunderstood. John Maynard Keynes has, of course, always cast a long shadow. Keynes's first biographer observed that the British had tended to think wrongly of White 'as some dim scribe, some kind of robot, who wrote ... an inferior version of the Keynes plan' for the IMF (Harrod, 1951, p. 537). A later biographer simply gave up trying to understand White's role, concluding that it was, 'like almost everything else in his career, mystifying' (Skidelsky, 2000, p. 424).

Closer to home, White's boss, Henry Morgenthau, admired and trusted him greatly (as did Keynes and Harrod). When the Japanese attack on Pearl Harbor drew the United States into the war, Morgenthau immediately elevated White and put him in charge of all international economic policy at the Treasury. 'I want it all in one brain,' he declared, 'and I want it in Harry White's brain' (Blum, 1967, p. 89). In truth, of course, White was no match for the intellect and imagination of Keynes, as he himself well understood. White's insistence on multilateral discussions no doubt in part reflected his personal discomfort at battling *mano a mano* with the great man. When planning the Bretton Woods conference, Keynes pleaded for a bilateral meeting of the US and UK Treasuries, whose governments would then become the 'founder states' of the new institutions. When White insisted on a conference of all of the allied nations, Keynes complained that it would be a 'most monstrous monkey house' of a gathering, from which nothing useful would emerge.[33] In the event, however, White's natural inclination for multilateral negotiation meshed well with his personal desire to maximize his chances of guiding the outcome. The conference of 44 delegations from every continent succeeded in three weeks in creating two institutions, the IMF and the World Bank, that have played key roles in the international economy for sixty years.

Notes

James Boughton is Historian of the International Monetary Fund. He wishes to thank Robert Leeson and Roger Sandilands for helpful comments on an earlier draft. This chapter expresses the author's personal views, not those of the IMF.

1. Three major biographies – Harrod (1951), Moggridge (1992), and Skidelsky (1983, 1992, and 2000) – and a thirty-volume collection of his writings are only the core of a vast literature.
2. For detailed biographies, see Nathan White (1956), Rees (1973), and Craig (2004). White (p. 71) is the source for information on Harry White's second heart attack, in the late summer of 1947. Craig (p. 201) speculates that White's dissatisfaction with US policies and his concerns over ongoing investigations of his loyalty to the United States may have been factors in his decision to leave the IMF in 1947, in addition to his declining health. There is, however, no direct evidence for that conclusion. Although White publicly disguised his health problems so as not to jeopardize his subsequent consulting career, he maintained privately that his health was the sole reason for his departure. The mission to nine South American countries that White led from 7 February to 15 March 1947 is described in several different files in the IMF archives in Washington. His illness, which eventually forced an early termination of the mission, is recounted in a report in the IMF file C/Ecuador/810. The information that the illness was a heart attack and that it precipitated White's retirement is from a file on White (file number 101-4053) prepared by the US Federal Bureau of Investigation (FBI), which is open to the public in the FBI's Freedom of Information Act Reading Room in Washington.
3. Much later (in 1983), Edward M. Bernstein – White's principal assistant in the technical design of the IMF – claimed that he wrote White's 1945 article in *Foreign Affairs*. The claim appears in an oral history transcript, Black (1991, p. 61).
4. Also see Boughton (2004).
5. For a description, see http://libweb.princeton.edu/libraries/firestone/rbsc/ finding_aids/hdwhite.html (accessed 16 March 2009).
6. Record Group 56: General Records of the Department of the Treasury; 56.12.3, Records of the Assistant Secretary relating to monetary and

international affairs. Textual Records: Records of Harry Dexter White including a chronological file, 1934–46; memoranda, 1934–46; records relating to US-French financial negotiations, 1946; and lists of assignments and activities, 1939–41. See http://www.archives.gov/research/guide-fed-records/groups/056.html#56.12.3 (accessed 16 March 2009). Blum (1959), which is based on the nearly 800-volume collection of Morgenthau's diaries and Treasury papers at the Roosevelt Library in Hyde Park, New York, provides invaluable context for the College Park materials.

7. See http://www.imf.org/external/np/arc/eng/archive.htm (accessed 16 March 2009).

8. 'Proposal for Amendment of Fund Agreement to Increase Level of World Trade,' Executive Board Document No. 347 (14 October 1948). IMF Institutional Repository, S1140, 'White Plan.' Also see 'Rough draft of a statement that might be used to introduce the proposed amendments on the agenda,' Harry Dexter White papers, Princeton (hereinafter, 'Princeton papers,' Box 11, Item 27f. The manuscript includes a typed date, '4/20/48,' at the end but is signed and dated 'HD White May 19, 1948' at the top of the first page.

9. For the original IMF Articles of Agreement, see Horsefield (1969, pp. 185–214).

10. 'Selection of a Monetary Standard for the United States,' report submitted to Jacob Viner (22 September 1934). Harry Dexter White papers, Princeton (hereinafter, 'Princeton papers') Box 1. The reference to adjustment in periods of stress is on p. 232.

11. Bordo and Kydland (1995) argue that the classical gold standard was implicitly a conditional rule under which governments and markets understood that the standard would be abandoned temporarily in wartime and that abuses would be disciplined internationally by the Bank of England's power to control access to international capital. During the interwar period, however, economists analyzing the gold standard typically viewed it as a simple rule.

12. Two drafts are in the Princeton papers. The earlier of the two, in Box 4, is hand-dated '2/25/40' at the top of Section IV. The more complete version, in Box 3, includes a typed date, '8-4-42,' and a handwritten date, 'Feb. 44,' in pencil.

13. The Princeton archive (Box 1, Item 4a) includes two reports on this trip, in the form of memoranda from White to Haas: 'Personal Report on London Trip' (13 June 1935) and 'Summary of Conversations' (same date). For White's assessment that the pound was not overvalued, see his earlier memorandum to Haas, 'The Sterling Situation' (31 May 1935), at College Park (Box 1). On the negative reaction by British officials to White's visit, see Drummond (1981, p. 192). Blum (1959, p. 139) conveys a more positive impression. Blum's account is based on Morgenthau's diaries and refers to the reactions of British businessmen as well as officials, whereas Drummond cites British Treasury archives.

14. 'The United Kingdom of Great Britain (draft submitted to Mr. Haas October 18, 1935),' College Park, Box 1.

15. US policy at the time permitted gold sales only to countries adhering to the gold standard.

16. Memorandum from Haas to Morgenthau, drafted by White, 'French Devaluation' (25 May 1936); College Park, Box 1. The specific proposal relating

to the Bank of England is in this final 38-page draft but not in the original 23-page draft dated 8 May. It appears therefore that someone, probably Haas, prompted White to be more specific about how he hoped to enlist the British in the effort to dissuade the French. The 'crux' quotation is from p. 24, and the 'hardly dare' passage is on p. 35.

17. Untitled memorandum from Haas to Morgenthau, drafted by White (4 June 1936); College Park, Box 1.
18. Blum (1959, pp. 155–76), describes the negotiations from Morgenthau's perspective. On White's role, see Rees (1973, pp. 60–2). Neither the Princeton nor the College Park archive offers any primary evidence on White's role in the discussions.
19. White to Mrs Klotz (Morgenthau's secretary), 'Secretary's proposal for the record' (11 December 1937); Haas to Morgenthau (drafted by White), 'Mexico' (22 December); and Haas to Morgenthau (drafted by White), 'Preliminary notes for Mexican program' (28 December); all in College Park, Box 2. For the context of the silver-purchase proposal, see Blum (1959, pp. 493–7).
20. White to Morgenthau, 'Plan to promote the monetary and industrial use for silver and to make important use of some of our silver assets' (27 June 1938); College Park, Box 2.
21. See Emilio Collado, oral history interview (11 July 1974), Truman Library website: http://www.trumanlibrary.org/oralhist/collado2.htm (accessed 16 March 2009). Rees (1973, p. 104), has an overview based primarily on papers and testimony for US Senate committee hearings in the early 1950s.
22. The quotation is from p. 30 of an unaddressed draft memorandum titled 'Monetary Policy,' which White drafted and submitted to Haas on 13 November 1935; College Park, Box 1.
23. This operation is described in detail in Bordo and Schwartz (2001). For the history of the ESF, see Schwartz (1997) and Henning (1999).
24. Note prepared by White and Herman Oliphant (general counsel of the Treasury) and sent to Morgenthau on 5 November 1938; College Park, Box 2.
25. When White sent the note listed in the preceding footnote to Morgenthau, the secretary set it aside and asked that someone else review it. Blum (1964), however, attributes the idea of lending to Brazil through the ESF to Morgenthau, and he states that White 'thought that Morgenthau should not proceed without express congressional approval' (p. 53). The apparent implication that White was reluctant to use the ESF for this purpose is belied by the archival record, since it clearly was White who proposed the idea in the first instance.
26. Memorandum from White (and drafted by White) to Morgenthau, 'Chile's Request for Assistance' (12 September 1940); and untitled memorandum from White to Morgenthau (drafted by a member of White's staff, Frank O. Southard) dated 27 May 1942; College Park, Boxes 3 and 7, respectively. The proposal for Chile was a repurchase arrangement similar to those used earlier in Mexico and other countries. For the context of this arrangement, see Blum (1964, pp. 320–3).
27. These developments are described in memoranda from White to Morgenthau, 'Liberian proposal to purchase US currency' (9 October 1939); from White to [Daniel W.] Bell (under-secretary of the Treasury), 'The need for more coins in Liberia' (16 March 1942); from White to Bell (drafted by J.S. DeBeers),

'Letter from Mr. Berle on Liberian Coinage' (23 April 1942); from Southard
and DeBeers to White, 'Meeting on Liberian coinage in the State Department, May 8, 1942' (9 May 1942); and from White to Morgenthau on May
27, described in the preceding note. As noted above, Adolph Berle was assistant Secretary of State. The 8 May meeting at the State Department was with
Harvey Firestone, Jr, president of the eponymous tire company.
28. On the ESF credit, see Henning (1999, p. 14 and Table 1).
29. See Horsefield (1969, pp. 42 (White) and 24 (Keynes)).
30. White's terminology for this recommendation was 'permanent control with
only periodic restrictions.' See 'Selection of a Monetary Standard for the
United States,' Chapter XVII.
31. Memorandum from Haas to Morgenthau (drafted by White), 'Cause of gold
imports, 1934–1935' (19 November 1935); College Park, Box 1. The quotation
is from p. 9.
32. Memorandum from White to Morgenthau, 'What should our answer be to the
British Treasury as to our attitude toward further depreciation of the franc?'
(30 April 1938); College Park, Box 2.
33. Letter to Sir David Walley (30 May 1944), in Keynes, *Collected Writings XXVI*,
p. 42.

References

Black, Stanley W., 1991, *A Levite among the Priests: Edward M. Bernstein and the
Origins of the Bretton Woods System*, Boulder, Colorado: Westview Press.
Blum, John Morton, 1959–1967, *From the Morgenthau Diaries. Vol. I: Years of Crisis,
1928–1938* (1959), *Vol. II: Years of Urgency* (1964), *Vol. III: Years of War* (1967),
Boston: Houghton Mifflin Company.
Bordo, Michael D. and Finn E. Kydland, 1995, 'The Gold Standard as a Rule: an
Essay in Exploration,' *Explorations in Economic History*, 32 (October): 423–64.
Bordo, Michael and Anna J. Schwartz, 2001, 'From the Exchange Stabilization
Fund to the International Monetary Fund,' NBER Working Paper 8100 (January).
Boughton, James M., 2001, 'Northwest of Suez: the 1956 Crisis and the Interna-
tional Monetary Fund,' *IMF Staff Papers*, 48: 425–46.
_____, 2002, 'Why White, not Keynes? Inventing the Post-War International
Monetary System,' in Arie Arnon and Warren Young (eds), *The Open-Economy
Macro-Model: Past, Present and Future*. Boston: Kluwer Academic Publishers,
pp. 73–96.
_____, 2004, 'New Light on Harry Dexter White,' *Journal of the History of Economic
Thought*, 26 (June): 179–95.
Clarke, Stephen V.O., 1973, *The Reconstruction of the International Monetary Sys-
tem: the Attempts of 1922 and 1933*, Princeton Studies in International Finance
No. 33. Princeton, New Jersey: International Finance Section, Princeton
University Department of Economics.
Craig, Bruce, 2004, *Treasonable Doubt: the Harry Dexter White Spy Case*, Lawrence,
Kansas: University of Kansas Press.
Drummond, Ian, 1981, *The Floating Pound and the Sterling Area, 1931–1939*,
Cambridge: Cambridge University Press.

Flanders, M. June, 1990, *International Monetary Economics, 1870–1960*, Cambridge: Cambridge University Press.

Harrod, Roy F., 1951, *The Life of John Maynard Keynes*, London: Macmillan & Co.

Henning, C. Randall, 1999, *The Exchange Stabilization Fund: Slush Money or War Chest?* Washington: Institute for International Economics.

Horsefield, J. Keith, 1969, *The International Monetary Fund, 1945–1965*, Vol. III, *Documents*, Washington: International Monetary Fund.

Keynes, John Maynard, various dates, *The Collected Writings of John Maynard Keynes*, 30 volumes, London: Macmillan & Co.

Laidler, David E.W. and Roger J. Sandilands, 2002, 'An Early Harvard Memorandum on Anti-Depression Policies: an Introductory Note,' *History of Political Economy*, 34(3) (fall): 515–32.

Moggridge, Donald E., 1992, *Maynard Keynes: an Economist's Biography*, London and New York: Routledge.

Rees, David, 1973, *Harry Dexter White: a Study in Paradox*, New York: Coward, McCann, & Geoghagan.

Schwartz, Anna J., 1997, 'From Obscurity to Notoriety: a Biography of the Exchange Stabilization Fund,' *Journal of Money, Credit, and Banking*, 29 (May): 135–53.

Skidelsky, Robert, 1983–2000, *John Maynard Keynes, Volume I: Hopes Betrayed 1883–1920* (1983), *Volume II: The Economist as Saviour 1920–1937* (1992), *Volume III: Fighting for Britain 1937–1946* (2000), London: Macmillan.

Taussig, Frank W., 1931, *Some Aspects of the Tariff Question: an Examination of the Development of American Industries under Protection*, third enlarged edition, continued to 1930, with the cooperation of H. D. White, Cambridge, MA: Harvard University Press.

White, Harry Dexter, 1933, *The French International Accounts, 1880–1913*, Cambridge, Mass.: Harvard University Press.

_____, 1934, 'Haberler's *Der Internationale Handel* and Ohlin's *Interregional and International Trade*,' *Quarterly Journal of Economics*, 48 (August): 727–41.

_____, 1943, 'Postwar Currency Stabilization,' *American Economic Review (Papers and Proceedings)*, 33 (March): 382–7.

_____, 1945, 'The Monetary Fund: Some Criticisms Examined,' *Foreign Affairs*, 23 (January): 195–210.

_____, 1947, 'The International Monetary Fund: the First Year,' *Annals of the American Academy of Political and Social Science*, 252 (July): 21–9.

White, Nathan, I., 1956, *Harry Dexter White: Loyal American*, Boston: Independent Press [for Bessie (White) Bloom, Waban, Massachusetts].

3

Building up a Multilateral Strategy for the United States: Alvin Hansen, Jacob Viner, and the Council on Foreign Relations (1939–45)

Sebastiano Nerozzi

3.1 Introduction

The establishment of the financial and economic order after the Second World War is undoubtedly one of the most studied and discussed phases in the history of international economic relations. Eminent historians and economists have devoted great efforts to describing its origins, features and effects.

This chapter considers those events from the peculiar perspective provided by a set of contemporary sources: thanks to the documents preserved in the Council on Foreign Relations Archive,[1] we will look at the shaping of the post-war economic order through the eyes of two outstanding American economists: Jacob Viner (1892–1970) and Alvin H. Hansen (1887–1975).

Actually Viner and Hansen were not only witnesses of those events: they were engaged with the preparation of the Bretton Woods agreements and, more generally, with the shaping of the American strategy in the design of a new economic order after the Second World War. Their activity was mainly, although not exclusively, related to the War and Peace Study (WPS), a project set up by the Council on Foreign Relations in connection with the State Department. Several quotations traceable in the literature suggest that Hansen's and Viner's post-war planning activity was not a minor one. Yet their work within the War and Peace Study has received little attention, at least in the historiography of economic thought and policy.[2]

The subject of this chapter will therefore be Viner's and Hansen's views and contributions to the post-war planning activity of the Roosevelt administration.

The chapter is structured as follows: first we describe the institutional framework of the War and Peace Study group; then we examine Hansen's and Viner's contribution to the general economic strategy of the administration before Pearl Harbor; we then recall, briefly, their proposals in the commercial field and devote more attention to the focal point of the paper, namely their contribution to the debate around the International Monetary Fund (IMF) and the International Bank for Reconstruction and Development (IBRD). Finally we consider their general evaluation of the Bretton Woods agreements and reach some conclusions.

There is much asymmetry within the documents we examine: in the first period, roughly from 1940 to mid-1943, the War and Peace Study group had a good deal of influence on the State Department, and therefore on the shaping of American foreign policy; nevertheless its contribution was mainly related to such general aims and topics as multilateral trade, full employment, and international cooperation in the commercial and financial field.

Only in 1943 did the WPS get involved in more technical discussion about the tools and institutions that were emerging from the official Anglo-American negotiations. Unfortunately at the very same time the group ceased to exert a strong influence on the administration: the commercial negotiations were blocked from September 1943 until the end of the war and the financial negotiations were led by the Treasury, with the State Department only in a secondary role. Despite this declining role of the WPS, many of its members continued to contribute to the negotiations, working in government committees or exerting their persuasion through personal relationships with the main players on the stage.

However heterogeneous these documents may be, their extensive analysis will allow us to describe the contribution of Viner and Hansen to American foreign policy during the Second World War.

3.2   The State Department's post-war planning and the War and Peace Study project

The United Nations conference held at Bretton Woods in July 1944 with the participation of delegations from 44 countries is considered a turning point in the history of international economic relations.[3]

It gave birth to the IMF and the IBRD, preparing the general framework for the establishment of the GATT and other international economic institutions.

This turning point was not, of course, a sudden event, but the result of an intense process of analysis, political debate and negotiation, especially between the American and British governments. This process was brought about at considerable speed under the pressure of dramatic events.

At the end of the 1930s it was apparent that the traditional Euro-centric structure of international relations, the so-called 'balance of power' system, which had barely survived the 1914–18 war, could no longer manage the several pressures and conflicts arising around the world.[4]

Even the traditional gold standard, which had governed international economic relations in the second half of the nineteenth century, supporting the functioning of a free trade system, had been restored after the previous war only after a long process of political and financial struggles, with considerable economic difficulties and high social costs. Moreover its resurrection was to be only temporary. In 1936 the classical gold standard survived only in Albania and few people believed it capable of a second resurrection or considered that this would be desirable.[5] Nevertheless some sort of international economic agreement was invoked to revert the tendency to increasing trade barriers, bilateralism and competitive devaluations. The issue was not only an economic one: unemployment, economic distress, and unfair trade practices were considered powerful factors in the rise of totalitarian dictatorships and military expansionism. The general political and economic instability of the 1930s induced many governments to change their minds about their previous commercial and monetary policy in seeking a way out of chaos.

In June 1940 the American public was shocked by news of German soldiers marching into Paris. A few months had sufficed for Hitler to conquer much of continental Europe. Only the strenuous resistance of Great Britain and its fleet divided the German menace from the United States: in September 1940 even that last bulwark seemed very likely to crumble. The old balance of power was now completely swept away. What sort of international order would result?

It was in this context that the War and Peace Study project – and the Economic and Financial Group within it – was set up. Actually the WPS was not a public project: it had been initiated in December 1939 by the Council on Foreign Relations, a private institution, very close to the New York business community and well-known for its twenty years of activism in the field of international studies.[6] The council therefore could be considered a private pressure group formed by 'internationally oriented bankers and corporate executives in New York and surrounding areas, as well as academic experts and journalists' (Domhoff, 1990, p. 115).

The private character of the WPS did not prevent it from assuming an important role within the administration: the project was set up in accord with the State Department and placed under the supervision of one of its high officials, Leo Pasvolsky.[7] The State Department received reports and recommendations from the WPS, which were delivered directly to the President and the Secretary of State, and in turn provided the WPS with information and data of its own.[8]

The reasons for this close collaboration could be traced to the strong personal relationships the council enjoyed within the State Department.[9] But there were also institutional reasons that led the State Department to rely heavily on the WPS. The State Department had in 1941 organized its own Division on Special Research to study post-war problems. This division, directed by Pasvolsky under the supervision of Under Secretary of State Sumner Welles, numbered only a few officials.[10] The WPS, on the other hand, funded with a huge grant from the Rockefeller Foundation, was able to devote to post-war planning studies a wide and articulated structure, with the regular participation of more than one hundred individuals during its five years of activity.[11]

With its personal connections and institutional framework, the WPS was able to exert much influence on the State Department, especially in the first three years of its activity, when an overall rethinking of the US national interest had to be worked out in order to guide short-term decisions and long-term strategies.

In building up a rationale for this purpose a leading role within the WPS was assumed from the beginning by the Economic and Financial Group (EFG), which was certainly well equipped for this task. The EFG was entrusted to the leadership of Alvin H. Hansen and Jacob Viner, both of them former presidents of the American Economic Association, respectively in 1938 and 1939.

It was not only status within the AEA that made Viner and Hansen well suited to representing the profession in its broader amplitude. Viner was a 'late' exponent of the classical school of international trade, which passed through John Stuart Mill and Alfred Marshall to his own 'master and friend' Frank Taussig; he was also an outstanding member of the 'early Chicago school', which in the following years came to be known for its resistance to the 'Keynesian revolution.'[12] Hansen, himself a resolute opponent of Keynesian ideas in the early 1930s and a brilliant exponent of the 'Austrian' way of reasoning, was now regarded, after his declared conversion in 1937, as the leader of the Keynesian school in the United States.[13]

In addition to Viner and Hansen, the EFG counted other distinguished economists within its membership: Lauchlin Currie (since January 1943), John H. Williams (only for a few months in 1940), Benjamin V. Cohen, Randolph Flanders (New York Fed), William Diebold Jr (junior researcher until 1943), Percy Bidwell, Winfield Riefler. Many of them were already working with other agencies and Viner and Hansen were no exceptions: Viner had been special assistant to Henry Morgenthau Jr at the Treasury since 1934; Hansen had been adviser to the NBER and the Federal Reserve Board.

Between 1939 and 1945, the State Department received 161 reports and recommendations from the EFG: they covered a wide set of topics,[14] mainly related to the impact of the war on the American economy, and the desirable aims for the post-war economic order.

3.3   From the Western Hemisphere to the 'Grand Area'

In 1940–41 the central effort of the EFG was to press the administration to adopt as its main strategy the building up of a multilateral trade area embracing most of the non-German controlled countries.

It was not an easy cause to promote: one of the most popular ideas of the time was the 'Western Hemisphere' project.[15] This represented a kind of trade bloc within the pan-American continent, designed to face not only Japanese and German expansionism, but also trade discrimination on the part of the British Commonwealth. A pan-American economic and political isolationism could appear a good safeguard against involvement in the war.

In the summer of 1940, under the leadership of Viner and Hansen, the EFG endeavoured to show the economic unfeasibility of this idea:[16] the Western Hemisphere project would have required a huge reorientation of the main commercial flows of the United States toward Canada and Latin America. This would not be an easy task: demand for American goods was fairly marginal in both regions, which were mainly oriented to European products; many of the goods and raw materials that Latin America could supply would have displaced, with their low prices, American agricultural output. The resultant gigantic transformation of the American productive structure would bring mass unemployment and distress for millions of farmers. That was the darker side of the picture Viner and Hansen were drawing, but there was more: essential raw materials for the American industry (rubber, tin) were produced outside the western hemisphere, mainly in Asia and the British Commonwealth; moreover most of the markets for American industrial goods were in Europe or English-speaking countries. The moral of the tale was quite clear: the United States could not let the Nazis conquer Great Britain and keep Europe and part of the British Commonwealth under its own economic control; they could not let Japan build up its own empire in the Pacific. In short, they could not afford to stand aside from the war.

The alternative solution, supported by the EFG, was to build up a much wider trade area, extended to the British Commonwealth and shaped along the principles of multilateralism and economic cooperation, especially in the financial field.[17]

The 'Grand Area', as it came to be called in the EFG reports, should be started as soon as possible, as a means to enhance American defensive power and maintain its living standards during the war. But it should also be a sort of acid test for the future structure of international political and economic relationships.

In the phase of uncertainty that followed the outbreak of war in Europe the administration needed sound political and economic evaluations to guide its foreign policy and effective arguments to overcome a strongly isolationist public opinion: the EFG provided both. Moreover it set out the sort of post-war economic order the United States had to fight for. In EFG analysis and recommendations, short-term and long-term objectives were strictly related. American foreign policy had to be oriented to the attainment of a new world order consistent with its liberal-democratic creed and designed to serve its national economic interest. The Grand Area project seemed to satisfy both of these requirements.

3.4 Multilateral trade and international stabilization of employment

The first step to building up the Grand Area was to negotiate a military alliance with the British; but, in order to design the war aims of the future economic order, American-British cooperation in economic and political fields had also to be established as soon as possible.[18]

The EFG itself took the initiative. In summer 1941 the EFG drew up eight points constituting its proposal for an economic 'charter': multilateral trade, economic cooperation, security for individuals against old

age, disease and unemployment, and national self-determination should
be the essential features of an alternative economic system, designed to
spread higher living standards throughout the world.[19] After the Great
Depression, laissez-faire and free trade had lost their shine and a novel
economic program was needed to be championed against the Nazis' 'new
order'. Even the accusation of a new Anglo-Saxon plutocratic imperialism, in the form of commercial and financial exploitation, was to be
answered: an economic program should be devised to preserve small
countries' autonomy and give them substantial advantages.

The eight points of the Atlantic Charter were declared in August 1941,
but they contained no statements about economic aims.[20] The declaration of an economic charter was not simple: different points of view
and divergent national interests, competition between the rising world
economic power and older centers of power, and inadequate knowledge
of each others' problems were not an easy ground on which to base
commitments about the future economic system.

Mutual understanding was needed and the EFG was ready to play
its part. In the fall of 1941 the EFG, together with the Royal Institute
of International Affairs – a sort of British parallel to the Council on
Foreign Relations, to which it was bound by longstanding intellectual
exchange[21] – organized two unofficial meetings with British economists
in Washington to discuss the main issues between the two countries and
the prospective problems of the post-war period.[22]

The differences of opinions between the two group of experts could
hardly be greater: the British were carrying on their struggle against Germany almost alone, supported by the financial and material aid of the
Commonwealth; their industrial system, widely devoted to warfare production, would have to meet a drastic conversion to peace production;
their massive purchases of foreign raw materials had piled up considerable 'sterling balances' that would place a sudden and huge pressure
on the external value of the pound after the war. The maintenance of
tight exchange controls and the imperial preference system, probably
enforced by bilateral trade arrangements outside the Commonwealth,
seemed to be the only available means of avoiding a dramatic collapse
of the British economy and standard of living after the war.[23]

Not surprisingly multilateral trade and peaceful economic cooperation
sounded ominous to most British ears: the American proposals could
appear as the final insolence of a young man who, smartly dressed and
comfortably seated on a sofa, was casually declaiming to his agonized
father the virtues of the new house he was going to build with the proceeds of his legacy. The EFG economists who, to be fair, were actually

supporting a more active and sensible attitude on the part of the administration, had to work hard to overcome the doubts of their counterparts.

In October 1941 Alvin Hansen went to London to meet a number of economists engaged in public service:[24] he proposed again the building up of a multilateral trade system after the war, but this aim was coupled with a wide program of public investment projects, led by an international reconstruction finance corporation, funded by industrial countries in favor of developing ones. If the idle financial holdings of the United States could be put at the disposal of foreign investment projects in backward countries, these funds would increase the demand for capital goods produced in Britain as well as in the United States; under these conditions Britain could lower its trade barriers with no fear of a major balance of payments deficit, harsh deflation or dramatic falls in employment and living standards.[25]

The United States possessed a huge – currently idle – mass of reserves that had been built up in the previous years; if they released even a minor part of that liquidity, its circulation could bring prosperity, security and peace across the barren fields of the world.

The Keynesian tone of Hansen's proposal had a chance of finding a sympathetic listener in Keynes himself. As the Harvard economist wrote to Viner:

> Keynes and Henderson saw, through this type of approach, the possibility of working on to the Hull type of multilateral trade and agreed that, if a broad attack of this sort could be made on the whole problem of active employment and trade, everyone would prefer the broadest possible trade relations rather than the narrow bilateral arrangements.
> (Hansen to Viner, 20 October 1941: box 13, folder 9, JVP)[26]

But others admired Hansen's message for different reasons:

> These proposals proved to be a way of bridging to a large extent the gap between those who, like Keynes and Henderson, have been favoring continuation of exchange control and bi-lateral payments agreements for England after the war, and those ... led by Lionel Robbins, who favor the multi-lateral trade approach. Robbins proved, I think, everything considered, my warmest supporter in these proposals.
>
> (Ibid.)

Hansen's informal proposals had now to find their expression in the official negotiations. The Lend-Lease Act of March 1941 provided the opportunity: in the fall of 1941 the Roosevelt administration was pressing the British government to define some kind of 'repayment' for US financial and material aid. No monetary or material transfer was expected: the repayment should be on political grounds. The aim of the State Department was to obtain from Britain the commitment to give up any trade discrimination. This declaration would have implied the abandoning of the imperial preference system, established in the Ottawa Agreements of 1932 between Great Britain, the Dominions, and India.[27]

In January 1942 the EFG proposed that the State Department sign a joint statement with the British: the two governments should commit themselves not only to refrain from any trade discrimination and to reduce trade barriers, but also to promote, by national and international measures, 'full use of each country's domestic productive resources of men and material.'[28]

The importance of the joint statement was stressed by John Miller, executive director of the WPS:

> The memorandum ... is probably the most important matter which has come before any of the Groups since the Project began. If the United States begins to assume international responsibilities, it is more likely to do so in an economic than a political form. The success of this plan might be the contribution of the project to American foreign policy.
>
> (EA-23, 29 November 1941, p. 12)

The article VII Mutual Aid Agreement, finally signed on 23 February 1942, after strenuous resistance from the British government,[29] contained a clear commitment to the elimination of any discriminatory treatment in international trade, together with tariff reductions and other trade barriers. Moreover it asserted that:

> agreed action, open to participation by all other countries of like mind, directed to the expansion, by appropriate international and domestic measures, of production, employment and the exchange and consumptions of goods ... At an early convenient date conversations shall begin between the two governments with a view to determining, in the light of governing economic conditions, the best means of attaining the above-stated objectives.[30]

Now the problem was to set up appropriate machinery for cooperation: that was to become the EFG's main task in the following months.

3.5   A set of international agencies

Between the spring and summer of 1942 the process of 'osmosis' between the Council on Foreign Relations' and the State Department's post-war planning reached its climax. In March a closer relationship had been formalized between the WPS and the State Department Division on Special Research, still guided by Leo Pasvolsky. At the suggestion of the CFR, the secretaries and researchers of each WPS group spent half a week in Washington supporting the division's staff, and for the other half continued their work on behalf of the CFR's project in New York.[31]

The time was now ready to develop concrete plans for the post-war order in negotiations with the British. In accordance with Pasvolsky's detailed requests, the EFG began to work out a complete set of proposals concerning various aspects of the post-war economic order.[32]

In August 1942 the EFG delivered to the State Department the project for an International Trade Agency (EB-55), elaborated by Percy B. Bidwell.[33] The ITA was entrusted with the control of tariff duty changes, the promotion of multilateral trade agreements and the settling of disputes between member countries.

> The Authority should also supervise … the development and execution of national foreign trade policies in order that they may promote rather than endanger world prosperity and the maintenance of peace.
>
> The constituent nations, and those which later become members of the General organization, should submit to the Trade Authority all proposed increase in import and export duties, and also all proposed changes in quotas, licensing systems and in customs laws and regulations which interpose new or additional obstacles to international trade, thirty days before putting them into effect.
>
> … The authority should have power to initiate investigations and to suspend the operation of the proposed increases for a period not exceeded ninety days.
>
> … if [the country] does not accept the recommendations of the Authority, should be obliged to re-enact the original proposals before they become effective. The Authority should make public, promptly, a report of its findings and recommendations.
>
> (EB-55, p. 2)

The EFG was well aware that the extensive powers given to the new agency were likely to provoke strong opposition from national public opinion.[34] To overcome this difficulty Viner and Benjamin V. Cohen stressed the importance of an international agreement underwriting a 'Code of Fair Trade Practices for International Trade': the ITA should be entrusted to promote and control the respect for that code, limiting its discretionary power:

> The only way to get around this [opposition] would be to set up, so far as possible, predicable standards which would to some extent limit the Authority's jurisdiction and protect it from the charges of political motivation ... Mr Cohen hopes that the development of standards might make the question before the Authority more comparable to 'justiciable' than 'non-justiciable' issues.
>
> (Ibid., pp. 4–5)

The proposal contained in memorandum EB-55, had many parallels with the plan for a commercial union formulated, at about the same time, by James Meade for the British Department of Commerce.[35] These two proposals became the basis of the agreement reached by the British and American delegations during the first official talks held in September 1943.[36]

Even the EFG's proposals in the employment field were broadly confirmed in the 1943 Anglo-American official talks. As we shall see, they provided for a set of international institutions coordinated by a general economic staff, in order to stabilize employment throughout the world.

Keynes's clearing union plan and White's IMF proposals had not yet been published, but were under discussion within government: the EFG was asked to provide suggestions for the State Department position. The man entrusted with the provision of analysis and the elaboration of proposals in this area was Alvin Hansen: his two memoranda were discussed within the EFG in spring 1942 and 1943 respectively.[37]

In Hansen's view the only way to build up a sound and durable international monetary system was to adopt national and international measures able to ensure high levels of employment, production and living standards in the leading industrial countries and economic and social development in the rest of the world. The experience of the 1930s had clearly demonstrated that no monetary system could survive the consequences of a deep depression.

> The main means to achieve international equilibrium are: (a) the promotion of full employment in the industrially mature countries, and especially in the United States; (b) the development and industrialization of the backward countries designed to change the structure

of their economies; (c) tariff reductions in the United States ... In order to effectuate these ... programs of adjustment it will be necessary to set up international institutions which will be concerned (a) with counter-cyclical policy and the maintenance of substantial full employment, and (b) with the development and industrialization of backward areas.

(EB-64, p. 4)

Viner and most members of the EFG agreed with him:

No currency system, no procedures of international investment, can be expected to withstand strains of the degree which the great depression involved without cracking. No country can be expected to adhere to a liberal foreign trade policy in the face of economic storms of the severity of that of the 1930s ...

Provision for joint international action to prevent or mitigate booms and depressions will therefore be an essential feature of a satisfactory program of post-war international economic organization. This will call especially for some measure of coordination by at least the most important countries of their fiscal policies and their internal and external investment policies.

(Viner, 1942a, pp. 133–4)

Widening his 1941 proposals, Hansen designed a set of international economic institutions, charged to manage the new economic system after the war, namely an international development agency, a world bank, a commodity corporation (whose objective was to stabilize the prices of international raw material), an IMF or clearing union, and an international trade organization. Their activity should be coordinated by a general economic staff.

This machinery should therefore support a coordination of national fiscal policy designed to maintain international equilibrium as well as full employment.[38] Expansionist fiscal policy on the part of surplus countries was, in Hansen's view, the best means to promote balance of payments equilibrium, avoiding placing the entire burden of adjustment on deficit countries:[39] the latter could escape drastic deflation policies and trade restrictions which would have otherwise impaired their living standards and level of employment, with an overall depressive effect on the whole world economy.

Meanwhile these proposals, which were very close to the final agreement signed during the September Anglo-American expert talks,[40] provoked a strong debate within the EFG and allowed Lauchlin Currie and

Allan Sproul, both skeptical about the establishment of an international monetary institution, to address a basic objection to Viner's and Hansen's similar approaches (EA-39, 9 January 1943, p. 14): if national fiscal policies had such an importance in the attainment of external equilibrium and monetary stabilization; if stabilization of production and employment should be the main goal from which all others derived, why engage in such a difficult enterprise as the establishment of an international monetary agency? Why give up such a relevant part of national economic sovereignty, when all that was needed was greater freedom in pursuing full employment policies? Why not simply look for a long-standing agreement with the British to harmonize fiscal policies and stabilize exchange rates?

This was not an extemporaneous criticism: Currie's and Sproul's arguments were addressed explicitly against both White's and Keynes's monetary plans. They recalled quite explicitly John H. Williams's 'Key currencies approach,'[41] certainly the most serious challenge to the establishment of such international institutions as provided by the Anglo-American proposals. Williams's approach was popular not only among businessmen and bankers (like Sproul),[42] who were unsure of international financial institutions, but even among New Deal reformers (like Currie), who were supporting a high degree of national freedom from external entanglements in order to pursue full employment policies.[43]

The answers provided, quite unanimously, by Viner and Hansen were technical and political in character.[44] Even if a sufficient and appropriate fiscal intervention were granted, the process to international equilibrium could not be a perfect mechanism: external stabilization loans were needed in many cases to provide sufficient time to take account of domestic adjustments and to prevent, in the meantime, undesired exchange-rate fluctuations.[45]

> Mr Hansen said that the idea of the international fund is to have a pool that enables countries to secure exchange ... regardless of whether or not they possess gold ... Using the agency it becomes possible to replace unilateral and competitive depreciation with a plan conceived according to the interest of all concerned. The pre-war basis was unsatisfactory, and it is obvious that we should get something better. Short term measures will be of the first importance in making basic adjustments successful by showing the need for them and by buying time to make them ...
>
> Mr Viner put the problem this way: short-run disturbances are not hard to handle if the world is running smoothly; they are dangerous

in depression or when related to political crises. In a depression it would be of great advantage to be able to ease a temporary exchange shortage.

(EA-39, 9 January 1943, pp. 15–16)

The second argument was perhaps a more ambitious one: it was a defense of the multilateral character of the new institutions. Multilateral institutions, with their voting quotas and mechanisms of choice were certainly hard issues to deal with, but they were also the only means to avoid that imperialistic or paternalistic use of US financial aid that Currie was addressing.

The fact that even small and poor countries were asked to contribute (in the case of the IMF); that they could take part in many decisions; that they could receive the needed help other than directly from other governments or private corporations, through the channels of a truly multinational institution of which they were members; all these were, especially in Viner's view, important guarantees against an imperialistic use of international finance[46] It was not only an altruistic attitude. The fear of a new economic domination would have prevented the establishment of the kind of international cooperation in the commercial field that the United States was pursuing: many countries would not have accepted the removal of trade barriers and exchange controls without sufficient confidence that they would not to be exploited and dominated by more powerful countries. Actually the EFG was not unanimous on this point,[47] but the supporters of a set of multinational agencies finally prevailed: in the EFG recommendations, an international monetary agency was needed to support the functioning of a new monetary order; Anglo-American leadership and effective control could not be given up; but other nations' financial and political participation had to be secured from the beginning. Now the problem was to design the lines of conduct of the new monetary agency.

3.6   The EFG and international monetary stabilization: Hansen's proposals discussed

Having provided the general framework for a set of international institutions for the attainment of stabilization of employment and production, the EFG finally analyzed the type of monetary institution the administration should promote. Viner and Hansen had been united in defending the case for an international monetary agency, but when the discussion addressed the features of these institutions, the two leading economists revealed how far apart they were.

Hansen's proposals supported the British 'overdraft approach'; moreover, he opposed the return to a full-fledged gold standard and proposed abandoning the monetary use of gold, at least as internal reserves, in order to ensure an adequate elasticity of liquidity supply for the whole world. In Hansen's view the time was propitious for the establishment of a fiat money system.[48]

If the dollar was emancipated from any entanglement with gold holdings, the banking system would have been able to accommodate the liquidity demand of member countries without any fear of reserve depletion and capital flows. At the same time the huge gold holdings of the United States should not remain idle: they could be used to settle foreign claims and, moreover, to provide other international institutions with adequate resources, allowing them to promote economic growth in backward areas and stimulate American exports.[49]

Another desirable consequence of a US fiat money system, would have been the cessation of unlimited purchases of gold on the part of the Treasury at the price of $35 per ounce. These purchases created internal inflationary pressures and compelled foreign countries to adopt tight credit policies in order to maintain at least the gold reserves needed to meet their international claims. During the 1930s, unlimited gold purchases on the part of the US and their sterilization on the part of the Federal Reserve had worsened the maldistribution of international gold assets and prolonged world-wide depression.[50]

A fiat money system in the US, and an international currency managed by a really multilateral banking institution like an international clearing union or a world bank, could be the best solution to the problem of world liquidity[51] and a powerful device to support the building up of a worldwide multilateral trade system. But this perspective seemed too revolutionary and was attacked by other members of the group: Viner took the lead in the discussion, defending the monetary use of gold.

> Mr Hansen's suggestions involve a major change from what important countries have been willing to do in the past; previously they have wanted to hold gold as a reserve and this plan calls for their holding foreign currency only ... It is unnecessary to assume that the United States will stop buying unlimited quantities of gold at a fixed price since the whole stabilization scheme is consistent with, and notably would require, stabilized monetary values for gold as well as stabilized exchange rates.
>
> (EA-29, 15 April 1942, p. 6)

The monetary stabilization scheme which Viner was referring to was, apparently, different from Hansen's. What Viner had in mind was:

> A modified international gold standard, under which, to prevent world-wide inflation or deflation, and also to permit orderly adjustment when needed of the exchange-parities of particular currencies, changes in the monetary value of gold for at least the major countries would be permitted – or perhaps ordered – by an international body operating under general rules embodied in an international agreement.
>
> (Viner, 1942b, p. 174)[52]

The basic problem, in Viner's view, was not scarcity or misdistribution of gold. It was the uncooperative way in which the gold standard had been managed in the previous decade, which had caused the collapse of the world monetary and financial system.[53] According to the Chicago economist, the best way of restarting an international flow of goods and long-term investments after the war was not to provide a huge supply of liquidity and an artificial redistribution of gold reserves: the main precondition for restoring confidence and avoiding depression, was, in the long run, the stability of the international monetary system, that is, of exchange rates (Viner, 1942b, pp. 173–4).

The new institution was intended to serve this purpose, providing short-term loans to support temporary deficits in the balance of payments and maintain the stability of exchange rates. More fundamental imbalances could be met with parity revisions, provided these did not afflict the stability of other member countries. A higher degree of flexibility could be assured by the power of the new institution to vary the international price of gold in order to avoid worldwide deflation or inflation (Viner, 1942a, p. 134; 1942b, p. 174). Anyway, unilateral action should be banned.

Different priorities led the two EFG economists to endorse different solutions: the provision of a high supply of liquidity was more effectively guaranteed under Keynes's plan, which was supported by Hansen; the restoration of exchange stability was the main purpose of White's scheme, which Viner preferred on this ground.

Despite these basic divergences, Hansen and Viner were ready to recognize that both plans, given suitable technical changes, could be made very similar, at least in strictly economic terms.[54] Nevertheless, in Viner's view, the American Treasury scheme seemed to have a greater political or practical appropriateness.[55]

After several meetings and sharp discussions, a broad consensus began to emerge between the two EFG leaders:

> Mr Hansen hoped we would tackle the gold production problem but wondered if it is so serious as is often made out. We tend to overlook the indirect advantage to the world of the great increase of monetary gold in recent years. There has been a great gain in liquidity and we may lose it if we cut off the gold flow too suddenly ... Mr Viner agreed that if the stabilization system works as well as we hope, it would provide sufficient liquidity. But it would be wise to see it in operation for, say, five years before dropping gold altogether.
>
> (EA-42, 3 April 1943, p. 2)

Even if no formal commitment was made to it, White's scheme was clearly recognized as more suitable to attaining 'substantial stability of exchange rates.' The group suggested that its liquidity provisions should be widened to $12 billion; its governing board 'should be given the power to recommend and approve the adjustment of exchange rates' and also 'to make reports and recommendations to member countries urging appropriate national policies that may involve tariff adjustments, foreign lending, control of capital movements, exchange-rate flexibility, internal expansionist programs, and other measures designed to promote equilibrium.' The EFG clearly stated also the need for a general economic staff to: 'coordinate the operations of an international program designed to counter depressional or inflationary tendencies, to promote international world-wide expansionist and development programs, and to foster adjustments leading toward international equilibrium' (EB-64, p. 1).

With these appropriate emendations, White's scheme was believed to provide a sufficient degree of flexibility to the world supply of liquidity. But loose management of international and national monetary policy should not be regarded as a safe method of preventing depression and economic isolationism.

The compromise between Viner and Hansen was shaped in the form of a rigid monetary policy coupled with an expansionist or flexible fiscal policy. Domestic as well as international affairs should be ruled according to monetary orthodoxy. Expansionist fiscal policy had a more active role to play in developing a more peaceful and cooperative post-war economic system: domestic fiscal policies could be pursued by international agreement or by autonomous action and, within certain limits, with the fund's financial support, without external drain of reserves or devaluations. Moreover international investment policies should be promoted on a wide scale, especially in the developing countries; the timing of their operations should be managed with the purpose of smoothing the international cycle, thus preventing the world from falling into a major new depression.

3.7 The shaping of the IMF proposal

The discussion within the EFG about the post-war financial order deserves our attention not only because of the recommendations the group was sending to the State Department, but also for the role that Viner, Hansen and other of its members were playing in other agencies directly involved in post-war planning.

As we noted earlier, Viner was special assistant to Henry Morgenthau Jr at the Treasury: in January 1942 the Chicago economist was called to Washington to help Harry D. White in redrafting his first proposal for the IMF and IBRD. Viner stayed at the Treasury until the end of March and worked on the second and third drafts of White's scheme.[56]

In May 1942 White's scheme was approved by Morgenthau and sent to an interdepartmental committee formed by representatives of many agencies, with Adolph Berle, Herbert Feis, Leo Pasvolsky, and Dean Acheson serving on behalf of the State Department. Whereas the committee was intended to exert political control over the course of negotiations, a technical sub-committee, under the chairmanship of Harry D. White, was set up to discuss and refine the Treasury proposals for the IMF and the IBRD (Horsefield, 1969, pp. 25, 30–2; Eckes, 1975, pp. 61–2). Two members of the EFG, Alvin Hansen and Benjamin Cohen,[57] attended several meetings of the technical committee (Notter, 1949, pp. 141–3; Shoup, 1975, p. 37).

In the technical committee Hansen was one of the representatives from the Federal Reserve Board. Together with colleagues, Emanuel A. Goldenweiser and Walter Gardner, who had previously worked out an alternative plan for the IMF,[58] he tried to introduce considerable changes in the White scheme, as we can see from this personal letter to White:

Since we had our conference with you, the staff at the Federal Reserve has again gone over the whole matter and Goldenweiser is sending you a summary statement of the main points.

I'm sending you this personal note since I can't come on Monday so you will know my own point of view. It seems to me that our suggestions can quite easily be incorporated into your plan. You have frequently stressed the importance of having a plan that could get the approval of Congress. In my judgement, the modification which we have suggested would help very much to get this approval, for the following reasons:

1. The American contribution would not be increased beyond the $2 billion you have suggested.
2. The contribution of other countries would be very greatly increased to $13 billion.
3. The Fund would be stronger in its gold holdings under our proposal. This, I think, would be pleasing to Congress.
4. The American voting power while small (rightly so with our relatively small contribution) would rapidly grow if we purchased large amounts of gold from the Fund.
5. The plan looks toward future limitation by the fund of new gold production. This meets one type of opposition to gold purchases.

(Hansen to White, 11 June 1943)[59]

Despite some divergence in their perspectives, Hansen and the other Fed specialists shared the same anxiety about the dangers connected with unlimited gold purchases on the part of the Treasury, which could cause worldwide depression as well as inflation in the United States. But White and Morgenthau were immovable on this point, and refused to grant the fund any real power to limit American gold policy (Eckes, 1975, p. 95).

Hansen and his colleagues were not able to alter the philosophy of White's scheme, but they succeeded in obtaining some important changes in the final American IMF draft, which was to be sent to London as the basis for the official talks with the British in September 1943: the liquidity provisions were widened from $5 to $8 billion, a higher degree of exchange flexibility was permitted in the first three years of the IMF activity, and the gold percentage of each country's quota was increased to 50 per cent (Domhoff, 1990, p. 176).[60] Pressures in the same direction came from Canada, where a plan designed as a compromise between the British and the American one was presented in May 1943.[61]

Whereas Hansen was trying to bring White's plan a little bit closer to the British requests, Viner was doing something similar with Keynes's.

In spring 1943 Viner sent to Keynes, forwarded by Dennis H. Robertson,[62] a first draft of a paper he was going to publish in the *Yale Review*, comparing the relative advantages of the British and the American plans. Keynes wrote him a long letter, commenting on the paper point by point. A brief but very intense correspondence started: in the four letters exchanged from May to October 1943, when the final preparations for the first official talks between British and American delegations were under way, Keynes and Viner discussed in detail the functioning of the two plans, finding a good deal of agreement on many issues. The letters, published in Keynes's *Collected Writings* (Keynes, 1940–44[1980], pp. 320–35), are widely cited in the literature, but it is worth recalling here some of their contents.

In his article Viner repeated his arguments about the fund's superiority over the overdraft plan. Viner stressed that Keynes's plan seemed to grant an inferior role to gold than White's plan did and for that reason could be regarded as less acceptable to gold-producing or holding countries. Moreover Viner pointed out that White's plan, providing the fund with means of payment other than gold, was as able as the Keynes plan to enhance the elasticity of the world liquidity supply and prevent the risk of a new worldwide fall into deep deflation. Inflation, in Viner's view, was the danger from which neither plan seemed to provide sufficient defense (Viner, 1943, p. 210).

After some attempt to defend his own plan from Viner's criticism, Keynes admitted the legitimacy of Viner's anxiety about inflation:

> Assuredly I share your concern about possible menace of inflation, or rather ... the possibility of redundancy of gold. Experience shows that what happens is always the thing against which one has not made provision in advance. These currency schemes are providing against the danger of an insufficiency of international money. For my own part, I should not be all surprised if, in fact, the actual danger which meets us turns out to be just the opposite, namely, an excess of international currency.
>
> (Keynes to Viner, 9 June 1943: box 16, folder 21, JVP)

Viner's opposition to granting large drawing rights from US financial resources was not grounded on the fear of depletion of the reserves owned by the American banking system: the real danger was quite the opposite. Many countries had lost most of their productive resources during the war and needed large amounts of food, machinery, and raw materials. The greater the provision of international reserves at their disposal, the greater the demand for goods which would fall on American industry. If this was coupled with industrial conversion to peace production, bottlenecks, scarcity of raw materials, and rapid inflation, instead of full employment, were likely to be the outcome.

Thus it was not only the worship of banking orthodoxy that moved American public opinion to a view of the Keynes plan as a dangerous mechanism:

> The absence in the C[learing] U[nion] of a rigid limit to the creditor obligations is of course very attractive per se to those who are debtor-minded but it is literally terrifying to those who anticipate being creditors. Whether inherently desirable or not, I think that limits to credit obligations will absolutely without question have to be conceded to make the new agency acceptable to all the essential countries.
>   (Viner to Keynes, 12 July 1943: box 16, folder 21, JVP)

At this argument, already exposed in the paper, Keynes was ready to concede:

> You here express the view that countries are not likely to accept an unlimited liability to be net creditors under a scheme. I should think it extremely likely that you are right about this. I have always felt that the difficulty is to find a satisfactory alternative.
>   (Keynes to Viner, 9 June 1943: box 16, folder 21, JVP)

Viner clearly stated the reasons why the British plan could not be acceptable to American opinion. On the other hand he admitted that a larger amount of resources and exchange flexibility should be permitted in the American plan, especially in the transition period.

This last point was particularly stressed by Viner: the transition period should be excluded from the activity of the new institution.[63] The heavy load of extraordinary imbalances in the early post-war years could not effectively be managed by the new institution, and certainly would have caused its collapse.

> Here I come to the most important point I want to raise with you. I think that discussion of both plans has been befogged by failure to distinguish between the international financial problems of the period immediately following the cessation of hostilities and those of the long run more stable future. The expectation that the US will be alone or almost alone as a creditor is plausible for the first period. Over the long pull ... I think the US is as likely to be short as to be long of foreign short-term funds. But the difficulties re size of voting quotas, size of borrowing quotas, motives [of the authors] of the plans, etc. largely arise because the two plans are being interpreted primarily as plans to

tide over the immediate post-war emergency period ... I think many
apparent conflicts of opinion would disappear, and that it would be
much easier to ascertain – and enlarge – the area of agreement.
(Viner to Keynes, 12 July 1943: box 16, folder 21, JVP)

Even on that point Keynes and the British officials came to agree with
Viner: 'We have not yet found the precise formula for defining the role
of the plan in the early period. But you may feel confident that on this
issue we are entirely of your mind' (Keynes to Viner, 17 October 1943:
box 16, folder 21, JVP).

Viner was well aware of the huge financial aid the British needed to
sustain their balance of payments in the transition period: only it had
to be provided outside the fund, through the traditional channels of
intergovernmental loans. Viner declared on many occasions that this aid
should be particularly generous (Viner, 1943, p. 213; 1947, pp. 337–8).[64]

At that time, Keynes, though convinced about the technical superiority of his plan, was becoming more flexible towards the possibility
of adopting other solutions in order to achieve some sort of agreement
(Skidelsky, 2001, pp. 301–2). This exchange of letters with Viner probably
added arguments to the case for putting aside his own plan and trying
to improve the American one. Moreover Keynes was aware of Viner's
reputation within the administration and his special relation with the
Treasury:[65] Viner's open mind or rigidity about certain critical points,
helped Keynes to guess the attitude of the American officials and to work
out a better strategy for the negotiations.[66]

Looking at the first tentative agreement on the IMF achieved during
the formal September talks between the British and the American
delegation,[67] we can say that it resembled in many respects the suggestions sponsored by Hansen and Viner during the summer.

Keynes himself seemed to be satisfied by the outcome of the September
talks. The only issue on which, writing to Viner, he revealed his annoy-
ance was the strong conditionality the Americans were imposing for the
fund's financial help to debtor countries, a point that Viner himself had
stressed in his last letter.[68]

Our view has been very strongly that if countries are to be given
sufficient confidence they must be able to rely in all normal circumstances on drawing a substantial part of their quota without policing
or facing unforeseen obstacles ... If the clearing union provisions were
applied to the lower quotas now contemplated, we gravely doubt
whether those concerned, particularly some of the smaller countries,

would feel adequate confidence ... This, therefore, is a point about which, after further reflection, I cannot agree with you. No doubt it's a difficult issue.

(Keynes to Viner, 17 October 1943: box 16, folder 21, JVP)

The British could not deny the American request for stronger conditionality for the fund's aid, but asked in turn a much higher degree of autonomy in declaring exchange rate variations for reason of 'domestic political or social policy', without interference by the fund.[69]

Viner argued against this provision: it would have seriously injured the stabilization function of the fund. It would have also exposed national monetary authority to political and social pressures for inflation and exchange devaluation. 'As the criterion for permissible (or compulsory) changes in "normal" times, I don't think relative trends in "efficiency wages" would suffice, although they would be important ... The wage criterion, moreover, accepts the business agent of the powerful trade unions as the ultimate and unlimited sovereign over monetary policy' (Viner to Keynes, 12 July 1943: box 16, folder 21, JVP).

In the following months, prolonged discussions between (and within) each side of the Atlantic added to the 'technicalities', in order to make the IMF acceptable to public opinion in both countries, and guarantee each nation against undue interference in their national affairs.[70]

The refusal of the Americans to concede adequate and automatic liquidity to debtor countries, coupled with the British determination not to give up their freedom in pursuing full employment policies, threatened the accomplishment of what could be regarded as the main content of the agreement: namely, international stabilization of exchange rates.

Viner's and Hansen's three-year long efforts to get the two sides of the ocean closer and cooperative had brought forth their first fruit. But the workability of this compromise formula risked being very narrow.

3.8   EFG and the IBRD (September 1943–July 1944)

In the EFG strategy, the other essential device to assure the functioning of the new economic order was an international development agency. As we have seen earlier, this new institution was intended to provide a huge flow of investments to the world, fostering reconstruction, favoring social and economic development and increasing global aggregate demand: only international measures adequate to prevent a new world depression could convince many countries to open up their economy and take part in a multilateral trading system. Did the official Treasury proposals shape up to this?

In August 1943 Secretary Morgenthau presented to the Interdepartmental Technical Committee a plan for an 'International Bank for Reconstruction and Development' for discussion with the British delegation.[71] During these official Anglo-American conversations the American proposal received a good deal of critical comment from Lionel Robbins and John Maynard Keynes. As a result, the project was sent back to the technical committee for further revision and Hansen was asked to write a memorandum stating the EFG position on this subject.[72]

Hansen could not hide his disappointment about the White plan: the proposed bank was mainly a guarantee scheme intended to encourage private foreign investments; the rate of interest was to be set at the market level; the projects should yield sufficient profits; the capital goods should be bought in the country where the loan was raised; White's proposals stressed the reconstruction and short-term character of the new institution.[73]

In Hansen's view the right approach to meeting the great need for foreign investment in the post-war world was quite the opposite. Hansen did not reject the private investment-inducing function of the bank, but he wanted it to be supplemented with other commitments:

> Basic public development projects which could earn only a low rate of interest could be financed by bonds sold in the capital market of the capital surplus countries and guaranteed by the development bank. Other projects which entailed the possibility of a return inadequate to pay market rates on public guaranteed issues might nevertheless be thoroughly sound from the stand point of the whole world economy in increasing productivity and standards of living and by reason of their general expansionist and developmental effects upon the entire economy of the borrowing countries.
>
> (EA-49, 13 November 1943, p. 14)

Moreover the bank should employ its resources not only in making loans, given their dangerous rigidity in case of adverse business fluctuations, but in guaranteeing new equity issues of private corporations engaging in development projects (ibid., p. 14). The Harvard economist was decidedly contesting the Treasury approach:

> Mr Hansen remarked that Lord Keynes had made the point that unless the International Bank took such risks, if, instead, lending were to

be based strictly upon 'banker' principle, the volume of loans would be small. He mentioned that the Treasury proposal did rest squarely and rigorously on the 'banker' principle ... Mr Hansen said that the reference [in a recent Treasury statement] to the 'budgetary position of the member Government guaranteeing the loan' had a nineteenth-century ring and seemed to imply the borrowing country would need to have a balanced budget.

(Ibid., p. 16)

We can see that Hansen's comments and proposals followed quite closely those of the British critics of the scheme, with which Hansen showed himself to be well acquainted.[74]

Many EFG members shared Hansen's broader perspective, which was well grounded in the group's previous analysis. Nevertheless a politically acceptable solution had to be found in order to overcome the strong opposition which was likely to come – especially from the banking community – and to obtain Congressional approval.[75] Public opinion in the United States was becoming more and more sensitive to the topic of government intervention; it was also anxious about giving away US financial resources to serve foreign countries' needs (Gardner 1956[1980], p. 98).

Hansen's proposal on equity investments and special interest rate provisions were finally approved by the EFG, with several technical amendments and after a long discussion, briefly reported on record. The final Hansen memorandum was shaped as a mixed formula between guaranteed and direct loans, private and public projects, remunerative and not remunerative investments, development and reconstruction purposes. Only the 'export-tied' character of the loans in the September Treasury draft, was unanimously rejected by the group: it was an apparent betrayal of the multilateral approach that the EFG was striving for. Viner was particularly rigid in refusing any compromise on this point:

Mr Viner pointed out that the bulk of the proceeds of Loans become diffused and generalized. A capital exporting country was not necessarily in the same measure a capital goods exporter. France, for example, lent capital abroad but not capital goods. If borrowing countries were to be limited, with respect to foreign loans, to that volume of capital goods, the result would inevitably be a drastic reduction of the investments under discussion.

(EA-49, 13 November 1943, pp. 15–16)[76]

The last point stressed by the EFG was that the operations of the bank should have an anti-cyclical timing. Invited by Eugene Staley and Viner,[77] Hansen agreed to add a paragraph dealing with this problem in his memorandum. It was the last attempt on the part of EFG to give life to an international stabilization agency in the new economic order:

> The International Development and Investment Bank should itself be prepared to engage in vigorous counter-cyclical programs. The international pool of funds, consisting in the first instance of the capital fund of the Bank should, in times of depression, be enlarged substantially by the flotation of new issues by the Bank in capital markets, where funds for foreign lending and investment are available on favorable terms. Particularly in periods of depression, guarantees of private funds and the flotation of new issues should be undertaken on a large scale.
>
> (EB-65, 8 January 1944, p. 4)[78]

Looking at the final American proposal for the institution of the International Bank for Reconstruction and Development, underwritten after a brief discussion and a few changes at Bretton Woods, we can notice its resemblance to some of the EFG's proposals. Development as well as reconstruction was the declared aim, the mixed formula of direct and indirect loans was confirmed, and tied loans were almost completely ruled out. But the conservative character of the new institution was apparent (Gardner, 1956[1980], pp. 117–19; Eckes, 1975, p. 132). The bank's direct lending functions were intended to be marginal and the immediate capital contribution from member countries was minimal; although its guaranteeing functions would have allowed a multiple investment of its capital endowment, the sum of the bank's loans and guarantees could not exceed 100 per cent of the total[79] and its lending operations should be selected with due regard to the capacity of borrowers to repay appropriate interest rates.

The American and British governments, though for different reasons, had strongly supported the establishment of such a conservative institution. Its appeal for creditors should be secured by the soundness of its assets and the security of its operations. The British, who did not expect to engage in the bank's operations, were satisfied to restrict its role. Even American bankers could be reassured that the new international bank was established not to compete with them, but, instead, to support and share the risk of their foreign ventures.

Therefore the more progressive features suggested by Hansen and the EFG were dropped. Tied loans were retained for 20 per cent of the bank's direct loans[80] while provisions regarding the anti-cyclical timing of international investment, low interest rates for high social and economic value projects, and equity investments on the part of the bank, were driven back to the world of Utopia or delayed in the hope of better times to come.

3.9 The post-war planners and the post-war world

Meeting in October 1944, Hansen, Viner, and most of the other EFG members declared their satisfaction regarding the final outcome of the Bretton Woods Conference.[81] Their words betrayed some feeling of national pride:

> Mr Hansen said the work of the conference had been largely a gigantic drafting job. It had been a big task to work out quotas, decide how exchange rates had to be set, settle when provisions were to come into effect, etc. ... Mr Hansen felt that in all important controversies the Treasury and the State Department had won out all around. The Fund had become more conservative and more liquid. Other countries had wanted an unabridged right to draw on the Fund. As the scheme now stood, they enjoyed no such right ... the scheme means very cheap short-term money.
>
> Regarding the relation of exchange rate changes and devaluation to internal conditions, Keynes felt strongly ... that the Fund should refrain from telling member countries how to run their economic affairs, but the American delegation won out: the Fund may make reports on relevant economic conditions and developments within member countries. In fact, on the score of both the Fund and the Bank, America's money bags prevailed.
>
> (EA-58, 29 September 1944, pp. 7–9)

The EFG members hoped that the IMF and the bank, as they now stood, would be able to overcome bankers' opposition and attain Congressional approval: consequently they were eager to lend their voices in support of the Bretton Woods institutions.[82]

Actually the outstanding value of the agreements lay not in their technical perfection (about which EFG economists had much to say), but in their political relevance: the hope of the post-war planners was that

Bretton Woods was just a first step in the building up of a peaceful, cooperative and multilateral economic system.

> It is proper, especially for economists, to appraise the Bretton Woods Agreements from a strictly technical point of view, in terms of their ideal appropriateness, independent of special time and political circumstances, for their technical special purpose. But final judgment should be based on a much broader, and less exacting, range of considerations. These agreements were but a first installment of what, if the negotiations progress favorably, will undoubtedly be a long series.
>
> (Viner, 1944, p. 232)

> It is also my conviction that the details of the plan are relatively unimportant. What is important is that an international institution should be set up with broad powers to act. Such an international institution will succeed or fail, not by reason of the specific detailed sections contained in the statutes, but rather by reason of the wisdom and statesmanship of the Board of Governors.
>
> (Hansen, 1945, p. 86)

The post-war planners had been stubbornly resolute in pursuing this first victory, and even if the score was not an exciting one, it was a promising beginning. Better outcomes should wait for better times.[83]

However, for many of the individuals involved the first match turned out also to be last: new players entered the game and the game itself changed.[84] Government interventions through multilateral institutions were arousing growing opposition in American public opinion. From the beginning the Truman administration reverted to traditional patterns of prudent and bilateral bargaining in the commercial as well as in the financial field.[85]

Moreover, given that no help would come from the IMF in the face of their balance of payments turmoil in the immediate post-war period, the British had to ask the United States government for a stabilization loan. That was the opportunity for the US State Department and Treasury, no longer guided by Cordell Hull and Henry Morgenthau, to press for the immediate abolition of any trade discrimination on the part of the British, that is, of the 'imperial preference system' (Gardner, 1956[1980], pp. 188–99). They finally obtained, in return for the $3.75 billion loan, the establishment of current account convertibility for the pound sterling within a year, much earlier than asked for by the Bretton Woods Agreement (Gardner, 1956[1980], pp. 213–21). The British balance of payments crisis was mainly the outcome of this untimely provision. American bankers, who in 1944 had been disappointed in their desire to see a devalued pound, finally succeeded in 1949 (De Cecco, 1969, pp. 56–7).

For many years to come the Bretton Woods institutions were to be 'frozen' and new developments ruled out (Gardner, 1956[1980], pp. 286–99). Nevertheless some of the proposals the EFG had formulated in the previous years were not to be completely without fruit, at least in the long run: the International Finance Corporation (1956) and the International Development Agency (1961), envisioned in some of their earlier proposals, were finally realized a decade or more afterwards.

In the meantime, the emergence of the Soviet threat renewed the urgency of treating Europe's economic diseases. Those large funds that the US administration had refused to grant at Bretton Woods were provided on a multiplied scale a few years later in order to support European reconstruction: they were given in exchange for political and social stability. In 1951 the European Payments Union finally realized a multilateral clearing system to promote trade and economic growth in Europe. Multilateralism prevailed, although in a different role, on a different scale and timing than dreamed of by the New Deal post-war planners.

3.10   Concluding comments

This analysis of the documents preserved in the CFR's archive demonstrates their considerable value: the insights provided by this source substantially enrich our understanding of the contributions of Viner and Hansen (and other EFG economists) to the post-war planning activities of the Roosevelt administration during the Second World War. In this respect a number of conclusions can be stated quite clearly.

First we can point to the importance of the institutional framework provided by the Council on Foreign Relations: the non-governmental character of the EFG gave its members a degree of independence of judgement; its formal link with the State Department and the personal attachments with many other agencies assured the EFG a good deal of influence, at least in the first three years of its activity; its international scope provided the opportunity to develop a program of informal meetings with other government officials and economists, preparing the ground for more formal negotiations. We have seen the role of these factors in enabling the EFG effectively to press the administration toward a multilateral strategy for the post-war world and to progress some of the early steps in Anglo-American understanding.

But the general aim of the EFG comprised more than the building up of a multilateral trade system, it also encouraged a wide program of international reforms designed to prevent the new economic system from sliding into a new depression. In the long run international stabilization was needed to defeat depression, but the reverse was also true: international exchange of goods, services, and capital could be developed and maintained only if 'internal' equilibrium was secured at least in the major countries. Hansen, the American 'Keynesian,' and Viner, the apologist of the classical approach to international economics, well represented the two poles of this strategy.

Their divergent viewpoints and theoretical backgrounds emerged clearly on several issues; nevertheless they were unanimous on the core of their effort: not only in championing a multilateral trade system and stabilization policies, but also in supporting the case for multilateral *institutions* to manage and develop the new international order.

Moreover their discussion within the EFG revealed a sort of alchemic box from which a new economic policy formula could be derived: Hansen's longstanding fear of world and national depression had come to be at odds with Viner's growing anxiety about world and national inflation. The outcome was to be a flexible fiscal policy coupled with a rigid monetary policy. This middle way attitude, exerted on many other issues, contributed to preparing the ground for a compromise between White and Keynes, the United States and Great Britain.

If the tale stopped in September 1943, or more generously, in July 1944, we could say that Hansen and Viner, as well as other post-war planners, had accomplished their mission: they had been able to overcome isolationism, bilateralism, the imperialistic attitude toward international economic relations, skepticism around the feasibility of international institutions; they had been able to impose on their politicians the grand rational design of a novel economic world order, shaped along the lines of a neoclassical-Keynesian synthesis. Up to a certain point this was true, and it cannot be considered a poor outcome. But, as we have seen, that was not the end.

More than sixty years have elapsed since Bretton Woods: the Cold War grew up and faded away, new international institutions were created besides the IMF and IBRD, old-fashioned colonialism came to an end; technological improvements transformed this world into a close community. Despite all these developments multilateralism is still a fragile creature, easily overcome or exploited by older and more deeply rooted attitudes.

Notes

This chapter is a revision of the paper presented at the VIII AISPE Conference held in Palermo, September 2004. I am grateful to Pier Francesco Asso, Duccio Basosi, Luca Fiorito, Riccardo Realfonzo and Roger Sandilands for their useful suggestions and detailed criticisms. The usual disclaimer applies.

1. In addition to the Council on Foreign Relations Archive in New York and Princeton, we resorted to the Jacob Viner Papers (indicated in the text as JVP) at the Seeley G. Mudd Manuscript Library (Princeton University) and the Morgenthau Diaries (MD) in the Roosevelt Presidential Library in Hyde Park (NY). The Council on Foreign Relations Papers are referred to in the following manner: EA (followed by a number) indicates the proceedings of discussions within the EFG; EB indicates the reports set out by the EFG. Both series of documents are published in volumes: EB is traceable in a limited set of libraries; EA is available at the Council on Foreign Relations Archive. Archival sources are quoted with permission respectively of the Council on Foreign Relations, the Seeley G. Mudd Manuscript Library (Princeton University) and the Roosevelt Presidential Library.
2. Some political inquiries into WPS's activity, with great attention devoted to the Economic and Financial Group, are Shoup (1975), Santoro (1987), and Domhoff (1990). Some references to Hansen's and Viner's work in WPS, concerning the Bretton Woods Agreements are also in Ikenberry (1993, p. 165).
3. See Bordo and Eichengreen (1993), Kirshner (1996), Eichengreen (1996), Harold (1996) and Cesarano (2001).
4. Concerning the balance of power system, see Spykman (1942), Newman (1968), and Sheehan (1996).
5. On the interwar record of the international monetary system see Drummond (1987), Flanders (1989), and Eichengreen (1992).
6. On the activity of the Council on Foreign Relations see Council on Foreign Relations (1947), Shoup and Minter (1977), Wala (1994), and Domhoff (1990).
7. Leo Pasvolsky was one of the officials most involved in Anglo-American economic planning during the war: he took part in most of the meetings held by the State Department with the British embassy, the US Treasury and the British expert delegation in September 1943. See *Foreign Relations of the United States*, 1942, VII, pp. 163–242; 1943, I, pp. 1054–126; see also Opie (1957, p. 134) and Goodwin (1998).
8. *Council on Foreign Relations, War and Peace Study Group*, in George W. Ball papers, *c.* 1933–94, Box 141, Mudd Library, Princeton University, pp. 9–10.
9. According to Domhoff (1990, p. 115), Norman H. Davis, CFR executive director, had 'long standing and close ... relationships with central decision makers in the State Department and White House ... He had direct and frequent

access to [President] Roosevelt and [Secretary of State Cordell] Hull in the years between 1940 and 1942'; moreover many State Department officials, like Sumner Welles, Leo Pasvolsky, Dean Acheson, Herbert Feis, and Myron C. Taylor had been members of the Council (Shoup, 1975, p. 25).

10. According to Aaronson 'Hull established a small staff of eight under Pasvolsky to develop America's long term goals for the peace. But these employees ... were overwhelmed with operational responsibilities. Pasvolsky and his staff devised an innovative approach to facilitate the committee's background work. Under a grant from the Rockefeller Foundation, the Council on Foreign Relations worked with the division to prepare a wide range of studies on international issues (Notter, 1949, pp. 53–6). This approach enabled the post-war planners to broaden their perspective without adding to the department's budget' (Aaronson, 1991, p. 174). According to Santoro, the personnel devoted to post-war planning were even fewer elsewhere in US government departments (Santoro, 1987, p. 187).

11. The WPS was composed of five study groups (political, territorial, peace aims, security & armaments, economic & financial), coordinated by a steering committee and each one placed under the leadership of two 'joint rapporteurs', chosen from the most eminent scholars in each field. Each group could also enjoy the full-time assistance of two junior researchers; George W. Ball papers, *Council on Foreign Relations, War and Peace Study Group*, p. 11.

12. On Viner's life and work, see Robbins (1970), Samuelson (1972), and Bloomfield (1992). On the debate over the 'early Chicago School' and its relations to the later Chicago School of Political Economy see, for all, Leeson (2003).

13. On Hansen's life and work see Tobin (1976), Barber (1987), and Mehrling (1997, pp. 85–157).

14. George W. Ball papers, *Council on Foreign Relations, War and Peace Study Group*, p. 10.

15. For a survey of the Western Hemisphere idea in American political thought, see Whitaker (1954) and Callcott (1968).

16. Hansen (1940) and Viner (1941). The most popular refutation of the Western Hemisphere project was Spykman (1942).

17. EB-19, *The War and United States Foreign Policy* (19 October 1940); EB-34, *Methods of Economic Collaboration: Introducing the Role of Grand Area in American Economic Policy* (24 July 1941).

18. With regard to Anglo-American negotiations during the Second World War, see Gardner (1956[1980]), Pressnell (1986), and Dobson (1995).

19. EB-32, *Economic War Aims: General Considerations* (17 April 1941). These aims were further developed in 11 points presented in the memorandum EB-36, *Economic War Aims: Main Lines of Approach, Preliminary Statement* (22 June 1941). For a comparative analysis between this second document and the Atlantic Charter, see Santoro (1987, pp. 200–7).

20. EB-42, *Economic Aspects of the Eight Points of the Atlantic Charter* (20 October 1941).

21. Anglo-American economic relations had been the subject of a parallel study in 1936–38 realized by the two institutions concerning financial problems (settlement of the old war debts) and perspectives for commercial cooperation. This project had been carried out especially by Herbert Feis, Winfield Riefler,

and Percy Bidwell, later to be deeply engaged in the WPS (CFR Papers, Princeton University, 2, VII).

22. EA-20, EA-25. The British experts who took part in the first meeting held on 20 September 1941 were Geoffrey Crowther (at that time editor of *The Economist*), Mr Kenneth Bewley (chief of the British Supply Council of North America) and Mr Hutton (whose identity I have not been able to clarify). The second meeting, on 24 January 1942, was attended by Sir Arthur Salter, Mr Tawney, Redvers Opie (economic adviser to the British embassy in Washington and a participant in the Hot Springs and Bretton Woods Conferences; later he was editor of the *Oxford Economic Papers*), and the Canadian economist Louis Rasminsky (at that time member of the Canadian exchange-control board, he took part in the Bretton Woods Conference and was Governor of the Bank of Canada from 1961 to 1973). About Anglo-American official negotiations between the summer and the fall of 1941, see Pressnell (1986, pp. 33–49) and Gardner (1956[1980], pp. 40–68).

23. With regard to early British forecasts on their own post-war economic conditions, see Pressnell (1986, pp. 1–5) and De Cecco (1969, pp. 53–5).

24. Hansen was a delegate to the international conference sponsored by the British Association for the Advancement of Science. Apart from attending the conference, he 'held numerous informal and unofficial discussions with people at Chatham House, London School of Economics, Lord Reith's Ministry of Reconstruction, the Group of Nuffield College, Oxford, working under G.D.H. Cole, and numerous government officials, many of them erstwhile academic economists. Discussion concerned the British balance of payments in the post-war years' (EA-22, 11 November 1941).

25. Hansen to Viner, 20 October 1941 (box 13, folder 9, JVP). See also Harrod (1951, p. 527).

26. In the second draft of his clearing union plan, Keynes inserted this statement: 'I believe that there is great force in Prof. Hansen's contention that the problem of surpluses and unwanted exports will largely disappear if active employment and ample purchasing power can be sustained in the main centres of world trade' (Keynes, 1940–44 [1980], p. 48).

27. About Anglo-American trade relations during the 1930s, see Rowland (1987) and Lake (1983).

28. EB-45, *Tentative Draft of a Joint Economic Declaration by the Governments of the United States and the United Kingdom* (3 January 1942). An early version of the draft had been circulated in Washington since the end of October (Hansen to Viner, 20 October 1941, box 13, folder 9, JVP). An EFG memorandum entitled *International Collaboration to Secure the Coordination of Stabilization Policies and to Stimulate Investments*, EB-44 was approved on 29 November 1941 and sent directly to President Roosevelt who 'referred the matter to Secretary Hull. Hull wanted to move slowly and therefore advised Hansen to continue this work and the discussions he had been having with the State Department' (Shoup, 1975, p. 36).

29. Pressnell (1986, pp. 49–58).

30. These references to expansion of production and employment, 'inserted to allay the British fears of an American slump' (Opie, 1957, p. 137), were absent in the State Department's July draft and were introduced in the final draft

after negotiations with the British Ambassador Lord Halifax and Redvers Opie (Gardner, 1956[1980], pp. 58–9). Article VII of the Mutual Aid Agreement is reproduced in Pressnell (1986, p. 372).

31. George W. Ball papers, p. 8. The Division on Special Research was established to serve an interdepartmental Advisory Committee on Post-War Foreign Policy authorized by Roosevelt in December 1941, under the chairmanship of Secretary Cordell Hull: of the 14 members of the committee, ten had long-standing links with the CFR, and six were involved in the WPS (Shoup, 1975, p. 25). According to Notter, in summer 1943 Roosevelt selected from the Advisory Committee six individuals in order to have a closer group to advise him on post-war planning: the so called 'Informal Agenda Group' was formed by Cordell Hull, Sumner Welles, Leo Pasvolsky, Isaiah Bowman, Myron C. Taylor, and Norman H. Davis: all of them, with the exception of Hull, were members of the CFR (Shoup, 1975, p. 38).

32. Between March and April 1942 the following six memoranda were discussed and approved by the EFG: *Problems of International Relief* (William Diebold); *Labor Problems and Social Legislation* (Carter Goodrich), *Problems of International Trade* (Arthur R. Upgren), *International Commodity Problems* (Eugene Staley), *Problems of Monetary Reconstruction* (Hansen); *Problems of International Long-Term Investment* (Viner), collected together in EB-49, *Post-war Economic Problems*. They had been requested from the State Department's Division on Special Research on 28 February 1942, just five days after the Mutual Aid Agreement had been signed. In May 1942 Pasvolsky and Harry Hawkins started, on behalf of the State Department, informal meetings with British embassy officials, drawing up and sending to London an agenda of a 'dozen of topics covering the broadest possible economic field … known as the Pasvolsky Agenda' (Opie, 1957, p. 140).

33. See also Bidwell (1943, 1944).

34. 'Mr Maddox asked if Mr Bidwell was definitely recommending the creation of an international authority which would be able to control national tariff schedules. There are very important political and economic implications to such a decision. Mr Bidwell said that … real international tariff control is possible only if states give up some power. Mr Viner agreed with Mr Bidwell on this last point and urged that the memorandum stated this very clearly' (EA-31, 15 June 1942, pp. 2–3).

35. Pressnell (1986, p. 99). The EFG might have been acquainted with the commercial union plan through Pasvolsky who had been one of the first to receive it from the US Ambassador in London, John G. Winant, in December 1942, *Foreign Relations of the United States*, 1943, I, p. 1103.

36. The State Department officials involved in the official Anglo-American talks of September 1943 were: Myron C. Taylor (who guided the delegation), Leo Pasvolsky, Herbert Feis, Harry C. Hawkins (chief of the Division on Commercial Policy), John D. Hickerson (assistant chief of the Division of European Affairs), Leroy D. Stinebower (chief of the Division on Economic Studies). For a brief summary of the September discussions around employment policies, see Gardner (1956[1980], pp. 104–6, 109). The Anglo-American documents on commercial policy, commodity policy, cartel policy, employment policy, called the 'Washington principles' are published in Pressnell (1986, pp. 390–6). The employment policy provisions followed quite closely EFG's

proposals of spring 1943. For a synthesis of those discussions see Gardner (1956[1980], pp. 102–6); Opie (1957, pp. 142–3).

37. EB-49, *Problems of Monetary Reconstruction* (25 April 1942); EB-64, *International Adjustment of Exchange Rates* (6 April 1943).

38. About Hansen's view on this point, see also Hansen (1941), Hansen and Kindleberger (1942) and Eckes (1975, pp. 84–5).

39. If a country had a balance of payments surplus with inflow of reserves, the government should produce a fiscal deficit in order to enhance its imports without reducing its exports; this expansionist policy should be brought about up to the point where full employment was reached and domestic prices began to rise; at that point a tight monetary policy should intervene to stop the outflow of purchasing power (EB-64, pp. 13–14).

40. The document containing the general statements shared by Anglo-American experts is named, at least in British records, 'The Washington Principles' (Pressnell, 1986, pp. 390–6). In the section on 'international co-ordination of measures for the maintenance of high levels of employment' it declared that: 'It is hoped that four new international institutions may ultimately emerge as a result of informal economic discussions: a) An international stabilization fund for currencies; b) An international investment bank; c) An international commodity organization; d) An international commercial policy organization.' About the 'Coordination of specialized international economic organization' the Washington Principles stated that 'Clearly the policies pursued by these different bodies should be ... coordinated ... and ... it is desirable that there should be some organization with wider terms of reference ... It is suggested that an advisory economic staff should be established as the nucleus and operative section of such an organization' (Pressnell, 1986, pp. 395–6).

41. On John H. Williams's monetary thought and policy prescriptions see Asso and Fiorito, Chapter 8 in this volume.

42. On bankers' views see Eckes (1975, pp. 86–7).

43. 'Mr Currie thought the whole concept of the agency rather paternalistic or avuncular. It might become the vehicle of a new kind of imperialism. The agency will have a bias against exchange controls' (EA-39, 9 January 1943, p. 16).

44. According to Eckes, Hansen, as adviser in the Federal Reserve Board, played an important role in determining the attitude of the board in favor of the White plan and against the key currency plan proposed by John H. Williams and supported by the Federal Reserve Bank of New York: 'Consultant Alvin Hansen who was instrumental in shaping the Federal Reserve position on this issue, asserted that, if Bretton Woods failed, there was little hope for supplementary economic agreements on investments, commodities and commercial policy. And, without a network of international ties, parallel political agreements designed to assure future peace would surely fail' (Eckes, 1975, p. 119; cited also in Domhoff, 1990, p. 179).

45. In its final version the EFG memorandum took into account Sproul's and Currie's criticisms: 'If the basic underlying condition for international economic equilibrium are present, it might be argued ... that stability of exchange rates would automatically follow and that there would be no need for any specially designed mechanism intended to regulate the system of exchange rates.

But this would imply a degree of perfection in the fundamental adjustments leading to equilibrium which cannot be reasonably expected. The essential purpose and function of an international monetary mechanism is to provide ways and means to soften the impact of disturbing forces tending to overthrow the equilibrium and to provide time for making the adjustments necessary to restore equilibrium' (EB-64, p. 8).

46. This point had been particularly stressed by Viner even during the discussion of Hansen's first proposal for an International Reconstruction Finance Corporation in 1941: 'Mr Viner commended Mr Hansen's memorandum for its recognition of the role of other nations than England and the United States in the organization of such an international lending authority. He urged that the difficulty be recognized even more explicitly. There is a natural uneasiness in small countries which find themselves facing two great naval powers with what looks like a financial monopoly able to impose its own conditions. To be successful the proposed body must avoid the odium of two-power imperialism' (EA-22, 1 November 1941, pp. 6, 9). See also EA-21, 11 October 1941, p. 8. Viner's view on this point did not change in the following years (Viner, 1946, 1947b).

47. 'Mr Viner thought it could be accepted as definite that no countries will surrender control over their national economies to an international agency if that agency then becomes subject to our goodwill. If that is so, said Mr Sproul, the alternative is for us to give up control over an agency in which we are Santa Claus. Mr Currie agreed, asking what national interest of the United States is advanced by participating in an agency for which we supply the money while the other countries vote its use ... Mr Staley agreed that there would be some difficulty in getting acceptance of an international agency, but surely it can be proved that doing things internationally we further the chances of promoting peace, so that our long run economic interests are necessarily involved. International problems must be met internationally and solved on a cooperative basis' (EA-39, 9 January 1943, pp. 13–14).

48. Cesarano (2001) stresses the importance of the Bretton Woods institutions as a first step along the transition from a commodity to a fiat money system.

49. 'It should not be overlooked that a high degree of liquidity, particularly in the leading industrial nations, is essential if we are to continue to maintain, as we should, low rates of interest in the money and capital markets ... The United States could implement its part of the overdraft plan without violent departure from established practice. The Treasury might buy "bancors" ... just as it has purchased gold. Against such "bancor" balances the Treasury could similarly deposit "bancor" certificates with the Federal Reserve, thereby rebuilding its balance and thus causing no drain whatever upon the budget ... The public could react more favourably to the Treasury accumulating a credit in "bancors" (which represents under the International Clearing Union a symbol for international collaboration to promote trade, economic expansion, and employment) than to the policy of buying gold and burying it in a hole in the ground of Fort Knox' (EB-64, pp. 10, 12).

50. EB-49, pp. 11–12; EA-29, p. 25, 15 April 1942, pp. 6–7; EA-40, 6 February 1943, pp. 8–9. On the economic consequences of the US gold policy on the international maldistribution of reserves, see Eichengreen (1992).

51. In the following years Hansen came to be more concerned about the inflationary consequences of full employment policies, see Leeson (1997, pp. 468–70).
52. Even Keynes's clearing union plan included such a proposal: the bancor should be tied to gold, but its gold content could be varied by the union (Horsefield, 1969, I, p. 18).
53. There was, in Viner's position, a good deal of historical reflection: the old gold standard was, in his view, the opposite of an automatic mechanism; even in the golden age before 1914, it was a 'managed' international standard, functioning through effective cooperation between the foremost central banks (Viner, 1937, pp. 388–436). This cooperation was mainly based upon a mix of common banking practices, informal consensus and personal relationships. But this informal cooperation had been revealed as too fragile to overcome the strains and imbalances of the 1920s and 1930s: conflicts over reparations and war debts, violations of the 'rules of the game' (particularly on the part of the United States), lack of agreement about the aims of monetary policy, and pro-cyclical management of central banking, caused the failure of any attempt to coordinate national monetary policies. Misdistribution of gold and the spreading of deflation were merely the symptoms or, at least, manifestations of a more basic disease: the lack of international monetary cooperation. Short-term capital flows, trade barriers, and the heavy load of reparations and war debts had finally caused the collapse of the international monetary system, the imposition of exchange controls and the general instability of the 1930s (Viner, 1932, 1943).
54. In Hansen's view: 'If the stabilization fund plan provided for national contributions in local currency only, exchange would be provided without reliance on gold and the plan would be virtually indistinguishable from that of overdrafts, provided overdrafts were limited to the same amount as was required as contribution to the fund. The big difference remaining would be that under the overdraft plan exchange would be provided only as it was needed whereas the fund provides a supply from the beginning.' Even Viner conceded that 'By various means you can make the fund and overdraft plans very similar economically' (EA-40, 6 February 1943, p. 7). 'Mr Hansen said that the discussion made it seem that the difference between the two stabilization plans was less than he had believed' (EA-41, 6 March 1943, p. 5).
55. 'Mr Viner thought that the memorandum overemphasized the case in favor of the overdraft method of stabilization as opposed to the fund arrangement. Both require the same basic commitment to be made in the first instance .... If a Central bank claimed it had no free assets when the Clearing Union wished to draw on the line of credit, no money might be forthcoming unless a priority had been legally arranged for. A country wishing to avoid its obligations might find it easier to cancel a line of credit than to seize a deposit of the International Fund ... We cannot assume that the integrity of London or New York money market will prevail everywhere. Some countries do not recognize a line of credit. A weak central bank might have trouble meeting its obligations even if it recognized them. The overdraft method of financing is not universally recognized; it is not used in the United States or even in Canada and Scotland. [It] leaves the decision actually to grant funds up to the country at a crucial time, when the temptation not to recognize an

obligation may be great and ability to meet it reduced' (EA-41, 6 March 1943, pp. 4–5).

56. Evidence of Viner's assistance to White is in MD book 483, p. 180 (quoted also by Domhoff, 1990, p. 169); book 498, p. 111; book 504, p. 212. On Viner's and White's collaboration at the Treasury from 1934 onward, see Rees (1973, pp. 43–4, 65).

57. On Benjamin Cohen see Lasser (2002).

58. The Federal Reserve Board plan is described in Eckes (1975, pp. 93–5) and Horsefield (1969, I, pp. 39–40).

59. The letter, preserved in the Hansen Papers in the Harvard University Archive, is cited in Domhoff (1990, pp. 175–6).

60. This last provision was strongly opposed by Keynes and the British negotiators who were trying to limit their gold contribution in order to retain a higher level of foreign reserves. They were at that time proposing a gold quota of no more than 12.5 percent, whereas White's plan drafted in April requested 25 percent. Provided some exception for poor countries, the latter was the quota finally agreed at Bretton Woods (Horsefield, 1969, I, pp. 60–1).

61. Given the special relationships between Canada, the United States and the United Kingdom, the Canadian plan was surely effective in the progress of the negotiations. Designed as a compromise between the ICU and the IMF plan, it adopted the fund framework, providing a greater amount of liquidity ($8 billion instead of $5 billion), a higher degree of exchange flexibility and an international monetary unit based on gold (Horsefield, 1969, I, pp. 37–42; Eckes, 1975, pp. 90–1).

62. Viner papers, box 16, folder 21, JVP. In 1943 Robertson was appointed economic adviser at the British Embassy in Washington.

63. On the economic problems of the transition period see De Cecco (1969) and Bordo (1993, pp. 37–48).

64. On this point, Lionel Robbins, one of Viner's closest British friends, recalled that: 'During the war my own duties as a temporary U.K. official brought me into many Washington contacts; and often, where there were enlightened counsels and sensible policies, I detected traces of his [Viner's] influence. An incident in which he was involved deserves to be placed on permanent record. In early Summer of 1943, Harry White of the US Treasury Department organized an informal international gathering of delegates returning from the Food Conference in Hot Springs. The proceedings, however were in the highest degree unfruitful. The US Treasury was not yet used to the organization of international meetings; and, apart from White's own exposition, delivered as it was from the bridge of a ship without a rudder in a stormy sea, there was little of great intellectual interest and much of political confusion. Towards the end, however, Jack, who had been asked in as an observer, was invited to comment. I do not remember the exact words in which he prefaced his candid expression of general disappointment with the perspective of the discussion. But I shall never forget the sentence in which he summed up his view of the irrelevance of the plans under discussion to the problems of the immediately post-war period. "I shall need" he said, "a bombproof shelter and you offer me an umbrella." Seldom can an economic prognosis have been more accurate' (Robbins, 1970, pp. 5–6).

65. Keynes asked Viner for some further explanation of the Scarce Currency Clause: 'Over here we find this feature of S[tabilization] F[und] rather obscure. Are you clear how it would work? Do you think that is a satisfactory way out?' (Keynes to Viner, 9 June 1943: box 16, folder 21, JVP).

66. The most recent and complete analysis of Keynes's shifting from the defense of the international clearing union scheme to an amelioration of the IMF scheme during the late spring and summer 1943 is provided by Skidelsky (2001, pp. 300–20). In this context the correspondence with Viner is regarded as an important factor in Keynes's preparation for the compromise with the Americans (ibid., pp. 303–5).

67. The agreement is reproduced and commented in detail by Horsefield (1969, I, pp. 58–77).

68. 'In this respect, I believe, neither plan has any historical counterpart whether in private or in public finance. I don't have any fully satisfactory solution, since I believe that the assured availability of credit upon demand is a most valuable feature of both plans. I would try to get the best of both worlds by limiting the unconditional quotas much more narrowly than you do, but making the conditional ones larger than the American draft does' (Viner to Keynes, 12 July 1943: box 16, folder 21, JVP).

69. Actually the formula 'domestic and social policies' was inserted later in the negotiations and finally subscribed at Bretton Woods. But the shape of the compromise was in that direction: 'The essential feature of the Anglo-American compromise was that in return for accepting the US principle of limited liability, Britain won a small increase in Fund resources, a greater freedom to devalue ... a promise of passivity at the right "temporarily to restrict the freedom of exchange operations" in a currency which the fund had declared scarce' (Skidelsky, 2001, p. 320).

70. On the British discussions following the financial compromise of September 1943, see Pressnell (1986, pp. 137–52), Skidelsky (2001, pp. 325–36). Concerning the American debate, see Gardner (1956[1980], pp. 133–43). The financial compromise reached in October 1943 was published only in April 1944. In a preliminary meeting held in June in Atlantic City, further elaboration continued, substantially strengthening the provisions about scarce currencies (Williams, 1944). The agreement was finally subscribed, without substantial modifications, by the governments of 44 countries gathered at the Bretton Woods Conference, between 1 and 21 July, but the final decision had to be made by each country's parliament. The US Congress began discussing the agreement in January 1945 and approved it in summer 1945. In England, where strong opposition rose against the plan, the ratification was achieved even later (Gardner, 1956[1980], pp. 143–4).

71. The Treasury proposal for an International Bank for Reconstruction and Development had been worked out by Harry D. White together with his exchange stabilization fund plan as early as Spring 1942, but it had not been released by Morgenthau, who preferred to refine and discuss the IMF plan first. Only on 18 August 1943 did Morgenthau present the project to other departments and ask the interdepartmental technical committee to refine it in order to get it ready in mid-September for discussion with the British delegation (*Foreign Relations of the United States*, 1943, I, p. 1083). The project,

rapidly worked out by White with the help of Emilio Collado and John Parker Young, two State Department officials (Asher and Mason, 1973, p.17), was finally presented in September 1943. It was strikingly less ambitious than the plan which White drafted in Spring 1942 (Eckes, 1975, pp. 101–3; Gardner, 1956[1980], p. 110).

72. Hansen probably received the Treasury draft from Pasvolsky who got it in mid-September from White's Technical Committee and took part in the discussion with the British experts (*Foreign Relations of the United States*, I, 1083, 1092). After a preliminary discussion on 16 October 1944 (EA-48), Hansen drafted a memorandum which was discussed by the group between November 1943 and January 1944 and finally issued on 8 January 1944.

73. See also Eckes (1975, p. 131).

74. Anglo-American discussion about the proposed bank are published in *Foreign Relations of the United States* (1943, I, pp. 1092–6). Keynes's criticisms are reported also in Eckes (1975, p. 103) and they resembled quite closely Hansen's comments. Only a few months later Keynes came to appraise the opportunities the American plan for the bank could provide for developing countries with only a minor financial effort on the part of England (Eckes, 1975, pp. 122–3).

75. In the following months even Hansen's position became less adverse to the Treasury proposals (see EA-58, 29 July 1944, p. 7). His own position might have been influenced by the positive appreciation that Keynes himself expressed from March 1944 onwards about the bank's guaranteeing functions (Opie, 1957, p. 145).

76. The same arguments had been used by Lionel Robbins during the Treasury plan discussion: 'Mr Robbins said it was impossible to make a distinction between proceeds spent in one country and proceeds spent in another country; that in the last analysis the process was interwoven. For example, in most projects the bulk of expenditures are for local labor and supplies; yet the project may stimulate imports and expenditures in various countries' (*Foreign Relations of the United States*, 1943, I, p. 1094). Anyway, Lauchlin Currie's and Eugene Staley's efforts succeeded in introducing into the EFG final report some exception to the general rule of multilateral trade in the use of loans (EA-50, 11 December 1943; EA-51, 8 January 1944): 'In a period of unemployment in the heavy goods industries, the government of a country like the United States, for example, might be permitted to make loans or direct investments which would require the purchase of equipment in the United States' (EB-65, p. 4).

77. 'Mr Staley asked whether the memorandum should include suggestions regarding counter cyclical timing, such as especially favorable rates for time order. Mr Viner said he could see no solution to the problem of the synchronization of anti-depression policy other than through the action of an international bank with a large capital investment fund. Consider how much more workable such an approach was as compared with attempts to tie solution into separate fiscal policies pursued by several different countries' (EA-50, 11 December 1943, p. 9).

78. The need for an international stabilization agency was also stressed by Viner (1946, p. 334).

79. For a synthesis of the Bretton Woods discussions on this point see Eckes (1975, pp. 155–7). White opposed such a restrictive measure, but finally accepted this proportion in order to overcome Congressional and bankers' opposition.
80. 'Mr Hansen said ... As to the bank, the capital was divided into two parts; the paid-in portion was 20 per cent, the unpaid part 80 per cent, and the tied-loans feature, prominent in the original Treasury draft, applied only to the former' (EA-58, 29 September 1944, p. 7). See also Eckes (1975, p. 132): 'The Bank might make direct loans, provided recipients agreed to spend the funds in the country supplying the currency.' Actually this interpretation given by Eckes and Hansen did not enjoy an explicit statement in the text of the agreement. It was probably a personal view about the way some of the provisions, for example the right of a member country to avoid the bank selling bonds in its own market, were likely to be used.
81. See also Hansen's and Viner's contribution to the Irving Trust Company symposium on the Bretton Woods Conference (Hansen, 1944b; Viner, 1944).
82. Viner (1944) and Hansen (1944b, 1945a,b).
83. 'No one familiar with the political realities of the time is likely to argue that a more ambitious scheme could have been approved' (Hansen 1965, p. 177).
84. According to Aaronson, in the fall of 1942 the State Department's post-war planning activities began to be entrusted to 'operational' officials, under Harry Hawkins's Division on Commercial Policy (Aaronson, 1991). A tighter control on the commercial field could be desirable in order to compensate the priority the US Treasury had gained in the financial field. This shift of relative power within the State Department in favor of operational control might have lessened the influence of Pasvolsky and his CFR aides.
85. The Trade Agreement Act passed by Congress in 1944 allowed the President to negotiate only selective tariff reductions, which should be proven to give substantial advantages to the American economy without seriously injuring any domestic industry (Gardner, 1956[1980]), pp. 151–61). Any across-the board tariff reduction was ruled out, to the great disappointment of the British (Penrose, 1953, p. 107).

References

Aaronson S., 1991, 'How Cordell Hull and the Postwar Planners Designed a New Trade Policy,' *Business and Economic History*, II series, XX: 171–9.

Asher R.E. and E.S. Mason, 1973, *The World Bank since Bretton Woods*, Washington, DC: Brookings Institution.

Barber, W.J., 1987, 'The Career of Alvin H. Hansen in the 1920s and 1930s: a Study in Intellectual Transformation,' *History of Political Economy*, XIX(2): 191–205.

Bidwell, P.W., 1943, 'Controlling Trade after the War,' *Foreign Affairs*, XXI(2) (January): 296–311.

———, 1944, 'A Postwar Commercial Policy for the United States,' *American Economic Review*, 34(1) (supplement): 340–55.

Bloomfield, A., 1992, 'On the Centenary of Jacob Viner's Birth: a Retrospective View of the Man and His Work,' *Journal of Economic Literature*, 30(4): 2052–85.

Bordo, M.D., 1993, 'The Bretton Woods International Monetary System: a Historical Overview', in M.D. Bordo and B. Eichengreen (eds), *A Retrospective on the Bretton Woods System: Lessons for International Monetary Reform*, Chicago and London: The University of Chicago Press., pp. 3–107.

Bordo, M.D. and B. Eichengreen (eds), 1993, *A Retrospective on the Bretton Woods System: Lessons for International Monetary Reform*, Chicago and London: The University of Chicago Press.

Callcott, W.H., 1968, *The Western Hemisphere: its Influence on United States' Policies to the End of World War II*, Austin: University of Texas Press.

Cesarano, F., 2001, *Gli Accordi di Bretton Woods. La Costruzione di un Ordine Monetario Internazionale*, Roma-Bari: Laterza.

Council on Foreign Relations, 1947, *The Council on Foreign Relations: a Record of Twenty-Five Years, 1921–1946*, New York: Council on Foreign Relations.

De Cecco, M., 1969, 'Origins of the Post-War Payments System,' *Cambridge Journal of Economics*, 3: 49–61.

Dobson, A.P., 1995, *Anglo-American Relations in the Twentieth Century: of Friendship, Conflict and the Rise and Decline of Superpowers*, London and New York: Routledge.

Domhoff, G., 1990, *The Power Elite and the State*, New York: Aldine De Gruyter.

Drummond, I.M., 1987, *The Gold Standard and the International Monetary System: 1900–1939*, London: Macmillan.

Eckes, A.E., 1975, *A Search for Solvency: Bretton Woods and the International Monetary System, 1941–1971*, London: Austin.

Eichengreen, B., 1992, *Golden Fetters: the Gold Standard and the Great Depression, 1919–1939*, New York : Oxford University Press.

———, 1996, *Globalizing Capital: a History of the International Monetary System*, Princeton, NJ: Princeton University Press.

Gardner, R.N., 1956[1980], *Sterling-Dollar Diplomacy in Current Perspective: the Origins and the Prospects of our International Economic Order*, new expanded edition, New York: Columbia University Press.

Goodwin, C.D., 1998, 'Vision Accomplished: Harold Moulton and Leo Pasvolsky of the Brookings Institution as Champions of a New World Order', in M. Rutherford (ed.), *The Economic Mind in America: Essays in the History of American Economics*, London, New York : Routledge, pp. 80–96.

Hansen, A.H., 1940, 'Hemisphere Solidarity: Some Economic and Strategic Considerations', *Foreign Affairs*, XIX(1) (October): 12–21.

———, 1941, 'The Importance of Anti-Depression Policy in the Establishment and Preservation of Sound International Relations', *International Conciliation*, April: 424–7.

———, 1944a, 'World Institutions for Stability and Expansion', *Foreign Affairs*, XXII (January): 148–55.

———, 1944b, 'The Views of Alvin H. Hansen', in M. Shields (ed.), *International Financial Stabilization: a Symposium*, New York: Irving Trust Company, pp. 19–35.

———, 1945a, *America's Role in the World Economy*, New York: Norton & Co.

———, 1945b, 'International Monetary and Financial Programs', in P.W. Bidwell (ed.), *The United States in a Multi-National Economy*, New York: Council on Foreign Relations, pp. 73–86.

———, 1965, *The Dollar and the International Monetary System*, New York: McGraw-Hill.

——— and C.P. Kindleberger, 1942, 'The Economic Tasks of the Post-War World', *Foreign Affairs*, XX(3) (April): 466–76.

Harold, J., 1996, *International Monetary Cooperation since Bretton Woods*, Washington, DC: International Monetary Fund.

Harrod, R.F., 1951, *The Life of John Maynard Keynes*, London: Macmillan.

Horsefield, J.K. (ed.), 1969, *The International Monetary Fund 1945–1965: Twenty Years of International Monetary Cooperation*, vol. 2, Washington, DC: International Monetary Fund.

Ikenberry, G.J., 1993, 'The Political Origins of Bretton Woods', in M.D. Bordo and B. Eichengreen (eds), *A Retrospective on the Bretton Woods System: Lessons for International Monetary Reform*, Chicago and London: The University of Chicago Press, pp. 155–98.

Keynes, J.M., 1940–44 [1980], *Activities 1940–44: Shaping the Post-War World, the Clearing Union, Collected Writings*, XXV, ed. D. Moggridge, London: Macmillan, Cambridge University Press.

———, 1941–46 [1980], *Activities 1941–46: Shaping the Post-War World, Bretton Woods and Reparations, Collected Writings*, XXVI, ed. D. Moggridge, London: Macmillan, Cambridge University Press.

Kirshner, O. (ed.), 1996, *The Bretton Woods-GATT system: Retrospect and Prospect after Fifty Years*, Armonk, NY: M.E. Sharpe.

Laidler, D., 1999, *Fabricating the Keynesian Revolution: Studies of the Interwar Literature on Money, the Cycle, and Unemployment*, Cambridge: Cambridge University Press.

Lake, D.A. (1983), *Power, Protection and Free Trade: International Sources of US Commercial Strategy, 1887–1939*, Ithaca: Cornell University Press.

Lasser, W., 2002, *Benjamin V. Cohen, Architect of the New Deal*, New Haven: Yale University Press.

Leeson, R., 1997, 'The Eclipse of the Goal of Zero Inflation', *History of Political Economy*, XXIX(3): 445–96.

———, 2003, *Keynes, Chicago and Friedman*, vol. 2, London: Pickering & Chatto.

Mehrling, P., 1997, *The Money Interest and the Public Interest: American Monetary Thought 1920–1970*, Cambridge, MA and London: Harvard University Press.

Newman, W.J., 1968, *The Balance of Power in the Interwar Years, 1919–1939*, New York: Random House.

Notter, H., 1949, *Post-War Foreign Policy Preparation: 1939–1945*, Washington: State Department.

Opie, R., 1957, 'Anglo-American Relations in War-Time', *Oxford Economic Papers*, IX(2) (June): 115–51.

Penrose, E.F., 1953, *Economic Planning for the Peace*, Princeton, NJ: Princeton University Press.

Pressnell, L.S., 1986, *External Economic Policy since the War*, Vol. 1, *The Post War Financial Settlement*, London: Her Majesty's Stationery Office.

Rees, D., 1973, *Harry Dexter White: a Study in Paradox*, New York: Coward, McCann & Geoghegan.

Robbins, L., 1970, *Jacob Viner (1892–1970): a Tribute*, Princeton, NJ: Princeton University Press.

Rowland, B.M., 1987, *Commercial Conflict and Foreign Policy: a Study in Anglo-American Relations 1932–1938*, New York and London: Garland Publishing.

Samuelson, P., 1972, 'Jacob Viner (1892–1970)', *Journal of Political Economy*, LXXX(1) (January-February): 5–11.

Sandilands, R.J., 1990, *The Life and Political Economy of Lauchlin Currie: New Dealer, Presidential Adviser, and Development Economist*, Durham, NC: Duke University Press.

Santoro, C.M., 1987, *La perla e l'ostrica. Alle fonti della politica globale degli Stati Uniti*, Milano: Franco Angeli.

Sheehan, M., 1996, *The Balance of Power: History and Theory*, New York: Routledge.

Shoup, L.H., 1975, 'The Council on Foreign Relations and the United States War Aims during World War II', *The Insurgent Sociologist*, Spring: 9–52.

—— and W. Minter, 1977, *Imperial Brain Trust: the Council on Foreign Relations and the United States Foreign Policy*, New York: The Monthly Review Press.

Skidelsky R., 2001, *John Maynard Keynes: Fighting for Britain (1937–1946)*, New York and London: Viking.

Spykman, N., 1942, *America's Strategy in the World: the United States and the Balance of Power*, New York: Harcourt, Brace.

Tobin, J., 1976, 'Hansen and Public Policy', *Quarterly Journal of Economics*, XL(1): 32–7.

Viner, J., 1932, 'International Aspects of the Gold Standard', in Quincy Wright (ed.), *Gold and Monetary Stabilization*, Chicago: University of Chicago Press, pp. 3–42.

——, 1937, *Studies in the Theory of International Trade*, New York and London: Harper & Brothers.

——, 1941, 'International Economic Relations and the World Order', in W.H.C. Laves (ed.), *The Foundation of a More Stable World Order: Lectures on the Harris Foundation 1940*, Chicago: Chicago University Press, pp. 35–73.

——, 1942a, 'The International Economic Organization of the Future', in *Toward International Organization*, Oberlin College Lectures, New York, Harper & Brothers, pp. 110–37.

——, 1942b, 'Objectives of Post-War International Economic Reconstruction', in W. McKee and L. Wiesen (eds), *American Economic Objectives*, New Wilmington, PA: Economic and Business Foundation, pp. 161–85.

——, 1943, 'Two Plans for International Monetary Stabilization', *The Yale Review*, 33 (Autumn): 77–107; reprinted in J. Viner (1951), *International Economics*, Glencoe, IL: Free Press, pp. 192–215.

——, 1944, 'The Case for the Bretton Woods Agreement', in M. Shields (ed.), *International Financial Stabilization: a Symposium*, New York: Irving Trust Company; reprinted in J. Viner (1951), *International Economics*, Glencoe, IL: Free Press, pp. 232–46.

——, 1945, 'The American Interest in the Colonial Problem', in P.W. Bidwell (ed.), *The United States in a Multi-National Economy*, New York: Council on Foreign Relations, pp. 1–17.

——, 1946, 'International Finance in the Post-War World', *Lloyd's Bank Review*, 1 (October): 3–17; reprinted in J. Viner (1951), *International Economics*, Glencoe, IL: Free Press, pp. 323–36.

——, 1947, 'America's Lending Policy', *Academy of Political Science Proceedings*, 22 (January): 51–66; reprinted in J. Viner (1951), *International Economics*, Glencoe, IL: Free Press, pp. 337–43.

——, 1951, *International Economics*, Glencoe, IL: Free Press.

Wala, M., 1994, *The Council on Foreign Relations and American Foreign Policy in the Early Cold War*, Providence: Berghahn Books.

Whitaker, A.P., 1954, *The Western Hemisphere Idea: its Rise and Decline*, Ithaca, NY: Cornell University Press.

Williams, J.H., 1944, 'The Views of John H. Williams', in M. Shields (ed.), *International Financial Stabilization: a Symposium*, New York: Irving Trust Company, pp. 91–104.

Archival sources

EA: Studies in War and Peace, Economic and Financial Group, Discussions, New York City, CFR.

EB: Studies in War and Peace, Economic and Financial Group, Reports, New York City, CFR.

MD: Henry Morgenthau Diaries, Roosevelt Presidential Library (Hyde Park, NY).

JVP: Jacob Viner Papers, Seeley G. Mudd Manuscript Library, Princeton University.

4
A Hands-off Central Banker? Marriner S. Eccles and the Federal Reserve, 1934–51

Matías Vernengo

Introduction

Central bankers are seldom known for their heterodoxy. However, periods of crisis demand unorthodox solutions, and sometimes produce unexpected leaders. When it came to explaining the Great Depression and what had to be done, Marriner Eccles was quite aware that he had 'challenged all that had been said up to that point and [that he] was practically alone in doing so' (Eccles, 1951, p. 104). Eccles was clearly for public works as a solution for the Great Depression, even when Roosevelt and several high-ranking government officials remained firmly in the camp of balanced budgets and sound finance (Stein, 1969).

In addition, Eccles imposed as a condition for accepting the appointment to the Federal Reserve Board (later chairman of the Board of Governors of the Federal Reserve System) that Roosevelt agreed to overhaul the whole system, centralizing its activities and effectively creating a modern central bank. Nonetheless, some authors argue that monetary policy was mainly passive during Eccles's tenure and that, if anything, it contributed to the 1937–38 recession (Meltzer, 2003). The main criticism of Eccles's policies is related to the view that he subordinated the Federal Reserve to the Treasury. On the other hand, during the controversy that led to the famous Federal Reserve-Treasury Accord of 1951 Eccles sided with the Fed and against the Treasury, and supported increased taxation and balanced budgets. Eccles's changing view on deficits irritated several people and, as one author put it, at the end of his long tenure at the Fed, Eccles 'was despised by the bankers, no longer trusted by the banker's enemies' (Greider, 1987, p. 326).

The main problem with the notion that monetary policy was in the back seat during Eccles's chairmanship is related to the lack of understanding of his views on the Federal Reserve and Treasury inter-action. Proper appreciation of Eccles's views on fiscal and monetary policy makes clear that he thought that in a recession the main role of monetary policy was to accommodate expansionary fiscal policy, but that in a boom the opposite would be the case. In particular, this explains why, contrary to several Keynesians in the Roosevelt administration and even in opposition to the fiscal conservatives, he was against fiscal and monetary laxity during the war.

This chapter will look at the evidence on Eccles's views on monetary and fiscal policy at some crucial moments of his time at the Fed. It is argued that despite his limited knowledge of dominant monetary policy theories before the Great Depression – fundamentally the so-called 'Real Bills Doctrine' – and of Keynesian developments – which to some extent he understood at second-hand from his close adviser Lauchlin Currie – Eccles had a refined appreciation of the interaction of fiscal and monetary policy, which is essential to understanding his policy stances and Federal Reserve policies during his long tenure as chairman.

In the back seat or holding the steering wheel?

Marriner Stoddard Eccles was born in Logan, Utah in 1890, and died in Salt Lake City in 1977. His father David Eccles had emigrated from Scotland to Utah with his parents, and had made a fortune in the lumber business. Marriner Eccles graduated from Brigham Young College, with a high school education, in 1909. After a two-year stint as a missionary in Scotland he returned to Utah, where he started to work in the family businesses. In 1912 his father passed away, and as the oldest son of David Eccles's second marriage Marriner became responsible for the economic interests of his side of the family, pitting him against his half-brothers over the management of the family businesses (Eccles, 1951, p. 39). He eventually displaced his half-brothers in the family enterprises and in the 1920s acquired a few small regional banks, which were incorporated as the First Security Corporation in 1928. The successful management of his banks during the Great Depression, and his peculiar views brought some attention from political circles in the east.

The Great Depression and the election of Franklin Roosevelt led to a complete reorganization of the Federal Reserve, which started with the Federal Reserve Act of 1933 (before Eccles joined the Treasury in 1934). In part, the emphasis on reform and regulation was the consequence of the views of the original Brain Trusters, Adolf Berle, Raymond Moley, and Rexford Tugwell,[1] who saw the Great Depression as the result of change in the competitive structure, which became more oligopolistic, creating a more rigid price structure. In this view, centralization and control were essential for planned capitalism and the reform of the Federal Reserve System was part of the concentration of power in Washington.[2]

Eccles also saw the centralization of power, particularly in the case of monetary policy power, in Washington and away from Wall Street, as an essential part of the reforms needed for promoting recovery. In fact, a reform of the Federal Reserve Board was a precondition for him to accept a position as governor (Eccles, 1951, p. 166).[3] It is important to note that Tugwell and others in the administration who saw industrial concentration as the main cause of the crisis, and sought reform and regulation as its solution, emphasized that experimentation was necessary to overcome the Great Depression.[4] Tugwell (1958, p. 47), in fact, argued that Roosevelt had 'a bulldog determination concerning objectives and a completely contrasting flexibility concerning means.'

Eccles's views on the Great Depression tended to emphasize the role of consumption and debt in promoting prosperity.[5] The best source for his views on the causes of the Great Depression are to be found in a talk given to the Utah State Bankers' Convention in June 1932 titled 'Depression: Its Causes, Effects and Suggested Remedies.' In that talk he argued that:

> The depression within our own country was primarily brought about by our capital accumulation getting out of balance in relationship to our consumption ability ... The difficulty is that we were not sufficiently extravagant as a nation. We did not consume what we were able to produce.
>
> (Marriner S. Eccles Papers, Box 72, Folder 2)

He also emphasized that international debt was an essential part of the Great Depression, for him 'the matter of international debts is the commencement, I believe, of our problems' (ibid.), and he understood that a worldwide recovery was heavily dependent on a recovery in the United States. For him, 'a revival in this country, a willingness to sit down and discuss world economy problems in the light of financial and business necessity would go a long way toward bringing the world out of this depression' (ibid.)

More importantly Eccles believed that the only institution that would be capable of turning the cycle around was the government. In particular, he argued that only the federal government had the capacity to increase debt without going bankrupt. In his own words:

> If a man owed to himself he could not be bankrupt, and neither can a nation. We have got all the wealth and resources we ever had, and

we do not have the sense, the financial and political leadership to know how to use them. We are trying to apply a theory of economy as obsolete as the Ark ... If the Government in order to finance the War [World War I] could spend billions of dollars in order to give protection to life and property, and not have a single thing to show for it when it is over but the destruction of the flower of the youth of the nation, then certainly the Government is justified in supplying sufficient credit or money to take care of the unemployed through public works, or an unemployment wage or a combination of both.

(Marriner S. Eccles Papers, Box 74, Folder 2)

In that respect, it seems that Eccles not only emphasized the importance of budget deficits at the federal government level, but also was not concerned with the increase of public debt – which he saw as a necessary condition to compensate the reduction in private debt.[6] Eccles suggested – in ways that foreshadow functional finance ideas to be developed a decade later – that the federal government would not be able to balance the budget in the recession. Only the federal government had the money-creating powers and could use debt on a national scale to end the depression (Eccles, 1951, p. 106).[7]

These views, expressed openly before Roosevelt's election, led to his defense of a five-point program that put the concept of a deliberately unbalanced budget at the center of the recovery and which he presented to the Senate Finance Committee in 1933. The program consisted of increasing transfers (as gifts) to states to take care of the unemployed, increase federal government spending, implement a program to control production and raise agricultural prices, refinance mortgages on a long-term basis at low rates of interest, and bring about a permanent settlement of inter-allied debts by promoting cancellation of debts (1951, pp. 91–113).

The program fundamentally emphasized the role of spending, that is, fiscal measures rather than monetary measures, and also tended to emphasize macroeconomic solutions for the Great Depression rather than institutional reforms. As noted by Eccles (1951, p. 113), his five-point program came close to the actual policies pursued by the Roosevelt administration, so much so that *Fortune* argued that if one compares Eccles's 'earlier general statements of economics with the economics of the present administration [one] will be forced to conclude that M.S. Eccles of Ogden, Utah, was not only a Mormon but a prophet' (ibid.) The emphasis on fiscal and macroeconomic solutions to the Great Depression expressed in Eccles's 1932 and 1933 speeches to the business community in Utah opens up the question of the intellectual influences that shaped his views.

Sydney Hyman (1976, pp. 71–3) suggests that William T. Foster and Wadill Catchings, an academic economist and a Goldman Sachs banker, respectively, who espoused under-consumptionist views in the 1920s, were more influential than Keynes in forming Eccles's notions about the Great Depression. Eccles later argued that 'the New Deal economists probably stressed the under-consumptionist forces in a depression economy to a greater extent than did the Keynes-Hansen school, which dwelt principally upon the lack of adequate private investment outlets' (Marriner S. Eccles Papers, Box 111, Folder 3). He also argued that his 'conceptions were based on naked-eye observation and experience in the intermountain region … [and that he] never read Keynes's writings except in small extracts' (1951, p. 132). In that sense, it seems reasonable to presume that under-consumptionist ideas were central to Eccles's understanding of the Great Depression. However, one should not overemphasize the importance of Foster and Catchings. Eccles's argument about the relative unimportance of Keynes on his views should probably be extended to all academic influences. In his early speeches in Utah, there is only a single reference to Foster (Marriner S. Eccles Papers, Box 74, Folder 3), and in the same vein there is only one quotation from Keynes, on the need for increasing spending (ibid.)[8]

More importantly Hyman (1976, p. 155) and Roger Sandilands (1990, pp. 62–4) emphasize the importance of Lauchlin Currie's intellectual influence on Eccles, and in fact sometimes Eccles's views have been described as 'Curried Keynes' (see Sandlilands, 2001, p. 232). The famous memorandum titled 'Desirable Changes in the Administration of the Federal Reserve System,' given to the President on 3 November 1934, and that Eccles took to his meeting with Roosevelt the following day, was drafted by Currie and clearly retains his intellectual imprint. The eight-point program of reform of the Federal Reserve System outlined in the memo emphasizes the importance of conscious control of the money supply for controlling the level of activity, and the importance of strengthening the authority of the Federal Reserve Board (Marriner S. Eccles Papers, Box 4, Folder 1).[9] Currie's emphasis on the importance of active control of the money supply, in part, follows from his correct understanding of the dominance of the Real Bills Doctrine in Fed practices up to that point (D'Arista, 1994; Meltzer, 2003).[10]

In that respect it seems that Currie's ideas in his early years at the Treasury and the Fed were less Keynesian than usually assumed, or at least that he perceived the control of money supply as a more important policy tool than Keynesians would have done at a later time. Yet as Keynesian ideas started to spread in the United States Currie became increasingly persuaded by them. He certainly had a crucial role in promoting Keynesian ideas within the administration. In a letter to Eccles in September 1936 Currie tells him that he is working 'on a simple exposition of Keynes' last book, which [he] thought [Eccles] and the other members of the Board might like to read' and he added 'the book itself is pretty tough reading' (Marriner S. Eccles Papers, Box 43, Folder 1). Currie's review of the *General Theory* (ibid., Box 111, Folder 1) most likely provided the only clear exposition of Keynes's ideas to Eccles.[11]

In contrast to his early views, which emphasized the efficacy of monetary policy, in a July 1937 paper titled 'The Objectives of Monetary Policy' – written at a time when concerns with a recession were increasing (Marriner S. Eccles Papers, Box 73, Folder 1) – Currie argued that 'there is no direct nor proportional relationship between changes in the volume of money and changes in the price level' and that 'the government action with reference to its taxation and spending policies has far more influence on the demand for goods and the general price level than have the policies of the Federal Reserve System.' Even though it might be unfair to charge Currie with repudiating his previous ideas, as Paul Samuelson did (Sandilands, 1990, p. 50), it seems justified to note that the emphasis on the relative efficiency of monetary and fiscal policy changed from 1934 to 1937.[12] In that respect, one may speculate – given Eccles's early defense of fiscal activism – that Eccles might have had as much influence on Currie as Currie had on Eccles's ideas.

Eccles's understanding of the Great Depression emphasized the relative conflict between debtors and creditors. He believed that 'after four depression years spokesmen for the creditor sections of the land were still our intellectual elite [and] labor and farm spokesmen, representing the debtors of the nation, enjoyed scant prestige as opinion-makers' (1951, p. 93). The relevance of the New Deal was that 'at last [the administration] turned its attention to debtor relief' (ibid., p. 94). He noticed that opposition to public debt was less a matter of the debt growth itself, but a simple question of who benefited from it. He argued that:

> For all their expressed opposition to the growth in public debt, the business leaders who appeared before the Finance Committee [in February 1933] were quite prepared to see debt grow when it meant the preservation of their own interests. They were quite prepared to interfere with 'natural' economic laws when their own enterprises were at stake ... These business leaders argued that the only way to

relieve the pressures on the unemployed was by means of the 'trickle down' method.

(1951, pp. 101–2)

These views, which are clearly influenced by populist ideas, are peculiar for a banker,[13] emphasizing the income distribution conflict involved in macroeconomic policies. Also, and more importantly, these views, which stress the distributive conflict between debtors and creditors, shed light on Eccles's policy positions as Federal Reserve Chairman.

It is often suggested that Eccles's Fed was passive, and that it submitted without a fight to the directions of the Treasury (for example, Calomiris and Wheelock, 1998; Meltzer, 2003). This criticism suggests that the Treasury maneuvered to obtain low interest rates in order to keep debt servicing expenses low. In this view, even though the Real Bills Doctrine was not the dominant theoretical position of the board, conventional wisdom suggests that the Fed under Eccles remained passive. Allan Meltzer (2003, p. 470) argues that Eccles 'did not seem to share Currie's strong beliefs about the need to abandon the real bills doctrine [and] he preferred to rely on judgment and wanted a large measure of authority to do what he believed was in the public interest.' In Meltzer's view Eccles was not only relatively uninterested in monetary theories – Real Bills or otherwise – but was happy in letting the Treasury take the steering wheel while the Fed sat in the back seat. For him:

> Eccles was much more interested in fiscal actions, housing, and advising President Roosevelt on these and other issues than in conducting monetary policy. The Federal Reserve took very few discretionary actions. Except for doubling reserve requirements in 1936–37, it was passive through most of these years. Despite the mutual antipathy between Eccles and Treasury Secretary Morgenthau, the Treasury usually led and the Federal Reserve followed.

(Meltzer, 2003, p. 575)

This interpretation fails to note that Henry Morgenthau was and remained always a balanced-budget, sound finance person. Hence, one would expect that if the Treasury led and the Fed followed, balanced-budget ideas would have prevailed during the period, a position that is hardly defensible, at least after the 1937–38 recession when by most accounts Roosevelt 'subscribed to the doctrine of a compensatory economy' (Eccles, 1951, p. 318).

More importantly, following the monetarist interpretation of the Great Depression as the Great Contraction of 1929–33, which underlies his views, Meltzer argues that the 1937–38 recession was caused by the increase in reserve requirements. In other words, monetary policy was not only passive, but also fundamentally responsible for Roosevelt's recession (2003, pp. 521–9). In this view, higher reserve requirements led to higher rates of interest and to the recession. Monetary policy 'did not change until 1938, when Morgenthau and the Treasury pressed for . . . reductions in the reserve requirements ratios.' However, the notion that no changes in monetary policy occurred during the recession is not accurate.

Eccles (1951, p. 293) notes that:

> Those who argue that the increase in reserve requirements was meant to tighten money rates and that this in turn parched the flow of credit into the economy and thereby precipitated the recession of 1937–8 could prove their case if they demonstrated that the increase resulted in any credit restriction or any material rise in interest rates. There was, it is true, a sharp rise in Treasury bills from very low rate in the latter part of 1936 of $\frac{1}{10}$ of 1 per cent to $\frac{3}{4}$ of 1 per cent at times in 1937. Also, the market yield rate on three to five year Treasury notes rose from around 1 per cent to over $1\frac{1}{2}$, and the average yield on long term Treasury bonds rose from about $2\frac{1}{2}$ to $2\frac{3}{4}$ per cent. But the levels reached were not high. Neither were the degrees of change large compared with those in previous periods, nor was the rise in rate long sustained.

The decision to increase reserve requirements was associated with the accumulation of idle reserves by banks.[14] The recession was for Eccles caused by a fiscal contraction, itself largely the result of two factors, the new social security law that increased taxes without initially disbursing payments, and the end of soldiers' bonus payments (Eccles, 1951, p. 295).[15] Peter Temin (1989, pp. 121–2) suggests that both fiscal and monetary policy caused the recession.[16]

Eccles (1951, p. 291) had guaranteed that if banks sold government bonds as a result of the increase in reserve requirements, the Federal Open Market Committee (FOMC) would intervene to stabilize the market.[17] Arguably, reserve requirements were increased to force banks to buy more Treasuries and support the government's deficit financing policies.[18] In fact, the FOMC did sustain the bond market and interest rate increases were not marked. It seems that Eccles and his advisers were correct in pointing out that the main cause of Roosevelt's recession was fiscal contraction, and hence, that the Fed was not passive in this crucial period, but tended to emphasize its own role as fiscal agent of the Treasury, something that was crucial for Eccles (Marriner S. Eccles Papers, Box 9, Folder 6). For him, supporting the bond market was essential to allow low interest payments on public debt, and for the expansion of public debt to go to expenditures that would go into current purchases.[19] The war and its aftermath would show that Eccles thought that under different circumstances, one in which full employment was achieved, the role of the Federal Reserve would be different.

The war and the Federal Reserve-Treasury Accord

John Kenneth Galbraith (1977, p. 221) famously noted that 'Hitler having ended unemployment in Germany, had gone on to end it for his enemies.' The New Deal turned the economy around but it did not lead to full employment.[20] Even though accumulated growth of real gross domestic product (GDP) between 1933 and 1939 was an impressive 41.2 percent, unemployment still remained at 17.2 percent in 1939. The rates of growth of the New Deal would be shadowed by the war effort, and unemployment would fall to a low of 1.2 percent in 1944.

From early on in the build up to war Eccles showed concerns about war finance and the great risk of inflation. In April 1942 Eccles discussed an anti-inflationary program with Roosevelt, and relayed his concerns about the dangers of runaway inflation.[21] Regarding Eccles's new found preoccupation with inflation, Meltzer (2003, pp. 636–7) argues that:

> Eccles's economic views seem confused. In the 1930s he saw no reason for Federal Reserve action because monetary policy was ineffective when interest rates were low in a recession. In 1946, a period of anticipated expansion, part of his argument was that policy would have little effect unless the Federal Reserve undertook large-scale operations and raised interest rates substantially.

In fact, even earlier than 1946, as we noted, Eccles showed serious concerns about inflation and suggested that fiscal and monetary action should be taken to avoid excessive inflation. For Eccles the main instrument for controlling inflation was fiscal policy. He argued 'that the most effective anti-inflationary measure has been and should continue to be a rigorous fiscal program to insure the largest possible budgetary surplus consistent with the Government's obligations at home and abroad' (Marriner S. Eccles Papers, Box 4, Folder 10).

The progressive press also noted that changed circumstances demanded a new course of action in which there was no contradiction. The editorial in *The Nation* of 11 January 1941 argued that

> in some quarters the proposals of Mr. Eccles and his colleagues are being treated as a slap at the Administration and a confession of past errors. This of course is sheer nonsense. Objections may be raised by the Treasury and other government departments to certain details of the Federal Reserve report, but informed supporters of the New Deal will certainly not carp at the general principle that a managed monetary system must restrain inflation as well as combat deflation.
> (Marriner S. Eccles Papers, Box 4, Folder 1)

It should be noted that during the war John Maynard Keynes (1940) also became concerned with inflation. Keynes argued that at full employment, if aggregate demand rose, output could not increase because of supply constraints. Excess demand would mean that the level of output that would be determined by the multiplier process would be higher than the full employment level, and, thus, the market-clearing level of output would not be achievable. Keynes referred to the difference between market clearing and full employment output as the inflationary gap. As nominal wages lagged behind prices in adjustment, the rise in prices would lead to a reduction in the real wage and a redistribution of income away from wage-earners. Further, as workers usually have greater propensities to consume than capitalists, the redistribution of income induced by the inflationary gap would lead to lower aggregate demand and close the gap.

Robert Skidelsky (2000, p. 88) argues that:

> The [British] Treasury's acceptance of Keynes's logic to deal with inflation did not imply acceptance of that logic to deal with unemployment. The idea of using the budget to 'balance the accounts' of the nation did not extend to augmenting purchasing power when the 'output gap' developed. For the inflation problem, the orthodox and Keynesian logic coincided: for the unemployment problem, they diverged.

Further, Skidelsky (2000, pp. 120–1) argues that 'the American Keynesians had all read [Keynes's] *How to Pay for the War*, but were more worried about stagnation than inflation ... The American Keynesians wanted to continue the New Deal in war, whereas Keynes wanted to convert the economy from peacetime to wartime production.' As noted above, that was clearly not the case, and some New Dealers, including Eccles, were as concerned about war finance and inflation as their British counterparts.

Eccles (1944, p. 226), contrary to many Keynesians[22] who thought that there was a great risk of a depression after the war, argued that 'our home front fight against inflation will have to continue for a considerable time after the war ends.' He believed that 'backlog needs' would imply that for a long time after the war consumption would exceed by far productive capacity. Yet, preoccupation with inflation did not mean forgetting the centrality of maintaining full employment. Eccles (1944, p. 237) was clear that 'underlying all that I have said is the fundamental purpose of avoiding either inflation or deflation – in other words, what we would like to have is full and sustained production and employment.' Hence, it would be unfair to argue that Eccles's preoccupation with inflation overshadowed his commitment to full employment.

However, Meltzer (2003, p. 671), argues that 'Eccles showed that he had forgotten why he came to Washington 1933.' Underlying this comment is again the fact that in February 1949 when the board recognized the signs of a recession Eccles suggested that some deflation 'was necessary and desirable if the economy was to return to a period of stability' (ibid.) Eccles, as we noted, thought that overall the postwar problem would be inflation and not unemployment. In addition, and not mentioned by Meltzer is the fact that when Eccles went to Washington – in 1934 not 1933 – unemployment rates were above 20 percent (in 1933, 24.9, and a year later 21.7 percent), while in 1949 unemployment was only 5.9 percent. Eccles had not forgotten why he went to Washington; he had already accomplished his objectives. Not only was unemployment virtually eliminated, but the Employment Act of 1946 had also established the importance of full employment for macroeconomic management.[23]

During the war, and in its immediate aftermath, when demobilization led to a fall in GDP of 11.1 percent Eccles maintained the view that a loose monetary policy was needed. He argued in 1947 that 'under present and prospective conditions it is essential to maintain the established 2½ per cent on long term marketable government securities' (Marriner S. Eccles Papers, Box 4, Folder 10). However, by 1950 – when Eccles was a member of the board, but had already been sacked from the position of chairman – he had changed his mind. In a letter to the *American Banker* in March 1950 in response to criticism about his changing views, Eccles remarked that 'the prospect in 1948 was that the post-war boom would wear itself out; the prospect today is for continuing inflationary pressures for an indefinite future' (Marriner S. Eccles Papers, Box 61, Folder 7).

Eccles was not alone in his increasing concerns with inflationary pressures.[24] In November 1950 a long list of economists – including several Keynesians, such as James Duesenberry, John K. Galbraith, Seymour Harris, Charles Kindleberger, Kenneth Kurihara, Hyman Minsky, Tibor Scitovsky, Arthur Smithies and Lorie Tarshis to name a few[25] – signed a declaration titled 'An Economist's Statement on Anti-inflationary Measures,' favoring contractionary fiscal and monetary policies, and also 'government controls over wages, prices, production and distribution' (United States Senate, 1951, p. 1531).[26] Contractionary monetary policy would disturb the implicit agreement between the Federal Reserve and the Treasury, which implied that the former would stabilize the market for government securities.

In this context, Eccles joined Allan Sproul, the governor of the New York Federal Reserve, to free the Federal Reserve from its obligations to the Treasury. In a letter to Milton Friedman in February 1951 Eccles argued that:

> The insistence of the Treasury on carrying over into the post-war period and into the defense period the same artificially low and frozen interest rate that was unavoidable [Eccles crossed out with his pen the word 'justified'] during World War II conditions is, of course, very unfortunate. In the early months after the War there was justification for a go-slow policy on significant rate changes since the belief was widely held that the adjustment from war to peace would be much more difficult than it turned out to be. But once the strength of the inflationary forces in the country became evident it was time to take appropriate monetary action.
>
> (Marriner S. Eccles Papers, Box 62, Folder 1)

Some have argued that this position implied a *volte face* by Eccles. Meltzer (2003, p. 723) emphasizes the importance of Eccles in promoting central bank independence and judges that Eccles's 'last days [at the Federal Reserve] were among his best' (ibid., p. 705, n. 222).

The view that central bank independence is essential for achieving price stability has become dominant in professional circles. Alternatively, Gerald Epstein and Juliet Schor (1995) developed a 'contested-terrain' theory of central banking, and use extensive archival evidence to suggest that distributive conflict is central for establishing policy regimes.[27] In their view, those who promoted the independence of the Federal Reserve System from the Treasury ultimately wanted to maintain adequate real rates of return for rentiers, to support higher profits for banks and by preventing full employment, to reduce the bargaining power of labor. In their view:

> Flexible monetary policy and a fully independent Federal Reserve System were major components of the conservative Keynesian policy structure developed in the postwar era. Just as the implicit 'accord' between labor's conservative elements and capital set the rules for direct labor and capital bargaining, the Accord between the Treasury and the Federal Reserve set the terms of the larger macroeconomic environment within which that bargaining would take place. And by freeing monetary policy from governmental control, it played a major role in establishing the terms on which capital would score a significant victory against labor in the 1980s and 1990s, namely through tight monetary policy.
>
> (Epstein and Schor, 1995, p. 8)

Epstein and Schor's 'contested terrain' theory provides a good framework for understanding the disputes between the Federal Reserve and the Treasury. The main concern of the Treasury Secretary, John Snyder, as had been the case of his predecessors, was with the cost of servicing public debt, which had swollen during the war and corresponded to 93.9 percent of GDP in 1950. John D. Clark, the vice-chairman of the Council of Economic Advisers (CEA) argued in February 1951 that 'we look at the cost of capital [the rate of interest] as being no different from any other cost of production and we believe that [it] is always desirable to have the costs of production, including the cost of capital, held [at] as low a point as social policy will permit' (Marriner S. Eccles Papers, Box 62, Folder 8).[28]

In addition, the Treasury, as much as the Federal Reserve Board, was permeable to political influences. Beyond their intention of minimizing interest payments, it is not clear that Snyder and others at the Treasury or the CEA were the standard-bearers of democratic monetary policy.[29] In fact, Eccles showed considerably more awareness of the distributive conflict involved in setting interest rates than his counterparts in the Treasury. Eccles knew that at the first signs of recovery there would be demands for higher interest rates. As he noted, 'at the end of 1936 and early in 1937 strong pressures were exerted by some financial circles for higher interest rates' (Eccles, 1951, p. 293). In that respect, he knew that demands for higher interest rates in 1950 were also cries for higher profits for banks, and rentiers' interests in general.[30]

In an address to the Executive's Club of Chicago in March 1951 Eccles argued that:

> The Federal Reserve System has been accused of seeking higher interest rates, which primarily enrich banks and other corporate holders. The Federal Reserve is not interested in higher interest rates as such, but only as they help in curbing the sales of Government securities which add to the reserves and deposits of the banking system. In order to curb such sales of Government securities, it is necessary that the market for them become more self-supporting and less dependent on Federal Reserve purchases. The incidental result of such a development, under current conditions, will be somewhat higher interest rates.
>
> (Marriner S. Eccles Papers, Box 62, Folder 5)

In other words, Eccles was not interested in increasing interest rates per se, and in fact the eventual increase was small. His main concern was to preserve the ability of the Federal Reserve to control excess reserves, and to make it less responsible for stabilizing the public bond market, since he believed that these activities might have been incompatible. Eccles also favored a certain amount of discretionary power for central bankers, and as much as he fought for central bank independence from Wall Street interests in the 1935 Bank Act, centralizing power in Washington and reducing the role of the New York branch, he fought against direct control from the Treasury. Ultimately what Eccles wanted was for the Federal Reserve to have discretionary power to deal with unemployment and inflation.

Further, the relations between Eccles and the banking community were never particularly good (Meltzer, 2003, p. 656). For that reason it is hard to argue that he was a champion of central bank independence, in particular if one suggests that 'the lasting reason for the separation of monetary and debt-management powers was the patent failure of cheap-money, low-interest-rate programs to achieve acceptable results' (Timberlake, 1999, p. 67).

The fight for central bank independence for Eccles was not a recantation of the New Deal policies he defended before. For him the question was how to create the conditions to implement his economic philosophy in conditions of full employment and inflationary pressures. Eccles (1951, p. 316) defined his economic philosophy in the following terms:

> I believe, however, that the most basic right of all is the right to live, and next to that, the right to work. I do not think that empty stomachs

build character, nor do I think the substitution of idleness and a dole for useful work relief will improve either the dignity or the character of the people affected. We cannot expect to preserve our free institutions in this country if we condemn a substantial proportion of our people to prolonged idleness on a bare subsistence level of existence. Further than the right to eat and the right to a position, I think the individual, whether rich or poor, has a right to a decent place to live. I think he has a right to security in old age and to protection against temporary unemployment. I think he has a right to adequate medical attention and to equal educational opportunities with the rest of his countrymen. The government expenditures ... have in large part been the means of translating these basic rights into realities.

Eccles's broad philosophy of economic rights, and the crucial role he played in the implementation of the New Deal, suggests that he should be considered among the central figures of the Keynesian revolution in the policy arena. His preoccupation with inflationary pressures after the war, and his latter-day defense of the Federal Reserve-Treasury Accord were perfectly compatible with his commitment to full employment and a more equitable and civilized society.

Concluding remarks

Conventional wisdom about monetary policy during the Great Depression holds that it was passive and that it did not contribute to the recovery. Eccles's positions during and after the war, when he became concerned with inflation, have sometimes been considered inconsistent. His support of the independence of the Federal Reserve from the Treasury is seen as a confirmation of the inconsistency of his views. This chapter suggests that, in part, these perceptions result from an incorrect understanding of Eccles's policy positions.

Rather than a hands-off central banker who subjugated the Fed to the Treasury, a more proper depiction of Eccles's tenure at the Fed would be as a Main Street chairman, one preoccupied with full employment and a more equitable distribution of creditors' and debtors' burdens in a recession. That is, he considered the role of the Federal Reserve as the fiscal agent of the Treasury as the essential one, in a situation where only expansionary fiscal policy could turn the economy around.

Also, much like Keynes, once full employment was achieved during the war Eccles became preoccupied with inflation. He considered that fiscal measures and income policies were necessary to contain inflation, but that monetary policy, which for him was quite ineffective in a recession, would be slightly more effective in the upturn. These concerns with inflation, and his predilection for discretion rather than rules, were behind his defense of central bank independence. He did not favor increases in interest rates, and envisioned a recovery in which public debt would gradually give way to the expansion of private debt, while maintaining full employment. In many respects the view that Eccles became more conventional at the end of his career is reminiscent of Keynes's reply to a friend who, after hearing of Keynes's appointment to the Bank of England, said he was becoming orthodox in old age. Keynes replied: 'You are wrong. Orthodoxy has caught up with me.'[31]

Acknowledgements

The author thanks Jane D'Arista, Per Berglund, Robert Leeson, Jim Rock and Roger Sandilands for their comments and the librarians of the Special Collections Department at the Marriot Library of the University of Utah for their capable assistance.

Notes

1. Tugwell was the main initial sponsor of Eccles within the Roosevelt administration, having met with him early in 1933 while he was still at Columbia University and after Eccles had presented his views to the Senate Finance Committee. Later in the same year Tugwell, then in the Department of Agriculture, invited Eccles to Washington and introduced him to several members of the administration, which eventually led to Eccles's appointment to the Treasury in 1934.
2. These views were to some extent influenced by Thorstein Veblen's *The Theory of Business Enterprise*. Veblen (1904) differentiated between business – the managerial profit-making activities – and industry – the technical and productive activities of society. Depressions were caused, in this view, by business behavior that disrupted the productive activities in the interest of maximizing profits. Interestingly enough, Eccles believed that ultimately Keynesian ideas dominated the New Deal, relegating institutionalist ideas to a secondary role. In a 1951 letter to Raymond Rasenberger – an instructor at Dartmouth – Eccles argued that: 'The social and institutional theories of Thorstein Veblen and of Wesley Mitchell have been less influential in New Deal circles in a specific sense than those of Lord Keynes ... Keynes' specific recommendations, on the other hand, that public investment expenditures be utilized in a period of unemployment to help offset deficiencies in the private demand for goods and services are clearly evident in New Deal economic philosophies' (Marriner S. Eccles Papers, Box 111, Folder 3). To a great extent, if Keynesian ideas prevailed over institutionalist ideas within the Roosevelt administration, Eccles was responsible.

3. Eccles's main criticism was that private interests – basically the big Wall Street investment banks – had dominated the system, and that political control in Washington should 'make the nation's financial centers useful servants of the national welfare' (Eccles, 1951, p. 166). The memorandum expressing most of the ideas that Eccles discussed with Roosevelt was prepared with the help of Lauchlin Currie, 'a member of the "Freshman Brain Trust"' (ibid., p. 166) who became one of Eccles's main economic advisers, and who was one of the early Keynesians in the administration (Hyman, 1976, pp. 154–61; Sandilands, 1990, pp. 60–8).

4. Galbraith suggests that he too believed in the idea that imperfect competition and a rigid price structure were at the heart of the unemployment problem before the publication of the *General Theory* (see Colander and Landreth, 1996, p. 136).

5. In that respect Eccles may be classified as a New Dealer Mark II – using Sandilands's (2001) classification – that is those who emphasized fiscal activism and became dominant after the 1937–38 recession. New Dealers Mark I focused on the countervailing power of the state to reduce the excesses of cartelization.

6. One should note that there was a long tradition in the United States, going back to Alexander Hamilton, of emphasizing the importance of public debt. However, in this respect Eccles seems to be closer to Abba Lerner's functional finance position than Keynes ever was. On Keynes's relative reluctance to increase the burden of debt see Lerner's conversation with Alvin Hansen in Colander and Landreth (1996, pp. 105–9). Hansen observes that 'Keynes was never interested in the national debt; he never really gave any serious systematic discussion, as far as I can remember, to the debt' (ibid., p. 105). Eccles on the other hand was keenly aware of the interaction between flow imbalances and the accumulation of stocks of debt. In a speech in Boston in February 1935 – when he was already a governor of the Federal Reserve Board – he suggested that his appointment 'was interpreted by some to mean that the "Great American Debtor" had come into his own' (Marriner S. Eccles Papers, Box 74, Folder 10).

7. Eccles several times expressed views that would be classified as part of the functional finance school. He believed that 'the budget comes into balance as the national income increases' and that 'there is no danger of bankrupting the Federal Government' (Marriner S. Eccles Papers, Box 6, Folder 11). More importantly, he argued that 'rising debt does not mean inflation. So long as many men are without jobs, heavy expenditures mean more goods and more employment, and not higher prices' (ibid.)

8. Also, one should note, that no book by Foster and Catchings is to be found in Eccles's Library of Political Economy (deposited at the Marriot Library at the University of Utah). For a discussion of influences on Eccles's economic ideas see also Israelsen (1985).

9. The first point of the memo, sub-titled 'Relation of Monetary Management to Business Stability,' indicates that 'fluctuations in production, employment and national income are determined by changes in the available supply of cash and deposit currency, and by the rate and character of monetary expenditures' (Marriner, S. Eccles Papers, Box 4, Folder 1). The memo also suggests that the main policy to increase national income at that point should be to raise government spending. However, Currie (1934) can be interpreted as a

forerunner of Friedman and Schwartz's (1963) monetarist interpretation of the Great Depression, as did Karl Brunner in his forward to the 1968 edition of Currie's book (Sandilands, 1990, p. 49). Eccles himself was always more cautious about the effectiveness of monetary policy. During the hearings on the 1935 Federal Reserve System Act, he appropriated the famous phrase coined by the ranking Democratic member of the House Banking and Currency Committee T. Alan Goldsborough of Maryland, according to whom monetary policy in the Great Depression was like 'pushing on a string' (Marriner S. Eccles Papers, Box 13, Folder 4). In addition, in a letter to Senator Willis Robertson, a Democrat from Virginia, dealing with a paper written in 1951 by several Chicago economists (including Friedman, Metzler, Mints and Schultz) titled 'The Failure of the Current Monetary Policy,' Eccles argues that the 'Chicago economists overstated somewhat the possible influence of monetary policy' (Marriner S. Eccles Papers, Box 61, Folder 2).

10. Orphanides (2003) argues that by the early 1920s the Federal Reserve had already developed the tools and methods of analysis approximating a modern Phillips curve-based approach to policy design. Even though the Real Bills Doctrine, and its emphasis on what might be called endogenous money, has some similarities with modern approaches to monetary policy, the evidence for a Phillips curve approach presented by Orphanides are thin, at best.

11. It should be noted that Currie's review of Keynes is very perceptive and does not fall into the trap that caught many other early Keynesians, *à la* Modigliani, of assuming that Keynes's main proposition rested on the notion of fixed wages. He clearly noted that 'in a downturn wage reductions are likely to result in an expectation of further reductions, a fall in prices, a diminished prospective yield of new capital, and, hence, lessened investment and employment' (Marriner S. Eccles Papers, Box 111, Folder 1).

12. Meltzer (2003, p. 479) quotes Currie's own argument that his 1934 book was 'partly obsolete when it was published.'

13. However, as Eccles noted he 'had not specialized in any particular line of business,' and the field of banking was a late addition to his business experience (Marriner S. Eccles Papers, Box 74, Folder 1).

14. Continued gold inflows in 1936 intensified concerns regarding the inflationary potential. One should note too that Eccles was still an advocate of easy money in 1937. In a statement in March 1937 Eccles argued 'I have been and still am an advocate of an easy money policy and expect to continue to be an advocate of such a policy so long as there are large numbers of people who are unable to find employment' (Marriner S. Eccles Papers, Box 9, Folder 8).

15. Lauchlin Currie produced a series of papers to show the impact of the fiscal contraction on the economy in which he notes the problems of lags in fiscal policy implementation and suggests automatic stabilizers as a solution (Marriner S. Eccles Papers, Box 73, Folders 5 and 8). Currie argues:

> It may very well be that much flexibility cannot be achieved within the budget. A large portion of the taxes are levied on the previous year's budget income and in accordance with prior enactments. The bulk of expenditures are determined by approximations made in advance of the period to which they apply. It may be that the solution lies in securing flexibility in large part outside the regular budget. For one thing,

the possibilities of providing for executive discretion in varying subsidies, and in maintaining, speeding up or retarding various types of
expenditures, might be explored. Another avenue of approach would
be the exploration of the possibility of securing appropriate compensatory variations in receipts and/or expenditures through the use of
automatic non-discretionary devices linking receipts and/or expenditures
to changes in the rate of consumption and production.

(Marriner S. Eccles Papers, Box 73, Folder 8)

These views were not only quite advanced for their time, but also highly
controversial (see Sandilands, 2001).
16. Conventional wisdom on the causes of the Great Depression and the reces-
    sion emphasize the roles of both fiscal and monetary policy, in particular, the
    contractionary stance imposed by the gold standard (for example, Kindle-
    berger, 1973; Temin, 1989). Hence, it was not just the macroeconomic
    policies, but more importantly the international policy regime, that forced a
    deflationary stance.
17. Meltzer (2003, p. 679) notes that monetary policy during the Great Depres-
    sion was misguided because of the 'failure to distinguish between nominal
    and real rates.' Deflation implied that real rates were higher, and having a
    negative effect on spending. In the 1937–38 recession, for example, the nom-
    inal rate on new issues of 3-month Treasury bills was around 0.05 percent,
    and consumer prices were falling at slightly more than 2 percent. Meltzer
    (ibid., p. 681) argues that the negative effect of higher interest rates was more
    than compensated by the positive effect of increased real balances on private
    spending. The war experiment with the massive increase in spending and the
    effective elimination of unemployment casts doubt on Meltzer's belief in the
    strength of real balance effects.
18. I thank Jane D'Arista for pointing this out.
19. Meltzer (2003, p. 507) suggests that Morgenthau was concerned with the
    effect of higher interest rates on investment. Eccles (1951, p. 314) was more
    concerned with spending in general, both private and public. In a letter to
    Senator Byrd he asked 'is it of no significance that, owing to the decline in
    the rate of interest, the total interest payments today [December 1938] is far
    less than in 1929?'
20. This led some Keynesians, like Hansen, to believe that it was the war experi-
    ence, and not the 1937–38 recession that led to the dominance of Keynesian
    ideas (Colander and Landreth, 1996, pp. 104–6). Samuelson, on the other
    hand, argues that 'it's completely untrue that the New Deal didn't work until
    World War II came and bailed it out' (ibid., p. 160). Stein (1969) takes a longer
    view, and suggests that Keynesian ideas did not triumph completely until the
    Kennedy administration.
21. The research director, Emanuel Goldenweiser, argued at that time that 'the
    greatest danger that we face on the economic front is the danger of runaway
    inflation' (Marriner S. Eccles Papers, Box 6, Folder 12).
22. Samuelson argued that 'the general profession ... laid a big egg for which they
    paid in acclaim, disesteem, recrimination. That is the famous prediction that
    there would be mass unemployment after the war unless the government

slowed down the return of soldiers and did a lot of deficit spending' (Colander and Landreth, 1996, p. 173).

23. The 1946 Employment Act per se was no guarantee of full employment or maximum employment, as defined in the Act. Leon Keyserling, chairman of the Council of Economic Advisers (CEA), an institution created by the Employment Act in the Truman administration, notes that it was difficult to define full or maximum employment. He recollects that Alvin Hansen was fearful 'that economists [would] take a higher and higher definition for what constitutes full employment' (Colander and Landreth, 1996, p. 233). See also De Long (1996).

24. Leeson (1997) shows how Alvin Hansen's ideas evolved from the notion that inflation was a dangerous problem to the view that some inflation could be acceptable and that it could be traded off for lower levels of unemployment, in other words, he developed a sort of Philips curve.

25. Surprisingly, given the advocacy of price and wage controls, the statement was also signed by economists who would be associated with monetarism, such as Arnold Harberger and George Stigler.

26. Fears of inflation were also connected to the international experience. In an internal Federal Reserve memo titled 'Lessons of Foreign Experience' the fear of pegging interest rates at low levels was explicitly analyzed. It was argued that 'under post-war conditions of higher employment attempts of monetary authorities to peg or lower interest rates have reinforced inflationary pressures and have contributed to balance of payments difficulties' (Marriner S. Eccles Papers, Box 62, Folder 3). The prime example of the failure of cheap money policies was Hugh Dalton's in Britain from 1945 to 1947.

27. Their theory is an alternative to the conventional wisdom dominated by the Barro-Gordon credibility model of central bank behavior, according to which central bank independence is a way of overcoming time inconsistency problems. For a description of modern views on central banking see Blinder (1998).

28. Clark seems to indicate that interest rates are a cost of production. Hence, increasing interest rates would lead to higher prices, something that Keynes referred to as Gibson's paradox, and that became known in the United States as the Patman effect, after the populist Texan Congressman Wright Patman.

29. In this, it is Congressman Wright Patman who more closely fits the bill. Patman clearly wanted to commit the Federal Reserve to a policy of low rates of interest. For example, in February 1951, in the midst of the debates that led to the Federal Reserve-Treasury Accord, he argued that 'we should not increase the interest rate unless it absolutely necessary ... There is no reason why we should pay more than 2½ per cent on long term paper, and if the Federal Reserve Banking System cooperates, we will not have to pay more' (Marriner S. Eccles Papers, Box 61, Folder 9).

30. As noted by Epstein and Schor (1995, pp. 16–17) the financial and industrial community favored what they call 'conservative Keynesianism,' meaning 'policies that maintained sufficient aggregate demand to maintain profitability and resist radical challenges to capitalism, while resisting government intervention which would interfere with the profitability or prerogatives of capitalists.'

31. The story is cited in Keynes's obituary in *The Economist*, 27 April 1946 (Marriner S. Eccles Papers, Box 111, Folder 2).

References

Blinder, Alan, 1998, *Central Banking in Theory and Practice*, Cambridge, MA: MIT Press.

Calomiris, Charles and David Wheelock, 1998, 'Was the Great Depression a Watershed for American Monetary Policy?' in Michael Bordo, Claudia Goldin and Eugene White (eds), *The Defining Moment: the Great Depression and the American Economy in the Twentieth Century*, Chicago: University of Chicago Press, pp. 23–65.

Colander, David and Harry Landreth, 1996, *The Coming of Keynesianism to America: Conversations with the Founders of Keynesian Economics*, Brookfield: Edward Elgar.

Currie, Lauchlin, 1934, *The Supply and Control of Money in the United States*, New York: Russell and Russell (reprinted 1968).

D'Arista, Jane, 1994, *The Evolution of U.S. Finance: Federal Reserve Monetary Policy, 1915–1935*, Armonk, NY: M.E. Sharpe.

De Long, J. Bradford, 1996, 'Keynesianism, Pennsylvania Avenue Style: Some Economic Consequences of the Employment Act of 1946,' *Journal of Economic Perspectives*, 10(3): 41–53.

Eccles, Marriner S., 1944, 'Possibilities of Postwar Inflation and Suggested Tax Action,' in Marriner S. Eccles et al., *Curbing Inflation through Taxation*, New York: Book for Libraries Press (reprinted 1971).

Eccles, Marriner S. (1951), *Beckoning Frontiers: Public and Personal Recollections*, 3rd edn (1966), New York: Alfred A. Knopf.

Epstein, Gerald and Juliet Schor (1995), 'The Federal Reserve-Treasury Accord and the Construction of the Post-War Monetary Regime in the United States,' *Social Concept*, 7(1) (July): 7–48.

Friedman, Milton and Anna Schwartz (1963), *A Monetary History of the United States, 1867–1960*, Princeton: Princeton University Press (reprinted1971).

Galbraith, John K., 1977, *The Age of Uncertainty*, Boston: Houghton Mifflin.

Greider, William, 1987, *The Secrets of the Temple*, New York: Simon & Schuster.

Hyman, Sidney, 1976, *Marriner S. Eccles: Private Entrepreneur and Public Servant*, Stanford, CA: Stanford University Graduate School of Business.

Israelsen, L. Dwight, 1985, 'Marriner S. Eccles, Chairman of the Federal Reserve Board,' *American Economic Review*, 95(2), May: 357–62.

Keynes, John M., 1940, *How to Pay for the War*, London: Macmillan.

Kindleberger, Charles P., 1973, *The World in Depression, 1929–1939*, Berkeley: University of California Press (reprinted 1986).

Leeson, Robert, 1997, 'The Eclipse of the Goal of Zero Inflation,' *History of Political Economy*, 29(3): 445–96.

Marriner S. Eccles Papers (1890–1977), Special Collections Department, University of Utah Libraries, Salt Lake City, Utah.

Meltzer, Allan, 2003, *A History of the Federal Reserve, 1913–1951*, Volume I, Chicago: University of Chicago Press.

Orphanides, Athanasios, 2003, 'Historical Monetary Policy Analysis and the Taylor Rule,' *Journal of Monetary Economics*, 50(5), July: 983–1022.

Sandilands, Roger, 1990, *The Life and Political Economy of Lauchlin Currie: New Dealer, Presidential Adviser, and Developing Economist*, Durham: Duke University Press.

Sandilands, Roger, 2001, 'The New Deal and "Domesticated Keynesianism" in America,' in Michael Keaney (ed.), *Economist with a Public Purpose: Essays in Honor of John Kenneth Galbraith*, New York: Routledge, pp. 219–46.

Skidelsky, Robert, 2000, *John Maynard Keynes: Fighting for Freedom, 1937–1946*, New York: Viking (reprinted 2001).

Stein, Herbert, 1969, *The Fiscal Revolution in America*, Chicago: Chicago University Press.

Temin, Peter, 1989, *Lessons from the Great Depression*, Cambridge, MA: MIT Press.

Timberlake, Richard, 1999, 'The Tale of another Chairman,' *Region* (Federal Reserve Bank of Minneapolis), June, 13(2): 32–5.

Tugwell, Rexford, 1958, *The Art of Politics*, Garden City, NY: Doubleday.

United States Senate, 1951, *An Economist's Statement on Anti-inflationary Measures*, Congressional Record, Senate, United States Government Printing Office, Washington DC, February 22.

Veblen, Thorstein, 1904, *The Theory of Business Enterprise*, New York: New American Library (reprinted 1958).

5
The Great Inflation of the 1970s: Evidence from the Archives

John Lodewijks and Robert Leeson

5.1 Introduction

In 1985 the Duke University Manuscript Department, in conjunction with the Department of Economics, began an Economists' Papers Project aimed at preserving the correspondence, writings, and related papers of a number of distinguished economists. These papers contain a treasure trove of useful information, particularly on the development of post-war economic theory.

This chapter will use these and other archival sources to provide insights into a number of issues. One issue that featured prominently in the debates between various macroeconomists concerned the causes of, and cures for, inflation. This issue was implicit in the early skirmishes between Keynesians and their opponents but was very explicit during the inflationary experiences of the 1970s and beyond. Section 5.2 examines the growing Chicagoan animosity felt towards John Maynard Keynes. Section 5.2 also examines the interactions between three 'permanent opposition' Left Keynesians (Joan Robinson, Richard Kahn, Michel Kalecki), an American Keynesian (Sidney Weintraub) and Keynes's biographer and disciple, Roy Harrod. (Daniele Besomi, 2004, should also be consulted as it deals with Harrod in far more detail.) Section 5.3 examines the validity of some New Keynesian assertions about Old Keynesians. Section 5.4 discusses more generally the insights into contemporary economics that can be provided by oral interviews by examining *The Changing Face of Economics: Conversations with Cutting Edge Economists*, by David Colander, Richard Holt, and J. Barkley Rosser (2004). Concluding comments are provided in Section 5.5.

5.2   Old Keynesian battle-lines

Between *A Treatise on Money* (1930) and *The General Theory* (1936) John Maynard Keynes was metamorphosized in Chicagoan eyes. This transformation was superimposed on a full-scale internal civil war that was engulfing the Chicago economics department. This was 'academic life on the battlefront' with Paul Douglas pitted against Frank Knight and his disciples, in particular Henry Simons (Stigler, 1988, chapter 12; Nef, 1973, p. 109; Patinkin, 1980, p. 5, n. 8). Milton Friedman recalled that Douglas and Knight were at 'very serious odds with one another. There was a feud' (cited by Blumenthal, 1986, pp. 96–7).

The *Treatise on Money* was apparently well received in Chicago. Douglas (1931, p. 9; 1933, p. 80) described it as 'brilliant' and 'the most stimulating single work on money'. But the *General Theory* was not well received: Simons (1936) stated that it could easily become 'the economic bible of a fascist movement.' Keynes's *Treatise*, like the *General Theory*, was 'full of brilliant insights and occasionally devastating criticisms of other writers'; but the *General Theory* was 'a revision (if not a repudiation)' of the first volume of the *Treatise*. Keynes had 'now' embarked on a mission that Simons found repellent: an authentic genius 'becoming the academic idol of our worst cranks and charlatans.' Roy Harrod (1951, pp. 448–9) noted that Keynes was becoming a widely 'hated' figure in some American circles.

The archives provide numerous insights into these developments. Frank Knight (1 May 1936) wrote to Oskar Morgenstern: 'What do you think of Keynes's book? I haven't got into it yet, but a couple of friends whom I consider pretty competent judges say outright that Keynes is losing his mind.' Three years later (8 November 1939) Knight wrote to Morgenstern:

I'm waiting expectantly to see what you will say about Hicks's Value and Capital. I put a class through it last spring, and am afraid it contributed something to my state of discouragement as to the state and prospects of our profession. I've never really 'gotten over' the shock I received from Keynes's General Theory, and even more the way it has been received by economists, particularly of the younger generation. If you can squeeze out the time and effort to give me any notion of what you are thinking on the general subject of 'what we might do to be saved,' I'll always be glad to hear from you. One reason I don't write letters more generally and promptly is the difficulty I find in thinking of anything to say that should not be suppressed rather than uttered![1]

It is interesting to note Keynes's response to Knight's review of the *General Theory*: 'Indeed with Professor Knight's two main conclusions, namely, that my book has caused him intense irritation, and that he has had great difficulty understanding it, I am in agreement' (Skidelsky, 2003, p. 545).

Two of Keynes's disciples, Joan Robinson and Richard Kahn, had appropriated the mantle of his heirs. In 1936, Harrod and Hubert Henderson complained that '2 people in Cambridge together with a few undergraduates' were propagating the belief that those who did not accept the *General Theory* were 'intellectually inferior beings' (cited by Clarke, 1988, p. 308). The reaction to Dennis Robertson's criticisms of the static nature of Keynes's analysis, and the ignoring of the forces of productivity and thrift on the rate of interest, is instructive:

> Robertson was starting to feel a 'back number' at Cambridge. Research students, he told Henderson, wanted to work with Kahn and Joan Robinson, not him ... [his] quarrels with Keynes and Keynes's young Turks, especially Joan Robinson, brought him close to a psychological breakdown. In 1938 he left Cambridge to take up a Chair at London University, driven out by the increasing hostility of Keynes's disciples.
> (Skidelsky, 2003, p. 545)

John King has reminded us that Joan Robinson actually did have a nervous breakdown in 1938, though whether Robertson can be blamed is uncertain.

Harrod (December 1970) complained to the American Keynesian, Sidney Weintraub:

> What I do object to is people attributing views to me that I have never held or expressed ... when I pointed out to Joan [Robinson] that she had erroneously attributed to me various things that I had never written ... she paid not the slightest attention, and went on to publish her note ['Harrod after 21 Years', *Economic Journal*, 1970] with the various misrepresentations of me thick upon it ... Oddly enough, at her suggestion, I re-read her little appendix about me in the *Accumulation of Capital* [Robinson, 1956]. I found that more or less (not quite) O.K. In the years that have passed since, she has built up in her mind ideas about me that are quite wrong ... What matters ... is that it misrepresents me and ...totally fails to understand me ... [She is] I think, addressing her mind to different problems.[2]

As we might have expected from someone who had the self-confidence to offer to write the Preface to Keynes's *General Theory* (oral communication, Claudio Sardoni, 14 December 2004) Robinson wrote to say that 'I think I understand Harrod's theory much better than he does' (see also King, 1998, for the Robinson-Kaldor exchanges). In a related context, Harrod (4 November 1970) wrote to Sidney Weintraub:

> I have just finished reviewing Kalecki on *Growth in a Socialist Economy* for *Kyklos*. It is an excellent book. It is a curious thing that I feel I have learnt more from this socialist than I have learnt in these recent years from all our capitalist growth theorists ... But perhaps I am prejudiced in favor of K because he is pure Harrod ... Now I have always believed that Domar had never read my piece, when he published his 7 years later, so I have never grudged him joint authorship. But I find it hard to believe that Kalecki had not read it. He was at Oxford for a long time during the war, viz. shortly after my article had appeared, and I had a number of talks with him. It seems unthinkable that we should not have discussed my article ... Not that I blame K for not expressing indebtedness. It is hard for a communist economist to express indebtedness to a capitalist.

Neither was Sidney Weintraub spared the critical responses of Kahn and Joan Robinson. In 1938–39, Weintraub spent a graduate year at the London School of Economics, where he was a student of Dennis Robertson and Lionel Robbins, and attended the LSE-Cambridge-Oxford seminar. What is interesting is that when he developed his critique of the mainstream interpretation of Keynes, only Robertson and Harrod came to his support. Others, who he regarded as natural allies, such as Kahn and Robinson, were critical of his contribution. The interchange starts with a 'wrist-slap' from Kahn to Weintraub (29 November 1960), followed by further letters to Kahn and Robinson in December 1960 and January 1961 in which Weintraub expresses astonishment at being subject to criticism from those he regarded as his natural supporters. There is a final letter from Robinson to Weintraub where she concedes that the 'semantic' misunderstanding has now been settled.[3]

Yet there was more at stake than mere 'semantic' issues. Weintraub's views regarding the role of government would not have been interpreted sympathetically by many of the English Post-Keynesians. Weintraub was 'interested in maintaining the market system, not dismembering it or replacing it' and stated that 'a great deal can be accomplished without involving any departure from our mutual dedication to freedom, and to a free, non-government coerced market economy.' Indeed, 'the *Journal of Post Keynesian Economics* was formed to offer reasonable, moderate, largely non-interventionist notions to improve on economic performance.'[4]

5.3   Keynesians: New on Old

Oral interviews are generally regarded as useful supplements to the professional correspondence found in the archives (Lodewijks, 2005). In the Lyndon Baines Johnson Library in Austin, Texas, there is a very detailed 156-page interview with Walt Rostow (Lodewijks, 1991b) plus two oral interviews with Arthur Okun. Another oral interview with Okun exists but is inaccessible. The interviewer had done nothing with it and has refused access to it. It is apparently still unpublished.

Okun (1928–80) was a highly policy-focused economist who died at the age of 51 of a heart attack at his home in Washington, DC. He was one of America's better-known economists and his early death was much lamented. Gardner Ackley regarded Okun as the best empirical economist and forecaster that he knew, while Geoffrey Harcourt thought that Okun surely would have been awarded a Nobel Prize had he lived longer. Paul Samuelson, who did win a Nobel Prize, acknowledged that Okun was the wisest and most creative economic policy adviser of his time (Lodewijks, 1988b).

Okun was born in Jersey City, NJ, and graduated from Columbia with a BA degree in economics (1949) and a PhD (1956). During his formative years at Columbia, Okun's research was directed by Arthur F. Burns, but he also came into contact with the works of A.G. Hart, J.M. Clark, F.C. Mills and G.C. Means and others influenced by the institutionalist tradition at Columbia. What Okun assimilated from this experience was a strong empirical orientation and 'respect for the facts.' One characteristic feature of Okun's later work was his persistent confrontation of economic theory with the facts in the form of empirical findings. Theory needed an empirical base in real-life observations and empirical generalizations provided the basis from which Okun developed new hypotheses about economic behavior. While working on his doctorate in 1952 Okun took up a position of instructor at Yale University. At Yale he was James Tobin's 'prize protégé' and was immersed there in Keynesian doctrine and the need for governments to actively manage the economy in order to achieve stabilization and economic growth objectives. Okun was to become one of America's leading Keynesians in the 1960s and 1970s. He became chairman of the President's Council of Economic Advisers (February 1968) and his early contributions related to forecasting and fiscal policy and the development of what was later to be called 'Okun's

Law'. Okun was most innovative in developing the policy component of the Keynesian approach to macroeconomics.[5]

When the Nixon administration took office (January 1969), Okun prepared to move back to Yale but was persuaded to join the Brookings Institution as a senior fellow. He stayed at Brookings for the rest of his career and there he joined a group of top-flight policy economists who moved easily between positions in academia, the Brookings 'think-tank' and government. These economists included Joseph Pechman, Charles Schultze, George Perry, Walter Salant, Ed Denison, Alice Rivlin and Henry Aaron. Perhaps Okun's major contribution while at Brookings was to begin (1972) a journal called the *Brookings Papers in Economic Activity* (with George Perry). This soon became one of the most frequently cited economic journals in the profession.

Milton Friedman described Brookings as 'the home away from home for Democrats out of office' (Friedman and Friedman, 1998, p. 93). The *Washington Post* reported that some Brookings economists circulated estimates that the money supply had to grow by 10–11 percent per annum to get unemployment down to an electorally acceptable level of 4 percent by 1972 (Rowen, 1970). President Richard Nixon repeatedly urged Fed chairman Arthur Burns to expand the money supply at a faster rate. Burns replied that some form of incomes policy was required (Evans and Novak, 1971, p. 370).

Brookings also attracted Nixon's attention for other reasons: he instructed his Treasury Secretary, George Shultz, to target Brookings (and other foundations) that 'had been used for left-wing purposes' (Ambrose, 1991, p. 19). Nixon believed that confidential and classified information was being held at the Brookings Institution: an academic research organization that he wanted to 'smash' (Ambrose, 1989, p. 448). Nixon (1978, p. 512) made it clear that he wanted the material returned 'right now – even if it meant having to get it surreptitiously.' One of Nixon's agents, Gordon Liddy, therefore targeted Brookings for fire bombing (Dean, 1976, pp. 316, 45; Woodward and Bernstein, 1976, pp. 324–5; Kutler, 1997, pp. 6, 8). Liddy (1980, pp. 225–6, 276, 438) planned to acquire an authentic looking fire engine so that a group of Cubans (later of Watergate infamy) could impersonate fire fighters whilst 'calmly loading the "rescued" material into a van.'

Okun's liberal views often got him off-side with some of the Brookings trustees and its then president, Bruce MacLaury. In a letter from Okun to MacLaury, dated 7 December 1979, Okun recounts the 'only significant unpleasant experience I have ever had in my affiliation with the Brookings Institution' where he was forced to take leave without pay because of the 'tenacity of some of the trustees during the election campaign of 1972.' He tells MacLaury in no uncertain terms that 'a recurrence of that situation' would be 'intolerable.'[6]

Gregory Mankiw (1992) highlighted what he sees as the substantial differences between New Keynesian economics and the views of early Keynesians. In particular he claims the early Keynesians were far too complacent about the costs of inflation and overly optimistic about the benefits of discretionary stabilization policy. This dichotomy seriously misrepresents the traditional Keynesians (see also Blinder, 1988, and Leeson, 1994). In this section we will show the usefulness of archival research in dispelling Mankiw's caricature of Keynesian economics through a case study of Okun, who Edmund Phelps considered to be for more than a decade 'the foremost practitioner of macroeconomics in the United States' (Lodewijks, 1989, p. 141).

What is noteworthy in Okun is his persistent and innovative attempt to make fiscal policy more practical and flexible in operation. Okun was fully aware of the constraints on the use of discretionary policy. On the revenue side, there was a 'political asymmetry which makes it easier to move to stimulus than restraint in outlays and taxes' and further, 'Every time we get into a debate about a cyclical change in taxes, up or down, we go through months of agonizing about what the right form and the right distributional aspect of that should be ... the whole can of worms has to be opened and inspected worm by worm, it seems' (Lodewijks, 1989, p. 151). Okun acknowledged that a two or three year delay in implementing tax proposals negated any possibility of their use as a counter-cyclical device, so he was an early advocate of providing the President with discretionary authority to execute prompt, temporary tax changes for stabilization purposes.

On the expenditure side, he repeatedly urged programs that increased private income, without committing the nation to future large expenditures, such as additional unemployment insurance benefits and Federal grants to states based on the amount of 'excess' unemployment. These expenditures would then steadily decline as the economy returned to full employment. Devising mechanisms yielding temporary stimulus but which would self-terminate as recovery ensued was a continuous preoccupation for him.

From the mid-1970s Okun shifted his attention to 'innovative fiscal measures' that would hold down *both* inflation and unemployment. His views on inflation are also somewhat at odds with the cavalier attitude that early Keynesians are supposed to have held, according to Mankiw. Okun was trenchant in his claims about the deleterious effects of inflation (even anticipated or steady inflation) that severely disrupted an economy based on the dollar yardstick. On 26 December 1975 Okun wrote to Sir John Hicks that 'Among American Keynesians, I have been nearly alone in regarding the inflation problem as real rather than as merely a figment of imagination or money illusion among the unsophisticated masses.'[7] By the late 1970s, Okun seemed shaken by the virulence of inflation. The weapons Okun proposed to control inflation were direct measures to hold down prices and costs that would then allow some relaxation of demand restraint. In that sense, they were alternatives to tough contractionary policies likely to generate high rates of unemployment. This was another theme in his work – developing a more 'humane' anti-inflation strategy.

What is particularly interesting is the evolution of Okun's thinking in the light of his perception of how the economy had changed over time. His *The Political Economy of Prosperity* (1970) can be seen as a favorable retrospective evaluation of the activist policy stance. Critics of discretionary policy had used the label 'fine-tuning' to characterize the Keynesian position. Okun preferred 'sensible steering', for he eschewed the notion that the dials of policy could be manipulated with precision; the objective was to turn the right dials in the right direction and to make adjustment as circumstances warranted. He favored small, flexible and frequent adjustments of policy instruments because: 'We can do far better by using our intelligence in diagnosing, forecasting, and prescribing than by adopting rigid formulas ... Events since early 1969 strengthen my conviction that the optimum amount of activism is a lot of it' (Lodewijks, 1988b).

Okun's doubts about the ability of forecasters to predict the economy's movements accurately increased over the 1970s, but in 1980 he was still confident that policymakers could forecast and control the course of nominal GNP, and indeed government economic estimates of this magnitude had been more accurate in the 1970s than they had been in the previous decade. However, he acknowledged that the split between the real and the inflationary component of GNP could not be controlled or forecast. From about the middle of the 1970s, as he absorbed the lessons of the previous decade and acknowledged the economy's faltering performance, he became more cautious in his policy advice:

> I am utterly confident that unemployment belongs in the wage equation for the United States *for 1954–69*. For that period, the evidence for that is as clear as for disposable income belonging in the consumption function, interest rates in the money demand function, and operating

rates in the investment function. During those good old days, U.S. performance fit the Phillips curve like a glove! In sharp contrast, I am not confident about anything for the decade of the seventies.[8]

An evaluation of the post-war record of monetary and fiscal policy could elicit only a judgment of 'mixed performance' from Okun in 1980. In an oral interview, he said that he saw only 'limited feasibility of pursuing counter-cyclical fiscal policy as a stabilization device.' He thought 'the whole question of discretion' was related to the state of our technical art and the information available to manipulate the policy tools and 'we don't know as much as we used to know' (Hargrove and Morley, 1984). Arthur Okun in early 1980 was saying that:

> most of the credit for increased economic stability should go to the automatic stabilizers – both fiscal and financial – and their impact on private behavior. And I do believe that public works and similar activist spending efforts have been so badly mistimed that they probably have done us more harm than good. But I also believe that most of the countercyclical tax actions and discretionary changes in transfer programs were on the whole constructive, even if they were not ideally timed. Even some of the things I call 'too much, too late' may have been better than nothing ever.[9]

Okun came increasingly to recognize the limited feasibility of pursuing a counter-cyclical fiscal policy as a stabilization device but persistently tried to make these instruments more flexible to override the political constraints on their use. At least with Okun, and perhaps others, it is the confrontation of established beliefs with the economy's actual performance that stimulates the recasting of ideas and beliefs. What Mankiw fails to appreciate is the development of thought and the honest attempt by practitioners to come to grips with the issues of the day. Building straw men and caricatures to juxtapose with extremist positions does little to advance the subject. Arthur Okun's views on macro policy provide a useful counter to Mankiw's Keynesian caricature. They also demonstrate the value of archival research in setting the record straight.

5.4   Other archival insights

Readers with more of an interest in contemporary economics should find the oral interviews collected in *The Changing Face of Economics:*

Conversations with Cutting Edge Economists, by Colander, Holt, and Rosser (2004) absorbing. This fascinating collection of conversations is a must-read for those intrigued by the diverse contributions that have characterized the recent history of our discipline. What follows is a very small sample of the delights that await readers. The first interview is with Deirdre McCloskey and we read that 'I was a communist, I was a man, I was a mathematical economist. I was all these things; now I'm not' (p. 30). Today, she describes herself as a 'post-modern, free-market, quantitative, English professor, Chicago School, feminist, Episcopalian female' (p. 34). The gist of the interview relates to her views on econometrics which she believes has 'become completely dominated by arbitrary tests that are rubbish ... 95 percent of economists are misusing statistical significance ... [and] the main devil was Tinbergen. Statistical inference came from him' (pp. 39, 43, 45).

Ken Binmore tells us that all of 'social science is just a branch of game theory' (p. 74). He forecasts that in 'fifty year's time, I think that economics will be classed as a science, like physics and chemistry [and] people will regard the present as the golden age of economic theory' (pp. 74–5). Moreover, what 'really exists in most markets is an adaptive dynamic process whose end product is the same *as if* there were a Walrasian auctioneer' (p. 69; emphasis in original). Binmore is particularly critical of behavioralists who design bad experiments – especially those designed to show that economic theory doesn't work (p. 63). He thinks that 'the current behavioral approach – that people somehow just have an intrinsic taste for fairness – is not only unsupported by the data but is downright dangerous when its advocates start trying to influence policy' (p. 65).

Herb Gintis, in his fascinating interview, says that 'Sam [Bowles] and I basically stopped doing Marxism. We were perfectly happy as clams doing neoclassical economics' (p. 89). They do not consider themselves 'heterodox': 'once we figured out that we could model the nature of conflict between capital and labor in the work process using a principal agent model and incomplete contracts, we just gave up on the labor theory of value' (p. 86). They stopped arguing with Marxists and just moved on. Furthermore, Gintis tells us that 'I could never get along with the Italians like Garegnani. For them, intellect is just a tool for communist revolution or something. It's a Talmudic exercise, and I've never treated it that way' (p. 87). He also considers himself a 'serious intellectual enemy of postmodernism in any form' (p. 90). A new passion has emerged however, he has 'fallen in love with general equilibrium theory' (p. 87).

Robert Frank reveals that he works in the intersection between biology and psychology and economics and finds that research out of business schools is more problem-driven and interdisciplinary than that emerging from departments of economics. Matthew Rabin similarly imports psychology into economics to develop a more sensible empirical economics. William Brock describes himself as a leftist libertarian concerned about externalities who loves the University of Chicago: 'I have never been to such a place that has such a commitment to pure science' (p. 164).

The interview with Duncan Foley is the second-best interview in the book, after Gintis. Foley works in the areas of nonlinear dynamics and complexity theory where he models a dynamic system that has endogenous instability rather than an alternative approach of using a stable equilibrium process subject to external shocks: 'at the core of the complexity vision is the recognition of a fundamental nonlinearity and instability associated with local increasing returns; this is what brings about multiple equilibria and the failure of the system to settle into equilibrium' (p. 185). Fascinating insights about the hierarchical nature of our profession and the power of key figures emerge. He describes his 'powerfully wrenching emotional experience' at MIT, and the pressures there to institutionalize and even monopolize cutting-edge work, while at Stanford he found the intellectual atmosphere was much more 'polarized, politicized and dogmatic' (p. 194).

Richard Norgaard gives a good account of the evolution of resource and environmental economics, and now ecological economics, in the US. He states that a perfectly efficient economy would deplete resources and leave future generations worse off and that we need to return to the approach of the classical economists who read widely in moral philosophy and the natural sciences.

Robert Axtell and Peyton Young, in another stand-out interview, provide valuable insights into agent-based modelling and the computational revolution in the behavioral sciences, particularly drawing on experiences at Carnegie Mellon. Work in cognitive science there was about observing how people solved problems and trying to understand how information was being processed. Current work stresses heterogeneous actors interacting through social networks and the evolution of norms and preferences. Thomas Schelling and Herbert Simon are the progenitors in this area. Peyton Young (p. 283) states that:

> Over the last ten years or so there has been a noticeable shift toward behavioral models that are built on rules of thumb and simple adaptive mechanisms ... buttressed by the results of laboratory

experiments ... [and] there has also been a renewed interest in the ways in which culture and social context affect decision making and in the possibility that culture, institutions and economic outcomes must be viewed as coevolving systems ... [so that] the study of institutions and the ways in which different institutional forms (including markets) evolve, is one of the most exciting areas of economic research today.

5.5   Conclusion

The interviews described above are entertaining and enlightening and provide a glimpse of the excitement at the research frontier. Yet it must be acknowledged that they (and archival research generally) are just useful supplementary sources of information to assist in interpreting the history of the discipline. They provide more pieces of the puzzle and need to be combined with textual exegesis and the other tools of the historian. In the case of Harrod a very useful source of information has been the publication of *The Collected Interwar Papers and Correspondence of Roy Harrod* by Daniele Besomi (2004). In the case of Sidney Weintraub, some caveats to the use of these archival materials have been provided. Roy Weintraub (2005), in his '2004 History of Economics Society Presidential Address', reminded us that misremembering is common and that using economists' reminiscences to construct historical narratives is problematic. While these oral interviews can provide a context, they must be used cautiously as we need to use other 'archival' and published materials as a reliability check on the accuracy of the observations made.

Notes

1. Both these letters were unearthed in the Oskar Morgenstern papers held at Duke University (Lodewijks, 1990b).
2. Sidney Weintraub papers, Duke University (Lodewijks, 1991a).
3. Box 1 Folders 11 and 12, Weintraub Papers, Duke University.
4. Box 4 Folders 1 and 3, Box 6 Folder 3, Weintraub Papers, Duke University; Lodewijks (1990b, 1991a).
5. Okun's papers are housed in the Lyndon Baines Johnson Presidential Library, Austin, Texas. There are two extensive oral historical interviews of Okun: one by David McComb (dated 20 March and 15 April 1969 on deposit with the L.B.J. Library) and the other is dated 24 February 1978, published in E.C. Hargrove (1984). A collection of 29 of Okun's articles appears in Pechman (1983). While Okun did not leave any complete bibliography of his works, Pechman (1983, pp. 645–52) has usefully assembled Okun's main publications. Personal tributes in memory of Okun appear in *In Memoriam: Arthur M. Okun* (1980), Brookings Institution; 'Arthur M. Okun: 1928–1980', *Brookings*

Papers on Economic Activity, I (1980); 'Portrait: Arthur Okun', *Challenge*, May–June (1980). For evaluations of his contributions to economics and the policy process see Lodewijks (1988a, 1988b, 1989) Phelps (1981) and Tobin (1983).
6. Box 21A, Okun Papers, LBJ Library.
7. Box 20B, Folder H, Okun Papers, LBJ Library.
8. Arthur Okun to Wynne Godley, 9 February 1979. Okun Papers, LBJ Library, Box 20A (emphasis in the original).
9. Arthur Okun to Martin Feldstein, 22 January 1980. Okun Papers. LBJ Library, Box 20A.

References

Ambrose, S.E., 1989, *Nixon: the Triumph of a Politician, 1962–1972*, New York: Simon and Schuster.
_____, 1991, *Nixon. Vol 3: Ruin and Recovery, 1973–1990*, New York: Simon and Schuster.
Besomi, D. (ed.), 2004, *The Collected Interwar Papers and Correspondence of Roy Harrod*, Vols 1–3, Cheltenham, UK and Northampton, MA, USA: Edward Elgar.
Blinder, Alan S., 1988, 'The Fall and Rise of Keynesian Economics,' *Economic Record*, The Economic Society of Australia, 64(187) (December): 278–94.
Blumenthal, S., 1986, *The Rise of the Counter-Establishment from Conservative Ideology to Political Power*, New York: Times.
Clarke, P., 1988, *The Keynesian Revolution in the Making*, Oxford: Clarendon Press.
Colander, D., R. Holt, and J. Barkley Rosser, 2004, *The Changing Face of Economics: Conversations with Cutting Edge Economists*, Ann Arbor: University of Michigan Press.
Dean, J., 1976, *Blind Ambition*, New York: Simon and Schuster.
Douglas, P.H., 1931, *World Unemployment and its Reduction through International Co-operation*, London: League of Nations Union.
_____, 1933, *Know America: its Ills and Cures*, Chicago: Buti-Lami Press.
Evans, R. and R. Nowak, 1971, *Nixon in the White House*, London: Davis Poynter.
Friedman, M. and R. Friedman, 1998, *Two Lucky People*, Chicago: University of Chicago Press.
Keynes, J.M., 1930, *A Treatise on Money: the Applied Theory of Money*, London: Macmillan.
_____, 1936, *The General Theory of Employment Interest and Money*, London: Macmillan.
King, J., 1998, ' "Your Position is Thoroughly Orthodox and Entirely Wrong": Nicholas Kaldor and Joan Robinson, 1933–1983,' *Journal of the History of Economic Thought*, 20(4) (December): 411–32.
Hargrove, E.C. and S.A. Morley (eds), 1984, *The President and the Council of Economic Advisers: Interviews with CEA Chairmen*, Boulder, CO: Westview.
Harrod, R., 1951, *The Life of John Maynard Keynes*, London: Macmillan.
Kutler, S.I., 1997, *Abuse of Power: the New Nixon Tapes*, New York: Simon and Schuster.
Leeson, R., 1994, 'The Rise and Fall of Keynesian Economics?' *Economic Record*, The Economic Society of Australia, 70(210) (September): 262–6.
Liddy, G.G., 1980, *Will*, Glasgow: Collins.

Lodewijks, J., 1988a, 'Arthur Okun and the Lucasian Critique', *Australian Economic Papers*, 27(51): 253–71.

_____, 1988b, 'Arthur M. Okun: Economics for Policymaking', *Journal of Economic Surveys*, 2(3): 245–64.

_____, 1989, 'Arthur Okun's Contribution to the Macroeconomic Policy Debates,' *Economic Analysis and Policy*, 19(2) (September): 141–66.

_____, 1990a, 'The Oskar Morgenstern Papers,' *HETSA Bulletin*, History of Economic Thought Society of Australia, 14 (Summer): 10–16.

_____, 1990b, 'Sidney Weintraub, the English Dons, and an Unpublished Obituary of Harrod,' *HETSA Bulletin*, History of Economic Thought Society of Australia, 13 (Winter): 8–17.

_____, 1991a, 'Sidney Weintraub and the "Noxious Influence of Authority",' *History of Economics Review*, 16 (Summer): 112–18.

_____, 1991b, 'Rostow, Developing Economies and National Security Policy,' in Craufurd D. Goodwin (ed.), *Economics and National Security*, Durham: Duke University Press, pp. 285–310.

_____, 2005, 'The ET Interview: Professor Jan Kmenta,' *Econometric Theory*, 21(3): 621–45.

Mankiw, N.G., 1992, 'The Reincarnation of Keynesian Economics,' *European Economic Review*, 36: 559–65.

Nef, J.U., 1973, *Search for Meaning: the Autobiography of a Nonconformist*, Washington: Public Affairs Press.

Nixon, R.M., 1978, *The Memoirs of Richard Nixon*, Sydney: Macmillan.

Patinkin, D., 1980, 'New Material on the Development of Keynes' Monetary Thought,' *History of Political Economy*, 12(1): 1–28.

Pechman, J.A., 1983, *Economics for Policy Making: Selected Essays of Arthur M. Okun*, Cambridge, MA: MIT Press.

Phelps, E.S., 1981, 'Okun's Macro-Micro System: a Review,' *Journal of Economic Literature*, XIX(3) (September): 1065–73.

Rowen, H., 1970, 'Burns Pressing Hard for "Incomes Policy",' *Washington Post*, 15 November.

Simons, H.C., 1936, 'Keynes' Comments on Money,' *The Christian Century*, 22 July: 1016–17.

Skidelsky, R., 2003, *John Maynard Keynes, 1883–1946: Economist, Philosopher, Statesman*, London: Macmillan.

Stigler, G.J., 1988, *Memoirs of an Unregulated Economist*, New York: Basic Books.

Tobin, J., 1983, *Macroeconomics, Prices and Quantities: Essays in Memory of Arthur M. Okun*, Washington, DC: Brookings Institution

Weintraub, E.R., 2005, '2004 HES Presidential Address: Autobiographical Memory and the Historiography of Economics,' *Journal of the History of Economic Thought*, 27(1) (March): 1–11.

Woodward, B. and C. Bernstein, 1976, *The Final Days*, London: Coronet.

6
An Archival Case Study: Revisiting *The Life and Political Economy of Lauchlin Currie*

Roger J. Sandilands

I had been closely associated with Lauchlin Currie (1902–93) for almost twenty years, as student and research assistant, before formally embarking on his biography (Sandilands, 1990) in 1987. Though by then nearly 85, Currie was still a senior adviser to the Colombian government, mentally very alert, and even physically fit enough to play tennis daily, and at weekends to hack terraces out of a Colombian mountainside where he experimented with the cultivation of irises. Over the next two and a half years I was able to interview or write to him on any aspect of his life and work on which I needed more information. He also gave me carte blanche to rifle through his extensive archives. My working conditions while in Colombia (June 1987–January 1988 and June–August 1988) were close to ideal. On weekdays I occupied an office next to Currie's in the Colombian Savings and Loan Institute, and at weekends I freely explored bulging cupboards and filing cabinets at his home.

His is not a household name, even among economists, though it was not always thus. At the launch of the Spanish translation of my biography in Bogotá, Colombia, in November 1990 (the English version having appeared in February), one of the speakers, Rudiger Dornbusch, brought with him a special message for the conference from his colleague Paul Samuelson. With the title 'Tribute to Lauchlin Currie' it read:

> Lauchlin Currie and Alvin Hansen, working through Marriner Eccles and Franklin Roosevelt, were the two economists most influential in converting the original New Deal from a program to reform the institutions of capitalism into a Mixed-Economy system of macro-economic stabilization. Before there was a Keynesian *General Theory*, Currie was one of the stellar band of economists who urged monetary

easing on the Federal Reserve to mitigate and prevent a devastating and unnecessary depression.

The world owes Lauchlin Currie a great debt. Connoisseurs among scholars know how much economic science owes to Currie's originality. On behalf of Harvard economists everywhere, on behalf of researchers yet unborn, I proclaim Lauchlin Currie's praises. Hail Caesar! Hail Nestor!

(Paul A. Samuelson, MIT)

This was gratifying recognition of Currie's many contributions to monetary theory, policy and institution-building in the 1930s.[1] However, Samuelson said nothing of Currie's work in the White House as peacetime and wartime assistant to Franklin Roosevelt, 1939–45, nor of his many years as a development economist since 1949. Currie's relatively low profile among mainstream 'Western' economists during these years can perhaps be explained by two considerations.

First, from early 1941 Currie was diverted from strictly economic work into wartime administration: as director of the Lend-Lease Program to China, 1941–43; as de facto head of the Foreign Economic Administration, 1943–44, where his work was mainly concerned with the procurement of strategic materials and with loan negotiations with British and Soviet officials; and as head of the allied delegation to Switzerland, January–March 1945, to secure a freeze on Nazi gold deposits in Swiss banks and to bribe the Swiss into denying further shipments of Nazi *matériel* through Switzerland to Field Marshal Albert Kesselring's army in northern Italy.

Second, after 1949 most of Currie's work was based in Colombia where he was relatively hidden from the mainstream. Though a top adviser there, this was not the same as being adviser at the Fed or the White House. Also, his day-to-day advisory work meant his writings were either in the form of unpublished memoranda designed to influence policy in a timely and effective manner, or academic articles not always sufficiently refined (or orthodox) to be publishable in the more prestigious mainstream journals. A related consideration is that Currie's reputation took a severe knock during the McCarthy era at precisely the time he was carving a new career in Colombia, and it suited some people to spread the notion that he was only there as a fugitive from justice.

It was my hope that a full-scale intellectual biography of Currie's unusual career would help to set the record straight and highlight his many insufficiently appreciated contributions to political economy both in the New Deal and in the field of development theory and policy.

Researching Currie's early years: records and reminiscences

Currie was born on 8 October 1902 in a small fishing village in Nova Scotia where his father had built up a substantial fleet of sailing vessels. But his father died when Currie was only four and his mother, a schoolteacher, moved to the nearby town of Bridgewater. He attended schools in Nova Scotia, apart from two years when his family stayed with relatives in Massachusetts and California. From 1920–22 he attended St Francis Xavier's University before enrolling at the London School of Economics. There his teachers included Edwin Cannan, Hugh Dalton, R.H. Tawney, Sidney Webb, and Harold Laski. After graduating from the LSE in 1925 he moved to the PhD program at Harvard where his chief inspiration was the legendary Allyn Abbott Young. His other teachers included Frank Taussig, John H. Williams, and T.N. Carver. Unfortunately for Currie, Young was lured to the LSE in 1927 to take over Edwin Cannan's chair of political economy but died suddenly in March 1929 during an influenza epidemic at the early age of 52. Currie was scheduled to be Young's teaching assistant in monetary economics had Young stayed at Harvard. Instead, John H. Williams became his formal PhD supervisor, but his research was initially guided by Young.[2] He was assistant to Young's temporary replacement, Ralph Hawtrey, in 1927–28, and later to Joseph Schumpeter. His PhD thesis, submitted in January 1931, was on banking theory and bank assets. Here he exposed the fallacies of the Real Bills Doctrine and was one of the very few who at the time blamed Federal Reserve Board policies for the Great Depression. His diagnosis was very similar to that given much later in Milton Friedman and Anna Schwartz's (1963) celebrated monetary history, in which, however, Currie's contributions were ignored (see Laidler, 1993; 1999, chapter 9).

Currie stayed at Harvard until 1934, producing important papers on monetary theory and policy in the *Journal of Political Economy* and the *Quarterly Journal of Economics*. A book on *The Control of the Supply of Money in the United States* appeared in 1934, dedicated to the memory of Allyn Young. Along with Harry Dexter White, his classmate and friend since 1925, Currie urged radical monetary and fiscal activism, the abandonment of the gold standard, increased fiscal deficits and inflationary finance as an escape from depression.[3] This did not please senior faculty members such as the department chairman, Harold Burbank, nor Gottfried Haberler and Joseph Schumpeter, not to mention Charles Bullock whom Currie described in his unpublished memoirs (1953, p. 26) as 'a violent reactionary, really, I believe, mentally unbalanced.'

In a letter to me, 28 June 1987, Currie denounced Schumpeter as a 'mountebank.'[4] A biographer may nowhere find in the published record such throwaway remarks. Yet this kind of information can cast new light on key events and characters and breathe life into the history. Access to the subject's other correspondence files, diaries, and memoirs also helps of course; but the biographer's own correspondence and interviews can add greatly to that body of informal information. Most helpful of all is the opportunity to listen to the subject in person and note the tone of voice: bitter or relaxed; mellow or rancorous.

In the case of Schumpeter, a policy nihilist in the depths of depression, one hears Currie relate contemptuously how in his lectures he would suddenly stop in mid-sentence, ostentatiously clasp his forehead, pull a paper from his pocket and scribble a note. 'It was probably his laundry list,' scoffed Currie. 'His only solution for depression was to let wages fall. Other than his own, of course. He even voted to reduce the tea ladies' wages.' In similar vein Currie would rail against Herbert Hoover's mean-minded Puritanism that upheld the virtues of 'fiscal rectitude' and balanced budgets. (This was in marked contrast to his reverential tone when describing Roosevelt's character.) Or I would hear him complain ruefully that Haberler, another policy nihilist of the Austrian School, voted against him in a close contest with Harry White for the prestigious Wells prize that would have guaranteed publication of his PhD dissertation.[5]

In these ways the Real Bills Doctrine, the quantity theory, going off gold, deflation, liquidation, mass unemployment, prohibition, departmental rivalries and patronage, opportunistic Johnnies-come-lately to intellectual and social fashions (his own Harvard rival Seymour Harris being the most despised example) need no longer be colorless names or dry ideas (except the case for prohibition!)[6] Instead, when struggling through a vast literature, I would often recall Currie's own vibrant take on the ideas and names that appeared before me. Thus I could fix and organize a mass of material into a more coherent narrative than would otherwise have been possible. No doubt this also biased my interpretations (usually, but not always, in favor of my subject's case), especially if subsequently I also had the opportunity to discuss the issues with him in person, as I often did. But the reader would surely get a more faithful impression of Currie's life, thought, and character than through a biographer without that advantage.

However, one incidental problem with writing Currie's life at the same time as he was still engrossed in his current writing and advisory work was that he was constantly badgering me to finish work on the early years and get up to date so I could spend more time discussing and helping him with his current work. He was very much a man of action to whom 'the past is poison' (as he once remarked ruefully, though in a different context) except as it provides useful lessons for today.

Naturally, the accompanying disadvantage of close association is the above-mentioned danger of lack of balance and an overly sympathetic, uncritical account of the subject's life. The biases can be reduced by contacting the subject's surviving friends and enemies. The object is to write biography not hagiography. The danger is clearly greatest, as in my case, when writing about an associate who is still alive and will eventually read the book. In this connection Charles P. Kindleberger (1991), in his *Journal of Political Economy* review of my 'remarkable book about a remarkable economist,' commented (after detailing my associations with Currie since graduate days in Canada in 1967):

> The preface emphasizes that Currie has allowed Sandilands complete freedom and that Currie in fact welcomed criticism and called attention to weaknesses. This then is not hagiography. While the account of Currie's life and work is strongly positive, there is frequent mention of failures, large and small, and of frustrations and disappointments.

On the other hand, Frank Steindl (1993), in his review for *Economica*, thought my biography too uncritical (especially where I gave a sympathetic account of Currie's advice to the Fed in 1936–37, advice with which Steindl disagreed). He wrote:

> Sandilands's forte is development economics, and so it is not surprising to find errors in his discussion of Currie's monetary analysis, ones against which Currie inveighed … The principal shortcoming of the book, however, is that Sandilands is too much of a disciple. Time and again, Currie was involved in disputes of ideas and analyses of significant import with formidable intellects – Friedman, Harris-Todaro, Hirschman, Keynes, Prébisch – and, with the single exception of one issue of second-order importance, Sandilands cannot have him being wrong! Now, of course, that is difficult to accept. In particular, I showed (*Journal of Monetary Economics* 1991) that Currie's analysis advocating doubling the reserve requirements in 1936–37 was mistaken.

I might defend myself here by noting that while Steindl's position on this latter episode is the majority view, it is not shared by everyone. For example, see Lester Telser (2001) of the University of Chicago, whose work I discuss in Sandilands (2004, pp. 181–3).[7] Be that as it may, here was a case where Currie had particularly strong feelings, for it was obviously uncomfortable to be blamed for causing a sharp increase in unemployment. We discussed this episode more intensively than any other from the 1930s. Naturally, I heard Currie's case more forcefully than any from the other side. However, I read and presented plenty of criticism, even some from Currie's close friend Walter Salant to whom I showed this chapter (and whom I later interviewed at the Brookings Institution). Steindl cannot complain that the alternative Friedman-Schwartz (1963) position was not given space in my book. Similarly, space was given to the views of Albert Hirschman (Currie's antagonist on planning in Colombia in the early 1950s),[8] Michael Todaro on rural-urban migration, Raul Prébisch on import substitution, and of the ILO and the Sussex School on employment strategies, so readers would be in a position to draw different conclusions from mine or Currie's. As it happens I came broadly to share Currie's views. Endorsement need not be hagiography.

Walter Salant was a friendly critic, and I admit to having been more inclined to contact Currie's friends than his enemies; partly, however, this was because his friends would usually have more to say or inside knowledge to impart: for the pre-Colombia (pre-1949) years these included Salant on the New Deal; Richard Goodwin on Currie as a teacher at Harvard and on his attitude toward Schumpeter; Don Patinkin on the Chicago School connection (and for advice on a publisher – he recommended Duke University Press, the publisher of his own book on the Chicago School; Patinkin, 1981); Byrd Jones on Currie's work at the Fed; and the Harvard historian John Fairbank and the veteran columnist Joseph Alsop on wartime China. For Currie's post-1949 Colombian career, I had the benefit of knowing quite well many of his close associates (and had even had brief meetings with two former presidents, Virgilio Barco and Misael Pastrana), having spent 12 extended periods in Colombia between 1968–90.

On Currie's work in the 1930s, Byrd Jones also sent extensive notes from his researches in the 1970s at the National Archives in Washington, mainly on Currie's unpublished Federal Reserve Board memoranda, not all of which were among Currie's own files in Bogotá. The Federal Reserve Board's own archives contain more information on Currie's work, and still more are to be found in the Marriner S. Eccles Papers in the Special Collections Department of the University of Utah libraries where the entry on Currie is the longest in the catalogue. Also useful is Princeton University's Seeley G. Mudd Manuscript Library where the Jacob Viner papers include a considerable correspondence with Currie dating from 1932, and where the Harry Dexter White papers include the important paper (mentioned above and only recently brought to light) that White co-authored with Currie and P.T. Ellsworth on anti-depression policy in January 1932 (Laidler and Sandilands, 2002). Some twenty-five of Currie's hitherto unpublished memoranda on monetary theory and policy were recently published in Sandilands (2004), mainly from the 1930s, but with a few from his time in Colombia. They cast fresh light on Currie's influence at the Federal Reserve Board, 1934–39, but these by no means exhaust the extensive information about this period in Currie's own papers.

The bulk of Currie's papers – over 31,000 items – has now been archived in Duke University's Special Collections and Rare Manuscripts Library, as part of their Economists' Papers Project (see Appendix 6.1). Time and resources did not allow me to visit the US during 1987–90 while I was writing Currie's biography, though since then I have spent some time in Washington (at the Library of Congress, at Brookings, and in the FBI Reading Room) and in California at the Hoover Institution at Stanford University where most of Currie's China papers are archived. Fortunately, Currie's personal archive in Bogotá was extensive and frankly more than I could cope with properly in the time available for work outside my home base in Scotland. Now that these papers are almost all at Duke or Stanford Universities they offer an opportunity for future biographers to prove David Reisman (1990) wrong when he described my effort as 'definitive.'

The Washington years, 1934–45

In June 1934, the US Treasury's special adviser, Jacob Viner, recruited Currie, Harry Dexter White, and others to his 'Freshman Brain Trust' to study specific topics related to the New Deal. Currie's brief was to outline an ideal monetary system for the US. In the Princeton University archives is a letter from Viner to Frank Taussig, October 1934, in which he wrote: 'I have had a few Harvard men working for me here, Currie, [Alan] Sweezy, and White, and have been very favorably impressed indeed with them, especially the two former. I think Currie has a tendency to dispose too summarily of arguments and difficulties which stand in the way of his pet ideas, but aside from this by no means rare shortcoming, I think he has an extraordinarily good mind.'

Currie's own correspondence files from the 1930s and 1940s are relatively thin (especially compared to those from early 1950, when he settled in Colombia and had less reason to discard files between moves), but are supplemented by the above-mentioned archives of correspondents such as Viner, White, and Eccles. It may well be that Viner's comment on Currie's 'tendency to dispose too summarily of arguments and difficulties' refers partly to the difference in their attitude to the gold standard in 1933 as an obstacle to more vigorously reflationist policies. Viner was one of twelve Chicago economists at the Harris Foundation conference in January 1932 who signed a cable to President Hoover recommending an increase in the free gold of the Federal Reserve System and expansionary open-market operations, 'with the double aim of facilitating necessary government financing and increasing the liquidity of the banking system.'

When in late 1933 President Roosevelt adopted his gold purchase policy with the avowed aim of raising the price of gold and reversing the decline in commodity prices, this was greeted by dozens of prominent economists with well-publicized cries of alarm and a call for a restoration of the gold standard 'to restore confidence.' A letter along these lines to the *Washington Post* on 4 November 1933 was signed by five Chicago economists including three who had signed the Harris Foundation message in January 1932. Viner was not one of the *Washington Post* signatories, though Currie has recalled that Viner was also worried at that time about the implications of radical policies for the gold standard (which Viner wanted to maintain) and avoidance of capital flight.[9]

Another strong attack on Roosevelt's monetary policies was published in the *New York Times*, 28 November 1933, signed by 38 Columbia economists. They included James Angell (another signatory of the earlier Harris Foundation cable), Wesley Mitchell, J.M. Clark, and H.P. Willis. It was endorsed by the Austrian economist Fritz Machlup.[10] These attacks prompted Currie and five of his young Harvard colleagues to write to President Roosevelt in an open letter to the *New York Times*, 25 January 1934 (reproduced in Sandilands, 2004, p. 261), in strong support of the gold purchase policy:

> What many authorities did not realize, and what has become increasingly evident, was that the departure from the gold standard was an absolutely indispensable prerequisite to the adoption of your other policies of reform and recovery. Otherwise, every proposal would have been opposed on the ground that it might endanger the maintenance of the gold standard. Any fears that expressed themselves in an outflow of capital and an export of gold would have been deflationary

in their effects and would have tended to intensify and prolong the depression.

Search the archives and one's memory of conversations and there are cautionary notes: in a letter to Alan Sweezy (emphasis in original), 22 August 1971, Currie wrote:

> I found the famous letter! I did some head shaking over it, but anyway our hearts were in the right place and our instincts were right, so what more can you ask? Anyway, despite what Walter [Salant] says, the *threat* of a run on gold was present at that time and going off gold (a) removed that threat for the time being (b) gave the 'man in the street' a feeling of bold leadership and (c) eased the gold and liquidity situation for many years to come.

Why the head-shaking? The letter to Roosevelt concludes:

> In the foregoing paragraphs, we may seem to have dwelt unduly upon the monetary means for recovery and reform. This emphasis arises from the immediacy of these problems. We would urge in conclusion, however, that we are not believers in the sole efficacy of monetary measures as a cure for our economic ills. Indeed, our primary interest is rather in the direction of your longer range programs for reform and here we feel admiration for the comprehensive view you have taken of the economic structure.

With hindsight, Currie has acknowledged that many of the regulations against big business, which in this letter he appears to have endorsed, were unhelpful to recovery. In a handwritten aide-memoir for a 1987 London Weekend Television interview on the Great Depression (among his papers at Duke and reproduced in Sandilands, 2004), he wrote that the recovery program of the Roosevelt administration was 'at first, rather confused and working at cross purposes. Monetary deflation continued in 1933. The Government sponsored a cost-inflation program called the NRA. Against all this, it had only a slow public works program. When NRA collapsed there was a recession. The mainstay was a cash deficit, but this was officially deplored.' No doubt his 1971 letter to Sweezy was also recalling the uneven pace of recovery, and in particular the sharp downturn in 1937 that he blamed on a failure to understand the need to maintain a steady 'net Federal contribution' to buying power.

Despite or because of Currie's forceful radicalism, Viner not only recruited Currie to his Freshman Brain Trust at the Treasury but also asked him to stay on as his assistant at the end of his initial three-month assignment. However, Currie's request for further leave from Harvard was rejected. This was not unrelated to the January 1934 letter to the *New York Times*. It had incensed Harvard's senior professors. So, with some bitterness, he resigned from Harvard, became a naturalized US citizen, and his three-month Washington stint eventually lasted eleven years.

At the Treasury he met and immediately hit it off with Marriner Eccles, another special adviser. When Eccles was appointed Chairman of the Federal Reserve Board in November 1934 he took Currie with him as his personal assistant. Together they drafted the bill that became the 1935 Banking Act that converted the Fed into a true central bank with greatly enhanced powers, including the power to double reserve requirements on commercial banks should this be deemed appropriate. These powers were indeed invoked in 1936–37, supported by Currie, at a time when banks' excess reserves had climbed from around $50 million in 1929 to $3 billion in 1936 as gold flowed in from a troubled Europe.

The raising of reserve requirements, as a precautionary rather than a deliberately deflationary measure, has been widely blamed for precipitating a sharp downturn in the economy in 1937. Several important memoranda on this subject in the Currie archives illuminate the continuing debate over whether monetary or fiscal influences were mainly to blame for the downturn. Today there is much support for the well-known view of Friedman and Schwartz (1963) that the Fed was to blame: see, for example, Steindl (2004). On the other side, University of Chicago economist Lester Telser (2001, 2003) has, like Currie, blamed the very sharp fiscal turnaround in 1937 compared with 1936. It may also be that the fiscal tightening was a more important (indirect) influence than the raising of reserve requirements on the deflation of credit and money in 1937. (See also Sandilands, 2004, pp. 181–8; and the review of Steindl, 2004, in Sandilands, 2005.)

Also revealing on this whole period are Currie's extensive correspondence files from the 1970s and 1980s. These included correspondence surrounding the session that John Kenneth Galbraith organized at the New Orleans meeting of the American Economic Association, December 1971, on 'The Keynesian Revolution and its Pioneers,' with contributions from Alan Sweezy, Byrd Jones, Robert Nathan, and Leon Keyserling. Other correspondents included Walter Salant, Tom Humphrey, and Don Patinkin. A good example is a letter to Paul Samuelson, 5 May 1978, in which Currie clarified the significance of his 1934 book on money, the contents of which Samuelson believed Currie had repudiated as soon as the ink was dry:

> Whoever told you that got the story a bit wrong. The book was specif-
> ically on the mechanism of the supply and control of money, and
> not on prices or incomes or the relative roles of money and the rate
> of interest. One of the chief findings was that a main determinant of
> the supply (and hence of control) was the extent of the indebtedness
> of the commercial banks of the large centers to the Fed. But by the
> time the book appeared and for a few years afterwards, the banks had
> an excess of reserves and were not in debt. My finding, valid for the
> 1920s and again since the late 1930s, ceased to be valid for some years
> in the 1930s, unfortunately, for me, just as the book was published!
>
> I would have agreed with your pragmatic attitude that the relative
> importance of money and interest rates changes with circumstances,
> and go even further and argue that under certain conditions neither
> may be sufficiently important to matter, which is why I devoted most
> of my time to deficit spending in the period 1934–39. The replen-
> ishment of the money stock in 1934–36 was helpful, as was the
> continuance of very low interest rates on riskless securities, but the
> 'causal' factor became, for a time, direct spending of old and new
> money. I don't imagine we would differ on that point.

During his years at the Fed, Currie became the acknowledged leader of the spending wing of the New Deal (see Stein, 1969, p. 165), based on pre-*General Theory* ideas and the development of statistical series on leakages and injections in the circular flow of income – vital for estimates of the size and composition of the federal budget required to arrest and reverse the depression. With this conceptual and empirical series he provided what may have been an original, albeit brief and informal, statement of the 'balanced-budget multiplier' concept (and on this too there is con-siderable retrospective discussion in his 1970s correspondence files, with Paul Samuelson, Walter Salant, and others).[11]

In *Federal Income-Increasing Expenditures, 1933–35*, written in late 1935 with Martin Krost (Currie and Krost, 1978 [1935]), he reported that any similarity between the 'net contribution' and the reported cash deficit was purely coincidental. The reported budget could be in balance while the net contribution was in heavy deficit. Thus there was no neces-sary conflict between those who wanted a balanced budget and those who wanted the government to provide a stimulus. In the unpublished appendix of Currie and Krost (1978 [1935]; original in Duke University archives, p. 30) 'By selecting income-increasing types of expenditure and non-income-decreasing methods of raising revenue, it is conceivable that a balanced budget could be maintained and at the same time a considerable stimulus given to business.' Investment subsidies, for example, could have a powerful stimulatory effect while a tax on undistributed profits might have only a small negative effect. However, there was no doubt in Currie's mind that the conditions prevailing in the mid-1930s called for much more than a balanced expansion of taxes and spending.

The size of the required deficit, whether in its cash or its 'net contribution' form, was calculated according to the size of potential, full-employment income (based on 1928 with adjustments for population and productivity growth) and the size of the leakages from that income that would need to be offset. If deficit finance was a precondition for the recovery of aggregate incomes and expenditures, it was also the main determinant of profits and business confidence. Strenuously opposing this view was Treasury Secretary Henry Morgenthau who believed that deficits destroyed business confidence.

In the fall of 1937, as the economy was plunging into renewed depression, Currie came to FDR's personal attention when, on the urging of Harry Hopkins, the President met directly with Currie and two other technicians (Leon Henderson and Isador Lubin) for an unprecedented four-hour conference on 8 November in which 'Curried-Keynesianism' was explained. The *New York Post* reported the next day that the advisers 'minced no words in giving Roosevelt a hard-boiled review of economic conditions and with equal bluntness and vigor they told him that a disastrous recession can only be averted by a resumption of big-scale government spending.'[12] As Currie later recalled in his New Deal memoirs (Sandilands, 2004, pp. 212–13):

> The President clearly did not understand what had happened to the recovery and was uncertain what to do. At this time he was receiving conflicting advice from many quarters. The conservatives were saying that the recession had been caused by the continued federal deficit (even though at that time the Federal Government was running a small cash surplus) and Morgenthau was influenced by their arguments. They also maintained that the undistributed profits tax was a factor and demanded its repeal. The President's faith in the basic New Deal policy of deliberately increasing a deficit to increase consumer buying power was obviously shaken. In any case, I always suspected that Roosevelt's adherence to that policy was based more

on humanitarian than on economic grounds, despite his statements to the contrary that could be quoted. He was glad to use economic arguments for something he wanted to do on other grounds.

In those circumstances Hopkins, I believe it was, said to him 'Mr. President, instead of always talking to the heads of departments, why don't you talk to the boys who actually write their memos and get some first hand dope on what is after all a highly technical matter?' The President assented and it was arranged that Leon Henderson, Isidor Lubin and I should see him. James Roosevelt, who at that time was acting as his father's secretary, included Paul Mazur to represent the Wall Street point of view. The meeting was set for November 8 of 1937 and with very little advance notice I prepared a memorandum which was signed by three of us. Our meeting, my first with the President, lasted an entire afternoon and received much publicity at the time. Unfortunately, the inclusion of Mazur led to much internal disagreement among the 'experts' and the President was again presented with conflicting views. I retained the objective of a balanced budget for 1939 since the fiscal year did not begin until the middle of 1938, and I had various ideas how the budget could be technically balanced while continuing a cash deficit.

The President was obviously very much interested in our meeting and, as always, took a vigorous part in the discussion. I was presented for the first time (although not the last) with the task of reconciling my great respect for the President, which would have led me to keep quiet, and my anxiety to make my point, which impelled me to break in and even differ, as respectfully as I could. That I succeeded in this reconciliation reasonably well in my first meeting was indicated by the President's reaction when my name was suggested to him as one of his new assistants in 1939: 'Currie? I remember him well. He can disagree with one without getting red in the face and pounding the table.'

Little tangible resulted from this meeting although probably it had its value in being part of the process by which the President finally made up his mind. Two days later Morgenthau made his then famous budget balancing speech, which, in the circumstances of the times, was widely hailed as a victory for the conservative point of view, particularly in his reference to the Government's future reliance on 'the driving force of private initiative'. With little objection from the Administration, Congress proceeded to repeal the undistributed profits tax. The only recovery measures we advocated that were promptly adopted related to housing, and this was in large part attributable to Eccles' brilliant manoeuvre in having them accepted and recommended by a distinguished committee of private citizens (see [Marriner Eccles's] *Beckoning Frontiers*, 1951, 302–303).

As Eccles says in his book, both he and the New Deal program for achieving recovery appeared, in the closing days of 1937, to be in the dog house. Since he was indisposed to try to see the President again for the moment, I decided that the most useful thing I could do was to re-examine the course of events leading up to the recession and present an explanation as well documented as I could make it. The resulting memorandum, on the *Causes of the Recession* was mimeographed and widely circulated and read in New Deal circles.[13] It probably had as much influence as anything I wrote in the Government. Although it was the fashion to accuse the Roosevelt Administration of favouring a planned society I argued that our current difficulties arose from the absence of careful planning. The juxtaposition of the payment of the veterans' bonus of $1.7 billion in 1936 (passed over the President's veto) and the beginning of collections of Social Security taxes in 1937 was wholly fortuitous and unplanned. The tremendous and highly disrupting wave of inventorying and then disinventorying was similarly unplanned as was also the excessive advance in building costs.

While this memorandum did much to restore or strengthen faith in the necessity of planning and for the Government to assume more active responsibility for the course of economic activity it left me dissatisfied with my own failure to forecast the severity of the recession well in advance of its occurrence. It was hindsight rather than foresight. It was particularly aggravating because I was aware at the time of the drastic fall in the excess of government expenditures over receipts, of the rise in building costs and of the probable excess of production over consumption, the difference going into inventories. I became aware of the chief mental hazard attached to forecasting – the reluctance to take a strong stand that business is going to be very different than it actually is. I think that in part this reluctance arises not only from a fear of being wrong, but also from an implicit awareness of the absence of reliable and current quantitative data. In the then state of our economic data, one naturally hesitated in taking a strong position which went contrary to existing trends.

Morgenthau continued to oppose proposals to increase deficit spending, but a few months later Roosevelt finally swung in favor of the spenders and the economy pulled out of recession in late spring 1938.

It is widely believed that J.M. Keynes was the key figure in altering attitudes toward the proper role of government in securing full employment in a mainly free enterprise US economy, greatly aided, after 1937, by Alvin Hansen's famous fiscal policy seminar at Harvard (conducted jointly with John H. Williams, and attended by the likes of Paul Samuelson, Lorie Tarshis, James Tobin, and John Kenneth Galbraith), together with Hansen's later, equally famous *Guide to Keynes* (1954). The Currie papers appear to uphold Galbraith's view that Currie has a claim to precedence, at least relative to Keynes's *General Theory* (1936), as an intellectual influence on New Deal macroeconomic activism. In an essay on 'How Keynes Came to America,' Galbraith (1971, p. 48; see also Sandilands, 2001) noted that 'Currie failed of promotion at Harvard partly because his ideas, brilliantly anticipating Keynes, were considered to reflect deficient scholarship until Keynes made them respectable.' However, the archives reveal that Currie was critical of *The General Theory* when it appeared. Nevertheless, he was happy to invoke its authority in support of policies he advocated on somewhat different intellectual and empirical grounds (the influence of Allyn Young[14] was at least as great as that of the early Keynes); and he teamed up with Alvin Hansen to defend activist fiscal policy in their joint testimony before the Temporary National Economic Committee in May 1939 (Sandilands, 1990, pp. 83–7).

In the White House in peace and war, 1939–45

In June 1939 President Roosevelt phoned the chairman of the Federal Reserve Board. Marriner Eccles (1951, p. 333) recorded the conversation thus:

> 'Marriner, I guess you are going to give me hell.'
> Without knowing what he had in mind, I replied: 'Mr. President, I do not know what good it would do to give you hell, even if I wanted to.'
> 'Well,' he explained, 'I am going to steal Lauch Currie from you. I need him here as one of my assistants.' He quickly baited the hook.
> 'I am sure you will realize,' he continued, 'that it is not such a bad thing after all as far as the Board and you are concerned. You, of course, see the advantages at once of having a friend in court who can represent and speak for *your* point of view.'

Thus in July 1939 Currie joined the White House staff as the President's administrative assistant for economic affairs, a post created in the 1939 Government Reorganization Act as drafted by Charles Merriam and Louis

Brownlow. One of the chief qualifications laid down for these advisory posts was 'a passion for anonymity.'[15] An interesting example of the need for this uncommon passion arose in connection with a March 1940 memorandum on unemployment statistics that he prepared for the President. As Currie recalled this work in his unpublished memoirs (Currie, 1953, pp. 154–7):

> There are probably very few writings on economic matters by Roosevelt extant that are unquestionably his own and reflect his own habits of thought, since the great bulk of them are the result of the collaboration or work of technicians. I happen to have one addressed to me, which is indubitably his own. It reflects so faithfully his particular habit of reasoning from the particular to the general, and throws such an amusing light on his attitude toward his own experts, that it is worth quoting in full. In the Spring of 1940 Dorothy Thompson and Arthur Krock presented estimates of unemployment considerably lower than the official government estimates and this touched off a great controversy. Assuming, of course, that the President was on 'our' side and perhaps mildly interested, I sent him a brief memorandum on March 14, 1940 setting forth briefly the basis of the then official estimates of unemployment of between 8.5 and 11.2 million and deriding the unacknowledged source of Krock's estimates, an economist of the Dupont Company.

To Currie's complete surprise he received back from the President a lengthy memorandum expressing skepticism toward all the official estimates and concluding that unemployment was no more than 6 million. For example, the President asked: 'Are the thousands of women who habitually take a month or six-week job in a retail store around Christmas time unemployed when the census taker arrives in April?' and 'Is my friend the skilled carpenter unemployed because temperamentally he cannot keep a job for more than two weeks – always having a row with his employer or his fellow workmen?' He also asked if his well digger at Hyde Park is unemployed 'even if he makes enough money in two or three months to last him the rest of the year.' After several similar examples, Roosevelt wrote that it seemed that 'what we mean by unemployed in this country are unemployed people who are eager to work and who really need work in order to feed, clothe and house themselves and their families,' and he did not believe that 'there are more than six million people in this country who fall into this category.' Already there were four million of these people receiving state aid, so only two million 'ought to have work provided for them in some way as a social and economic need. That's not bad at all.'

'Needless to say,' wrote Currie in his memoirs, 'I guarded this memorandum carefully as a mere intimation of its contents at that time would have been a political bombshell.' He composed a careful reply that classified the President's examples and defended the official estimates. He wrote that he heard no further on the matter. 'I don't imagine that my reasoning carried conviction, as it was probably too abstract for the President, but at least it intimidated him so that he never expressed his heretical views in public.' This of course is another illustration of the importance of archival material for economic and political historians. Currie wrote that the President's memorandum (a copy of which is presumably in the National Archives, though I know of no reference to it in the literature) 'illustrates both his down-to-earth practical type of thinking, and also the weakness of this method to solve certain types of economic problems.'

Another example of Currie's many efforts to educate Roosevelt came in a memorandum on full employment submitted to the President on April 27.[16] The preface read:

1. It represents the progress to date of a line of investigation I initiated at the Reserve Board and which is today being carried on by the brilliant group of young economists in Harry Hopkins' office. The basic analysis is that of J. M. Keynes. Since Professor Hansen and I testified along these lines before the TNEC [Temporary National Economic Committee 1939], it has become generally the New Deal economists' diagnosis of and prescription for our economic problem.

2. I have come to suspect that you are somewhat bothered by the apparent conflict between the humanitarian and social aims of the New Deal and the dictates of 'sound economics'. I feel convinced that in place of conflict there is really complete harmony and for that reason only the New Deal can solve the economic problem.

3. I think you should know the basic economic theory that underlies the suggestions and positions taken by your assistant. In treating special problems I have the basic problem and solutions, as I see it, constantly in mind and although feasibility and timing must always be given proper weight, I try to fit every specialized problem into the broad program.

4. In connection with the pressure currently being brought on you to call a Conference on Unemployment, my view is very naturally

that unless the conference can come out with the diagnosis and type of solution outlined in the attached memorandum it will be fruitless and probably harmful. Unless very carefully selected and stage managed, the likelihood of its so coming out is not promising.

5. You asked me to do some work on the problem of post-war reconstruction. This problem is, however, but one special case of the overall problem of securing and maintaining full employment.

In conclusion, let me say that I don't for a moment think that this type of analysis can be sold politically. Its value lies solely in the proper orientation of our own thinking in developing a coordinated program. The program itself, I think, must be sold on the specific appeal of its component elements.

The memorandum is long but even so is greatly compressed. I should be delighted to go into greater detail on any points that you think are crucial and 'unproven'. After having had to interview and read the outpourings of numberless cranks and crackpots, I feel a little abashed at coming forward and saying, 'I know the answer'. I trust, however, that you will make the distinction!

So here are examples of the anonymous backroom adviser quietly informing, educating, persuading and protecting – as the technician (who once described himself as 'inflexibly unenthusiastic' in a 1941 interview) rather than the politician. However, the anonymity rule could not always apply, and Currie's name, photograph, and even cartoon image appeared from time to time in national newspapers and magazines. Shortly after Currie's first official mission to China, Eliot Janeway wrote, in a *Time* magazine article (5 May 1941) on Roosevelt's diplomatic war against Hitler:

China affords the most concrete example of how Roosevelt proposes to win this [diplomatic] war. Last summer, after the Fall of France, Britain again started appeasing Japan by closing the Burma Road. Chiang Kai-shek asked himself whether the democracies understood in whose interests he was fighting ... Then, with characteristic diplomatic indirection, word trickled through to Chungking that it might be profitable to invite Lauchlin Currie, one of the President's most anonymous administrative assistants, to come to China. Currie, the No. 1 U.S. disciple of John Maynard Keynes, is also the No. 1 New Deal economist. He is not a politician. He has the immense prestige, so important in China of a scholar, moreover, a scholar who has taught at Harvard. He has the confidence of the President. He was the perfect choice…

Chiang agreed to call off the civil war long enough to sound out America's latest emissary … What could he lose? If Currie had just come to *talk* friendship, Chiang would find it out when Currie returned to the States. In that case, he could go back to feuding…

Currie's ostensible mission was to give China a budget. But the central government has no income to speak of. It simply prints notes … The average peasant pays 60% of his income (cash and crop) in rent. In return, the landlords, mainly militarists, are supposed to give the peasants police protection. But the militarists pay almost no taxes to Chiang's government. To make his budget, Currie apparently argued that Chiang should stop being a front man for the landlords, and to take them into partnership instead, i.e., tax their incomes. Some of the income could then be routed back to the commodity-starved peasants via a benefit program. Thus inflation, hoarding, the feudal independence of the landlords and the political orphanhood of the peasants would all be attacked at once. It dawned on the Generalissimo that he could overnight become a popular leader on the Roosevelt model if he let the peasants feel that the nationalist war, in addition to being a war for China's freedom, was also a war for social justice.

One question remained unanswered: could the professor deliver? Until the Chinese knew that, his ideas were merely something to think about. But deliver he did. Four days after Currie's return, the President made his speech to the White House correspondents about his plans under the Lend-Lease Act. 'China expresses the magnificent will of millions of plain people to resist the dismemberment of their nation. China, through the Generalissimo, Chiang Kai-shek, asks our help. America has said that China shall have our help.'

Thus China was added to America's Lend-Lease program and Currie put in charge of its administration (as well as the development of the Flying Tigers program for China under the command of General Claire Chennault, with authority to arrange for the release of planes and US airmen). In the event, Chiang had little interest in a New Deal for China's peasants but the Lend-Lease program served US and democratic interests by helping to keep China in the war against Japan. After the defeat of Japan it was not long before Chiang's corrupt Nationalist government met its almost inevitable overthrow by Mao's communist army in 1949. Currie was one of the 'China hands' who was then blamed for 'losing'

China during a rising tide of anti-communist hysteria. A full account of Currie's involvement in China policy, 1941–43, and his work as de facto head of the Foreign Economic Administration, 1943–44, is in Sandilands (1990, chapter 4). Currie's role in China is also dealt with in a major new biography of Mao Zedong by Jung Chang and Jon Halliday (2005), partly based on papers supplied to Chang and Halliday from my own archive.

From Grand Alliance to Cold War

Currie's wartime role in foreign economic affairs was to come under intense scrutiny soon after Roosevelt's death in April 1945. The Roosevelt administration had been assiduously promoting good relations with its Soviet ally and hoped that the close wartime cooperation would be continued post-war. Currie had been intimately involved in negotiations with the Soviets over wartime loans and their participation at Bretton Woods in late 1944 when it was still hoped that they would join the new multilateral institutions being established there.[17]

Another of Currie's official involvements with the Soviets followed upon his high-profile assignment in January 1945 as head of an allied delegation to Bern to persuade the Swiss to block Nazi gold stored in Swiss banks and to prohibit further shipments through Switzerland of *matériel* for Kesselring's forces in Italy. Currie's personal memoirs (in a transcript of some oral history tapes) refer to his last interview with President Roosevelt upon his return from Switzerland in March 1945. The Swiss President had asked Currie to convey a private message to President Roosevelt that the Swiss were disturbed by their very poor relations with the Soviets, and that 'they would appreciate it very much if Roosevelt would use his good offices to prepare the way for a better relation, to stop the attacks by the Moscow press on them as they would like to establish diplomatic relations.' (The Swiss feared their own interests were under threat with the Soviet advance into Central Europe.) Roosevelt said, 'I don't think I'd better give in the idea officially. You know everybody in the Swiss Embassy and in the Soviet Embassy.' Currie then mentioned having met the Soviet cultural attaché. Roosevelt said splendid, and urged Currie to make the appropriate connections himself, informally, since 'he was confident that what had to be done surely had to come from me.'

The 'Soviet cultural attaché' actually turned out to be the Soviets' chief KGB officer in the Washington Embassy, Anatoly Gorsky. Many of Gorsky's wartime coded cables to Moscow were later partially decrypted by the National Security Agency, some as early as 1946. This work, now famously known as the 'Venona' project, was top secret until the release of some 2900 decrypted cables in 1995–96. Persons mentioned in these cables were scrutinized during the Cold War for evidence that their involvement with the Soviets was espionage rather than part of their official duties. Currie and his old friend Harry Dexter White were among those mentioned in the cables and both came to very public attention when in 1948 they were named by former Soviet agent Elizabeth Bentley in open testimony before the House Committee on Un-American Activities (known as HUAC). Though she had never met them herself, she claimed that White and Currie had passed on information to other Washington economists who were consciously abetting her own espionage activities. Currie and White both demanded to appear before HUAC to rebut these charges. White, in particular, caused a sensation with his robust handling of pointed questions from Congressman Richard Nixon. Their testimony appeared to satisfy the committee at that time, though the strain contributed to the fatal heart attack that White suffered on his way home from the hearings.[18]

Currie's memoirs remind us that much diplomacy is of necessity covert and that official US-Soviet relations between 1941–45 were totally different from those that prevailed during the Cold War. Roosevelt's reluctance to be seen to be interceding personally in the Swiss-Soviet affair may have been related to two big issues concerning the Russians at that time (March 1945). First, he was having trouble with the press and Congress over proposed voting rights for the Soviet Union in the United Nations Assembly. Second, and relevant to Swiss-Soviet relations, was the bitter protest that Stalin had lodged when he learned of the secret feelers that the Germans had recently initiated in Bern with OSS agent Allen Dulles (whom Currie had himself met in Bern) to discuss the possibility that Kesselring might negotiate the separate surrender of the German forces in Italy. Stalin demanded to know why the Soviets had been excluded from these talks. He feared that a separate peace with America and Britain would leave the Germans free to continue war with Russia. Roosevelt was able to assuage Stalin's fears, and in a personal letter to Churchill from Warm Springs on 11 April 1945, the day before he died, Roosevelt wrote:

> I would minimise the general Soviet problem as much as possible because these problems, in one form or another, seem to arise every day and most of them straighten out as in the case of the Bern meeting.
> We must be firm, however, and our course thus far is correct.
>
> (Freidel, 1990, p. 602)

Currie left his position at the White House in June 1945 to go into business as an economic consultant in New York; later he was recruited by the World Bank to head a comprehensive country study of Colombia in 1949–50. His mission report was published in September 1950 at which point the Colombian government appointed him as adviser to a committee set up to study the report and act upon its recommendations (Sandilands, 1990; Alacevich, 2005). Thus began a new career as a development economist in Colombia that would stretch for more than 40 years. It is beyond my current remit to review this period in any depth but, as Alacevich has shown by delving into just one brief episode of Currie's time in Colombia, there is a wealth of information on this career in the voluminous memoranda, manuscripts, memoirs, and letters now archived at Duke University. These show that Currie was active almost uninterruptedly as a top-level presidential adviser and development economist right up to his death, aged 91, in December 1993.

When as a naturalized US citizen he attempted to renew his passport in the poisonous atmosphere of 1954, this was refused, ostensibly on the grounds that he was now residing abroad. However, the reality was probably connected with the 'Venona' project and other allegations about his wartime involvements in China and with the Russians. He had recently married a Colombian and was settled in Colombia, despite a military coup in 1953 that caused him to retire temporarily from his economic advisory work. Instead he devoted himself to the raising of Holstein cattle on a farm outside Bogotá.

With the return of civilian government in 1958, President Alberto Lleras personally conferred Colombian citizenship upon him and he returned to full-time advisory work for a succession of presidents. However, between 1966 and 1971 he served as a visiting professor in North American and British universities: Michigan State (1966), Simon Fraser, Canada (1967–71), Glasgow (1968–69), and Oxford (1969). He returned permanently to Colombia in May 1971 at the personal behest of President Misael Pastrana to prepare a national plan of development known as the Plan of the Four Strategies, with focus on the 'leading sectors' of urban housing and export diversification. (On Currie's theory of leading sectors see Chandra, 2005.) The plan was implemented, and the institutions that were established in support of the plan played a major role in accelerating Colombia's urbanization.

For most of his professional life Currie was an eclectic mixture of economic liberal and economic planner. Understanding the cultural and intellectual roots of this admixture requires much more than a reading of his published output. We need to know how his writing is influenced by upbringing, training, personal characteristics, and experience, both personal and professional; and the constraints of time and place. This is what makes a wide-ranging archive so invaluable. On the eclecticism of his planning and advisory work in light of that experience, Currie best summed up his approach at a conference in Panama in 1975 (as reported in Sandilands, 1990, p. 372):

> Although I have a great respect for the power of economic incentives and the efficacy of decentralized decision making, I am still an inveterate planner. Despite my good intentions, the State reappeared, but I hope in acceptable collaboration with the use of economic incentives. The 'invisible hand' became two hands, the traditional one working more or less silently through economic incentives, and the more visible one of national economic policy making. The resulting strategy is a mixed one, difficult to classify. I distrust labels. Personally, I would not call myself a monetarist nor a Keynesian, nor a believer in intervention nor the market, nor a structuralist nor a neo-classicist but a little of all of these, and am prepared to use policies involving elements of all these approaches when the attainment of certain goals appears to make their use appropriate.

Currie remained as chief economist at the National Planning Department for ten years, 1971–81, followed by twelve years at the Colombian Institute of Savings and Housing until his death in 1993. There he doggedly defended the unique housing finance system (based on 'units of constant purchasing power' for both savers and borrowers) that he had established in 1972. The system thus continued to boost Colombia's growth rate and urban employment opportunities year by year. Currie was also a distinguished urban planner and played a major part in the first United Nations Habitat conference in Vancouver in 1976. His 'cities-within-the-city' urban design and financing proposals (including the public recapture of land's socially created 'valorización', or 'unearned land value increments', as cities grow) were elaborated in his *Taming the Megalopolis* (1976). He was a regular teacher at the major universities in Bogotá and published widely in international journals. His writings were heavily influenced by his Harvard mentor Allyn Young. A paper on Youngian endogenous growth theory was published posthumously (Currie, 1997), pieced together by the present writer from several incomplete drafts, notes, and tabulations that were on his desk when he died, and that are now among his papers at Duke University. On the day before he died, of heart failure, President Cesar Gaviria presented Currie with Colombia's highest honor, the Gran Cruz de Boyacá, for services to his adopted country.

Appendix 6.1   Archives of papers of Lauchlin Currie

The main archive of Currie's papers is in the Rare Book, Manuscript, and Special Collections Library, Duke University, under the title 'Lauchlin Bernard Currie Papers, 1931–1994 and n.d. (bulk 1950–1990)'. The extent is currently 60.35 linear feet and 31,370 items. Before the originals were shipped from Bogotá to Duke, most were first photocopied under the direction of Elba Cánfora of the Universidad Nacional de Colombia, thanks to a major grant from the Banco de la República, for deposit in Colombia's Luis Angel Arango Library in Bogotá. For details of the Duke collection see http://library.duke.edu/digitalcollections/rbmscl/currie/inv/ (accessed 25 February 2009). Currie's papers are part of Duke University's 'Economists' Papers Project' (http://scriptorium.lib.duke.edu/economists [accessed 25 February 2009]). This growing collection includes the papers of Kenneth Arrow, William Baumol, Arthur Bloomfield, Martin Bronfenbrenner, Jesse Chickering, Robert Clower, Max Corden, Lauchlin Currie, Paul Davidson, Evsey Domar, Frank Fetter, Nicholas Georgescu-Roegen, W.M. Gorman, Earl Hamilton, Clifford Hildreth, Homer Jones, Juanita Morris Kreps, Axel Leijonhufvud, H. Gregg Lewis, Carl Menger, Karl Menger, Lloyd Metzler, Franco Modigliani, Oskar Morgenstern, Douglass C. North, Don Patinkin, Mark Perlman, Benjamin Ratchford, Albert Rees, Tibor Scitovsky, Martin Shubik, Vernon L. Smith, Joseph Spengler, Wolfgang F. Stolper, and Sidney Weintraub.

Currie's China papers are archived at the Hoover Institution of War, Revolution and Peace, Stanford University, under the title, 'Register of the Lauchlin Bernard Currie Papers, 1941–1993'. The extent is five manuscript boxes and one envelope of photos, and is summarized in the catalogue as: 'Correspondence, notes, memoranda, reports, and summaries of interviews, relating to American aid to China during World War II, conditions in China, and military operations in the China-Burma-India Theater.' See http://www.oac.cdlib.org/findaid/ark:/13030/tf2779n58h (accessed 25 February 2009).

The Marriner Eccles papers at the Marriott Library, University of Utah include a large number of letters and memoranda from Currie. His is the largest single entry in the catalogue. (http://www.lib.utah.edu/portal/site/marriottlibrary [accessed 25 February 2009]).

See also material on Eccles and Currie in the records of the Federal Reserve Board that are located in the US National Archives at http://www.archives.gov/research/guide-fed-records/groups/082.html#82.1 (accessed 25 February 2009).

Notes

1. A few years earlier, one of Samuelson's Harvard teachers, Wassily Leontief, was passing through Bogotá. He told his minders that there were only two institutions he wanted to visit: the famous gold museum and Lauchlin Currie. (This, at least, is how Currie told the story to me.)
2. Currie visited Young in London in the summer of 1928 while collecting information on English banks. A moving letter from Currie to Young's widow in March 1929 was uncovered after my biography appeared, and is reproduced in Sandilands (1999) in an article on Young's influence as a teacher. That article benefited greatly from my access to Charles Blitch's archive on Young that he had built up for his biography (Blitch, 1995).
3. Currie, White and Paul Theodore Ellsworth wrote a long memorandum on anti-depression policy in January 1932 that was later discovered among White's papers in the Princeton University archives. It was then published (Currie, Ellsworth, and White, 2002) with a foreword by Laidler and Sandilands (2002) explaining its significance and possible influence on what has sometimes been considered the 'unique' Chicago tradition in monetary theory and policy.
4. In a letter dated 16 October 2004, Mark Perlman told me of a similar judgment from Paul Samuelson who 'launched into a vehement anti-Schumpeter speech at the 1980 International Economic Association Congress in which he denominated JAS as a mountebank and a hollow show-off.'
5. In Sandilands (2004), three chapters of Currie's PhD thesis – on the theory of banking and control of the business cycle – were finally published.
6. He often revealed his animus against Irving Fisher, the famous champion of prohibition – and Currie's diary for 1926–27 records several visits to illegal bootleggers with his Harvard classmates. Apart from disliking his Puritanism, Currie complained that the conservative Fisher was a monetary reformer mainly because he hoped that those measures would make broader government action unnecessary. He criticized Fisher's 'transactions' version of the quantity theory as simplistic and misleading, and found his frequent crusading visits to the Fed irritating and time-wasting. Nevertheless, Fisher had a high regard for Currie and I learned later (from Steindl, 1993) that he took credit for getting him appointed to the White House as Roosevelt's assistant for economic affairs. I think Currie would take that claim with a pinch of salt.
7. Concerning this 2004 publication of some of Currie's memoranda from the 1930s and beyond, Telser wrote me on January 9, 2005:

> I have been reading and learning from Lauchlin Currie from your *Journal of Economic Studies*. It has very important material so that I hope you can get it read by the right people. I am going to bring it to the attention of

some of my colleagues. Especially striking to me are the essays I have read so far on deposits and the 100 percent reserve plan. People like Douglas Diamond, Calomaris, Friedman, Neil Wallace, Peltzman et al. who have studied bank runs and panics are woefully ignorant of the facts. Bob Solow should get a copy of your journal. He wrote me a very perceptive letter on my veterans' bonus piece and I am sure would welcome your work on Currie ... Congratulations!

8. Michele Alacevich spent the summer of 2004 in the Duke archives research-ing Currie's World Bank mission to Colombia, 1949–50, and its follow-up, including the period in 1951–53 during which he and Hirschman worked in uneasy partnership (Alacevich, 2009). I am also indebted to Alacevich for unearthing in the archives of the University of Milan the Italian text of an otherwise unknown lecture that Currie gave to the Istituto di Studi Internazionali, Milan, on 5 March 1946, while president of the board of the Council of Italian-American Affairs, on 'Italy in the Postwar World,' in which he urged the importance of Italy's democratic integration into the world economy and the need to avoid an overvalued exchange rate.

9. Personal communication and as indicated in comments on Viner in Currie's (1990, p. 13) recollections of Allyn Young: Young did support the gold standard, but Currie wrote that he 'would immediately have seen the fallacy of composition in the argument of the budget balancers. The logic of his 1928 *Economic Journal* article would have led him to stress the role of demand and the ultimate consumer and to downgrade the independent role of "confidence" in itself rather than as a reflection of demand ... But he might have felt, with Viner, that a deliberate unbalancing of the budget might have resulted in a flight of capital.'

    Similarly, in a letter to J. Ronnie Phillips, 27 July 1993, commenting on a draft of Phillips's book on the 'Chicago Plan' for monetary reform (Phillips, 1995), in which Currie's 1934 proposal for a 100 percent reserve banking system was discussed, Currie wrote that 'Viner was a very able economist but not very daring ... I doubt if he passed my paper [on the 100 percent reserves plan] to Morgenthau, who was also timid.'

10. I am indebted for this information to Hansjoerg Klausinger, working on Machlup's archives, and to Masazumi Wakatabe who sent me the *Washington Post* and *New York Times* letters.

11. The original formal mathematical statement of the balanced-budget multi-plier theorem was by Walter Salant's brother William while he was an assistant to Currie in the early 1940s. In various unpublished memoranda written in the late 1970s, Currie again questioned the practical relevance of the theo-rem, and also criticized its assumption that a rise in the tax rate would have no effect on the marginal propensity to save or, as Currie would prefer to express it, on the marginal propensity to hold money in the face of a need to replenish depleted cash balances. In the latter case the value of any multiplier effect would be far less than unity.

12. Extracts of the report that was laid before the President are included in 'Editor's Introduction' (Sandilands, 2004, pp. 185–6). The full report and contemporary newspaper commentaries are in the Currie archive at Duke University.

13. This was subsequently published, with an introduction by Byrd Jones, in Currie (1980).
14. For Young's influence on Currie's monetary economics see Sandilands (1990, chapter 2) and Laidler (1993, pp. 1083–4); and for his influence on Currie's thinking on development economics see Currie (1997) and Mehrling and Sandilands (1999, p. xi).
15. Currie was the first professional economist to work as a presidential adviser in the White House. The Employment Act of 1946 formalized this role with the creation of the Council of Economic Advisers. One of Currie's postgraduate students at Simon Fraser University, 1967–68, was Martin Neil Baily who was appointed by President Clinton as Chairman of the CEA in 1999.
16. Currie's memoirs record that he finished this 18-page memorandum (plus nine charts) on 18 March, but that he quietly 'kept it on my desk until April 27 when I finally submitted it with apologies for its length. Apparently the ostensible occasion was agitation for a National Conference on Unemployment, which could easily have turned into an attack on New Deal policies.' Part of this memorandum was reproduced in Sandilands (2004, pp. 366–8).
17. A revealing insight into contemporary attitudes toward the Soviets and hopes for continued economic and political cooperation after the war is given by the erstwhile Assistant Secretary of State, Sumner Welles, *The Time for Decision* (October 1944). Currie was close to Welles from the summer of 1940 when they were both involved in embargo policies against Japan. Currie's memoirs (Currie, 1953, pp. 152–3) record that Welles was 'unquestionably one of the most competent persons I encountered in Government' and that he 'could understand why the President always preferred to deal with Welles [rather than Secretary Cordell Hull] when he could.' Currie contrasted Welles's 'competence and forcefulness' with Hull's 'jealousy and vindictiveness', which eventually forced Welles's resignation in August 1943.
18. For an examination of the evidence against Currie and White (concluding that both were innocent of espionage), see Sandilands (2000), James Boughton (2001), and Boughton and Sandilands (2003). After reading the latter paper, Major-General Julius Kobyakov, deputy director of the KGB's American desk in the late 1980s, wrote to me on 22 December 2003 to confirm our conclusions. After extensive archival research on Soviet intelligence in the US in the 1930s and 1940s he found that 'there was nothing in [Currie's] file to suggest that he had ever wittingly collaborated with the Soviet intelligence ... However, in the spirit of machismo, many people claimed that we had an "agent" in the White House. Among the members of my profession there is a sacramental question: "Does he know that he is our agent?" There is very strong indication that neither Currie nor White knew that.'

References

Alacevich, Michele, 2009, *The Political Economy of the World Bank: the Early Years*, Palo Alto: Stanford University Press.
Blitch, Charles P., 1995, *Allyn Young: the Peripatetic Economist*, Basingstoke and London: Macmillan.

Boughton, James M., 2001, 'The Case against Harry Dexter White: Still Not Proven,' *History of Political Economy*, 33(2) (Summer): 221–41.

Boughton, James M. and Roger J. Sandilands, 2003, 'Politics and the Attack on FDR's Economists: From Grand Alliance to Cold War,' *Intelligence and National Security*, 18(3) (Autumn): 73–99.

Chandra, Ramesh, 2005, 'Lauchlin Currie's "Leading Sectors" Strategy of Growth: an Appraisal,' *Journal of Development Studies*, 42(3) (April): 490–508.

Chang, Jung and Jon Halliday, 2005, *Mao Zedong*, London: Stanley Paul.

Currie, Lauchlin, 1934, *The Supply and Control of Money in the United States*, Cambridge, MA: Harvard University Press. Reprinted, 1968, by Russell & Russell, New York.

——, 1953, 'Memoirs,' unpublished manuscript, Duke University archives. Parts of chapters 2 and 3 are published in Sandilands (2004, pp. 198–234).

——, 1976, *Taming the Megalopolis: a Design for Urban Growth*, Oxford: Pergamon Press.

——, 1980 [1938], 'Causes of the Recession,' *History of Political Economy*, 12(3) (Fall): 303–35.

——, 1990, 'Recollections of Allyn Young,' in Roger J. Sandilands (ed.), *Nicholas Kaldor's Notes on Allyn Young's LSE Lectures, 1927–29*, Special issue, *Journal of Economic Studies*, 17(3/4): 10–13.

——, 1997, 'Implications of an Endogenous Theory of Growth in Allyn Young's Macroeconomic Concept of Increasing Returns,' *History of Political Economy*, 29(3) (Fall): 413–44.

—— and Martin Krost, 1978 [1935], 'Comments and observations on "Federal Income-Increasing Expenditures, 1933–35",' *History of Political Economy*, 10(4) (Winter): 507–48.

——, Paul Theodore Ellsworth, and Harry Dexter White, 2002 [1932], 'Memorandum on Anti-depression Policy', *History of Political Economy*, 34(3) (Fall): 533–52. Reprinted in Robert Leeson (ed.), 2003, *Keynes, Chicago and Friedman*, London: Pickering & Chatto, pp. 271–90.

Eccles, Marriner S., 1951, *Beckoning Frontiers*, New York: Alfred A. Knopf.

Freidel, Frank, 1990, *Franklin D. Roosevelt: a Rendezvous with Destiny*, Boston: Little, Brown and Company.

Friedman, Milton and Anna Jacobson Schwartz, 1963, *A Monetary History of the United States, 1867–1960*, Princeton, NJ: Princeton University Press.

Galbraith, John Kenneth, 1971, 'How Keynes Came to America,' in *Economics, Peace and Laughter*, London: André Deutsch, pp. 43–59.

Hansen, Alvin H., 1954, *A Guide to Keynes*, New York: McGraw-Hill.

Keynes, John Maynard, 1936, *The General Theory of Employment, Interest and Money*, London: Macmillan.

Kindleberger, Charles P., 1991, 'Review of The Life and Political Economy of Lauchlin Currie,' *Journal of Political Economy*, 99 (October): 1120–2.

Laidler, David, 1993, 'Hawtrey, Harvard and the Origins of the Chicago Tradition,' *Journal of Political Economy*, 101 (December): 1068–103.

——, 1999, *Fabricating the Keynesian Revolution*, Cambridge: Cambridge University Press.

—— and Roger J. Sandilands, 2002, 'An Early Harvard Memorandum on Anti-Depression Policy: an Introductory Note,' *History of Political Economy*, 34(3)

(Fall): 515–32. Reprinted in Robert Leeson (ed.), 2003, *Keynes, Chicago and Friedman*, London: Pickering & Chatto, pp. 251–70.

Mehrling, Perry G. and Roger J. Sandilands (eds), 1999, *Money and Growth: Selected Papers of Allyn Abbott Young*, London and New York: Routledge.

Patinkin, Don, 1981, *Essays on and in the Chicago Tradition*, Durham, NC and London: Duke University Press.

Phillips, J. Ronnie, 1995, *The Chicago Plan and New Deal Banking Reform*, Armonk, NY: M.E. Sharpe.

Reisman, David, 1990, 'Review of *The Life and Political Economy of Lauchlin Currie*,' *Singapore Economic Review*, 35(2) (October): 125–7.

Sandilands, Roger J., 1990, *The Life and Political Economy of Lauchlin Currie: New Dealer, Presidential Adviser, and Development Economist*, Durham NC and London: Duke University Press. (Spanish edition: *Vida y Política Económica de Lauchlin Currie*, Bogotá: Legis Editorial, 1990.)

——, 1999, 'New Evidence on Allyn Young's Style and Influence as a Teacher,' *Journal of Economic Studies*, 26(6): 453–79.

——, 2000, 'Guilt by Association? Lauchlin Currie's Alleged Involvement with Washington Economists in Soviet Espionage,' *History of Political Economy*, 32(3) (Fall): 473–515.

——, 2001, 'The New Deal and "Domesticated Keynesianism" in America,' in Michael Keany (ed.), *Economist with a Public Purpose: Essays in Honour of John Kenneth Galbraith*, London and New York: Routledge.

—— (ed.), 2004, *New Light on Lauchlin Currie's Monetary Economics in the New Deal and Beyond*, Special issue, *Journal of Economic Studies*, 31(3/4): 170–403.

——, 2005, 'Review of Frank Steindl, *Understanding Economic Recovery in the 1930s: Endogenous Propagation in the Great Depression*,' *Journal of the History of Economic Thought*, 27(2) (June): 226–8.

Stein, Herbert, 1969, *The Fiscal Revolution in America*, Chicago: University of Chicago Press.

Steindl, Frank G., 1993, 'Review of *The Life and Political Economy of Lauchlin Currie*,' *Economica*, 60 (November): 491–2.

——, 2004, *Understanding Economic Recovery in the 1930s: Endogenous Propagation in the Great Depression*, Ann Arbor, MI: University of Michigan Press.

Telser, Lester G., 2001, 'Higher Member Bank Reserve Ratios in 1936 and 1937 did not Cause the Relapse into Depression,' *Journal of Post-Keynesian Economics*, 24(2): 205–16.

——, 2003, 'The Veterans' Bonus of 1936,' *Journal of Post-Keynesian Economics*, 26(2): 227–43.

Welles, Sumner, 1944, *The Time for Decision*, New York: Harper and Brothers.

7
New Evidence on Allyn Young's Style and Influence as a Teacher[1]

Roger J. Sandilands

There has been in recent years a revival of interest in Allyn Abbott Young (1876–1929). Charles Blitch (1983) wrote on the 'curious case of professional neglect' of Young and a comprehensive biography followed (Blitch, 1995). This documented his wide-ranging contributions to methodology, statistics, the index number problem, value theory, public utility regulation, the trade cycle, monetary policy, and monopolistic competition. Blitch also examined Young's role as a teacher, notably his PhD supervision of Frank Knight on risk and profit and Edward Chamberlin on monopolistic competition. Laidler (1993, 1998) and Mehrling (1997) have recently highlighted Young's influence on American monetary economics; and Kaldor (1972, 1985), Thirlwall (2002), Romer (1989), and Currie (1981, 1997) have explored the implications for growth theory of Young's famous paper on 'Increasing Returns and Economic Progress' (Young, 1928b). See also Chandra and Sandilands (2005).

His contributions appear to have been as much indirect, through his inspirational teaching, as direct through his writings. J.M. Keynes, in a letter (in the files of Young's biographer, the late Charles Blitch, now in my possession) of condolence to Mrs Young upon the sudden death, aged 52, of her husband in London in March 1929, wrote: 'His was the outstanding personality in the economics world and the most lovable. His influence as a teacher and a critic and as one who would always share with others all his best ideas was far greater than anyone would suppose who knew only his printed words; for it was his own work – unfortunately perhaps – which always came last.'

Young has had the reputation of a brilliant economist who wrote little. Partly this is because much of what he did write was published in obscure places, including anonymous contributions to encyclopedias.

Joseph Schumpeter (1937, pp. 514–15), who first came to Harvard in 1927 as Young's temporary replacement when Young left to take up the chair vacated by Edwin Cannan at the London School of Economics, wrote: 'Rarely if ever has fame comparable to his been acquired on the basis of so little published work. What there is consists of mere fragments written in response to chance occasions.' He indicated that no enumeration of his publications can give an adequate conception of his contribution to economics. 'He was first and last a creative teacher, and it was through his teaching rather than his writing that he influenced contemporary thought.' Young's LSE colleague, T.E. Gregory (1929, p. 300), also emphasized his greatness as a teacher and colleague: 'Until one had come into personal contact with him, it was not easy to understand precisely how his great influence in the American economic and academic world had arisen … [P]robably no living economist has had as much influence as Young had through the spoken, rather than the written word.'

Gregory noted that Young's extraordinary range of interests and experiences was too wide to make systematic writing easy. He was convinced that:

> economic truth was not the monopoly of a single school or way of thinking, and that the first duty of a teacher and thinker was to see the strong points in every presentation of a point of view. Such an attitude of mind, combined with great personal modesty, made for unsystematic writing: for scattered papers and articles and not for a comprehensive treatise. In many respects he resembled Edgeworth, for whose work he felt a growing admiration; and if Young's work is ever collected, it will be seen that, like Edgeworth's, it amounts in sum to a very considerable and impressive achievement.
>
> (Ibid.)

It was 70 years after Young's death before such a collection of his writings was put together, with a comprehensive bibliography of some 100 items (Mehrling and Sandilands, 1999). It supports Gregory's statement. The collection includes a large portion of the 36 unsigned chapters that Young contributed to the Grolier Society's *Book of Popular Science* shortly before he died. These had been virtually unknown and resurfaced only recently. Gregory (1929) wrote that in London Young had begun a systematic treatise on economic theory and had resumed the writing of the work on monetary theory that he had begun at Harvard.[2] Young's Harvard colleague Frank Taussig (Taussig et al., 1929, p. 347) also alluded to these projects. However, it seems that in the hasty departure from London by his wife, who was nearly blind, his manuscripts were lost.

Oskar Morgenstern (1929) wrote that Young:

> was stopped short by death while engaged in the execution of important projects. One of these was a large work on the theory of money which was already at a very advanced stage. He had developed his thoughts over the years in his Harvard lectures and his theory, which would certainly have represented a milestone, has become part of the oral tradition at Harvard in the same way as Marshall's monetary theory at Cambridge ... [Nevertheless] reading the entirety of his publications shows one only a fraction of his achievement. He found it difficult to decide to publish anything, being extremely modest and self-critical in a manner which made him say something important in a casual aside; but he greatly inspired his pupils and patiently and constantly made himself available to them. Many of the best of those who have today made a name for themselves beyond America went through his hands and acknowledge the most lasting encouragement they received from him.

And Wesley Mitchell (1929, p. 201) wrote:

> For economic investigation Young was remarkably endowed. He united in rare measure mathematical powers, historical learning, and philosophical grasp. Indeed, his versatility was an ever-lurking temptation to disperse his attention. Many were the colleagues and the students who sought his critical and his constructive advice. Because his range was so wide and his insight so quick, as well as because he loved to help others, Young found it difficult to say 'No'. Few American economists of his generation are represented in so many books which bear other men's names. And Young's prefaces written to help others get a hearing would make a slender volume ... All of us value his published work highly, for though slender in bulk, it is of rare quality. But Young was not satisfied. He felt, and with increasing intensity as the years went by, that he must carry through the larger projects – particularly a systematic study of monetary problems – on which he had long been working. Those who saw fragments of the investigation could not but sympathize with his longing for time to finish what he sketched.

On the other hand, the following is Paul Samuelson's measured judgment, in a letter to the present writer, 4 June 1997, on his reading of 'the skimpy Young output, including Ely chapters influenced by him and various encyclopedia boiler plate.' He wrote that:

> Young was wise, deep, and a great personal influence on colleagues and pupils. But he wrote so little, not only because he was so poor and so encumbered by family responsibilities but also because he had never worked out a coherent macro paradigm that differed creatively with the received notions of Marshall, Fisher, Pigou, and that crowd. Bullock, Carver, Burbank, Mason, Harris, Crum, Williams, Ohlin, Taussig – all those who knew him well in the 1920–27 Harvard years, talked to me and others about what a great economist Young was but none could guess what would be in the great book he planned to write but never did. (Young's influence on Knight and Chamberlin, which is manifest but should not be exaggerated, has nought to do with Laidler's macro.)[3]

The recent revival of interest in Young's published output, and the surfacing of much of his writing that had hitherto been almost unknown, may belie Samuelson's judgment regarding an absence of a distinctive macro paradigm in Young.[4] Be that as it may, to the extent that Young's fame was based more on personal recollections than on his published work, that fame has tended to fade with the passing of his colleagues and students. Today none survives to tell of the personal magnetism and enormous erudition upon which so much of his reputation was based. However, in the 1970s Charles Blitch, himself encouraged by Milton Heath, a student of Young's at Harvard, contacted many of Young's students and colleagues to seek their reminiscences of Young the man and teacher, and his influence upon their work. Space limitations imposed by his publisher meant that Blitch could use only a fraction of this material in his 200-page biography. He has, however, kindly given permission for his correspondence – nowhere else available – to be published here. This material provides additional insight into Valdemar Carlson's (1968) semi-autobiographical paper on 'The Education of an Economist before the Great Depression: Harvard's Economics Department in the 1920s'. Carlson speculated on the influence of Harvard upon the subsequent careers of some prominent New Dealers attracted to Washington in the 1930s, notably Harry Dexter White, Lauchlin Currie, and Gardiner C. Means (see also Mason, 1982; and Barber, 1996).

Several of Blitch's correspondents, such as Nicholas Kaldor, Colin Clark, and Bertil Ohlin are especially well known. Kaldor was the only one to preserve comprehensive notes of Young's lectures. These were published in Sandilands (1990b) along with a commentary on Kaldor's notes by Lauchlin Currie (1990), a student of Young's at Harvard, 1925–27. Currie's doctoral dissertation, *Bank Assets and Banking Theory* (1931) was initiated under Young's direction, and his *The Supply and Control of Money in the United States* (1934a) was dedicated to Young's memory. Since Currie's letter to Blitch has already been published (Currie, 1990), it is not included here. Instead we include a letter of condolence to Young's widow (March 1929) that surfaced just a few months before Currie died in 1993, together with extracts from his diaries, 1926–27,[5] that include references both to teachers such as Young and Taussig and also fellow students such as Harry White and Gardiner Means, the New Dealers mentioned by Carlson (1968).

Blitch's other correspondents include Melvin M. Knight, brother of Young's more famous student Frank H. Knight whose regard for Young was such that in 1928 he tried to recruit him as head of the economics department at Chicago. Another was Eleanor Dulles (John Foster Dulles's sister), whose PhD dissertation on *The French Franc* (Dulles, 1929) was published with a foreword by Young (reprinted in Mehrling and Sandilands, 1999, chapter 42). The other letters are from James Angell, Melvin de Chazeau, Arthur H. Cole, Howard Ellis, Frank W. Fetter, Earl J. Hamilton, Seymour Harris, Richard S. Howey, Geoffrey Shepherd, Overton H. Taylor, and Gilbert Walker.[6] In some cases the correspondents say how their own careers were influenced by Young; and reveal aspects of Young's thought that are absent or only hinted at in his published work. But their main value probably lies in the picture they give of the character of the man: of the wisdom and humanity that informed, but are naturally only partly revealed in, his professional writings.

Not all of his students were completely sold on Young. Frank Fetter dropped out of Young's course in money and banking because Young had said that he didn't believe everything he had written, for the sake of simplicity, in the Ely text (Ely et al., 1923), and that he, Fetter, 'didn't want to spend a term getting the ideas of a man who didn't know what he believed.' (However, in a letter to his father in May 1924 – copy sent to Charles Blitch – Fetter wrote: 'Our good friends Kemmerer and Fisher had better look to their laurels as practical economists, as Harvard has a rival in the person of A.A. Young ... Young certainly rates big around here.') Richard S. Howey, in a letter to a Professor Dewey, 28 March 1988 (copy sent to Charles Blitch), referred to Young's absent-mindedness, and stated that 'everyone, except Lionel Robbins in his autobiography, overlooked Young's faults.'

Robbins (1971, p. 120) acknowledged Young's 'massive erudition', but suggested that his time at the LSE was not a great success because 'he was generally not a good lecturer,' nor a good administrator. He gave the impression of a profoundly unhappy man with a tortured temperament, ill at ease in his surroundings and difficult to talk to. In a letter to the present writer, 2 January 1989, Lauchlin Currie (who studied at the LSE, 1922–25) commented on Robbins's views: 'What mattered to Robbins was verbal facility (which he had) and administrative detail (Beveridge had Mrs. Mair for that) ... [Young] never for a moment gave me the impression of being an unhappy man. I remember his bright smile and eager interest in the subject at hand – which he apparently didn't have with Robbins!' Kaldor's letter to Blitch (below) confirms how untidy was Young's office; but for him this was a source of amused delight! Sir William Beveridge (1929 [1990]) paid this tribute in his memorial address:

Of the arts by which men commonly seek success he had none. He did not seek success. What brought it to him in abundance? First, was the high standard of scientific work that he set for himself as for others. He was at once the kindest of men and the severest of judges ... Second, he was by taste a great teacher, interested in young minds, able to make them share his own sense of the high issues involved in what they studied with him, believing and making them believe in the importance and the possibility of finding truth. Third, there was in him a total lack of certain things which the gods do not always remember to leave out when they mix god-like reason with human clay. He had no envy, jealousy, or harshness; of sarcasm, cynicism or flippancy he was incapable. Sensitive he was, but with the sensitiveness not of vanity but of most genuine diffidence. He was ever the last person, not the first, to be persuaded of his own successes.

With reference to Fetter's views on Young's apparently indecisive thinking, what to Fetter was a fault to others was a virtue. Eleanor Dulles commented that 'none of his conclusions as to others' views were frozen, all were to be reexamined in the light of new experiences. Never have I known such a combination of sound knowledge and willingness to speculate and reconsider.' Melvin de Chazeau wrote that he 'impressed his students with the importance of seeking out the truth wherever it might be revealed.' To Earl Hamilton 'he was the least prejudiced of all the scholars ... I have ever known.' And for Lauchlin Currie (1990, p. 11):

> Professor Young was the most inspiring teacher I ever had. While Frank Taussig ... was a fine teacher, for example, inasmuch as he aroused heated discussions on such abstruse topics as what Böhm-Bawerk really meant, his impact on me was that economic theory was complete and it was up to the student not to criticise or contribute but to try to master that theory. The enquiring mind of Young, on the other hand, gave me a feeling that the field was wide open and that it was possible and proper to criticise and explore new and different approaches. In short, he inspired as well as taught.

Some years ago, while I was enthusing excitedly over something by Young, Currie admonished me not to read Young as one might the Bible. That was not in the spirit of Young, for whom the subject of economics was wide open to modification and improvement.

Currie's recollections are echoed by Carlson (1968, p. 107):

> Taussig tolerated no half-formulated ideas in his pedagogical pursuit of developing the student's logical thinking. Young took the least glimmer of insight or understanding expressed by a student and clothed it with an amazing amount of significance ... He was the Toscanini of the classroom, referring neither to outline nor notes while lecturing ... In Young we were privileged to experience the thinking process of a great mind who shared his ideas with his students in an amazingly democratic manner.

Finally, the obituary in the London *Times*, 8 March 1929 stated:

> No man was more ready to see all the sides of an argument; he had none of the intellectual arrogance which sometimes accompanies great mental gifts; and if he ever felt anger it was with those who refused to acknowledge merit in the work of other schools or of modern writers of a tendency opposite to the received tradition. These qualities of mind and character, which made him a great teacher, made him also the most sympathetic and helpful of colleagues. No one could go to Young without receiving enlightenment, and, since his range of knowledge was extraordinary, without the impression that here was a man who was an absolute master in his chosen field.

Perhaps we have in the above character sketches, and those presented below, a clue as to why there was no distinctive, lasting 'Harvard tradition', oral or otherwise, comparable, say, to the renowned Chicago tradition (see the exchanges on this subject between Laidler, 1998, and Tavlas, 1998, for example). Young was extremely open-minded, keen to inculcate into his students the art of critical and creative thinking, and insistent that economics should be both abstract and concrete, concerned with the ever-changing communal problems of economic life. Young disapproved of doctrine based purely on abstract deductive logic. 'Economic theory', he said in his inaugural address at the LSE (Young, 1928a),

> divorced from its functional relations to economic problems, or with those relations obscured, is no better than an interesting intellectual game. It gives endless opportunities for dialectical ingenuity. But it cannot advance knowledge, for it leads up a blind alley [pp. 4–5] ... Economics will have to make room for new conceptions and new sorts of abstractions if it is to make effective use of the new facts which the statisticians are uncovering [p. 10] ... The most important thing a student of political economy gets from his training is not the possession of a body of 'economic truth' but command of an intellectual technique. Confronted by a new problem he knows how to find his bearings and how to work his way through to some sort of reasoned conclusion. He knows how to pick up new facts and find a place for them in some consistent view of the mechanism of economic life. That is why economics is on the one hand a discipline to be taught, and on the other hand an almost limitless field of research [p. 14].

The best testimony of Young's success as a teacher, as measured by the criteria he posited in that LSE inaugural, is not that he left as his legacy a Youngian school with disciples to espouse the true faith, but that so many of his students became eminent in diverse fields of research, and indeed even developed contrasting perceptions and generalizations from their investigations in the same field (witness, say, Angell, 1933, versus Currie, 1933, 1934b, on monetary theory and policy; or Kaldor and Chamberlin versus Currie in the analysis of the relationship between growth and the structure of industry; Sandilands, 1990a, chapter 12; and Chandra and Sandilands, 2005).

This may explain why so many of his students' recollections are not so much of the specifics that Young taught, important as those might be, as of the sense of the even greater importance he gave to intellectual integrity, judgment, and relevance. Possibly Currie (1990, p. 12) spoke for them all when he remarked that 'after 50 years I do not recall specific points. I should say that Young's enduring contribution concerned more an attitude of mind. I gained more confidence and was not so impressed by authority. He gave me more courage to think things out for myself.'

* * *

The following are the full statements (except insofar as courtesies and so on are edited out) made by Blitch's correspondents, together with some related material.

From James W. Angell
   West Chop
   Massachussetts
   April 6, 1973

Dear Professor Blitch,

... Professor Young had a greater and more stimulating effect on me than any other teacher I can recall, yet my contacts with him were in a sense not very extensive. I took his famous graduate course in money, in 1920–21; wrote one paper that year which he worked over for me; and then, partly under the sponsorship of Professor Taussig but chiefly under Young's, went abroad for most of a year to do the main part of the work on my Ph.D. dissertation. I also served as Young's assistant in a seminar in Williamstown in the summer of 1923. But these were almost the whole of my personal contacts with him – these, and the correspondence my dissertation entailed. I never took his seminar in economic theory, did not see him often in his office, and myself left Cambridge in 1924. Yet I felt that I knew him quite well, and – like most of his students – was almost irrationally devoted to him. It is this last aspect that you especially inquire about.

The foundations of the great influence which Young had on his students, the necessary though not sufficient conditions, were both his own great intellectual capacity, and the wide range of knowledge not only of economics but also of other fields which he brought to bear on specific economic problems. I can no longer cite concrete examples, but I still remember my repeated excitement at analogies he often pointed out between what we were talking about in class and the propositions of some of the physical and biological sciences. He made our horizons seem wider, and the air fresher.

A second large source of his influence was the remarkable clarity, simplicity and persuasiveness of his expositions, especially in his lectures. He found easy paths for us through the many tangles; and one never had the slightest inclination to question his conclusions.

But these things alone might have been insufficient. The key factor, I am sure, was some sort of warm personal magnetism (a charisma, in the literal dictionary sense?) that seemed to flow from him to his students, and that made them both trust him personally and believe in him intellectually. What more can I say?

It must be 45 years or more since I last talked with him, a year or two before his death, but I can still see the massive head and shoulders, hear the rich and unusual tones of his voice, and instinctively respond to the remembered glow in his eyes.

From Colin Clark
  Monash University
  Australia
  7th December 1972

Dear Prof. Blitch,

... I was not a student of Allyn Young, but his research assistant. I was appointed in October 1928 and he died in February [sic; actually it was March] 1929, so I did not see much of him.

My friend Prof. Gilbert Walker ... attended some of his lectures, and I suggest that you write to him. I remember his quoting some of Young's epigrams. 'Productivity, or scarcity – they mean the same thing', and, after drawing an elaborate diagram on the blackboard, challenged his class 'Show me consumer's surplus in that!'. Except for his very pregnant article in the Economic Journal just before he died, Young wrote comparatively little; his work has mainly survived in oral tradition. One of Young's ideas, which certainly startled his audience, was that what Britain needed was a population of 100 million; this would facilitate sub-division of processes, and raise productivity almost to an American scale. (I regard it as a characteristic Americanism on Young's part that he always thought of the internal market, and that it did not seem to occur to him that a country could attain economies of scale by working for a world export market – this is the explanation of the present high level of productivity in small economies such as Switzerland and Sweden). Young certainly stressed the importance of sub-division of processes, as against the idea then fashionable that what were needed were very large individual plants covering every process – though already by the late 1920s Henry Ford's way of doing things was obviously becoming discredited. The work on which Young employed me was an attempt to obtain evidence of increasing returns from the US manufacturing statistics, in the deplorably crude form in which they were then published – we made no headway at all.

Young took a great interest in the pioneer work of one of his research students, G.T. Jones, who was killed in a car accident in 1928.[7] I had the job of editing his manuscripts, which eventually appeared as a book entitled <u>Increasing Returns</u> (Cambridge University Press, 1933). Jones's methods were greatly in advance of his time, and I think clearly show Young's influence. It really was a remarkable event when, in 1955, a student taking my course at Oxford, also called G.T. Jones, turned out to be the posthumous son of this writer; he had inherited all of his father's econometric ability and more.

I trust that you have a record of the interesting legend of Young's conversation with President Harding. Harding had consulted Young as President of the American Economic Association, and disliked the advice he received. 'I am not sure that you are the man I want', said the President, 'I think that I ought to send for the President of the American Statistical Association'. 'What do you want to send for me for – I am here' Young replied.

I remember conversations with Young on the Harvard system of Economic forecasting in the 1920s, which was to be proved so disastrously wrong in 1929. Young was sceptical at a much earlier date. The system was largely designed by Bullock – Young respected him, but considered that he had overstrained himself.

Ibid.
27th December 1972

My recollections of Young are quite clear. He was large in build, with a slow and relaxed manner of speaking, and a delightful sense of humour. He was mild and friendly in his dealings with his subordinates. At a time when Americans were not so well known in England, and there was some prejudice against them, he did much to enrich the American 'image' (as it would be called nowadays). His health appeared good, and his sudden death took us all by surprise.

From Arthur H. Cole
   Cambridge
   Mass.
   April 1, 1972

My dear Professor Blitch,

… I was an old friend of Professor Heath, and did overlap in service here at Harvard with Professor Young. I had already become pretty well sunk into economic history research when he did join the faculty here at Cambridge, and mostly I may be able to help you with your recollections of his personal life. I do still quote a passage in his essay before the English economic association, and do believe him to deserve your scholarly attention.

A better man for you to interrogate relative to Professor Young's intellectual accomplishments is Professor Edward S. Mason, now emeritus at Harvard but still active intellectually.[8] I believe that he studied under Young, and surely was close to the revivification of economic theory – as Professor Taussig's influence diminished and before Professor Schumpeter took the first rank here. I have a distinct impression that Professor Young was responsible for Edward Chamberlin's innovation into monopolistic competition and the like. Mason would know this story well.

I do not know what Professor Heath may have told you about Professor Young's private life and his personal character. I will list a few elements and let you ask for such data as I possess:

Mrs. Young was totally blind, and Professor Young devoted much time to caring for her;
A sister of hers lived with the Youngs as well as an orphan girl and boy, the children of a third sister;
The Youngs had a son who never lived up to his potentials …;
Professor Young was quite absent-minded. Also he had the condition of lapsing into a brown study as he lectured or, according to stories, even as he carved a turkey or roast of beef at his table – carved for the family.
He was a somewhat wild golfer – slicing his drives all over the course.
He was tall, loose jointed, but rather noble looking – at least with a commanding, serious mien. Everyone respected him and his students were surely very fond of him.

From Lauchlin Currie (to Mrs Allyn Young in London)
Cambridge
Mass.
March 1929

Dear Mrs Young,

Altho I am a stranger I cannot resist writing you how very deeply I sympathise with you in your terrible loss. I was a student of Professor Young's from 1925–27 and am now assisting Professor Williams in his old course in money and banking at Harvard, which position I owe to his kind recommendation.

I wish that I could convey to you how deeply we students loved and revered Professor Young and what a tremendous inspiration he was to us. He was our mentor and we referred to him and talked about him constantly. He was always available and gave of his precious time all too freely. We can only try to show our appreciation and make amends for our encroachment on his time by acknowledging continually our deep debt to him for any creative work we may accomplish.

I, perhaps, was closer to him than many of his students in recent years. I had taken my degree at the London School and he used to like to talk over his plans with me before he left. I was in his special field of banking and he took a keen interest in my thesis. During my visit to London last summer he was so kind in giving me introductions and assisting me in every way possible. I shall never forget the afternoon that I last saw him when he entertained four of us – all former Harvard students of his – at your house. He had just finished his Presidential Address and was in excellent spirits. I have rarely enjoyed an afternoon so much and came away longing to accomplish something worth while – something to show him that I was worth a little of the time and consideration he had given me. I realize now more than ever how much my desire to write something worth while was activated by that sole motive. I could never tell him all I felt but I do so hope that he realised that both his genius and his charming personality were fully appreciated by his students.

* * *

The following are extracts from Currie's diary for 1926–27. Most refer to Young, but other extracts are included to give some of the atmosphere and flavor of economics education at Harvard at that time. They include references to some of the other students and staff, such as Melvin de Chazeau and Arthur Cole (see below), and other prominent persons such as Frank Taussig and Harry Dexter White.

May 22nd [1926]. In morning talking to Young re L.S.E. There is a strong probability that he'll accept the offer. It's a compliment to Cannan, Beveridge and Young. I don't think Y. would like it as much as here. His going wd. be a calamity from my own view point as I wished to work under him. A truly gt. economist.

May 28th. Last Ec 11 class. Taussig spoke on the future of econs. He made me feel ashamed for all the hard things I've said about him. Once, in speaking of the newer schools conducting investigations by means of their statistical tools, he said that it made him feel like a back number. Then I did feel mean. The future, to him, belongs to the econ. statistician and 'institutionalism'. Deprecated utility of work we're at now but said it was necessary – an indispensable groundwork, on wh. he is quite right. I've got something I did not get with Cannan and which I could or rather would not have got by myself. Besides it was good training in critical reading and thinking.

Sept 17th. In the evening de Chazeau and Vosper came in and stayed till 12. A good talk. de Chazeau is going with a girl w. expensive tastes and his thots are turning to money. He is seriously thinking of deserting the academic field for business as a consequence. He said sg. which has often depressed me viz that at present we know nothing *definite* and are nobody. Most sciences seem to have a fairly coherent subject matter – ours hasn't. The system here prevents us from ever thinking a thing thru – because that is a mighty slow process and we have no time. There are always exams in the offing. When we do get our degree on theoretical econ. there is nothing we can do except teach. Promotion is slow and it may be years before we can even own a home. On the other hand the life attracts me very much. There are no joys to be compared with intellectual joys. I have always had sufficient money to learn that after a certain point more or less income has little effect on our happiness. The deepest pleasures of life, love, friendship, enjoyable work and intellectual achievement, cannot of course be bought w. money. Again I feel that by an intelligent study of business trends, etc. I will be able to make a bit on the side by speculating in stocks.

Sept 18th. Reading Wallas, Nearing and Memorials of A. Marshall. They all bear more or less on the art of thought and the art of teaching. I've been thinking a good deal about these topics lately. I firmly believe that there is an art of thot tho I think that it is largely an individual art. Nevertheless it is very helpful to learn the methods of great thinkers. Teaching is one of the most difficult of all arts and I mean to devote a good deal of time and thought to it. However there is no use trying to be a good teacher unless one is also a great scholar or scientist. I have found that the men who have inspired me and whom I respect have been men who I know were thinkers – who thought with the class. One can hardly teach others to think unless he thinks himself.

Sept 24th. Consulted Young re my course and, among other things, he strongly advised me to take pol. theory – which means more work for me. Said that he understood that Mrs [Evelyn] Burns was coming to Harvard this year [from the LSE]. I certainly hope so.

Sept 27th. Spent the morning in trying to see how much material was available for my thesis and was very disappointed. No Canadian financial journals are in Boston. I may have to go to N.Y. for them. I feel that the subject is a big one and an important one and I should not like to give it up.

Sept 29th. Lectures began w. MacIlwain and Young – I'm going to enjoy them both.

Oct 18th. Heard Dr Schultz-Gauvernitz [sic; Gerhart von Schulze-Gaevernitz] before the Seminary. Rather superficial. Talking to Young in afternoon when he signed my application for Ph.D. and in evening. I fairly worship him. A five minute talk w. him sets me up for the day. Talking to [G.T.] Jones, and walked home w. [H.D.] White and [M.M.] Bober – a regular talking orgy.

Nov 27th. Letter from Taussig telling me that one of Viner's students is working on Canada's Trade Balance 1913–25. Cut the ground from under my feet.

Nov 28th. Sunday. Spent most of the day struggling w. net and gross terms of international trade and discussed the subject w. White in night.

Nov 29th. About 5 p.m. I was in the depths of despair and I've only slowly pulled myself out of it. There is only one thing which bowls me over is the realization of my mental inferiority. Days pass and even weeks when nothing occurs to disturb my peace and then just when I'm beginning to feel some degree of confidence in myself something happens to remind me forcibly of my mediocrity. To-day it was Young's class. He was discussing some aspects of Jevons utility value theory, and while White and de Chazeau and I suppose others followed the discussion keenly I did not understand some of it and found the rest difficult to follow. Young simply overwhelms me. I came home like a woman thoroly disheartened. But even while I was saying that I should give up this work and get in some line of work in which men are never called to meet the acid test of ability, I knew that I will simply hang on and go thru with it. I can't resign myself to the role of second-rater.

Prof. Edie spoke on Institutional Economics before the Seminary in evening.[9] His arguments were very weak. White, Silverman, Bober and I walked home together and needless to say that one Gentile among three Jews gets very little chance to get a word in edgeways!

Nov 30th. Long talk with Young who called me by my name for the first time. Advised me to continue on my Canadian subject. Doesn't think much of Viner's book and imagines that a study by one of his men will be on the same lines. Suggested some other subjects such as the theoretical aspects of branch banking vs U.S. system; saving among working classes; velocity of banknote circulation; causes of bank failures etc. Taussig in his class and afterward to me suggested this problem: international trade adjustments occur very quickly and yet the influence of specie takes place slowly and yet this is the orthodox mechanism by wh. changes are supposed to be brought about. Explanation? I told T. that I did not think that I was statistically minded enough to attempt it.[10] Any probs. I investigate must be those requiring a minimum of stats. and a good deal of judgment of weighting diff. factors and seizing on the important thing. Whatever strength I have lies in such directions. Working at German all day.

Jan 10th. Busy all day and evening. Wrote out a point I raised in international trade for Taussig which I think is valid and wh. he has apparently overlooked. Feeling a bit of my old time ambition to master econ. theory. To study, think, teach and write ...

Jan 11th. Talking to Young. He is going to L.S.E. for about 3 years w. the intention of returning then to Harvard. I have been very fortunate in having Young – his reputation is going to grow steadily. A genius. Working at report. Spent evening at Whites. Looking over past exams. in Young's course and, as always, got an attack of cold feet. Reading over my old econ. exam papers in London and marvelled that I ever got a 2nd class. What a wonderful feeling of liberty I should experience when I've finally passed my last exam. It's been an awful grind all my life.

Jan 19th. Last lectures for the half year. Met Taussig to-day and he stopt and said that he had a good mind to ask me on my exam paper what was wrong w. the point raised in the note I gave him the other day. I said 'Wasn't there anything in it?' To which he replied w. brutal frankness 'Nothing'. But I'm sure there is sg. in it and that T., who differs so from Young, in this respect, did not consider the question sympathetically in an effort to see where the truth or error lay. Many people are complaining or rather remarking on the extreme disinclination T. has to reopen any question upon wh. he has made up his mind. He seems weary of thinking and is becoming more and more dogmatic. He will prob. retire soon.

Jan 30th. Sunday. Long walk w. Harry in night. He was quite enthusiastic re my prospects in the academic field and rather made me feel better about it all. Finished my report for Young.

Feb 4th. Talking to Young in afternoon. Said I couldn't expect much due to my lack of teaching experience. He is full of his English plans.

Feb 9th. Talking to Young about a travelling fellowship and other things ...

Feb 13th. Sunday. Another good day's work – I felt a true zest for it to-day. Told Harry about J. and he thinks I did the right thing. This doubt is very distracting. Reading Macaulay's fascinating essay on Machiavelli. Let the pedants gravely shake their heads, he has a marvellous style. Such a blessed relief after the desperately written econ. books. I find Nietzsche splendid tonic. If I could lose myself in my work for a time I might accomplish wonders. My attention is *always* divided. When I think that I've used the outer crust of my mind, as it were, I marvel that I have got as far as I have. If

I could only expel that blighting consciousness of self and really concentrate!

Feb 14th. Interviewed Young and Williams and they are going to recommend me for a Sheldon Travelling Fellowship.

Feb 15th. Williams' course on International Finance is excellent – he is a good man and likeable ...

Feb 17th. Got an A in Ec 33 – Taussig's Foreign Trade – The last exam I ever write.

Feb 21st. Got an A– in Young's Modern Schools of Econ. wh. I believe is a good mark in that course. Recommended for a $2000 instructorship in the Hunter College of N.Y.C. It looked good at first but when I found that it is a ladies college and that the Econ. is part of a Social Sc. course I did not feel so keen about it. Talking a long time to Greef about jobs and on his advice wrote to Chicago Univ. asking if there were any teaching assistantships going. All very distracting and I have so much work to do.

Feb 23rd. Talking to Williams in morning and Young in afternoon and as a consequence cd. do little work. Young most amiable. Thot N.Y. a good place to start and said I sd. hold out for $2500 – he had written to Dawson about me. I told him about my Chicago hopes and he was quite enthusiastic – thinks Chicago a fine place and Viner a very able man. However as there are very few jobs going advised me to hedge on the N.Y. job. Told him I heard that it might prove a blind alley as I was depending on him to get me away from it next year and he wd. be in Eng[land]. He said that that put a diff. complexion on it and that if I got to Chicago I might find somebody there to push me. Has nothing good to say about Columbia or Brookings School. Slated Seligman ... Told me his plans with regard to L.S.E. Told him that I thot he had treated me rather well in Ec 15 exam mark and he admitted that he had but that I deserved sg. for my courage in tackling the question I did as I was the only one in the class who did choose that question.

March 7th. Young sent for me and told me to turn down the N.Y. offer. He had been thinking it over and decided that I am too good for that post! Unless I get a good offer from Chicago he thinks that

Harvard will be able to look after me, i.e. I will get an instructorship providing two instructors leave this year. Then he went on talking about London and for the fourth time told me his present position on credit creation. I came home treading on air and dropt in to White to tell him the news. If I get it I would be *made*. I haven't even hoped for such a thing. But I'm afraid that Hunt and Beach are both after the post and their qualifications are far better than mine.

March 14th. Jones spoke before econ. society in night. The numerous qualifications to his conclusions due to his data rather took the teeth out of his contention that what little increasing returns there had been in Brit industries 1860–1910 was entirely due to inventions.[11] Talking to Young a little. He says Burbank has the power of selecting instructors tho Y. had mentioned my name to him.

March 17th. Amusing Ec 39 class. De Chazeau got excited and talked of 'growing cheese'.

March 18th. No summer travellingships being granted this year. Feel as tho I had lost $300. Young asked me if I would like to teach at Dartmouth. I said 'yes' so he said he that altho they had written particularly about Erb he wd. mention me. Also Smith College.

March 18th. Called on Burbank and apparently a $1200 job ('mainly tutorial') awaits me next year at Harvard. Dropt in to Young's office to tell him the news and thank him. He seemed to want me to have the Ec 3 assistantship if Marget leaves but I'd much rather be an instructor.

March 21st. Date of exam. fixed for April 11 – earlier than I expected. Young, (Bullock), Burbank, (Gay), Miller, Cole, Wright. Talking to Burbank – little prospect of getting an instructorship as very few vacancies. Discussion w. White on Ec 11 notes. The next 3 weeks will be contracted misery.

March 23 – April 5th. A solid grind. During the first part of it I became pessimistic – had to drive myself at work and lay awake at night thinking what I wd. do when I failed. Made up my mind to chuck econ. and go to England and write. Then I rec'd a letter from Dartmouth so decided to apply for the post there.

April 10th. White and I worked all day at pol. theory.

April 11th. Up late, pottered around, laid down after dinner until it was time to leave. Met Taussig on the way and he told me to keep my wits about me. Chatted w. Dr Wright, a young chap, before the exam. Young began and I was a little nervous to start with. Got all balled up over the 18th Century. Contractual vs institutionalized view of society's natural order in U.S. and the Empire too. Found my footing for a moment on rent but lost it again in contrasting Marshall's extension of concept [of] rent with that of Jevons. Altogether I did poorly in ec. theory. Next was Wright on pol. theory. He was very generous and I was able a little to guide the discussion. Next came Usher (Gay was supposed to be on the Board) and I fared passably well with him. Then Cole who instead of asking me sg. about the theory of international trade confined his questions to protection and the tariff and the Webb-Pomerene Act – about all of wh. I knew very little and plainly showed it. But the worst was yet to come with Burbank on public finance. He literally browbeat me. Then Young asked me to leave the room – I walked out amid deep silence – a terrible feeling. At the end of 5 minutes Young hurried out and shook my hand for a minute, congratulating me. What I owe to him! It is my firm opinion that he got me thru. I told him that I was ashamed of my performance in his subject and he said that his questions were very hard. Said that while it was not a brilliant exam still it was quite alright. Then Burbank came along and congratulated me tho I doubt if he passed me …

All night long till 5 a.m. I kept thinking of what I should have answered and didn't. Felt as discouraged as tho I had failed.

April 12th. Went to class in afternoon and the news had evidently preceded me and everyone congratulated and asked me the questions. I felt better when I saw that the questions stumped them.

April 15th. White failed in his generals. He was handed a raw deal and treated most unjustly in pol. theory and ec. hist. I couldn't have answered the questions in those subjects and indeed no one cd. unless they made a life study of the subjects. White, with a better brain and a fuller knowledge of the subjects, failed and I passed; merely because our boards were different and the types of questions different. So much for the 'generals' as a test of one's ability. We were all perfectly sure of White's passing as he is abler than any of the men passed so far this year.

April 16th Letter from Prof [E.W.] Goodhue of Dartmouth regretting that I'm staying at Harvard and implying that I wd. have got the post at Dartmouth.

April 25th. Talking to Young – said I got a straight pass in my exam. Reading a monograph on branch banking in the U.S. by J. Steels – in French.[12]

May 3rd. Attended dinner to Young at Harvard Club. He gave a splendid address. Every time he speaks he says sg. worth while. I was talking to him a minute afterwards and he told me that his family was English and had come over in the 17th C.

May 19th. [Gardiner] Means failed his Generals.

May 31st. Last class w. Young.

* * *

From Melvin G. de Chazeau
  Cornell University
  Ithaca, N.Y.
  Oct. 3, 1973

Dear Professor Blitch:

It was my good fortune to have had a course in money and banking and a seminar in the development of economic thought under Allyn Young at Harvard. I came to regard him as one of the best, if not the very finest teacher, I have ever known. He impressed on his students the importance of seeking out the truth wherever it might be revealed; and he practiced so religiously his admonitions to others that his untimely death robbed the profession of many a contribution to the literature that he was preeminently fitted to make.

My most vivid mind-picture of Prof. Young in the classroom is of him wiping off the blackboard with his coat sleeve as he altered or modified notations and diagrams. He seemed always to finish his lectures well dusted with white chalk. This was an endearing mannerism in a person whose depth of understanding, breadth of knowledge and sensitivity to the reactions of others could not help but make an indelible impression on those with whom he came in contact. Indeed he had the superb ability to pick up any comment or suggestion from a student, no matter how stupid it might appear, dust it off analytically, provide it with historical or tangential substance and relevance, and transform it into a meaningful contribution to the subject under discussion – all without blasting or belittling the person who first proffered it. It was Allyn Young's basic modesty and his sensitivity to others, not any desire on his part to demonstrate his profound knowledge, that led him to exercise this talent especially in his seminar where circumstances were more propitious ...

From Eleanor Lansing Dulles
  Washington, D.C.
  December 31, 1974

Dear Professor Blitch,

... Allyn Young was a professor who kept developing his ideas with his class. His students participated in this development – he was nearly a perfect teacher.

A large, square-shouldered man with slightly rumpled tweeds, he would look into space with a long range perspective while his hands groped for a handkerchief – usually not there, and we wondered whether we should give him one. But his words never failed him.

Every year he progressed with new concepts in the field of monetary theory. None of his conclusions as to others' views were frozen, all were to be reexamined in the light of new experience. Never have I known such a combination of sound knowledge and willingness to speculate and reconsider.

In the years I knew him, from 1924 to 1927, much new material was becoming available. When he approved my undertaking a study of French inflation and I went to Paris in 1925, I felt I had his full sympathy and support.

When two Columbia professors, Robert Murray Haig and James Harvey Rogers tried to persuade me to give them my material and retire from the project, I wrote him, saying I wanted to continue. He cabled at once, 'Stick to it. You are on the right track.'

I returned in March, 1926, to the United States with a bundle of notes, much enthusiasm, and the expectation of turning in a thesis by April 1. Professor Young was, I later learned, dismayed. He did not tell me he saw no hope of my gathering the material into shape by the deadline.

I hired a crackerjack secretary and worked 20 hours a day. On April 1, at 3:30, I staggered up the stairs to his office with my new manuscript. He was intensely relieved. He cared. His introduction to my book, with its recognition of the psychological, is an essay on inflation which is highly pertinent to today's world.

When we were told he was leaving to be on the faculty of the London School of Economics, Emily Huntington, later Professor of Economics at Berkeley, and I, who knew what a mess his office was in, offered to help. He let us help him sort papers and throw some away. It was an interesting chore and one that gave me a better understanding of his dedication and sense of values.

He cared little for the trivial. We knew his wife was blind. He had no regular secretary. He was baffled by the mass of papers.

Allyn Young died too young and wrote too little. We who were his students owe him much.

From Howard S. Ellis
  Berkeley
  California
  November 1, 1973

… Concerning Allyn Young, let me first observe that my first teacher of economics was Frank H. Knight, then at the University of Iowa, Iowa City. For some reason or other Knight 'took up' with me, a mere undergraduate, but I came to know him very well. I have no hesitation in saying that Young, as a professor at Cornell, was Frank's chief inspiration and mentor, and remained so as long as he lived.

My bosom friend at Ann Arbor, later at Cambridge and as long as he lived, was Edward H. Chamberlin. We were room-mates in both places and were so much Damon and Pythias that people often confused our identities. Thus I can feel some confidence in saying that Young was Ed Chamberlin's chief mentor and inspiration, in economic theory, though both Ed and I held Taussig in high esteem as an applied economist (lacking somewhat in Young's theoretical acumen).

I was a member of a graduate course in Statistics at Harvard which was taught by Edmund E. Day (later Dean of the School of Business at Michigan and subsequently President of Cornell). It was in this connection that I knew Allyn Young directly; after the first semester, Day left and Young took over. After the crisp, business-like demeanor of Day, Young seemed very much abstracted, sometimes a bit dreamy, but always modest, kindly and attentive to students and always a bit more profound than the books we were advised to read, including G. Udny Yule and Chichec (Czizek? *sp.*a bit uncertain after 50 years). In my estimation, all students particularly interested in economic theory gravitated toward Young. (Since my interest was particularly in money and monetary theory I turned to John Williams. He befriended me notably; but I wrote my dissertation, which won a Wells Prize, in virtual isolation at Heidelberg and Ann Arbor, Michigan).

I always felt that Young was a truly great man, original and productive in economic theory with a strong sense of relevance and importance ...

From Frank W. Fetter
  Hanover, N.H.
  February 20, 1984

Dear Professor Blitch:

... When I was a graduate student at Harvard in 1923 I signed up for Young's graduate course. (The exact title I don't recall, but it dealt with monetary theory.) As I recall it he sat on his desk, talked in what I felt was rather disorganized way about the complexities of monetary theory, and in substance said that he didn't fully believe in the more simple explanation that he had given in his contribution to the revision of Ely's text. As I recall it, my reaction was that I didn't want to spend a term getting the ideas of a man who didn't know what he believed, so I dropped out of the course after the first meeting and transferred to Henry Jackson Turner's course on the Frontier in American History.

As I look back this was a youthful simplistic view of mine, for from all I have heard Young had a very fertile and imaginative mind, but my impression is that at the undergraduate level he was not regarded as an outstanding teacher ...

From letter from Frank Fetter to his father,
   May 18, 1924:

Dear Dad,

... Our good friends Kemmerer and Fisher had better look to their laurels as practical economists, as Harvard has a rival in the person of A.A. Young. There was recently long article in the Boston Evening Transcript giving his opinion on the Dawes report. The writer said of Young, that 'he is regarded by leading financiers of Boston as "the most able bankers" economist' – meaning by that the most able judge of immediate practical values as well as of long range movements – 'which the present generation has produced.' Young certainly rates big around here.

For Williams' course we have recently been reading the new books on international finance, that is; Keynes 'Monetary Reform', Cassel 'Money and Foreign Exchanges Since 1914' and Moulton and Maguire 'Germany's Capacity to Pay'. I have been very much disappointed in this course and about all I seem to be getting out of it is a rebellious spirit. Williams avowedly is very ready to have discussion but somehow people who start discussions don't get very far so have been just raring to go for an argument. Almost all the talking in the class is done by Gardner who is not enrolled in the class but sits on the back row and chimes in on the discussion whenever he feels like it. Williams stands for the thesis that the increase in paper currencies in Germany has been the result and not the cause of the increase in prices, which to me is the rankest sort of heresy. He also takes issue with Cassel when the latter claims that the huge selling of German marks on the international markets depressed the price of the mark. Williams says this is one of the most naïve statements he has ever read, and says that the fact that so many marks were bought ought to have raised the price of the mark. I understand that Young also takes the same position as Williams, but for the life of me I can't see how they figure it out.[13] By their reasoning a huge offering of drafts on London in New York, which are purchased by New York bankers, should greatly raise the price of the Pound because the fact that so many are bought shows that there is a great demand for sterling exchange. If the class were one in which discussion was carried on I would welcome such issues but as it is it is bad for my spirit. Perhaps it would be a good thing if there were some discussion and I would get some of the conceit knocked out of me for as it is I feel quite confident that I am right. But the class hasn't been a total failure as Williams has some suggestive ideas and I have got a good bit from the reading.

From Earl J. Hamilton
  University of Chicago
  February 14, 1973

Dear Professor Blitch:

… It is a pity that I could not foresee your request for information concerning Allyn Young before I began packing to leave Duke, for I took extensive lecture notes under him in two major courses and preserved them until 1944. One thing that my notes taken in 1924–1926 conclusively showed was that every worthwhile idea in E.H. Chamberlin's subsequent work on imperfect competition had been clearly expounded by Allyn Young in class long before Chamberlin put pen to paper. Curiously, Young credited Cournot for most of what he said! He was the epitome of modesty.

Nevertheless, Young either did not prepare his lectures or prepared them very poorly. Nothing could have been more disorganized than he was in class. Consequently, as much as 90 percent of the time I spent in his classes was wasted. But in the remaining time I got something that was so original, so profound, so meaningful and so impossible to get anywhere else that the total time I spent with him was invaluable. In the years I was at Harvard the Department of Economics was clearly the best in the United States, and Allyn Young was far and away the most innovative thinker in the Department. He was the least prejudiced of all the scholars or even persons I have ever known. Yet he constantly said that he had no knowledge of this or that, that he only had prejudice. Incidentally, his downright prejudice against Gustav Schmoller was colossal. But I never detected any other prejudice toward anybody or any thing. I must say, however, that Young never criticized Schmoller without prefacing his remarks by a strong reminder that he was chock full of prejudice against him. I must qualify what I have said above by pointing out that some of Young's prejudice against Schmoller was reflected in Young's attitude to his colleague Edwin F. Gay, who studied under Schmoller and was his disciple.

I am sure you know that Young was handsome and that he had a magnetic personality.

You may be interested in knowing that Irving Fisher told me several times that Allyn Young was decidedly the best mathematician among living American economists. As you probably know, Fisher's Ph.D. was in mathematics, not in economics. I believe I am right in thinking that Young never had a course in mathematics beyond the sophomore level in college.

My admiration for Young is enormous, and I am eternally grateful for what I learned from him. What I treasure most of all is the inculcation of his firm belief that the world is full of interesting problems about which we know next to nothing and that if one tackles them and really studies them, there is no limit to what one can achieve except limitations inherent in himself. He made me feel this strongly when I left almost every class I ever had under him.

One thing that you will need to read and re-read until it becomes a part of you is the article by Nicholas Kaldor, on 'The Irrelevance of Equilibrium Economics,' in *The Economic Journal*, December 1972, pp. 1237–1255 which has just reached me and that I have just read. It is largely devoted to the brilliant and path-breaking thought of Allyn Young. I expect to read this at least twice more myself. You can easily guess how infrequently I do this with any article.

Perhaps you know that, although Allyn Young was there less than three years, the London School of Economics bought Allyn Young's books that he had with him, installed them in a room with a splendid portrait of him and calls this the Allyn A. Young Room. Offhand, I cannot think of another prestigious institution anywhere in the world that is shorter of space than the London School. I do not know but suspect that papers of Young are in that room too ...[14]

You may know that the late Frank H. Knight wrote his doctoral dissertation under Allyn Young, and the two were very close until Young died. I know that in Knight's papers there is a lot of material pertaining to Allyn Young ...

Incidentally, Mrs. Hamilton and I took one full-year course together under Allyn Young. She fully shares my exalted opinion of him.

From Seymour S. Harris
  University of California
  San Diego
  April 18, 1973

Dear Professor Blitch:

... I wrote my thesis with Professor Young when I was at Harvard and knew him reasonably well. As you may know, Professor Young took an examination at the Peace Conference in 1918, and he wrote the best paper on the economic issues of the peace, and therefore was invited to join the peace group in Paris.

As soon as he came to Harvard, he virtually took over the graduate school, and all the bright students wrote their theses under him.

He unfortunately died, as the result of a bad cold, in London, and also, most unfortunately, he did not carry through his life insurance policy. The University took care of his widow for over 40 years.

Professor Young had a very close connection with the New York Federal Reserve Bank and was frequently an adviser for the bank. He was a charming man, a great teacher and a first rate scholar, though he did not write very much. He was one of the first to get into the field of mathematical economics ...

From Richard S Howey
University of Kansas
January 3, 1980

Dear Professor Blitch:

In the academic year 1925–1926, my last year as an undergraduate at Harvard, I attended Allen [sic] Young's lectures in Economics 3 (Money and Banking). Unfortunately I would be at a loss to reproduce now any of their contents. All my class notes I gleefully destroyed in a happy celebration at the end of my senior year. There are two things, however, that I do remember: the setting of the lectures, and the style of Young's delivery. I recall that the lectures were held in Harvard Hall, a building no longer used for classrooms. My copy of the 1924–1925 *Harvard University Register* gives '6' as the number of the room, and the figure '2' as the time of the class. The classroom must have held as many as two hundred graduate and undergraduate students, seated on Harvard College chairs behind long planks mutilated by countless pocketknives. There was an aisle down the middle. Entrance was from the back, where clustered a few Radcliffe girls. Young lectured on a slightly raised platform bearing a desk with a moveable lectern upon it. His style was unique. He brought no notes. His delivery consisted in a string of silences, some quite long, after each of which would come forth a complete freshly composed sentence. Once, at the end of a very long composing silence, during which he was leaning on the lectern, he accidentally pushed it off the desk and it clattered on the floor.

After graduation I returned to Southern California where, in the first part of 1929, I read in the *Harvard Alumni Bulletin* of Young's death in London. That summer I gave the examinations and graded the class papers of Thomas Nixon Carver who was a visiting professor at U.S.C., having just completed his long tenure at Harvard. I mentioned Young's death to him, and was astonished when he told me it was the result of a combination of London fog and Scotch whiskey. Later Carver's secretary informed me that Carver received 50 cents a word for writing in support of prohibition. Carver also said that Hawtrey, who had been sent to Harvard to secure some teaching experience so that he could take Young's post at the L.S.E. when Young returned to Harvard, was now going back to London. Carver added that it was felt that he had rather resume his position with the Treasury than to take the L.S.E. professorship. This is what did happen, and Robbins followed Young. Carver mentioned that this chair was the highest paid in the British Empire, and that there had been 'murmuring' when it was filled by an American.

The remainder of what I know about Young concerns his interest in, and teaching of, the history of economic thought, knowledge that I largely acquired from the Seligman papers deposited in the rare Book Room of Butler Library at Columbia University, and from the archives of the Baker Library at Harvard.

I suspect that in all the major places that he studied and taught he had some connection with the history of economics. I found a letter from Young dated March 30, 1910 at the time Young was on the point of moving to Harvard from Stanford – this time he spent only one year in Cambridge – saying 'I have been continuing Veblen's course in the History of Political Economy and have put a lot of work on it; but that, I imagine is covered by Bullock and Gay.' This, of course, was true. At this point in my notes I wrote 'There are several interesting letters from A. Young.' If you have not used these you might profit if you can uncover them at Columbia. In 1964, when I looked at the Seligman archive, it was 'unprocessed', in more than one hundred and twenty-five boxes. In recent years the Library has been processing the Seligman archive which should make the search for particular items easier, but I wouldn't be too sure of that. The high esteem that Seligman had of Young is shown by a letter Seligman wrote September 30, 1929 [sic] to Young, then in London, saying that, if he had not gone to the London School, Seligman would have made him his first assistant on the *Encyclopedia of the Social Sciences*. 'I was determined,' he wrote, 'to make the offer so attractive that you would not be able to refuse it.' Instead he appointed Alvin Johnson.

When Young went to Harvard in 1920, he taught, in addition to his main course 'Economics 3', two smaller courses, one a half course

'Economics 15hf.' With the title 'Modern Schools of Economic Thought,' a course in the history of economic thought descended from 'Economics 22' which Gay had been teaching in 1910. Young repeated this course every year thereafter until he left for London. His hours for student consultation listed in the *Harvard University Register*, '3:30 to 4:00 Monday and Wednesday,' may seem puzzling in light of his reputation as a professor more interested in his students than in publishing, but at least they compare favorably with those of other professors of that period.

From the Seligman correspondence I learned that Young's wife was left in a sad financial plight by his death. Seligman played a leading part in bringing her some financial assistance. I wondered if you have located Young's only son or his descendants, and if there were any literary remains, with them, in Widener at Harvard, or elsewhere.

Another role in which Young appeared was that of adviser to Dean Donham of the Harvard Business School at the time when negotiations for the purchase of a Foxwell library were in progress. Here Young was seen as an expert in old books, a bibliophile sufficiently well grounded to confer and bargain with Foxwell in Cambridge. It was in the course of these negotiations that Young died. All the information I have on this episode I found in the archives of the Baker Library at the Harvard Business School. There was no correspondence from Young except a cable, but some of the letters and memos mentioned Young and showed the esteem in which he was held.

From Nicholas Kaldor
  King's College
  Cambridge
  June 1979

Unfortunately I only knew Young for a short time. I attended his lectures in the session 1927–28 (which was his first year as Professor at London University) and in the following year, when, as a second year undergraduate, I decided to take economics as my special subject. I was formally supervised by Young and was invited to one of his weekly classes. He divided his students into small groups of eight or ten, and held a two hour discussion with each group once a week in the early afternoon. He had a magnetic personality and in a short time all of us who attended his class fell under his spell. This was partly because of his transparent sincerity and his ability to talk to young students as if they were his intellectual equals, and mainly perhaps because he talked about the things that interested him most at that particular moment. In this way we had a running account of his correspondence with Pigou on the cost controversy and of the critical line he took on the particular measure then introduced by the Conservative Government headed by Mr. Baldwin, the so-called De-rating Bill, which exempted industrial establishments from the 'rates' which is the local property tax in England. Young's view was that since local property taxes were part of overhead costs, it was a mistake to think that their removal would lower the prices of the products of British industry and thereby make them more competitive in exports. (The discussion arose out of a paper he asked me to prepare on Marshall's concept of 'quasi-rent'.) His chief quality as a teacher (which he shared with Keynes) was his ability to make the subject of economics an exciting one, by making his students feel that they were participating in forming a judgment on the main issues of economic policy. He made one feel that by being a member of his discussion group, one was brought into the centre of things.

He held these classes in his room which was extremely untidy. His desk and tables were full of letters, papers, books, notes, etc. Being a very untidy man myself I often recalled the memory of Young's desk which made one feel that untidiness on one's desk need not necessarily go together with untidiness in thought.

His unexpected illness (after a brief Christmas trip to the U.S.) and death from pneumonia was felt as a tragedy by all his students. There was a memorial service at St. Clement Danes's in the Strand (two minutes from L.S.E.) which was attended by almost everyone from the School and at which Sir William Beveridge, the Director of L.S.E., made a memorable oration.

From Melvin M. Knight
  University of California
  Berkeley
  22 Dec/73

Dear Professor Blitch,

Eleanor Dulles, who visited here recently, told me you were writing on Allyn Young. He edited a book of mine on the Ec. Hist. of Europe to the end of the Middle Ages, then a second volume on Modern Times (this with Fluegel and Barnes).[15] He was a highly conscientious and helpful editor. I sent both to him by chapters on which he made quite extensive comments, discussing some questions of theory which I asked him in accompanying letters. There were problems about the modern part in particular. Fluegel was an excellent but somewhat conventional student of history. His doctorate was in economics, but he had been teaching economic history here before I came in 1921 (for summer school – I joined the Berkeley faculty in 1928). Barnes is probably best labeled an historical sociologist. He was a fast and rather careless writer (on econ. hist.), given to large generalizations. Young had the tedious job of correcting Barnes' chapters. He backed me in the discard of several. There was a notable amount of friction over this. While finishing the modern part, I was in Paris, intermittently, while working on some French colonies. Young was in London where I visited him at Xmas time, 1927, to talk over some of the problems of this volume. He was a close friend of my brother Frank (now deceased), and I had known his brother Evan, Minister to Santo Domingo while I was working on the American occupation there. In 1926, this would have been. The first volume was an 'idea book,' written by an evolutionist trained originally in genetics. It was Young who suggested publishing it separately, as it was solely my work, and the second volume was straying from the evolutionary scheme of the first. I last saw Young in 1929 or 1931 – you would know when the Am Ec Assn met in Chicago.[16] He died shortly afterward, as I now remember it, in London and of pneumonia.

This was a loss to me in more ways than one. At the meeting (29 or 31), Young was full of a project to assemble a rather small group. One aim was to do some 'integrating' of theory, history and other general approaches to economics ...

It was Young who put me on to Simiand, who had been most helpful to him during the 1919 peace conference. He was Eleanor Dulles' major professor. A Columbia professor insisted on seeing her unpublished MSS on the French franc. I told her to refuse flatly, and wrote Young about it in London. He said 'of course.' Then her brother John Foster came to Paris, and took the opportunity to tell our would-be pilferer where to go ...

From Bertil Ohlin
  Stockholm
  December 21, 1978

Dear Professor Blitch,

Thanks for your letter. I took a very stimulating course for [sic] professor Young at Harvard in 1922–23. The subject was history of Economic Doctrine. He impressed me immensely. I am inclined to believe that he was a man, who knew and thoroughly understood his subject – economics – better than anyone else I have met.

I tested him by means of a question about the 'Wicksell effect', i.e. the special aspects of the marginal productivity of capital, which at that time was practically unknown in most countries outside of Scandinavia. He immediately gave a fine account in a five minutes speech before the students.

What characterizes Allyn Young as an economist was that he had deep understanding of all fields of economic theory while other economists knew well one third of the theory and had only superficial knowledge of the rest.

I looked him up in London, where he spent one year, to ask for his advice on a question of great importance for my own scientific work (around 1928). See 'Festschrift' to Roy Harrod in 1970, footnote on the first page of my paper.[17]

I am sorry that I don't remember any anecdote about him. He was exceptionally friendly, spoke with an even voice and gave the impression that he was often plagued by long and severe headaches.

From Geoffrey Shepherd
  Iowa State University
  December 1, 1975

Dear Dr. Blitch:

I took one of Professor Young's graduate courses in economics in 1926–27. I developed the greatest respect for him as a man as well as an eminent scholar.

His erudition was tempered by kindliness and good humor. Because he had moved several times in his professional career, he referred to himself as a member of the peripatetic school of economics. He told us how he had been teaching at Cornell, and received an offer from Harvard. After due consideration, he declined the offer. With a smile, he said that after a year recovering from the shock, Harvard made another offer. This time he accepted. Clearly, he was not a professional climber.

After one year of our classes with him, one of my classmates whispered to me, 'You feel you are close to greatness, don't you?' He was right.

A seminar was held with Lionel Edie, who had founded his own successful business firm. One or two of the Harvard professors, including Taussig, roasted him a little in the field of economic theory, which, they thought, would be his weakest point. But Young disdained such ungentlemanly conduct. He commended Edie for his work, on broader grounds, with charity and appreciation. He was indeed a gentleman and a scholar.

From Overton H. Taylor
  Nashville
  Tennessee
  October 15, 1973

Dear Professor Blitch,

A good book about Allyn Young's life and economic thought would be wonderful. But I can't help doubting the possibility of learning much – even enough to be worth-while – about his economic thought. He wrote *so* little – as you are finding out. I think that each time, as soon as he had satisfied himself with his study of one subject, he at once shifted his attention to another, different subject, without pausing to write anything about the first one. The only writings of his that I know of at all are contained in his slender little book, 'Economic Problems New and Old'. What else you may have found in the Harvard Archives I have no idea. I think the best thing for your purpose in the 'Econ. Problems' book must be his review of 'The Trend of Economics' by R.G. Tugwell and others – the joint manifesto so to speak of a large number and variety of dissatisfied economists writing in the 1920s. It might help you to study, together, much of that book – the included essays dwelt upon in Young's review – *and* his review. The flavor of Young's own thought comes through pretty well, in his comments on those diverse essays.

Young did give much orally to us who were students in his Harvard classes; but as one of them I cannot now, after all this time, recall enough of what he taught us, to help you much; but I'll gladly do what I can here. His lectures were always lucid, penetrating, brilliant, but a bit unsystematic, being punctuated with many questions to and from the class. He had a wonderful trick of taking a student's often 'dumb' question to him in class, re-stating it with a twist which turned it into a brilliant question, and then answering *that*, to the great benefit of all of us. We all admired him enormously – he was our intellectual hero – yet as I've said I now remember, of the substance of all he said to us, very little.

I 'took' his two graduate courses in widely different fields – the one on Money and Banking, I think in the academic year 1924–25, and the other on 'Modern Schools of Economic Thought', I think the next year, 1925–26; though I'm not quite certain I have these years exactly right. In the M. & B. course, he explained the terrible German inflation of that period – heavily stressing, I remember, the immense rise of 'V' in the money-quantity as the Germans fled from depreciating money into goods and appreciating non-money assets. Our text-book in that course was R.G. Hawtrey's 'Currency and Credit', and Young made us understand Hawtrey's version of the Cambridge (Marshallian) 'cash balances' idea (Hawtrey's 'unspent margin') and its uses. He (Young) was critical, however, of Hawtrey's stress on the effects of high and low short-term interest-rates on 'traders' and thus on the level of economic activity. I'm pretty sure we also, in that course, studied the early Keynes 'Essay on Monetary Reform', and *its* use of the 'cash balances' or variable liquidity-preference concept. And we also studied, critically, the Foster and Catchings book – title I can't remember – attributing depressions to insufficient purchasing power in the hands of the people, and advocating 'pump-priming' through governmental public works expenditures as the remedy.

Young's <u>main</u> influence <u>on me</u>, however, was exerted through his other course, on 'Modern Schools of Economic Thought'. That began with a few brilliant introductory lectures on the Physiocrats and Adam Smith, which I will refer to again below; and went on to deal with the 'classical school' or Ricardo and his disciples, and J.S. Mill and others;

and Jevons, the Austrians, and other 'marginalists', and Marshall; and various socialist writers – tho' I don't think he did much with Marx; and the German historical schools; and the American Institutionalists – chiefly Veblen and Wesley Mitchell. Young in that course was in the main friendly to the main theory tradition, or classical and neo-classical analysis, and adversely critical of all of the 'insurgent schools' – but not extremely 'biased' in that way. He defended the classical tradition as having created 'some of the nineteenth century's distinguished intellectual achievements'. And he strongly rejected Wesley Mitchell's Veblenian view of the great influence of Bentham's psychological hedonism upon classical economic theory. As between those two things, he maintained, the relation or influence ran mainly in the other direction; <u>from</u> the older assumption that in business dealings men tried to maximize their economic gains, <u>to</u> Bentham's broader generalization that <u>all</u> human behavior tries to maximize the net gains of 'pleasure' or 'happiness' for those doing the 'behaving'. The more basic influence behind classical economic thought, Young believed, was British empiricism in philosophy; the basic premises of deductive economic theory were <u>not</u> *a priori* axioms, but inductive generalizations from experience and observation of economic activities themselves. – I recall nothing of whatever was said in the course about socialist economic thought[18] – not even what contributors to or examples of it were taken up. But I'm sure Young was no crusader either against or for socialism, nor a strongly partisan critic or defender of capitalism or private enterprise.

The part of the course dealing with the German historical schools was interesting, but I retain very little of definite matter from it. I think his main general conclusion about them was that although they produced some good and useful work in economic history they unfortunately failed to put history and theory together in the right way or relation to each other. (Nor did Young himself make clear, I fear, what that relation should be!)[19]

His treatment of the vague American 'institutional economics' movement was in the main adversely critical. Veblen and Mitchell got most of his attention in that area. He was personally fond of Mitchell and admired his empirical work, but thought M's admiration of Veblen an aberration of no great importance. And he thought there was no real institutional 'school', and the people who used the term as a banner contributed little, and went too far overboard in their wholesale rejections of main-tradition theory. But he laid much of the blame for <u>that</u> at the door of J.B. Clark who he thought made his own special variety of such theory too inviting a target.

The part, however, of that course of Young's which made the greatest impact <u>on me</u> was the very first part – those few introductory lectures on the Physiocrats and Adam Smith; yet I can't remember with any specificity what he said in them! I know they included some explanation of and commentary on the prevalent eighteenth century ideas about (natural-and-social-scientific) 'natural laws', and the ethical-and-juridical body of 'natural law' or ideal justice in human relations and institutions, men's 'natural rights', and the mainly harmonious 'natural order' existing in the universe and to be created in human societies by the right use of experience and reason in organizing, developing, and operating social institutions. Whatever it was Young said on that set of topics so aroused my interest that I went on to write my doctoral thesis precisely about it; and I'm sure that thesis owed very much of its substance and of whatever merit it had, to Young; but what in it was his contribution, and what was my own, derived from other sources, I don't know at all. My thesis as such was never published. But about two years after I completed it and got my doctorate, I re-worked most of it into the 'pair' of articles that I got published in the Q.J.E. (of Nov. 1929 and Feb. 1930 I believe) on 'Economics and the Idea of *Jus Naturale*'. (Those were much later reprinted – in 1955 by the Harvard Press – in the small volume of reprints of my various journal articles entitled 'Economics and Liberalism'.) – I wrote the thesis under Young's nominal supervision, but it was only that; I went to see him only a few times while working on it, and he did very little for me in connection with it. That was my fault. I was timid about taking up his time, and confident of my own ideas and abilities – as the doubly foolish young man I was. But I know he did read it all and thought well of it on the whole. In the summer of 1928, right after getting my doctorate, I went to England and some more of Europe with Ed Mason, and we called on Young at the London School to which he had just moved from Harvard, and Young spent an evening with Ed and me and Harold Laski whom he invited in for the evening to meet us (or have us meet Laski, rather!). And I recall my young pride when Young praised my thesis to Laski, especially its part on the natural law, etc philosophy of the Physiocrats, and commended that to Laski as something that he, Laski, might well learn a good deal from! (Laski had published writings on the history of 18th and 19th century 'liberal' thought, interpreting it all in a very different way, and I think Young meant that from my study Laski might get another point of view that would usefully modify his own[20]).

Well! This letter is too long and still contains too little that is likely to be useful to you. I'm tempted to suggest that you read my 'natural law' articles, and the first five chapters of my 'A History of Economic Thought' (McGraw-Hill 1960), as work by a disciple of Young's thought. But apart from the immodesty I know that, as I say, there is no distinguishing in my stuff what comes from Young from what does not ...

From Gilbert Walker
    University of Birmingham
    England
    7th February, 1973

My dear Professor Blitch,

Clark and I came down from Oxford in 1928. I had read Modern Greats: he had read in Chemistry; and been turned into an economist by his interest in the statistics of unemployment, by active attendance at Professor D.H. McGregor's 'informal instructions' (in Oxford at that time, a professorial seminar) and by participation each Monday evening during term in the proceedings described by Margaret Cole in her biography of her husband, of the 'Cole Group'. We made our way after graduation, both of us, to the London School of Economics: he to a research assistantship in Economics; and both of us to continue at the L.S.E., the education in economics begun at Oxford.

I certainly, and I think Clark also, attended Allyn Young's seminar for graduate students. No notes have survived – if indeed I took any. Nothing I am afraid remains now of the part taken by Allyn Young in those seminars but the sketchiest and least relevant detail – of Allyn Young himself, heaving around in his big comfortable chair, emitting as I recall, faint but distinctly ambiguous noises!

You mention Allyn Young's paper on 'Increasing Return'. Now this I do remember and for this very good reason. After two years on an Oxford graduate Scholarship, swanning around L.S.E., Hamburg, Berlin and back to Oxford, I responded to an advertisement put out by Trinity College Dublin, inviting applications for appointment as Lecturer in Economics. Applicants sat six papers and attended in Dublin for via voce examination. This was concluded with a lecture, delivered by the candidate rigged out in full fig and 'sub fusc' (at that date by T.C.D. taken seriously indeed – tail coat, boiled shirt, white waistcoat and white tie; and all at 11 a.m. of a fine June morning in 1930.)

The lecture was delivered before Examiners and a gala audience of Dublin society gathered in the College Hall. Among the topics offered as choices was 'Increasing Returns'. Fortified by those seminars with Allyn Young at L.S.E., this I chose in preference to alternative, more conventional (?) topics selected by my competitors.

Developing the argument, I lost my way and would have collapsed in confusion I imagine, had I not glanced over my lectern and observed among the Examiners, A.L. Bowley seated right below me, doodling on a pad. He was in fact illustrating as I went along, and for his own amusement, the model of increasing return developed by Allyn Young in that paper you mention and in those lectures at L.S.E. which earlier, Clark and I had been attending!

I was saved. I did not, I have to admit, win the appointment. That went to George Alexander Duncan. Not being appointed, to those scholarly (and literate) Irish minds, I was *dis*appointed. Later at lunch, seated between Bowley and a really lovely Irish girl, I was complimented by the former both on the topic I had chosen for my lecture – judged by contemporaries at that time as among the less tractable issues in economic theory – and upon the assurance with which I had expounded Allyn Young's theorem!

Forever since, I have been entitled to describe myself as Meritorious Disappointed Candidate of Trinity College Dublin. The distinction is unusual, as I am sure you will agree. It is owed, I believe, to Allyn Young – and to the fortune which lead [sic] me from Oxford to that seminar he conducted at L.S.E. during session 1928/29.

Concluding remarks

The above testimonies to Young's style and influence as a teacher give a rounded picture of the breadth of his learning, his capacity to convey a sense of the evolution of ideas and their practical utility in the affairs and well-being of the world; and so to inspire his students to carry the torch forward. A further extract from Sir William Beveridge's memorial address makes a fitting conclusion:

> Allyn Abbott Young from earliest manhood found one call after another pressed on him for help. As to the kind of work that he would do, he never really wavered; the life of thought and teaching and help to the coming generations was his by deepest nature. The University of Wisconsin, fine home of free traditions, made him an economist. Three great universities in his own land he then served in turn – Stanford, Cornell, Harvard. Before he went to the last of these he had been called on for public work of first importance, in the Great War and after. At the end of seven years at Harvard he held a position of enormous influence; the economic faculties of America were filled with men who had learned to venerate him as students; his fellow economists in all the world looked on him as a leader. When in London two or three years ago the time came to find a successor to Edwin Cannan, and fill the gap left by withdrawal of an influence and inspiration of thirty years, our thoughts went easily to Allyn Young. When we knew that he, who had the choice of universities in his own land, who already held the best that it could offer, was ready to come to us, that he thought it an honour to be asked, we felt that a turning point had been reached in our own history, a milestone of progress and recognition passed.

Appendix

Oskar Morgenstern wrote an obituary notice in German for the *Zeitschrift für Nationalökonomie*, Vienna, 1(1), May 1929, where his review of Young's *Economic Problems New and Old* (1927) also appears. This obituary is to be found in the Oskar Morgenstern papers in the Special Collections Library at Duke University. I am indebted to Susan Sirc of Glasgow University for preparing the following English translation for this volume.

Allyn Abbott Young †
by
Oskar Morgenstern, Vienna

The news of Allyn Young's death on 7th March 1927 comes as a painful shock. At the age of 52, at the peak of his career and in the process of putting great plans into practice, he was struck down by pneumonia.

Allyn Abbott Young came from an old New England family, but was born and raised in the Mid-West of the U.S.A. in Wisconsin. Yet neither his external appearance not his inner approach revealed provincial narrowness; on the contrary, he was a man of the world with panache. He began as a musician, an organist and as such was offered a post at an important church in England which he turned down. At that point he presumably had no intimation that he would later accept a second offer of a job, this time as Edwin Cannan's successor at London University. He gave up his musical profession, being more engaged with social problems and took up an academic career, becoming a Professor at Leland Stanford, at Cornell and Harvard. In 1927 he went to London and appreciated the honour of being given a chair in London as a foreigner. America tried to recall him. Chicago, which wanted to create an impressive field of influence for him, had the best chance. He was also asked to do a lot for his government and for individual state authorities. 1918–1919 he was head of the Economics Division of the American Peace Delegation, and later he presided over the American Commission for the preparation of the World Economic Conference. Since he took part in this and other ways, in the great international economic questions, his academic approach also acquired a basic breadth and humanity as its main characteristic feature. There were social successes as well; he became President of the American Economic Association, the American Statistical Association, and in England he was given the especially rare and covetable honour for a foreigner of becoming President of the celebrated Section F of the British Association.

I can think of no other scholar whose academic achievements and significance would prove so difficult to outline in a few strokes. For in his case personality and work were unusually closely connected. Reading the entirety of his publications shows one only a fraction of his achievement. He found it difficult to decide to publish anything, being extremely modest and self-critical in a manner which made him say something important in a casual aside; but he greatly inspired his pupils and patiently and constantly made himself available to them. Many of the best of those who have today made a name for themselves beyond America went through his hands and acknowledge the most lasting encouragement they received from him. One of the best recollections of him are the numerous evening discussions he had at his home at Harvard from January 1927 until deep into the summer at which everybody young in body and spirit who was working on economic theory at Harvard was present.

Allyn Young had a marked gift for theoretical research. He was a sovereign mathematician, hence also statistician, acquainted with the latest methods of this discipline which gained a number of brilliant analyses from him. He absorbed a lot from Alfred Marshall but seems to have valued Edgeworth even more highly. The task of reconciling the Austrian School with that of Lausanne seemed to him to be a task which time only made all the more urgent. And doubtless he was right. He disliked the way in which theory was often handled in Germany and he constantly singled out the Austrians, since he saw in their achievements the only contribution from the German-speaking countries which was able to secure international recognition and even take the lead. For this reason he was closely interested in the latest direction taken by economic theory in Vienna.

He was stopped short by death while engaged in the execution of important projects. One of these was a large work on the theory of money which was already at a very advanced stage. He had developed his thoughts over the years in his Harvard lectures and his theory, which would certainly have represented a milestone, has become part of the oral tradition at Harvard in the same way as Marshall's monetary theory at Cambridge according to Keynes. Only those who are aware of this and who recognized the move toward a new synthetic conception of pure theory which would have been expounded in a large book will be able to assess the true extent of the loss which we mourn here. A man like Young, who had new ideas and in addition the synthesizing skill to take into account various schools from different nations and languages is a rare phenomenon considering the present state of our discipline. His death just before concluding and formulating the final version of his book will perhaps have made it impossible for economic theory to take a step forward at the right time for it possibly to introduce a new phase.

Those who not only remain in his debt academically but were also close to him personally, mourn in Allyn Young one of the most valuable and noble human beings.

Notes

1. This chapter is a revised version of a paper of the same title published in *Journal of Economic Studies*, 26(6): 453–79, together with a new appendix, an obituary notice for Allyn Young by Oskar Morgenstern. We are indebted to Emerald Group Publishing for kind permission to reproduce the original material.

2. Chapters 33–8 of Mehrling and Sandilands (1999) are Young's chapters on money and banking for the Grolier encyclopaedia, and may be part of a draft of the treatise that Gregory alluded to.

3. The reference is to Laidler (1993) on the alleged links between Young and the Chicago School of monetary thought. Later, 7 April 1999, Samuelson wrote that 'My words about Knight and Chamberlin were to correct an impression that each of these were mere dummies who spoke with the voice of the master ventriloquist. Young himself spoke *against* such exaggerated rumors – which was not to deny that he did them lots of good.'

4. One may also note Schumpeter's judgment that 'in his concise and unassuming analysis of national bank statistics, there is enshrined the better part of a whole theory of money and credit' (Schumpeter, 1954, p. 876). Schumpeter lamented that 'this great economist and brilliant theorist is in danger of being forgotten.' He remarked that 'one of the reasons why his name lives only in the memory of those who knew him personally was a habit of hiding rather than of emphasizing his own points.'

5. Reproduced with the kind permission of Elizabeth Currie.

6. Among Young's other PhD students (at Cornell and Harvard) were Holbrook Working, A.P. Usher, G.P. Watkins, M.M. Bober, Arthur Marget, Myron W. Watkins, and Gardiner C. Means. Young also initiated the PhD work of W. Edwards Beach (see Beach, 1935, pp. vii–viii). When Young left Harvard the supervision passed to John H. Williams (as also in Lauchlin Currie's case).

7. George Jones arrived at Harvard as a Laura Spelman Rockefeller Fellow in September 1926 from Cambridge, England 'to make a study of the variations in costs and in profits among different industries.' Letter from Lawrence Frank to Allyn Young, 17 September 1928 (Charles Blitch's files).

8. Mason (1982) has an account of the Harvard economics department in the 1920s.

9. See Melvin de Chazeau's letter below.

10. This, however, was the topic that H.D. White (1933) was to choose for his well-known dissertation under Taussig.

11. See Colin Clark's letter above.

12. Young (1926) wrote an introduction to this book.

13. See Blitch (1995, p.102) for an explanation of Young's position as expressed at a conference in Williamstown in 1924. Young rejected both Keynes and Cassel in favor of Hawtrey's explanation of the monetary situation, in his *Monetary Reconstruction*. Young attributed inflation to speculation by the German people against the mark. The resulting depreciation adversely affected the government budget, forcing the government to print money, resulting in a cumulative upward spiral of prices. (See also letter from Overton H Taylor below.)

14. There is no longer any trace of Young's books or papers at the LSE.

15. Knight (1926) and Knight et al. (1928). Young wrote introductions to both of these volumes.

16. December 1928.

17. Ohlin (1970).

18. Young's lectures on socialism at Washington University, St Louis, 1912, are reprinted in Mehrling and Sandilands (1999, chapter 7).

19. Young's view of the German historical school is expounded in a survey, 'Economics', for the *Encyclopaedia Britannica* in 1929 (reprinted in Mehrling and Sandilands, 1999, chapter 11).
20. Laski (1925).

References

Angell, James W., 1933, 'Money, Prices and Production: Some Fundamental Concepts,' *Quarterly Journal of Economics*, November: 39–76.
Barber, William J., 1996, *Designs within Disorder: Franklin D. Roosevelt, the Economists, and the Shaping of American Economic Policy, 1933–1945*, Cambridge: Cambridge University Press.
Beach, W. Edwards, 1935, *British International Gold Movements and Banking Policy, 1881–1913*, Harvard Economic Studies No. 48, Cambridge, MA: Harvard University Press. Reprinted by Greenwood Press, Westport, Connecticut, 1972.
Beveridge, Sir William, 1929 [1990], 'Allyn Abbott Young: Memorial Address, 11 March 1929,' *Economica* (April): 1–3; reprinted in *Journal of Economic Studies*, 17(3/4): 16–17.
Blitch, Charles P., 1983, 'Allyn A. Young: a Curious Case of Professional Neglect,' *History of Political Economy*, 15: 12–17.
———, 1995, *Allyn Young: the Peripatetic Economist*, London and Basingstoke: Macmillan.
Carlson, Valdemar, 1968, 'The Education of an Economist before the Great Depression: Harvard's Economics Department in the 1920s,' *American Journal of Economics and Sociology*, 27: 101–12.
Chamberlin, Edward H., 1933, *The Theory of Monopolistic Competition: a Re-orientation of the Theory of Value*, Cambridge, MA: Harvard University Press.
Chandra, Ramesh and Roger J. Sandilands, 2005, 'Does Modern Endogenous Growth Theory Adequately Represent Allyn Young?' *Cambridge Journal of Economics*, 29(3) (May): 463–73.
Currie, Lauchlin, 1931, 'Bank Assets and Banking Theory,' PhD dissertation, Harvard University.
———, 1933, 'Money, Gold and Incomes in the United States,' *Quarterly Journal of Economics*, November: 77–95.
———, 1934a, *The Supply and Control of Money in the United States*, Cambridge, MA: Harvard University Press.
———, 1934b, 'A Note on Income Velocities,' *Quarterly Journal of Economics*, February: 353–4.
———, 1981, 'Allyn Young and the Development of Growth Theory,' *Journal of Economic Studies*, 8(1): 52–60.
———, 1990, 'Recollections of Allyn Young,' *Journal of Economic Studies*, 17(3/4): 10–13.
———, 1997, 'Implications of an Endogenous Theory of Growth in Allyn Young's Macroeconomic Concept of Increasing Returns,' *History of Political Economy* 29(3) (Fall): 413–43.
Dulles, Eleanor, 1929, *The French Franc*, New York: Macmillan.
Ely, R.T., T.A. Adams, M.O. Lorenz and A.A. Young, 1923, *Outlines of Economics*, 3rd edn, New York: Macmillan.

Gregory, T.E., 1929, 'Professor Allyn A. Young,' *Economic Journal*, 39 (June): 297–301.

Kaldor, Nicholas, 1972, 'The Irrelevance of Equilibrium Economics,' *Economic Journal*, 82: 1237–55.

——, 1985, *Economics without Equilibrium*, Cardiff: University College of Cardiff Press.

Knight, Melvin M., 1926, *Economic History of Europe, to the End of the Middle Ages*, Boston: Houghton Mifflin.

Knight, Melvin M., H.E. Barnes and F. Fluegel, 1928, *Economic History of Europe, in Modern Times*, Boston: Houghton Mifflin.

Laidler, David, 1993, 'Hawtrey, Harvard, and the Origins of the Chicago Tradition,' *Journal of Political Economy*, 101(6) (December): 1068–103.

——, 1998, 'More on Hawtrey, Harvard and Chicago,' *Journal of Economic Studies* 25(1): 4–24.

Laski, Harold, 1925, *Political Thought in England from Locke to Bentham*, London: Williams and Norgate.

Mason, Edward S., 1982, 'The Harvard Department of Economics from the Beginning to World War II,' *Quarterly Journal of Economics*, 97 (August): 425–8.

Mehrling, Perry G., 1997, *The Money Interest and the Public Interest: American Monetary Thought, 1920–70*, Harvard Economic Studies, No. 161, Cambridge, MA and London: Harvard University Press.

—— and Roger J. Sandilands (eds), 1999, *Money and Growth: Selected Papers of Allyn Abbott Young*, London and New York: Routledge.

Mitchell, Wesley, 1929, 'Allyn Abbott Young,' *Journal of the American Statistical Association*, N.S. 24 (June): 200–1.

Morgenstern, Oskar, 1929, 'Allyn Abbott Young,' *Zeitschrift für Nationalökonomie*, 1 (May): 143–5 (translated by Susan Sirc). See also A Schotter (ed.), 1976, *Selected Economic Writings of Oskar Morgenstern*, New York: New York University Press, pp. 487–8.

Ohlin, Bertil, 1970, 'Model Construction in International Trade Theory,' in W.A. Eltis, M.F.G. Scott and J.N. Wolfe (eds), *Induction, Growth and Trade: Essays in Honour of Sir Roy Harrod*, Oxford: Clarendon Press, pp. 325–33.

Robbins, L., 1971, *Autobiography of an Economist*, London: Macmillan.

Romer, Paul M., 1989, 'Capital Accumulation in the Theory of Long-run Growth,' in Robert J. Barro (ed.), *Modern Business Cycle Theory*, Cambridge, MA, and London: Harvard University Press.

Sandilands, Roger J., 1990a, *The Life and Political Economy of Lauchlin Currie: New Dealer, Presidential Adviser, and Development Economist*, Durham, NC, and London: Duke University Press.

—— (ed.), 1990b, 'Nicholas Kaldor's notes on Allyn Young's LSE Lectures, 1927–29,' *Journal of Economic Studies*, 17(3/4): 18–114.

Schumpeter, J.A., 1937, 'Allyn Abbott Young,' in Edwin R.A. Seligman and Alvin Johnson (eds), *Encyclopaedia of the Social Sciences*, XV, New York: Macmillan, 514–15.

——, 1954, *History of Economic Analysis*, Oxford: Oxford University Press.

Taussig, Frank W., Charles J. Bullock and Harold H. Burbank, 1929, 'Minute on the Life and Service of Allyn Abbott Young,' *American Economic Review*, June: 346–8.

Tavlas, G., 1998, 'More on the Chicago Tradition,' *Journal of Economic Studies*, 25(1):17–21.

Thirlwall, A.P., 2002, *The Nature of Economic Growth*, Cheltenham, UK and Northampton, MA, USA: Edward Elgar.

White, Harry D., 1933, *The French International Accounts, 1880–1913*, Cambridge, MA: Harvard University Press.

Young, Allyn A., 1926, 'Introduction,' in Jean Steels, *La Banque à Succursales dans le Système Bancaire des États Unis*, Ghent: A. Buyens, pp. vii–xx. Reprinted in Mehrling and Sandilands (1990, chapter 40).

——, 1928a, 'English Political Economy,' *Economica*, 8(22) (March): 1–15. Reprinted in Mehrling and Sandilands (1999, chapter 2).

——, 1928b, 'Increasing Returns and Economic Progress,' *Economic Journal*, 38(152) (December): 527–42. Reprinted in Mehrling and Sandilands (1999, chapter 5).

8
A Scholar in Action in Interwar America: John H. Williams on Trade Theory and Bretton Woods

Pier Francesco Asso and Luca Fiorito

8.1 Introduction

Interwar economic events were a powerful source of inspiration for those economists who studied the relation between theory and current problems with a view to prescribing original solutions for policy authorities. If we examine the presidential addresses at the annual meetings of the American Economic Association (AEA), we see that the difficulty in reconciling past economic doctrines with the events which were profoundly disturbing the working of the economic system was frequently deplored. Many scholars denounced the inherited corpus of economic theories as inadequate and misleading. Others asked whether the causes of economic maladjustments could exclusively be grouped in the short term of cyclical fluctuations which characterized the transition between equilibrium positions. Still others, more pragmatically, believed that there were major imperfections in economic policies and the institutional framework which needed to be profoundly rethought and redesigned.[1]

In the US, this challenge to orthodoxy was cultivated by at least two distinct groups of professional economists. The first brought together those who throughout their education and formative studies had shown a strong preference for the study of international economic problems. From this perspective, the First World War, together with the new international role of the United States in the management of world economic and financial affairs, had provoked a blossoming of research activities in the fields of international monetary reform, trade regimes and stabilization policies. These were subjects that – with few exceptions – had traditionally been neglected by the most authoritative economists since the foundation of the AEA. On the other hand, a powerful movement towards the elaboration of new ideas, techniques and policy proposals came from those scholars who, at some juncture of their academic career, had the opportunity to serve within the public administration. The war had greatly increased the demand for economists as government consultants and policy advisers. Their successful performance as members of public boards, think-tanks and research institutes had paved the way for more systematic exchanges and marked the beginning of a new era that was characterized by a proliferation of economists 'in the public service' as Fisher (1919) put it. Brilliant professional accomplishments were also achieved because the group was led by some of the most eminent authorities in the fields of money, trade and economic analysis: Irving Fisher, Frank Taussig, and Wesley Clair Mitchell were among those who most vigorously encouraged younger colleagues to follow their lead as economists in the public service.[2]

After the 1929 crash, this new breed of 'international scholars in action' made important contributions to the growth of economics, favoring the opening of new fields of enquiry and the establishment of new research methods. As more recent interpreters have argued, the creation of new professional opportunities in the fields of international economics and economic policy advice contributed significantly to the triumph of pluralism in US economics (Morgan and Rutherford, 1998; Rutherford, 1998; Bernstein, 2001).

In this group, together with Edwin Kemmerer, Henry Parker Willis, Jacob Viner, and a few others, was John H. Williams. He was undoubtedly one of the most prominent international political economists of the interwar years, with a profound knowledge of classical economics together with a strong preference for applied studies and the inductive verification of inherited theoretical models. Williams was also a renowned authority on monetary reform and international finance, combining theoretical expertise with a strong bent for the practicalities of the everyday world. It was in the fields of international trade and finance that as a young economist he began to act as adviser to policy authorities.

John Henry Williams was a man of two careers.[3] He studied at Harvard where, in 1919, he completed a PhD under the direction of Frank Taussig. His dissertation on the Argentine balance of payments (Williams, 1920a) was published by Harvard University Press and provided one of the first critical accounts of the classical approach to external adjustment. Until 1925, Williams held temporary teaching positions at Brown, Princeton and Northwestern Universities, before he returned to Harvard as associate professor of economics. He gained a full professorship in 1929 and, in 1947, was appointed as the first dean of the Harvard Business School. As an economist in the public service, Williams's career started in 1918 as assistant in chief at the Department of Commerce. After a brief period as research economist at the American Bankers Association (ABA), on 1 May 1933, Williams joined the Federal Reserve Bank of New York as an expert in international monetary affairs. While retaining his professorship at Harvard, he became an assistant Federal Reserve agent.[4] Three years later he acquired a senior administrative position as vice-president and research director. At the New York Fed, Williams wrote a vast number of proposals for the reform of the domestic and international monetary system and fought hard to modernize the art of central banking after the poor performance exhibited by the federal monetary authorities during the depression. His professional life continued up to the 1950s, when he held advisory positions in the US post-war commission on foreign economic policy and in the Economic Corporation Administration in Paris.

Several authors have already recognized Williams's originality as an international economist who made innovative contributions to economic thought and policy (Clarke, 1977 and 1987; Cohen, 1998; De Cecco, 1976; Fishlow, 1989; Gardner, 1980; Flanders, 1989; Ikenberry, 1992; Rowland, 1976).[5] Williams is well known for his early studies on the structure of the US balance of payments,[6] for his critical interpretation of the classical theory of international trade (Williams, 1920a and 1929), and for his unconventional analysis of the international gold standard (Williams 1932a, 1932b, 1934). The intense research activity which Williams conducted in these areas gave him a focus on the importance of macro-structures, economic history and empirical verification which he never lost, and deeply influenced his activities as a public servant and monetary reformer.

As an economist in the public service, Williams started as an assistant to Herbert Hoover at the Department of Commerce. There he was commissioned to prepare reliable statistics on the US balance of payments, with particular responsibility for capital transactions and the 'invisible' items. As William Barber (1985, p. 206 n. 83) has observed, 'in the history of the statistical work of the Federal government, this was a signal event. It marked the first occasion on which government itself generated the primary data, as opposed to relying on private organizations to supply them.' At the New York Fed, Williams began to get deeply involved in the study of monetary affairs, an area that soon fascinated him and was to remain a major interest throughout his life. According to his own private records,[7] between May 1933 and May 1954, Williams produced almost 200 pieces – mainly memoranda to the governors, bank committees or other parties but also reports, legislative proposals, and statistical enquiries. The subjects of Williams's activities ranged widely from monetary and exchange rate policy to domestic and central banking. Some historians have studied Williams's monetary theory and his activities at the New York Fed: 'in the contributions of Williams more than anyone else,' David Laidler (2003 [1993]) has found evidence in support of the pervasiveness of an early 1930s' Chicago tradition in monetary economics.[8] In his recent biography of the Federal Reserve, Allan Meltzer has confirmed that Williams contributed to shaping Federal Reserve monetary policy: he had 'considerable influence on policy throughout [his] long career at the Federal Reserve and was an ardent proponent of international coordination' (Meltzer, 2003, p. 436 n. 42).[9]

It is also well known that the most relevant portion of Williams's activities at the Federal Reserve dealt with the elaboration of plans for international monetary stabilization. In particular, Williams's writings have been considered as originating the so-called 'key currency approach' to the reform of the international monetary system. Peculiar to the key currency approach is the assumption that the world is hierarchically divided into countries, regions, and currencies which are characterized by unequal economic size and importance (Cohen, 1998). On the other hand, established doctrines – such as the Ricardian theory of comparative advantages or Hume's price–specie–flow mechanism and, above all, the conventional interpretation of the classical gold standard – were based on the flawed principle of homogeneous countries and perfectly symmetrical markets which found no correspondence in the real world. On these grounds, Williams thought that the preliminary condition for restoring stability and optimality in the post-war monetary system was to redesign the responsibility of key countries and set new rules for their currencies. The idea of key currency was also influential on the development of plans for monetary reforms based on a restricted number of countries or on a variable speed of participation. Among others, Robert Mundell (1961, 1997) has acknowledged the importance of Williams's writings in a paper devoted to the reconstruction of his theory on optimum currency areas.

By the mid-1930s the key currency approach had been brought onto the diplomatic agenda (Williams, 1937). In close cooperation with the Taussig group of international economists, who had by that time joined the Roosevelt administration (most particularly, Jacob Viner and Harry Dexter White), Williams strongly advised Treasury Secretary Henry Morgenthau to start informal discussions with France and Great Britain to re-establish some form of cooperation and stable relations in the management of exchange rates. Following these conversations, in 1936 the three countries signed a Tripartite Agreement which operated as a daily fixed exchange rate system between their respective currencies.[10]

Subsequent developments of the key currency idea led Williams to become the most authoritative voice opposing the two official plans that formed the intellectual backbone of the Bretton Woods agreements. Williams wrote an influential 'third' plan that appeared in spring 1943, at about the same time that the White and Keynes plans were published and became the object of official negotiation. In a series of articles published in professional journals and in *Foreign Affairs*, in his activities at the New York Fed as well as in Congressional hearings, Williams raised a number of critical concerns in opposition to the proposal for the establishment of new international monetary institutions.[11] His views received a wide audience and elicited comments and replies from several economists in government. His opposition created serious conflicts within the administration and between the US Treasury and the Federal Reserve.

Williams's plan was known as the 'key currency plan.' From the outset, the main target of Williams's campaign was White's scheme for an international stabilization fund. Williams was particularly concerned about its technical functions and about the likely consequences of its failure on the post-war economic and political order. He believed that the new spirit of universal multilateralism had to be supported by the stabilizing role of hegemonic powers. Rather than an outright alternative to White's scheme, his approach was conceived as a preliminary, more realistic step before post-war reconstruction was completed and the prospects for multilateral convertibility were put on more solid foundations. In the meantime, the key currency plan was meant as a challenge to the strong and hegemonic countries to recognize and to assume their responsibilities before the effective launching of new world organizations.

While some scholars have argued that the Harvard boys under Frank Taussig in the 1930s were as influential as the Chicago boys under Milton Friedman in the 1970s (Liu, 2002), Williams's role in the discussions and negotiations of the post-war international monetary system has been unduly neglected. Many have dismissed it with the observation that, for different reasons, Williams's key currency plan soon ran up a blind alley. First, unlike the situation in the 1920s, at this period the Federal Reserve held only an insignificant role in international monetary affairs and diplomatic negotiations. After the depression, the wave of bank failures and the 1935 banking reform, central bankers in the US had lost most of their powers in monetary policy while responsibility in international negotiations rested firmly in the Treasury's hands.[12] Second, Williams himself was initially involved in the discussions of the Economic and Financial Group at the Council for Foreign Relations which provided much of the intellectual background to White's plan. Headed by Jacob Viner and Alvin Hansen, Williams was soon obliged to drop out of the council because of his firm advocacy of an alternative plan.[13] Third, most delegations at Bretton Woods never seriously considered Williams's counter-proposals as part of the diplomatic agenda which eventually elaborated the final Articles of Agreement.[14]

However, as we shall see in this chapter, drawing extensively on archival material, Williams actively participated in the discussions and, to some extent, managed to influence the development of the drafts which finally evolved to the Joint Statement of Experts and to Bretton Woods. From its first publication, Williams's proposal had gained some support within influential financial and intellectual circles – particularly among New York bankers and the leaders of small and open economies. Perhaps as a result of these circumstances, in the most crucial stages of the negotiations, Williams had two long meetings with Keynes at the New York Fed. Detailed minutes of these meetings were kept by a Federal Reserve economist and by Williams himself and provide a full, sometimes vivid, account of the group of experts at work. Indeed, this episode has already been mentioned in the literature on the making of the Bretton Woods agreements, even though one of its most detailed accounts has downplayed its importance (Van Dormael, 1978). By contrast, our examination of the full minutes of these meetings – together with other archival materials – will lead us to argue that Williams's views managed to exert some 'conditionality' on the final articles of agreement ratified at Bretton Woods in 1944. We shall also show how Keynes himself agreed with many of Williams's critical arguments and how the 'key currency' idea can be considered a part of the architecture of the post-war international monetary system. Allan Meltzer (2003, p. 585) has recently reinforced our evaluation that 'as the system developed, Williams' proposal for an international system based on the dollar soon supplanted many of the features of the Keynes–White plan.' As Charles Kindleberger (1989, p. 51) wrote, Williams's plan was 'an example of an idea that had difficulty in catching hold but finally won out.'

In this chapter we first intend to investigate the analytical background of Williams's key currency approach to the reform of the international monetary system. Sections 8.2 and 8.3 present a succinct overview of Williams's main contributions to international trade theory and to the interwar debate on the reform of the international monetary system. Particular attention will be devoted to his early academic writings, which contained different critical arguments against the two main tenets of classical international economics: the Ricardian theory of comparative advantages and the gold standard. These criticisms formed the theoretical rationale of his key currency proposal. Then, in Section 8.4, we analyze the contents of Williams's proposal and reconstruct his main criticisms of the two official plans presented by John Maynard Keynes and Harry Dexter White. Section 8.5 is devoted to the examination of Keynes's and White's reactions and to the elucidation of which aspects of Williams's ideas managed to influence the shaping of the agreements. Section 8.6 presents some conclusions.

8.2   Williams's criticism of classical trade theory

According to Williams, since the first industrial revolution, international trade and integration had played a crucial role in determining the rate of economic growth and technological change, as well as the cyclical downturns and the spreading of depressions.

As were many other thoughtful international economists who had worked under Frank Taussig's supervision,[15] Williams was motivated by the presumption that the pattern of comparative advantages did not tell the whole story in international specialization and the evolution of the patterns of trade. He believed that only under very specific conditions did terms of trade variations and nominal price changes represent the most important variables in the adjustment process to external shocks. Starting from these premises, Williams's critical appraisal of the classical theory of international trade was based on four issues which were meant to undermine both its methodological foundations and the peculiar nature of its essential assumptions.

8.2.1   On method

Having acquired a highly critical attitude toward Ricardian economics from his reading of Walter Bagehot and Thomas Cliffe Leslie, Williams disputed the pretension of universality which characterized classical economic laws from his earliest writings.[16] As a methodological device for theoretical exposition, Williams was convinced that the classical approach retained some usefulness and validity, even though it had severe limitations if applied to such post-war problems as German reparations or currency instability (Williams, 1920b). Perhaps it was also the proximity of Schumpeter at Harvard and his personal friendship with Jacob Viner that led Williams to extend the dangers of a Ricardian vice to the mainstream tradition of international economics. In fact, as many contemporary inductive verifications confirmed, the classical theory of international trade was based on very restrictive assumptions, which ruled out the really dynamic forces at work. In Williams's view 'the classical theory assumes as fixed, for purposes of the reasoning, the very things which in my view should be the chief objects of study if what we wish to know is the effects and causes of international trade' (Williams, 1929, p. 24).[17]

Historically, Williams believed that the international transfer of productive factors – mainly capital, labor and entrepreneurship – had played a paramount role in the long-run changes of the industrialized world which the comparative static nature of classical trade theory did not fully take into account. Therefore, he suggested that particular attention ought to be directed to revealing the connections between foreign investments, short-term capital movements, commodity trade and income growth. Reliance on Ricardo's model had rendered these connections extremely weak even though they were the 'more significant part of the explanation of the present status of nations, as to incomes, prices, well being, than is the cross-section value analysis of the classical economists, with its assumption of given quantities of productive factors, already existent and employed' (Williams, 1949 [1929], p. 25). As an alternative, Williams suggested that international trade and capital movements should be studied 'from the point of view of history' and primarily 'from the point of view of their effect on the development of nations' (Williams, 1928; quoted by Dorfman, 1959, V, pp. 584–5).

From a methodological point of view, Williams (1929) observed that international trade issues raised the most intriguing questions about the optimal relation between theory and policy. If international economists had not been able to provide satisfactory responses to the economic consequences of the war and to the world depression, again much of the blame fell on abstract theorizing. Post-war events had not changed this attitude in any significant way: 'one of the greatest paradoxes of recent times is that, while since 1914 the world has been in a state of profound and virtually continuous disturbance, formal international trade theory has continued to emphasize equilibrating tendencies' (Williams, 1952a, p. 24). On these grounds, most modern refinements of the Ricardian model were also based on the mistaken tendency 'to run away from the actual problems by putting them under an expansible umbrella labelled "short run"' (ibid.)

8.2.2 Trade, growth, and economic geography

According to Williams, factor endowments and different cost ratios, as well as the distortions induced by protectionist commercial policies, provided only a partial explanation of the patterns of trade. Again he started from the premise that the world was composed of heterogeneous countries whose economic systems were characterized by markedly different stages of development. Countries of unequal size and divergent economic structures could be grouped as either center, 'key' countries or peripheral countries. Asymmetric patterns of adjustment were also a common feature in international economic relations: 'This is not a world with many countries mutually held in balance through compensatory internal adjustments ... [but] a world with one or two predominant key countries and with many peripheral countries which are all subject to profound changes also in their attitudes towards internal adjustment ... at least until some decisive steps are made toward common sovereignty' (Williams, 1951, pp. 40–1).

In many of his writings Williams (1953b, p. 10) interpreted 'the development of international trade as a process of expansion from a center' which profoundly affected the economic performance of its periphery. Thus, 'key countries' played a paramount role in the determination of international cycles and trends. Recent history, in fact, taught that periods of growth (as well as depressions) were generally originated in the core country while countries outside the center owed their development to the movement of factors as well as of capital goods from the center. Williams also argued that the establishment of a stable network of peripheral countries was often indispensable for the survival of the center, since it provided cheap labor and a steady demand for exports in the technologically most advanced sectors.

This stadial interpretation of economic development was refined with two closely connected considerations: first, the international monetary system – particularly whenever it was based on a common standard – was a powerful mechanism of propagation of shocks from key countries to their periphery; second, any theory of international trade which did not approach the subject matter in this way (dynamic interactions between core and periphery) had very serious limitations as a guide to policy. Here again, Williams strongly suggested that any international economist should feel the inadequacies of static equilibrium analysis. Economists were facing just another 'great paradox' of modern economic theory: 'though international trade has been peculiarly characterized by growth and change, economists have continued to discuss it theoretically in static terms' (Williams, 1953b, p. 9).

Williams (1929, p. 31) also drew attention to the fact that exploitation of comparative advantages could be limited by market imperfections and failures which classical economists did not fully take into account or – again – simply assumed away. In particular, peripheral countries suffered from 'inferior organization of capital and labor ... inferior domestic banking, inferior internal means of communication, inferior perception of economic opportunity.' More than their relative natural endowment of productive factors, such a relative domestic backwardness in capital markets was a further determinant of the international hierarchy among countries and of the way the patterns of world trade followed the patterns of the world 'key' investors. It was not by chance – Williams (1929) noted with great perceptiveness – that the performance of developing countries depended greatly on their capacity to build a cosmopolitan center within their region which had a strategic importance for the intermediation of foreign finance, and where the presence of large-scale foreign enterprises mainly in the extractive and transport industries was particularly high. Thus, capital transactions had a great impact in the performance of the domestic economy and for the determination of the structure of commodity trade.

Relative positions between core and peripheries were not intrinsically static: on the contrary recent events showed that there was much room for processes of cumulative change. Williams often observed (Williams, 1932a, p. 272) that 'the greatest single change which has occurred since 1914 has been in the comparative international position of the United States and England.' It basically depended on the real long-run factors which affected levels of productivity and on the political processes that historically influenced stages of integration or disintegration of a regional or multilateral nature. Again, in order fully to understand the nature of these changes specific attention had to be devoted to the effects of the relative movement of productive factors – primarily capital.

8.2.3 Mobility of factors

Williams thought that the most disturbing element of the Ricardian model was to be found in the international mobility of capital which the classical economists had generally assumed away for reasons of formal accuracy or for the prevailing 'home bias' sentiments.[18] Under Taussig's guidance, Williams (1920a, 1929) developed critical arguments against classical monetary theory, whose discussion of factor mobility was largely confined to problems connected with the balancing of international payments. In contrast, capital movements and the international environment had pride of place in Williams's explanation of economic growth and domestic stability. In his view, the real functioning of the pre-1914 gold standard relied to a significant extent on the stabilizing function of short-term capital movements. What was even more relevant was that the factor immobility assumption had to be rejected in order to understand not only recurrent episodes of panic and crisis in financial markets but also business cycles, market failures, and the efficacy of economic policy.

Williams shared the heterodox view that productive factors had traditionally moved more freely between – rather than within – nations (Williams, 1929, pp. 24ff.)[19] Countries at different stages of economic development had experimented with episodes of massive migration and capital movements which had important effects on their long-run economic performance. In his empirical studies, he also showed the existence of important interactions between the capital account and the current account; the former generally exerting the more powerful influence upon the latter by means of exchange rate and interest rates variations. On the whole, capital movements were an endogenous factor in the adjustment mechanism, a crucial element in exchange rate variations, a key determinant of the stability of macroeconomic aggregates. Their overall significance was greater than the one played by changes in the terms of trade and in comparative factor productivity.[20]

Capital and labor movements also represented the most important single factor that favored a shift in relative growth rates. Neglect of 'core-periphery' implications served to explain why most recent contributions to neoclassical trade theory failed to pass the test of reality. Massive migration of capital and labor did not bring about an intrinsic tendency towards income or price equalization on a world scale (Williams, 1929, p. 30). In his writings, Williams discussed at some length the circumstances under which foreign direct investments could stimulate a more rapid rate of advance of productivity in the lending country than in the borrowing country and thus create further disparities in the patterns of growth. The recent surge of US foreign direct investments in the 1920s, he wrote (Williams, 1951), had significantly contributed to the expansion of its domestic economy, setting in motion a virtuous circle: increasing returns, higher profit margins, and the establishment of a more efficient network of productive capacity which, in its turn, was the reason for new investments and a further cumulative rise of productivity.[21] Foreign investments by US enterprises were also interpreted as a sort of indirect insurance against domestic market failures. Among them, Williams considered the frequent incidence of phenomena of adverse selection which had affected the US credit market in the 1920s.

8.2.4 Criticism of equilibrium analysis

In his early studies on Argentina's balance of payments, Williams criticized the comparatively static approach which generally pervaded the theory of international trade. Both classical and modern models, in fact, were designed in terms of a partial equilibrium framework, placing different emphasis on the equilibrating forces at work. Rather ambitiously, Williams tried to establish connections between trade flows, foreign investments, output, employment, and the balance of payments. Again, his approach rested on empirical verification which showed the non-existence of alternative stages of equilibrium. In fact, international trade and finance were influenced by a series of overlapping changes – 'working some times in the same direction, some times at cross-purposes' (Williams, 1920b, p. 51) – which rendered equilibrium analysis rather meaningless. Particularly if countries adopted inconvertible monetary standards, 'this reasoning from artificially simplified stages of equilibrium through periods of transition to new stages of equilibrium' had little interpretative value. For Williams (1920b, p. 52) it remained 'a characteristic product of the Ricardian mode of thought.'

Therefore, in the interwar years, the distinction between short-term factors – whose operation created instability and maladjustments – and long-run forces – which inevitably worked on behalf of stable equilibrium – was deemed to be utterly misleading. On the other hand, transitions from one core to another – like the one that occurred between Great Britain and the United States after the First World War – produced a shift away from equilibrium and smooth adjustment, in part also because of structural changes. For example, the emergence of the US economy as the core trading nation had managed to produce a number of shocks which negatively affected international stability and confidence. Among them Williams (1952b, p. 176) emphasized the great size and strength of the US home market; its diversified resources and large exports surplus; its comparative self-sufficiency; and its more rapid pace of innovation and productivity growth. Using similar arguments to Albert Hirschman's (1945) analysis of the 'influence effects' applied to the Nazi economy, Williams argued that all these features generated a greater dependence of the rest of the world on the US economy, rather than the converse. They represented objective circumstances that explained deep-seated, long-term imbalances in international payments and led him to suggest the diagnosis of chronic 'dollar shortages'.

In retrospect, one could say that Williams's contributions to international trade theory and his criticism of standard economic theory

lacked formal accuracy and suffered from vagueness.[22] Nevertheless, they
contained many original seeds which grew to have a profound influence
on subsequent developments of trade theory and policy. For Williams,
what mattered was that they were also useful in evaluating the orthodox
interpretation of the real functioning of monetary systems and adjustment mechanisms – beginning with the international gold standard. This
was another crucial step toward the development of new principles for
the reform of the international monetary system and must be considered
in detail.

8.3   Williams's criticism of the gold standard and monetary policy

On several occasions, Williams disputed the conventional interpretation
of the gold standard as a monetary system which provided an automatic
mechanism for balance of payments adjustment and a neutral set of rules
for economic policy authorities. In his view there was nothing intrinsically automatic in the functioning of the gold standard. Williams's
criticism moved from the specific nature of the assumptions and his
interpretation echoed many arguments which we have already found in
his writings on international trade theory (Williams, 1932a, 1932b).

In what follows we have chosen to discuss three points that recur in
his writings. They concern the role of capital movements, their effects
on economic performance, and the efficacy of monetary policy.

8.3.1   Capital movements and the adjustment process

According to Williams (1944a, p. 173), the gold standard was a monetary system which operated on the basis of a core-periphery structure: its
stability depended on the existence of a common center 'with which
the other countries were connected through trade and finance.' The
smooth working of the pre-war international monetary system in its
heyday depended on the strategic and hegemonic role played by key
countries – particularly Britain – which helped to enforce policy discipline and international coordination. Williams was among the first
economists to suggest that up to 1914 the system was based on a sterling
standard rather than on gold and that the reasons why the system worked
so well were to be found in the specific roles that countries – both at the
core and at the periphery – agreed to undertake. Williams noted that
exchange rate stability depended on sterling acting as the 'key currency'
of the system. 'Key' in the sense that sterling was the vehicle of all international transactions on both the current and the capital account while

a growing demand for sterling-denominated assets financed Britain's structural external deficits. Consequently, the crisis of the system coincided with the relative decline of the British economy. In this respect, Williams (1953b) thought that the war had simply hastened a process of change which was already well under way.

This picture contrasted sharply with the traditional gold standard theory based, as it was, on the interaction between homogeneous countries of approximately equal economic size and structure (Williams, 1944a). The gold standard had the great merit of providing a clear and definite objective to monetary policy. However, Williams criticized as false and abstract the dilemma – which Keynes had emphasized in 1923 – between internal and external stability: modern economic systems were characterized by a growing interdependence between internal and external components of aggregate demand. For peripheral countries, economic growth greatly depended on the performance of leading economies. If the latter were unsuccessful, the former could not be maintained, regardless of policy attitudes or nominal flexibility in price or wage setting.

Williams agreed with many interpreters that the most serious defects of the gold standard as a mechanism of adjustment depended on the growing rigidity of internal prices and costs, which ultimately explained the phenomenon of gold mal-distribution. In the most advanced countries prices remained insensitive to gold movements, particularly downwards. The presence of rigidities also reduced the opportunity to confine monetary policy to the objective of exchange rate stability: 'in the view of many economists, we must find ways of lessening rigidities or find ourselves forced to give up the free price-quantity system of economic adjustment altogether' (Williams, 1937). Moreover, gold standard rules required pro-cyclical policies which most governments were quite unwilling to follow, particularly those who were forced to accept contraction and unemployment whenever gold flowed out.

However, apart from the reduced flexibility of contemporary economies, the second and most serious source of troubles 'for any international monetary system' was to be found in the mobility of productive factors – most specifically, capital. Study of Argentina had shown that capital inflows had a great impact on the gold premium, with unfavorable connections to exchange rate variations and the burden of the public debt service. The stability and the adjustment of the Argentine economy depended not only on domestic conditions or price flexibility but were also connected to the vagaries of the international cycle and to the abrupt decline of inward capital flows.[23]

Starting from these premises, Williams wrote many essays in which he discussed the perverse role of capital movements in the stability of any international monetary system and as a major cause of economic recessions and their international propagation (Williams, 1944a). In this context, Williams denounced contemporary economists for not having given proper consideration to the causes and effects of short-term capital movements. They had passively accepted the classical doctrine which assumed that capital movements held a balancing function in the adjustment process of external shocks. Most of the time, however, their behavior followed different rules of the game than were generally assumed by classical economic theory.

Again, factual knowledge and empirical research helped. Economists could discover that not only was capital an extremely mobile and fluctuating item of the balance of payments – indeed its most mobile and fluctuating element – but that it basically flowed in the opposite direction from the one assumed by Hume's mechanism. In fact, inductive verifications had shown that there was no offsetting tendency between domestic inflation and the export of capital: rising prices were often accompanied by further capital inflows, since net foreign investments were attracted by surging economic activity and favorable profit expectations. On the other hand, in times of sluggish business confidence and economic depression, economies generally experienced a flight from their currencies, which worsened the external account (Williams, 1932a, pp. 272ff.) Williams was also struck by how quickly and easily the current account adjusted to – and was dominated by – the capital account, rather than the other way round. Even if the terms of trade changed in the direction predicted by the classical theory, these changes were too small to have been responsible for the recorded shifts in the balance of trade.[24] Moreover, for some countries free access to the international capital market was a major cause of intergenerational problems and structural imbalances: in fact, it served to postpone fundamental readjustment of their economic system by offsetting long-term capital exports with short-term capital imports.

For all these reasons, it followed that the gold standard was not a reliable corrective mechanism of capital movements. For many countries, its rules of the game did not operate while the quantity theory of money had a rather limited validity. Other effects stimulated by aggregate expenditure and the transfer mechanism held primary responsibility for external adjustment. Since the early 1930s Williams had shared Keynes's belief that the addition of a borrowing authority to supplement the use of a central bank's reserves represented a major step forward for the implementation of international stabilization plans (Williams, 1931).

8.3.2   Capital movements and the propagation of cyclical instability

Williams also discussed at length the possibility that international capital movements could become the vehicle for worldwide booms and depressions. The network of financial connections between core and peripheral countries served to explain why the gold standard was a means for spreading 'depressions, and sometimes booms, from one country to another' (Williams, 1944a, p. 171). In times of crisis, the gold standard could become a mechanism for growing disequilibria and disturbances which extended to neighboring countries. Adherence to an exchange rate commitment and to schemes of international coordination inhibited monetary authorities from undertaking stabilization policies.

Consistent with his functional interpretation of the gold standard, Williams again found the main seeds of contagion in the growing interdependence between the external and the internal economy: a sudden cessation of capital movements and the burden of fixed interest charges produced depressive effects in the capital-importing countries which 'then may spread back through the channels of trade to the capital-exporting, interest-receiving countries' (Williams, 1932a, p. 273). Whenever the drain of foreign capital had reached abnormal levels, capital movements provoked the familiar sentiments that had fuelled the world depression and unemployment far beyond their cyclical swings: uncertainty, distrust and speculative excesses tended to produce cumulative one-way movements. While monetary policy had limited powers to offset them, it was no coincidence – so Williams wrote in 1932 – that most episodes of booms and depressions had international capital movements as one of their most prominent features (Williams, 1932a).

From what we have seen, it is not surprising that Williams remained a life-long advocate of exchange controls. In his view, abnormal capital movements from core to peripheral countries were the international counterpart of domestic runs on the banks and other forms of 'internal money panics' which had played such a large part in economic history. Being 'the most volatile item of the balance of payments' (Williams, 1937, p. 29), capital movements managed to dominate and even nullify alternative corrective policies which were designed to support macroeconomic stabilization. What was worse, it some-times occurred that they produced real policy dilemmas and reduced the efficacy of monetary policy. One possible explanation was that, in the presence of unfettered capital movements, expectations tended to become 'self-fulfilling.' Many historical episodes provided interest-ing evidence in this respect: raising the rate of discount to protect the internal economy against capital flight had often intensified deflation-ary pressures and had been taken as a symbol of fear that further flight would undermine the stability of the exchange rate, 'which has led to further flight.' Other situations may occur whereby 'a rise in the rate designed to curb internal expansion may attract short-time funds from abroad' (Williams, 1937, p. 29). Finally, the destabilizing nature of capital movements also depended on the weak connections between the finan-cial and the real sectors of the economy. Empirical research supported this conclusion, showing how frequent it was that the main purpose of international capital movements was not to create new productive capacity but to meet extraordinary expenses of an unproductive nature (Williams, 1932a).

In terms of policy, throughout the 1930s Williams advocated world economic cooperation as the best method to cope with contractions of output and employment. With the rise of rival financial centers after the end of the First World War, Williams believed that stability of interna-tional agreements and policy coordination depended on the negotiation of credible commitments. In a meeting with Keynes, Williams main-tained that the gold standard was just 'a short-hand phrase for exchange stability' which was achieved by monetary discipline imposed by a coun-try's sense of its obligations to other countries and by informal central bank cooperation.[25] Commitment credibility was an important requisite to increasing policy efficiency and counteracting downward cyclical vari-ations of the relevant macroeconomic magnitudes. Thus, the best way for monetary authorities to discourage destabilizing speculation and con-trol the volume of capital movements was through their 'demonstration of purpose and capacity' to maintain a system of fixed exchange rates by mutual exchange of information, by the practice of currency swaps, and by a declaration of unlimited support of each other's currencies in case of need.[26] Since 1935 Williams had advised Roosevelt to sign an agreement on exchange rate stability to be achieved by a daily gold set-tlement at fixed nominal rates of the three key international currencies. With respect to the other requirements of international cooperation, he remained well aware that the framework of the Tripartite Agreement was disappointing and weak.[27]

8.3.3 Monetary policy and the art of central banking

In the 1930s Williams made important contributions to the analysis of monetary policy and to the interpretation of the Great Depression. While at Harvard and at the New York Fed, he tried to understand the mechanisms of the transmission of monetary forces and the ways in which monetary authorities could increase their capacity to stabilize the economy, both domestic and international. His early criticism of the quantity theory of money did not prevent him from pointing out the danger that, in the 1930s, monetary theorists had swung too drastically from overemphasis to extreme underemphasis of the role of the money supply. He believed that monetary authorities could regain control over the economic system by strengthening their capacity to control the credit market and increasing their level of independence from the Treasury.

Williams's essays on monetary policy together with his reports on banking reform contained critical remarks on Federal Reserve policy before and during the depression. Williams espoused the thesis – which had been elaborated by his PhD student, Lauchlin Currie, by Jacob Viner and others – that the Federal Reserve System was responsible for precipitating the US economy in the Great Depression. In a report for Secretary Morgenthau, he saw serious policy errors in the banking crisis that in the first half of the 1930s brought the US credit system very close to collapse. Under different perspectives the Federal Reserve System was faulty. It basically lacked effective powers of banking supervision and had no capacity for safeguarding the solvency of banks.[28]

Williams put forward some interesting arguments to substantiate the widespread skepticism towards monetary policy and its capacity to maintain macroeconomic stability. In the worst days of the economic depression, he declared little faith in the effectiveness of interest rate policy to stabilize business conditions and to reflate the economy. His perceptions were based on a negative correlation between a cheap monetary policy, the safeguarding of the profit margins of the banking system and the restoration of business confidence. Anti-depression policies did not require a countercyclical expansion of the monetary base because interest rate reductions had perverse effects on the solidity of bank assets and provoked a deterioration of the balance sheet of commercial banks.

Skepticism about the effects of monetary policy also depended on the weak connections between the banking sector and the real sector. Interest rate policy exerted little influence on investment decisions while borrowers' discrimination and credit rationing practices were more important factors influencing the money market (Williams, 1931, 248ff.) The main channel of transmission of monetary policy depended on the impact of interest rate variations on the availability of bank credit. From his reading of Keynes's monetary essays Williams added two further considerations: first he believed that small changes in interest rates did not have any great effect on economic activity and prices, while large changes were likely to have negative effects on business expectations. Second, he thought that the fundamental cause of the depression was the persistent gap between long-term and short-term interest rates. He believed that Keynes's *Treatise* had not succeeded in explaining causes and remedies of this discrepancy. In his 1931 review article of the *Treatise*, Williams argued that Keynes's monetary theory was built on the wrong assumption that the long-term financial market was sensitive to changes in the bank rate. By contrast, reality showed that a wide gap fragmented the capital market while there were non-monetary difficulties which basically affected aggregate demand and which '[we]re not sufficiently amenable to monetary action' (Williams, 1931, pp. 252ff.) In this context, the distinction put forward by Keynes and other business cycle theorists between the market rate and the natural rate of interest did not represent an important theoretical advance: it was rather a rhetorical gimmick, since 'the natural rate is not visible; it is an abstraction' (Williams, 1931, p. 248).

Williams thought that the Federal Reserve System had been dominated by advocates of the 'real bills doctrine' who denied any relation between their acts and inflation. The system's adherence to the real bills doctrine – combined with a belief that a 'natural' purging of speculative excesses was necessary to set the stage for stabilization and recovery – led to the failure of monetary policy. Whatever the intellectual origin of the Federal Reserve Act, Williams believed that the real bills doctrine was of little use in designing post-war monetary policy. In particular, after the 1919 economic recession, many business concerns 'shied away from banking loans, with the result that commercial paper, already diminishing in relative importance before the war was reduced to only 12% of bank assets in 1929 and 8% today.' The notion of 'eligible paper' should be replaced by the notion of 'sound assets' (Williams, 1936, p. 257).

These changes in the character of central and commercial banking, as Williams (1945) observed, coincided with the emergence of a new phenomenon in the credit market. Banks developed a strong preference for the selection of comparatively low-risk operations, such as the purchase of government securities at the expense of the investment needs of private enterprises. The growth of public debt had produced revolutionary changes in both central and commercial banking, and Williams watched with interest the growing tendency of banks to hold secondary reserves of government securities. High bank earnings coincided with periods of low but stable interest rates which determined an increasing volume of safe transactions in the market for public issues. On the other hand, commercial banks had become extremely vulnerable to interest rate changes because most of their assets were concentrated in government bonds. As a consequence Williams (1945, p. 219) feared that all economic subjects – 'the public and the Treasury, as well as the banks' – were developing strong vested interests in the stability of interest rates which, in fact, had become the primary objective of monetary policy.

On these grounds, and in order to increase the efficiency of monetary policy, Williams frequently wrote in support of the creation of a modern central bank machinery for credit control and the maintenance of economic stability. In his writings and in his official activities, Williams favored legislation which extended the scope of reserve banks' lending operations and reorganized the Federal reserve system with a view to increasing its powers of direct credit controls and supervision. Central monetary authority needed to be transformed from an agency which provided an elastic credit supply to meet the needs of investment and trade into an agency for credit control. As he wrote in a report to Morgenthau on central banking, the philosophy that had inspired the 1913 Federal Reserve Act needed to be reconsidered: 'there has arisen since the War a great diversity of views with respect to the status and functions of central banking institutions; their relations to government and to the commercial banks; their responsibility for currency and credit control.'[29]

In terms of positive proposals, Williams dismissed as unrealistic all proposals which found inspiration in the recent wave of European banking reforms and policy innovations. Major conversion operations of the public debt would have shaken confidence in the solvency of the Treasury, and Williams opposed the transformation of commercial banking into state-owned enterprises. His unpublished writings contain several suggestions regarding possible reforms in the art of central banking.

First, he denounced the fact that the Federal monetary authorities lacked the means for efficient banking supervision. They had no powers to prevent banking excesses and ensure the solvency of banks, particularly in relation to non-commercial assets. Williams observed that credit controls were no longer a question of measuring the adequacy of reserve requirements but needed to be exerted over the quality of bank assets: 'inability of the banks to borrow from the reserve banks upon sound assets … was not due … to defects in the machinery of organization and utilization of reserves, but to a general impairment in the value of banks assets so great as to reveal very strikingly the underlying weakness in our whole system of banking organization and supervision' (Williams, 1936,

p. 266). Williams put the blame for the comparatively higher failure rate of US banks on bad loans and limited diversification.[30] The modernization of the banking system required the development of more efficient methods of 'relationship banking' between central and commercial banks. The inadequacy of contacts was viewed as one possible explanation of the reasons why the 1929 stock-market crash had turned into a general collapse of the credit system. In particular, at the worst stage of the depression, many banks suffered from the absence of a lender of last resort and found themselves forced to dispose of sound assets by sale, thus contributing heavily to the general deflation and undermining their own solvency (Williams, 1936).

Second, Williams proposed that central banks should be given a considerable amount of discretion and independence when dealing with the system of commercial banks on the one hand and the government on the other: 'as regards commercial banks, the Central bank must have power to control them unaffected by profit-seeking considerations.' Regarding the difficult relationship with the Treasury, Williams believed that central bank credibility for credit and currency control would be strengthened if greater independence in monetary policy decisions was among its prerogatives: greater discretionary powers were 'desirable and necessary in order to safeguard against the possibility of hastily considered or politically determined actions.'[31] Proposals in this direction ranged from a general prohibition against buying government securities other than in the open market to an increase in the salaries of board members in order to enhance their status and autonomy. Williams favored increased centralization of credit controls without impairing the regional character of the reserve system. The concept of the Federal Reserve Board as a board of review of policy decisions of the reserve banks without powers to initiate changes in policy had created confusion, an excessive diffusion of responsibility, cumbersomeness, and delay. The establishment of an open market committee was a real piece of central bank machinery and the right solution to clarifying the policy responsibilities of the reserve system in matters of credit policies.[32]

8.4   Williams's plan for international monetary reform: the key currency approach

8.4.1   Official plans under criticism

From the beginning of the negotiations for a new monetary order, Williams was involved in the discussions that eventually led to the

Bretton Woods agreements. Williams's activities ranged around three main aspects which will be the object of our analysis in this and the following section. They regarded: (i) a detailed criticism of the two official plans; (ii) the elaboration and defense of an alternative plan based on the stabilization of the world key currencies; and (iii) participation in the negotiations in order to introduce amendments in the official plans in line with the key currency approach.

As a monetary reformer, Williams received widespread recognition. He believed that the key currency approach did not offer an outright substitute for a full-scale international agreement on exchange rate stabilization nor a new mechanism for balance of payments adjustment. As he wrote to the Bank of Canada economist, Louis Rasminsky, he had 'no desire to be the spearhead of any countermovement.'[33] However, he thought that the introduction of the White plan needed to be preceded by the stabilization of key currencies in order to make the establishment of a new monetary system more gradual and sustainable. In this manner, he felt sure that the risks of failure of the new institutions would be greatly minimized.

Williams's criticism was equally addressed to White's and Keynes's plans. However, at least initially, he thought that the former deserved greater support for reasons of political opportunity: among them he mentioned the fact that a clearing union would put the Fed in a difficult position because of its inflationary bent. As he put it in a letter to the Board of Governors of July 1943, 'the provision of foreign exchange resources to other countries on the scale suggested by Keynes would be an extremely hazardous undertaking from the standpoint of this country.'[34]

Williams found several shortcomings in the two official plans which were respectively related to their theoretical vision, technical provisions, and institutional design.

First of all, the proposal to establish a multilateral system of fixed but adjustable exchange rates was too abstract and ambitious: the two plans were 'like a mirage', being full of 'high sounding words and sentiments that do not get us anywhere.'[35] Lessons from the stabilization plans of the 1920s warned against the immediate determination of new exchange rate parities. Williams thought that the current exchange rate structure was meaningless, and that member countries needed time to find a sustainable relationship between their respective currencies. For a long time after the end of the Second World War the initial par value of all currencies could not be determined with any degree of scientific accuracy. In this respect, the stabilization fund's resources were utterly inadequate for the task of re-establishing an international payments system and they would be burnt in defense of a fixed exchange rates regime (Williams, 1943, 1944b).

The lessons of the 1920s had not been learnt too well from another standpoint. Williams recalled that under the weak supervision of the League of Nations a wave of doubtful loans was launched in attempts to support uneconomic levels of fixed exchange rates. He also added that interwar monetary reforms had had disastrous effects for Wall Street and the network of peripheral countries, because 'we lent too freely and then stopped altogether.' As he wrote in a report for the Federal Reserve Board, Williams feared that the process of establishing new parities could provoke a massive wave of destabilizing speculation and disorder in financial markets. Should that occur, the stabilization fund risked being discredited for a long time: it would be doomed even before it had officially started its lending operations. A more viable solution was to reach a bilateral agreement on the sterling-dollar exchange rate and to follow the method of trial and error, beginning with the key currencies.

Second, official projects were premature. Williams's most telling criticism of both plans was that they completely failed to distinguish between the problems of the transition and the problems of peace, between Western Europe's immediate financial requirements and the shock-absorbing activities of the new stabilization fund (Williams, 1943, pp. 151ff.) In a vast number of essays and reports he tried to prove that both plans were characterized by a serious lack of attention to transitional issues. The stabilization fund and the World Bank could not cope with them. They had limited resources, and uncertainty over the future of Europe and economic performance was great. Williams anticipated that it would take at least five years before Great Britain could be ready for multilateral trade and the elimination of current account restrictions because of the large volume of inconvertible sterling balances accumulated in foreign countries.[36] He also feared that the setting up of an International Monetary Fund could obscure the need to arrange relief and reconstruction and be a scapegoat for US responsibilities as the 'key' country.

At this stage, Williams was among the first economists to warn against the danger of a possible scarcity of key currencies – a dollar shortage – if the IMF was employed in the transition or to finance the settlement of sterling blocked balances. Williams pointed out that an increased demand for dollars could not be satisfied by the fund's resources, while the new institution would soon be converted into a stagnant reservoir of unwanted currencies: 'Very soon after the beginning of operations the

Fund will be long of the weaker currencies and short of the key currencies in which international transactions are actually carried out.'[37]

As the negotiations proceeded, the dilemma described by Williams began to receive widespread consideration and new technical provisions against the dangers of a dollar shortage were approved by the delegations of experts. Williams believed that some of them represented important improvements in the monetary mechanics of the fund. Particularly those which introduced the scarce currency clause, imposed progressive interest rate charges and established forms of repurchase agreements went in the right direction. In his opinion, however, these remedies still remained a 'second best' solution, if compared to the approval of a transitory system based on the key currency plan. Williams dismissed as politically unfeasible the option that – should the dollar shortage occur – the fund could impose 'buy backs' of weak currencies with dollar reserves that member countries possessed outside the fund. Moreover, he was convinced that the fund machinery did not technically allow for a dollar appreciation because this decision could never be taken unilaterally without a previous Washington consensus.[38] As a consequence of the dollar shortage, Williams correctly anticipated that the fund might soon need to be refinanced by borrowing arrangements with the leading financial powers: this contributed to the undermining of its authority and political independence.[39]

Moreover, the official plans had theoretical and technical shortcomings. For the author of the key currency plan, three of them were particularly noteworthy.

First, both plans bore too close a family relationship with the textbook type description of the gold standard and their success depended on surplus and deficit economies behaving in a flexible and symmetrical way. As far as the adjustment mechanisms of external disequilibria were concerned, Williams (1944a, p. 171) observed that the rationale of both plans was weak: not only did they neglect the role and weight of domestic policies in ensuring prospects for stability and growth but what was worse they almost completely failed 'to mention the need for internal adjustment.' Stabilization, in fact, was just a misnomer since 'all the stabilization measures are left out.'[40] Drawing from his early academic writings, Williams wrote that international stability depended mainly on the domestic stability and growth of the leading economies, while both plans followed a global approach and were based on a principle of equality in the world's currencies which simply did not exist.[41] Key countries, he urged (Williams, 1937, p. 49), must express a strong and explicit commitment to economic stabilization: 'The best prospect for general stability is to be found in internal stability in the leading countries' while 'economic conditions of young countries primarily reflect the conditions existing in the great world markets, for which they are only secondarily responsible' (Williams, 1943, p. 152). Stability and mutual cooperation at the center produced positive externalities to peripheral countries: 'There is no dilemma between internal and external monetary stability as has been frequently emphasised in abstract analysis.'

From the outset, neither Keynes's nor White's proposals for a new international institution considered the kind of corrective measures that countries would be obliged to impose in order to regain domestic economic stability as a prerequisite of international stability. Undoubtedly, the reasons for this omission were 'in part political,' because core countries were unwilling to subscribe to hard commitments or surrender national sovereignty (Williams, 1944a). However, having been a long-time reader of Keynes, Williams was surprised by 'the lightness of touch' he had found in the clearing union plan on domestic economic reforms and stabilization policies (Williams, 1943, p. 151). He found one plausible answer in Keynes's confidence that the new world organization would soon become a forum which provided a form of efficient world government. This was a rather platonic vision of the world, as Williams privately wrote to the Bank of Canada economist, Louis Rasminsky, since the establishment of a system of fixed exchange rates was quite a long way from complete surrender of national sovereignty to a bunch of enlightened technocrats.[42]

Second, the two plans would soon reach deadlock in what is nowadays called the 'impossible trilemma.' Williams feared that the mechanics of the fund would feed an insoluble alternative between fixed exchange rates, free capital movements, and the independent pursuit of monetary policies. In his reports to the Board of Governors, Williams recalled that, as Keynes himself had shown in the *Treatise*, this trilemma could again find a solution in a world ruled by a supra-national authority which effectively exerted its coercive powers on capital movements. Such a world, Williams warned, simply did not exist. On the contrary, as it was expected that in the post-war era most nations would follow independent economic and monetary policies, countries would not be able to defend their exchange parity in the presence of perfect capital mobility. Williams also warned against the technical difficulty of distinguishing between transactions on current account – which should remain free – and those on capital account – which the fund temporarily allowed to be prohibited by the retention of national systems of exchange control.[43]

Third, neither plan provided a workable condition for the eligibility of IMF loans. They contained no definition of what was meant by temporary disequilibrium of the external accounts nor adequate solutions for when and if key countries ran persistent current account deficits. On this account, Williams denounced both plans as containing only a sketchy treatment and no precise definition of the principle of conditionality. Again, the Harvard economist anticipated that the fund would never be influential enough to promote – and in some cases impose – the appropriate financial policies on the borrowing countries. He feared that most members of the new institution retained an unconditional and automatic drawing right, regardless of their creditworthiness. Making use of his familiar distinction, he believed that key countries would never accept a curtailment of their economic sovereignty or submit their policy decisions to the sort of necessary scrutiny implied by conditionality.

Williams's remarks on conditionality showed great perceptiveness of what would become the real burning issue in the history of the IMF. If the fund became a passive transfer agent with no active discretionary authority, Williams wrote that its resources would not be preserved for long and that its credibility would rapidly be undermined and the seeds for its failure be sown. On this issue, he thought that Keynes's plan fared better, because whatever conditionality the stabilization fund managed to acquire, it would sooner or later be weakened by the US refusal to grant borrowing powers.

These criticisms struck home and were the origin of a violent controversy within the administration. Although the rate of his publications was reduced as the conference date approached, Williams anticipated that the Bretton Woods agreements were doomed to fail. In an official statement to the Board of Governors, Williams characterized it as a 'rubber stamp conference.'[44] After two years of negotiations, what remained of the original Keynes's plan or of all the projects related to investment and commercial policy was of little substance: 'teeth should be put in this plan while the experts have taken out everything that expressly could suggest that there are any teeth in this plan to maintain exchange stability.'[45] On the grounds of the insurmountable difficulties in presenting a uniform view, he supported Governor Eccles because 'he has not made up his mind, re[garding] the Board position on the fund.'[46]

8.4.2 The key currency plan

In March 1943, at the time that discussions on the new international monetary system began to gain momentum, Williams presented his key currency plan (Williams, 1943). Like the Keynes and White plans, Williams's plan drew on the experience of the interwar years. One could speculate that while the two official plans were more strongly influenced by the debates of the 1930s and New Deal policies for avoiding international disintegration, Williams was more concerned with the failure of the 1920s League of Nations stabilization policy.

When the plan came out, most contemporaries observed that its strength lay more in the criticism of the official plans than in its own technical and institutional innovations. Keynes himself contributed to forming this judgment. In his personal copy of Williams's first *Foreign Affairs* article, Keynes had noted with approval: 'A very intelligent and moderate criticism.' Twelve months later, when the Joint Statement was about to appear in the press, in a personal letter to Lord Catto, Keynes added the following comment: 'this is an able article, but its criticism is much better than its constructive proposals – which are almost nil.'[47]

Williams was somewhat upset to find out that the various official drafts that crossed the Atlantic contained 'not a word about my preferred approach of going from the big countries to the smaller ones. A world-wide approach to an International Monetary Fund is the wrong approach, based as it is on an inadequate theory of international trade organization. Bad idea to apply one system to all countries since they are at different stages of development and have different functions.'[48] Nevertheless, Keynes was right and, as a matter of fact, the technical clauses of Williams's plan were never spelled out in great detail, even though careful examination of his published writings, Congressional hearings and written reports provide a slightly different picture. His plan contained some original insights – particularly for what was regarded as the rationale of a more limited approach to international monetary reform. In what follows we will briefly examine some of its most interesting features.

The exchange rate system

Williams's plan was based on the premises that the currencies of member nations were not of equal quality and acceptability in international transactions and that in a multilateral trading system most transactions were settled with just two or three currencies (Williams, 1943). By definition, key currencies were those most commonly demanded as international means of payment. On these grounds, Williams believed that one crucial condition for post-war recovery of world trade and international investment was the stability of the 'key currencies' exchange rate. As he put it in a meeting at the Federal Reserve Board, 'the essence of monetary stability is to stabilize the major currency and all else flows from that. If you do that it is much easier to permit of exchange controls and exchange rate variations for the younger countries. This does not really affect stability.'[49]

Thus, Williams's plan favored a two-speed approach to monetary reform by permitting different paths to convertibility and multilateralism. The first stage was characterized by the stabilization of the key currencies – notably the bilateral dollar/sterling exchange rate – with flexible fluctuations of all other currencies. Only in a later phase, in fact, would non-key countries be allowed to join an international monetary system based on fixed exchange rates and managed by supranational institutions.

The cornerstones of Williams's exchange rate agreement between the two key currencies were also quite simple and were represented by a modernized version of the 1936 Tripartite Agreement: they basically consisted in an exclusive monetary agreement between Great Britain and the United States with the fixing of a new exchange rate parity; parities could not be changed without preliminary consultations while both central banks were required to purchase each other's currency in specified amounts and with specific safeguards against losses; more currencies were gradually included in the new agreement once their external value was sufficiently in line with purchasing power parity in terms of key currencies.[50]

The institutional setting

One fundamental implication of the plan was that, in a very imperfect world, no major effort of institutional design should be undertaken, at least until more stable economic and political relations between trading countries were restored. In particular, Williams advised strongly against the establishment of an International Monetary Fund before serious progress was made in the post-war transition. New economic institutions could be designed only after the foundation of a new political institution. As he wrote to Rasminsky: 'A world organization for monetary stabilization ought to be a sub-head under whether there is to be some sort of a United Nations political set-up.'[51] The fund was opposed as a matter of timing, not principle. It was unwise to have it at a time when there was no hope of restoring multilateral trade and convertibility.

Allan Meltzer adds interesting details to this point. Meltzer shows how Williams and Sproul caused a stir when, alone among Fed officials, they testified in that vein before Congress in 1945. During the negotiations and in his meetings with Keynes, Williams endorsed the project of a world development bank, viewing it as a more appropriate vehicle for easing the severe dislocations in the immediate post-war period.

He suggested that the bank should be assigned the limited function of providing specific reconstruction loans. When the establishment of an international stabilization agency appeared inevitable, Williams forcefully suggested that it should be transformed into a special department of the World Bank.

Nature of commitments

Williams suggested that credibility in commitments helped to create a more stable international monetary order. While discussing the key currency plan, he acknowledged that the establishment of soft but credible commitments increased the efficacy of stabilization policies and strengthened central bank cooperation. On these issues, he agreed that the Tripartite Agreement lacked effective mechanisms for enforcing coordination. Conversely, the White plan was based on 'too many rules and regulations, too many pains and penalties, and too many functions for the new world governing body.'[52] If his predictions were correct, the general commitment to a fixed exchange rate regime would soon become hard to respect and would create credibility failures for the new institution, inevitably leading to disasters of the League of Nations kind. As he put it in a statement at a meeting of the Governors Board, 'we risk a setback in the cause of international cooperation.'[53]

Although the key currency approach called for a closer coordination of domestic monetary policies between the leading economies, Williams never explained the way this objective could be practically achieved.

Optimal currency areas

His interpretation of the functioning of past monetary systems – together with his preference for a two-speed monetary integration – led Williams to believe in the optimality of currency areas, which implied the participation of a limited number of countries. As he put it (Williams, 1944b), different kinds of countries require different kinds of monetary systems, and he often wondered about the optimal degree of monetary integration. He thought that the establishment of fixed exchange standards had more relevance for the few advanced countries than for the many 'less developed countries.' In most cases, their economic systems depended on the production of few primary commodities with extremely volatile terms of trade. Moreover, they were often characterized by a very low degree of trade integration which reduced the potential gains from a fixed exchange rate regime. Particularly during the presumably long period of transition and reconstruction, small and open economies would have all the advantages in maintaining flexible exchanges as a shock absorber policy instrument. Therefore, for them, greater exchange rate flexibility and control were the most appropriate policy and this was a further point on behalf of the key currency plan.

US Treasury economists found some merit in this argument, and Edward Bernstein agreed that greater exchange rate variability was needed to offset asymmetric shocks and the deterioration of the terms of trade (Bernstein, 1944, 1968). However, Williams's proposal was dismissed because it was agreed that less developed countries could get what they needed as insiders of the new international monetary order after consultation with the fund, rather than as outsiders who decided to act unilaterally. On their part, during the negotiations, small countries with open economies were favorable towards the possibility of adopting a key currency approach to monetary reform and felt that more time was needed for exchange rate negotiations to be put on a stable and realistic basis. France and Holland, among others, presented a lengthy memorandum which sponsored the adoption of Williams's plan.

Balance of power or hegemony?

Williams saw geopolitical rationales favoring the key currency approach. He was skeptical that the United States was really ready to face its global responsibilities as the world's largest creditor nation. According to the Harvard economist the United States was unwilling to manage its economy in such a way as to assure stability and growth to the rest of the world. He expressed these feelings in his meeting with Keynes with great frankness. 'I said we were a creditor country in a very mixed sense ... This makes our problem vastly more difficult than England's in the 19th century. To put it in a few words, we were apt to be self-righteous about currency stability but unwilling to live up to the obligations of a creditor nation' (Appendix 8.1). Also for these reasons, the gradualism and flexibility inherent in the key currency approach was more fit to steer the US administration through the obstacles of isolationism and the like.

8.5 In the heat of the negotiations: Williams, White, and Keynes

8.5.1 First reactions

Williams's proposal was discussed in the crucial months between the first draft of Keynes's clearing union plan and the Bretton Woods conference (Beckhart, 1944; Bernstein, 1944, 1968; Bogen, 1944; Borneuf, 1944; Brown, 1945; Mikesell, 1945).

At least in the very early stages of the negotiations, the key currency approach was viewed sympathetically, particularly in British quarters and among experts representing small and open economies (Horsefield, 1969, pp. 32ff.) Oxford economist Redvers Opie confessed that when the proposal came out he found some attraction in it, although as economic adviser to the British Ambassador in Washington he felt compelled to support the case for a broad international solution (Opie, 1957). In a private correspondence with a Federal Reserve economist, Roy Harrod recalled a long conversation with Keynes on Williams's project, even before the clearing union proposal had been fully conceived or put down on paper.[54] Other British economists thought that some preferential arrangement between the two reserve currencies could become part of the Lend-Lease agreement and a possible concession against the promised reduction of British trade discrimination. The Bank of England and the British Treasury supported Williams's plan as a prerequisite for the survival of the sterling area. Also Ralph Hawtrey favored the establishment of a close Anglo-American partnership, with the understanding that each country maintained domestic price stability and mutually supported the exchange rate.[55]

From the outset things were quite different in Washington where most reactions barred the possible adoption of Williams's proposal from the diplomatic agenda. In particular, the State Department never considered the key currency plan as a realistic solution. On the contrary, in order to make article VII of the Mutual Aid Agreement a credible commitment, the State Department required that most nations were to be brought into the White plan on a fully equal basis. The issue – as Roy Harrod recalled in a letter to Robert Roosa – was not 'one between the British (or Keynes) and the Americans' and the option on Williams's proposal was never seriously considered: 'it was settled by the definite attitude of the State Department, *well before* Williams' proposal [was formulated in detail]. By 1943 it was *chose jujee* [sic!].'[56]

The US Treasury and the Federal Reserve Board also reacted strongly to Williams's plan. On various occasions, the Federal Reserve Board attempted to silence Williams and Sproul. An official note was circulated through the Federal Reserve System which cautioned that 'public expressions of differences of opinion within the System would tend to impair effective representation at the international conference and to destroy any influence that the System might have' (Meltzer, 2003, p. 620). At Morgenthau's request, Eccles recommended that Williams desisted from criticism of White's plan. The governor's injunctions were unusually severe: he threatened not to renew Williams's appointment, tried to prevent his Senate testimony, and finally asked the board to dismiss him because 'his part time job [as vice president and research director] left him free to make public statements.' On their part, Williams and Sproul made no commitment to be bound by the board's position and refused to accept the restriction that their comments remained within the framework established by the official proposals (Meltzer, 2003, p. 523). The New York Fed voted unanimously in October 1943 and June 1944 to endorse the position taken by the two top senior officials.

When the debate heated up, Williams became the leading spokesman for the New York financial community and many statements were made in support of his plan. The bankers' conservative attitudes were sympathetic towards the more modest approach of the key currency plan, and open tributes were paid to its greater realism and far-sightedness. Williams's plan was more useful in transition, it provided greater prospective stability and it proposed ad hoc stabilization agreements tied to gold. Fraser (First National Bank), Riddle (Bankers Trust), and Aldrich (Chase National Bank) were among the most influential bankers who supported the key currency approach. US bankers generally resented their loss of control over international monetary affairs when authority was shifted from the New York Fed to the US Treasury under Secretary Morgenthau.[57] In this respect, Williams's rejection of the new international institutions was favored by the ABA as a way to reduce the loss of monetary sovereignty. His plan also had some support in Congress, because – as some members saw it – it called simply for a resurrection of the gold exchange standard, with the dollar performing the role that sterling had played previously (Ruggie, 1982).

Most of these reactions coincided with the Washington monetary talks of September to October 1943. In the history of the negotiations which prepared the Bretton Woods agreements, this round of meetings between experts was perhaps the most influential episode. For more than three weeks the two official plans were confronted, readapted, and redrafted. By the end of October, both plans were merged into what became the skeleton of the Joint Statement of Experts which provided the intellectual and technical background to the Bretton Woods agreements. Only a few specific points were still left undecided. When the two delegations adjourned it was agreed that the new international monetary system was to be based on White's stabilization fund. In exchange the British delegation obtained important concessions on a number of technical points, the most important of which were a greater amount of exchange rate flexibility, a greater amount of members' contributions, a more rigid maintenance of exchange controls over capital movements, and the approval of more liberal conditions to withdraw from the new institution.[58] In his accurate reconstruction, L.S. Pressnell (1986, p. 116) has observed that 'these informal, non committal talks of September-October 1943 ... were the most important Anglo-American exchanges on economic issues not only during the war but also for many years before and since. They were indeed unique; they were conducted at a high intellectual level, ranging frankly over virtually the whole field of economic policy ... these talks had a lasting ... significance: ... they registered and clarified issues and points of agreement.'

It was at this crucial stage of the negotiations that Williams had the opportunity to discuss his ideas with Keynes and White. Although Williams was not allowed to participate in the Washington talks, following Morgenthau's advice Keynes sought to gain the blessing of the Federal Reserve Bank of New York in order to strengthen the prospects of Congressional approval. In his visit to the New York bankers Keynes found that they were less obstinately opposed to the fund project than had been considered to be the case in Washington. Keynes was convinced that most of the problems with the US monetary authorities lay with the decision taken by the Roosevelt administration in the mid-1930s to confer on the US Treasury full powers in the management of monetary policy rather than in an insurmountable opposition to the plan. 'The real evil,' so James Meade confided in his wartime diary (22 October 1943), was that central bankers and the financial community 'were left so ignorant of the real intentions of the US Treasury' (quoted in Howson and Moggridge, 1990).

In their meetings with Williams, Keynes and White took into consideration some of the arguments of the key currency plan. They both disagreed on the fundamental issue of the two-speed approach and argued that reopening the discussion would not produce a better agreement, but found some merit in Williams's ideas. We will briefly discuss their reactions.

8.5.2   White's reactions

On July 1943, two months after the official plans were published and on the eve of the invitation of 46 countries to participate in their discussion, Harry Dexter White wrote an anxious letter informing Keynes that Williams's *Foreign Affairs* article on the key currency plan appeared 'to be having rather wide distribution.' Enclosed with his letter, White sent a copy of Williams's article with the purpose of letting Keynes have the taste 'of the kind of opposition there is developing in the United States to efforts for any comprehensive scheme of post-war monetary proposals' (Keynes, 1980, p. 337).

White's reactions generally followed a geopolitical focus: he repeatedly noted the existence of numerous political hurdles which would hinder the adoption of Williams's plan. He thought that Williams and the advocates of the key currency approach were reasoning in a political vacuum.[59]

First, White thought that it was politically unwise to appear to impose Anglo-American leadership or, to put it otherwise, to leave many European countries outside the agreement and unable to contribute to the new monetary order. Should the key currency approach be followed, Europe would never be fully integrated into a new multilateral payments system. Second, the adoption of Williams's plan was viewed as a possible threat to dollar supremacy; it artificially restored an international role for sterling while tending to underestimate the financial needs of British reconstruction. To put it more explicitly, White argued that the key currency approach was a gift to England and its desire for some spare hegemonic supremacy. Emphasis in the official US plan on convertibility, multilateralism, and stable exchange rates were all designed to limit London's capacity to organize a separate trading bloc, while Williams's plan deferring the establishment of a truly international system could be functional to British interests of continued trade discrimination. White also believed that exchange restrictions and discriminatory currency arrangements would be maintained – if not strengthened – by the adoption of the key currency approach, which would not guarantee the solution of the scarce currency problem. Finally, as is well known, White was a fervent advocate of eastward enlargement and argued that, for political reasons, China and Russia could not be excluded from the new monetary order.[60]

There were also more technical motivations underpinning White's opposition to the key currency approach. He believed that it was likely to favor the perpetuation of closed trading systems with trade conducted on a bilateral rather than on a multilateral basis.[61] He also noted that too many countries could have their own key currency with respect to single commodities while non-key currency countries accounted for over 75 per cent of world trade. The absence of an international organization – which the key currency approach implied – rendered more difficult the adoption of common rules and standards with respect to exchange and foreign investment practices. On this issue, he strongly affirmed that the fund had essential functions to perform during the period of transition. Although the demand for reconstruction loans could not be satisfied,

nevertheless the new institution could usefully operate to re-establish world confidence in a system of orderly exchange rate variations. Finally, White expressed his conviction that the key currency approach bore too close a resemblance to the Norman plan which dramatically failed to stabilize the international economy in the 1920s under the League of Nations. If Britain were to be granted the status of 'key country' she was quite likely to refuse to participate in major programs of external financing because foreign loans would drain resources and produce deflation and unemployment at home.[62]

White also stated that the most convincing aspects of the key currency plan were already embodied in his proposal.[63] The dollar was bound to become the key currency of the new system. His plan provided some safeguards against the risks of a premature participation of countries which were not yet qualified to operate with the IMF: the new institution had the powers to delay the beginning of lending operations with particular areas or countries, and it could take the decision to refuse to fix the initial parity.[64] On matters of exchange rate policy, White believed that Williams's plan would excessively increase exchange rate flexibility and provide incentives to ease unilateral alterations of exchange rates (Horsefield, 1969, p. 84). On this point, he feared that the British delegation might see some reasons to recognize the cogency of Williams's ideas. However, Keynes promptly reassured White that he no longer had a strong faith in the expansionary role of exchange rate depreciations and that the British would not support Williams's plan on this issue.

8.5.3   Keynes's reactions

Keynes's critical reactions to Williams's proposal were in part inspired by reasons of political opportunity and in part by theoretical conviction.

As the negotiations preceded, Keynes was persuaded that the official plans were not intended to deal with transition problems (Appendix 8.1).[65] However, in his conversations with Williams, Keynes insisted that the institutional machinery for the long run should be put into operation immediately after the war. Only in this way could international multilateralism in trade and finance be restored. He gave several reasons which largely depended on political opportunity rather than on any greater technical efficiency. As he confessed to Williams (see Appendix 8.1),

> one was the familiar one that we now have the opportunity, if ever, and if we wait we may lose it. Another was that there had now been so

much consulting of other governments that both the British and the US Treasury feel that there can be no turning back. Another was that there will be work for the stabilization plan to do even from the outset, that some countries will already be in proper shape for it, and here he mentioned the United States, the Dominions, the Latin American countries, and England (assuming that England has found ways for handling her immediate problems).

In his October 1943 meeting with Williams, Keynes also made it very clear that Britain and sterling no longer held a key position in international trade and finance. To restore its role as a key country she needed US assistance, and he guessed that she would prefer to apply to the fund and reap the advantages of anonymous borrowing rather than 'come to us with her hat in her hand and ask for help' (Appendix 8.1). As a founding member of the new stabilization fund Britain may be able to aggregate consensus from small countries and would not always prefigure a subordinate role dependent on US loans.[66] This point had already been dealt with at a meeting of Treasury experts in September 1943 where a further concern was raised against the adoption of the key currency plan:[67] it was observed that the divergent rates of the various currencies showed that members of the sterling area were already pursuing independent monetary policies while Britain was not in a position to dictate policy rules to the sterling area as she might be required to do under the key country approach. Finally, Keynes added that the Bank of England and Montagu Norman had not been keen on entering into a borrowing arrangement with the US, 'they couldn't live up to' (Appendix 8.1). In many British quarters it was hoped that the new institution could provide more favorable conditions.

However, unlike White, Keynes's objections to the possible adoption of the key currency plan also depended on its technical features. Keynes accepted several aspects of Williams's criticisms of the fund. In particular, he agreed that: (i) its resources were rather disappointing in relation to the future growth prospects of world trade and that the surrender of sovereignty was too limited; (ii) its machinery was not a cure for post-war problems and that loans from the fund had never been conceived of as something vital for western European reconstruction, but rather 'as oil for the machinery … breathing space';[68] and (iii) the discipline of conditionality was the really weak point in the Joint Statement and that it was bound to remain the burning issue of the fund's operations for a long time. In their private conversations Keynes justified the vagueness of the principle of conditionality in terms of political feasibility. In his opinion, the fund 'would not last two years if it were butting into domestic policies',[69] while it was doubtful that 'England or any other country would accept interference with its domestic policies' (Appendix 8.1). Quite to the contrary, in an effort to increase its authority and independence during the first period of operations Keynes thought that the fund must be 'kept clear of internal problems but it is entitled (though he should be careful) to make a report as to what it considers the cause of the basic disequilibrium.'[70] Therefore, Keynes agreed with Williams's basic observation that much work and a lot of time were required in order to make the new commitments realistic and efficient. He objected, however, that the system could not contemplate the gradualism implied by the key currency approach nor the maintenance of flexible exchange rates for all other members. On this point, Keynes confessed – to Williams's surprise – that he had little faith in the use of exchange rate variations as a macro stabilization instrument. Contrary to what he had advocated in the early 1920s, he favored exchange stability and agreed that nations ought to preserve some measure of freedom to change the parity, although he thought that this freedom had to be used very rarely, and 'only when it was clearly proved that this is the best method of adjustment' (Appendix 8.1).[71]

In line with Williams's philosophy, Keynes favored the redefinition of the nature of the general commitment in order to increase IMF credibility among member countries. These latter were to be persuaded to take all the necessary measures to respect soft but realistic commitments. Keynes believed that a clear opt-out clause might help: 'one way to do it was not the key currency approach but to allow free right to withdraw.' In fact, this concession would lessen fears of member countries 'about the extent of their commitment and encourage a general acceptance of the plans, and that afterwards, when they were in, they would find themselves under a strong moral compulsion to stay in and work out their differences within the framework of the plans' (Appendix 8.1). Williams replied that this was a good point but still thought that the risk of failure of the new institutions should not be minimized. Countries might even go 'to the length of destroying the plan, and the world could not stand another fiasco in the field of international cooperation' (Appendix 8.1).

Keynes consulted with Williams on a number of issues. They found themselves in complete agreement on the granting of member countries' freedom to maintain exchange controls. In Williams's report of their first meeting, it was at this point that Keynes admitted that one further reason for controversy with the US administration remained the question of exchange control. Keynes spoke against the US Treasury view which pressed for the earliest possible abandonment of all currency restrictions. In contrast, he favored a high level of post-war planning of foreign trade and exchange transactions, warning against the feasibility of any distinction between the capital account and the current account. As he put it, the control of capital movements implied an overall system of exchange control: what had been learnt in the 1930s should not be lost in the post-war world and British authorities had acquired strong reputations in the effectiveness of controls. As Williams recalled (Appendix 8.1):

> Keynes said he thought he had done some educating of our Treasury on this point, that his assistant (I think he said Mr Ausland) was a Bank of England man who understood their exchange control thoroughly, and he had been taken Bernstein aside and apparently having considerable effect upon him. Keynes said that the British view now is that we must control capital movements and cannot do so without an over-all exchange control. The transactions that they wish to leave free they authorise under a general license, but all transactions have to be reported. He urged us strongly to send a man over to the Bank of England to study their exchange control.

Williams and Keynes also agreed on the greater efficacy of direct methods of intervention, which ranged from import quotas to voluntary export restraints on the part of creditor countries. Again, in Williams's recollection, 'we asked whether under his scheme there could be also a control of exports of merchandise, and Keynes replied that he didn't see why not if that were really necessary. All this interested me very much' (Appendix 8.1). They were persuaded that efforts should be made to avoid the blocking of foreign assets in order to stimulate direct investments. 'What we need, therefore, is a partial control, giving a country control over its own capital, and this would probably be sufficient to handle the hot money problem' (Appendix 8.1).

However, concerning the official plans under discussion, Keynes, unlike Williams, saw positive externalities in the establishment of a stabilization fund. Among them, the fund was likely to strengthen international cooperation and the quality of information in monetary affairs, thus increasing the efficacy of monetary policy. He also believed that the fund would acquire 'considerable authority' in international monetary coordination and decisions, thus becoming 'the platform where central banks will come together and consider matters of public interest.'[72] The new institution could usefully act as 'the current barometer and give clear warnings on changes in weather conditions.' In terms of its technical mechanics, Keynes strongly rebutted Williams's criticism, affirming that the fund will provide 'a code of conduct with regard to exchange practices and orderly methods of making exchange changes and to constitute a consultative body.'[73]

Williams remained unconvinced by Keynes's arguments in defense of the fund. He replied that the art of central banking was based on selectivity while the fund's approach was too general and unconditional. On this occasion he spoke in favor of the clearing union plan as a real piece of institutional innovation and as a real international monetary authority with full corrective powers which were exercised through interest rate policy and discretion. Keynes replied that while quotas were maxima of right, the fund had the authority to increase them and even to create new means of international liquidity. These decisions largely depended on its authority, independence of judgment and reputation.[74]

8.6   Conclusions

Williams's plans and actions towards the establishment of a new monetary order were part of one of the most fascinating episodes in the history of economic ideas and policymaking.

In this chapter we have examined Williams's contributions as an international economist and monetary reformer, showing the theoretical rationale of his key currency approach and the reasons why he so fiercely campaigned against the two official Bretton Woods plans. His policy proposals were the outcome of his doctrinal rejection of the two main tenets of classical economics in the international field: namely, the Ricardian theory of comparative advantages and the gold standard. From his early academic writings Williams found the inspiration to create a stabilization plan which put special emphasis on the unequal size and importance of nations, on the international repercussions of key countries' domestic economic policies, and on the disturbing effects of international capital movements. Drawing extensively from the private collection of his papers, we have also shown the many and prestigious reactions which Williams's plan managed to provoke, together with the contents of his conversations with Keynes on the pros and cons of the monetary system under construction. The two economists had convergent views on a number of issues regarding the new architecture of the world monetary system. Keynes clearly admitted that political reasons prevented the British delegation from considering more carefully the inclusion of

Williams's plan in the diplomatic agenda, the most relevant being that Britain no longer held a 'key country' position in the post-war world.

From this reconstruction, what general conclusions can be drawn?

Williams was able to foresee many problems of the post-war world. He correctly anticipated that it would for a long time be dominated by renewed forms of bilateral and payments agreements and that to be successful all efforts towards the restoration of convertibility and outright multilateralism needed time, strong leadership and a lot of 'green cheese.' He was also right to anticipate the failure of the Morgenthau-White international economic policy and its substitution with a policy that recognized the reality of US hegemonic power and political interests. For a long time, the United States operated unilaterally outside the institutions they had worked so hard to establish. The International Monetary Fund remained inactive during the transition and for quite a long time afterwards.

At least indirectly, Williams succeeded in contributing to the improvement of the negotiations which were marked by the publication of the Joint Statement of Experts in April 1944. The Joint Statement clearly recognized the difference between the transition years and the long run, and the difference between exchange rate stability and exchange rate rigidity; it also approved the maintenance of national forms of active controls over capital movements. All these issues became evident during the October 1943 money talks and contemporary discussions on Williams's plan helped to bring them to light.

One final point which was somehow related to the key currency approach was conditionality. Discussions on conditionality and the dollar shortage were stimulated by Williams's writings. In his writings he urged that the fund's modest financial resources should not be used to liquidate war-time indebtedness. Gaining strong support in financial quarters – beginning with the open blessing of the ABA – Williams feared that the International Monetary Fund would be called upon to embark on a policy of making doubtful loans in order to defend the fixed parity of weak currencies. Automatic lending procedures would increase the fund's holding of poor currencies and decrease its holdings of valuable assets, running the risk of repeating the disastrous free lending policies of the 1920s which ultimately brought about a sudden reversal and a crisis. In line with Williams's writings, the final articles of the Bretton Woods agreement recognized that the fund was not intended to provide facilities for relief or reconstruction or to deal with international indebtedness.

Appendix 8.1   J. H. Williams, 'Our Meeting with Lord Keynes, October 20, 1943' (Archives of the Federal Reserve Bank of New York, Williams Papers)

It was a very helpful meeting. First, some facts about the present stage of the plans. The conferences in Washington have been concluded, and Keynes is on his way home. He will take the Clipper from Baltimore early next week. He also said that Robertson will be leaving soon. Keynes feels that a good deal of progress was made on this visit. He told us confidentially that before he came over there was a Cabinet meeting on the plans, and he was given instructions, which I gathered were all in the nature of making sure to safeguard the British position. He will go home now to submit the results of the negotiations and everything so far as the British are concerned that has been done on this visit will be subject to Cabinet approval. He said that there had been many meetings, well attended by the other branches of government, and he mentioned especially the State department, but that the most faithful attendants outside the Treasury had been Goldenweiser and Gardner, and that they had been very helpful. Toward the end, the negotiation took a most favorable turn he thought, and White and the others had been most generous and made some very real concessions. He told us confidentially about the proviso for a 10 per cent change in the rate every ten years without approval by the governing body, and that there could be a second 10 per cent change with the approval of the governing body which must give its decision within two days of being asked. (these and other changes I think I have from Tamagna's memoranda). He also said something about their having tried to find a common formula as between the fund and the clearing union, and that they had worked the differences down to such a point that it really made very little difference whether you used the clearing union idea or the stabilization fund idea.

I told him that on strictly monetary grounds I thought the CU was preferable because it provided a way for clearing only the ultimate balances on multilateral trade, and I asked him if it wouldn't be possible to preserve that idea and still provide the limits on our commitment and on the size of the debits of other countries which our Treasury has been contending for. He showed interest at once and said that had been exactly what they had been working for, but they had found now that it really made very little difference which way you go at it, except that there remained that curious inversion of the accounts whereby under the stabilization fund arrangement the surplus country's position is not shown by a credit but by a liability. I told him I was a little mixed up on this, and he said he would be glad to know what we thought when we saw the new set-up, that it really boiled down to the difference between the fund having accounts with the central banks, and the central banks' having accounts with the fund. I think it is the same difference which I noticed before, namely that in White's scheme an American surplus, for example, would be indicated by a shortage of dollars in the Fund, rather than by a surplus of bancor. I guess the point is that once you have limited each country's contribution and its right to draw, the scheme inevitably becomes a fund rather than a clearing union. I tried to clear this up by coming back to it two or three times, but all I got was an admission toward the end that the new scheme is really based on the stabilization fund idea rather than the clearing union idea and that once you introduce the limitations on the particular countries this is what you inevitably get anyway no matter which way you start out.

As things are now left, both sides are drafting a statement of principles, rather than the details of plans. He said, for instances, that one draft recently drawn up took only 4 or 5 sheets of paper. The two groups of experts are going to try to agree on a single draft, and when they have done so, this will be presented to the United and Associated Governments. But he told me afterward that they did not intend to go into any great detail in their negotiations with the other governments. If enough of them accept the principles, this draft of principles will be presented to congress and to parliament for debate, rather than the plans. I asked him if there would be a meeting of finance ministers, and he said yes, but only toward the end, and I thought he meant that this meeting will follow, rather than precede, the parliamentary action.

I think this is good procedure because there ought to be a better chance of getting favorable action from parliament and congress on a simple statement of principles than on elaborate technical plans, but I don't know how Congress will react. Now the plans have been published, they may insist on knowing just what the statement of principles will result in; they may want to see the plans.

What we mainly talked about today, however, was not the nature of the plans and possible compromises between them but some of the broader aspects of the problem. He surprised me greatly by saying at the very outset of the meeting that his plan was never intended to deal with immediate post-war problems. He said he had in mind a transition period of 2 or 3 years which would have to be handled in some other way. He admitted that the English had not given enough thought to just how these immediate problems were to be handled, and one of the things he is taking home from this visit is the clearer realization that concrete plans will have to be worked out for the immediate post-war period. He said later that this talk today and the one last night had been particularly helpful on this point. But he insisted that the machinery for the long run must be put into operation immediately after the war. He gave several reasons: one was the familiar one that we now have the opportunity, if ever, and if we wait we may lose it. Another was that there had now been so much consulting of other governments that both the British and the American Treasury feel that there can be no turning back. Another was that there will be work for the stabilization plan to do even from the outset, that some countries will already be in proper shape for it, and here he mentioned the United States, the Dominions, the Latin American countries, and England (assuming that England has found ways for handling her immediate problems).

I told him I thought we were on the horns of a dilemma, in that I agreed that this is the most favorable time to get a decision on a long-run plan but that one could not make up one's mind about the chances of its success without knowing much more than we do at the present about the short-run plans, because if the long-run mechanism is set up, it will inevitably be a catch-all, and if the short-run plans aren't adequate countries will inevitably run up deficits and surplus positions in a stabilization plan which will make it lop-sided and put all countries under compulsions to balance their accounts for the wrong reasons. England for example would have to behave as a debtor country is supposed to do under the plan, not because of anything in her normal situation but because of her transition difficulties. In this way the plan might be seriously impaired in its early years. He agreed and said that when he got home, he was going to emphasize this aspect of the problem very strongly. He said the trouble had partly been that England could not very well take the lead, that she couldn't come to us with her hat in her hand and ask for help. I said it was common gossip around here, and that I heard it from a number of the experts who had worked on the plans, that England preferred not to have the help, that that was the only way I could interpret the many references I had heard to the advantages of anonymous borrowing. He said there was an element of truth in that, that Montagu Norman and others, for example, had been keen on not entering into a borrowing arrangement with us they couldn't live up to, especially as their trade runs in other directions, and that they would therefore rather take their chances on some sort of generalized loan arrangement. But I said that the trouble with this was that the only generalised loan arrangement that I could see was the currency plan itself, and this, as he had just agreed, would be a misuse of the plan.

We then talked a little about the Reconstruction Bank, and whether that could be the generalised loan agreement, designed to protect the currency plan. I gathered he is not at all clear about this Bank. It seems to be the creation of our Treasury rather than the British. He wondered whether such a bank could be truly international or would have to [be] American. I said that was what bothered me. If England is to have a debtor position how can she contribute to a world bank? He said White had dressed the bank up with various gadgets so that, while it would appear as a world bank, it would seriously raise its funds in creditor country markets, but Keynes doubted whether this kind of camouflage would be persuasive with the public or would operate effectively anyway.

To sum this point up, I take it that the British are now thoroughly impressed with the necessity of working out the arrangements for the transition period and agree that they can't expect any agreement on the long-run currency plan until this has all been spelled out, and they confess that they hadn't previously been as clear about this as they are now, but they do say in their own defense that it is the kind of situation in which they couldn't very well take the lead. Keynes said he felt encouraged by the opinions expressed last night and today about the American willingness to help work out these problems. I feel entirely convinced in my own mind that the British did quite deliberately intend to use this plan for both purposes. I think the language of Keynes' white paper makes that abundantly clear, but they now see that this is not acceptable to us, or even desirable from their own standpoint.

This was perhaps the main thing that I got out of the meeting, but two other things also interested me very much. One was our discussion of the lines of compromise in working toward currency stabilization. On this he started off by saying that the British simply would not accept the old gold standard and he did not think England or any other country would accept interference with its domestic policies; but the ensuing discussion brought out some interesting things. Keynes said he had never favored a freely flexible exchange, that he had wanted a stable, but not a fixed, rate and an orderly method for change. He said he had come to believe, and here he said he thought his ideas had changed somewhat, that the situations in which a nation could benefit by exchange depreciation were rare. Without saying anything, I took all this with a grain of salt, because I think nothing could be clearer than Keynes' advocacy of flexible exchanges a decade or more ago. But that is water over the dam, and it really doesn't matter. What is now most interesting is that Keynes favors exchange stability and goes so far as to say that while a nation

224 American Power and Policy

must preserve some degree of freedom to change the rate, that it should be used very rarely and only when it is clearly proved that that is the best method of adjustments. ([P]erhaps this is what Geoffrey Crowther meant when he said that he would find Lord Keynes very different from John Maynard Keynes, and that he had undergone a fundamental change of heart on the whole subject).

At this point I made quite a long speech. I said that I felt a good deal better in my mind about the plans because of his frank recognition that we must separate out the transition problems, but that coming to the long-run problem itself, I was still a good deal troubled about whether the two countries had really thought out the nature of the compromises involved in any attempt to stabilize currencies, and this was why I had favored a gradual approach which could be more tentative and exploratory in character and would not confront the nations later on with a great failure and a collapse of the plans. Just before this, he had said that one new feature of the plans was to be the free right of any country to withdraw at any time and without the governing body insisting on a period of time before withdrawal. He thought this would lessen their fears about the extent of their commitment and encourage a general acceptance of the plans, and that afterward, when they were in, they would find themselves under a strong moral compulsion to stay in and work out their differences within the framework of the plans. I said I thought he had a very good point, but I was still unsure what the countries would actually do in some future concrete situation, and they might actually find that they would even go to the length of destroying the plan, and the world could not stand another fiasco in the field of international cooperation.

What I wonder, in other words, is whether either country has really thought through the nature of the problem and what it is prepared to do as its contribution to currency stability. To take the American problem first: I said we were a creditor country in a very mixed sense and then went along the lines of my note of last week. This makes our problem vastly more difficult than England's in the 19th century. To put it in a few words, we were apt to be self-righteous about currency stability but unwilling to live up to the obligations of a creditor nations. I said I thought it did very little good to reproach us because our problem actually is a very complicated one. See last week's notes.

Then, turning to England's problem, I said I doubted if the English had thought their problem through sufficiently to be prepared to say what they would do in particular circumstances. Different individuals might think that they knew (I said this in response to Keynes' interjection that the problem had been thought about for a long time, which I took to mean that we ought by now to be agreed about the theory of it – I might have added how much he had change[d] his mind about it himself), but could it be said there was anything approaching a general national opinion about it, or was England likely to find itself in a serious conflict at home. I said they didn't want the old gold standard and would never again put themselves in the straitjackets of 1925–1931, but I wasn't at all sure they knew what they meant by these statements as a nation. Gold standard is only a short-hand phrase for exchange stability to be achieved by discipline imposed by a country's sense of its obligations to other countries. I referred to the London Economist and their recent statement that neither plan would be acceptable, which I interpret to mean that they preferred exchange freedom even though it meant going back to bilateral trade. The Economist said this was 'second best', but they didn't define their first best, and left me with the suspicion that this so-called second best was what they really wanted.

This was what led up to Keynes' remark that he now feels that there are very few situations in which a country could benefit by exchange depreciation. But to my mind that still leaves open the whole question of what the English public really feels, and how to interpret their statement that they don't want the straitjackets of 1925–1931. Do they merely mean that that wasn't the right rate and that the problem is one of finding the right rate, or do they mean that they will resort to exchange depreciation as their primary method of adjustment? If they mean that, it is useless to talk about currency stabilization. If they don't know what they mean, it would be better to experiment with the dollar-sterling rate until we can find out what degree of international discipline is tolerable on both sides. To go out into a grand international scheme without having thought through such fundamental questions on both sides seems to me very risky. The more I think about it, the more I believe that this will be the main point of my next paper if I really do it. This I can discuss without needing to know too much about the present plans.

The other main point that interested me came up at lunch. I asked if there had been as yet any meeting of minds about exchange control, that I thought I had sensed the differences on this point since the beginning, our Treasury looking toward the earliest possible abandonment of exchange control (in their first draft they said within a year), and the British seeming to lean toward retention of exchange control, at least for capital purposes.

Keynes said he thought he had done some educating of our Treasury on this point, that his assistant (I think he said Mr Ausland) was a Bank of England man who understood their exchange control thoroughly, and he had been taken Bernstein aside and apparently having considerable effect upon him. Keynes said that the British view now is that we must control capital movements and cannot do so without an overall exchange control. The transactions that they wish to leave free they authorise under a general license, but all transactions have to be reported. He urged us strongly to send a man over to the Bank of England to study their exchange control. He then discussed control of capital movements very interestingly. He said the general principle they feel should be adopted was to control the export of capital by English residents, so as to safeguard against panicky and speculative movements, but at the same time they wished to leave free the capital assets of foreign countries (in other words, there should be no blocking of foreign assets. If for example the Guaranty Trust Co. has funds on deposit or invested in England, there should be no interference with their withdrawal etc.).

I thought this was excellent, because one of the arguments against control of capital movements has been that a market loses its international standing and repels capital, both short and long-term, which might otherwise come to it and be desired, by the threat that the funds might be blocked. What we need, therefore, is a partial control, giving a country control over its own capital, and this would probably be sufficient to handle the hot money problem. This is part way between those who have favored a complete control and those who say that no international money market can afford any capital control at all, that it must create the conditions, economic and political, to prevent panicky movements of capital, and have reserves large enough to take care of such movements when they do occur.

I then asked him whether they would ever use their exchange control under his scheme for controlling movements of merchandise; why, for example, when a country is faced with the necessity of adjusting its balance of payments, should it always adopt the change-of-the-rate method. Why not go straight to the mark and make the adjustment in the balance of payments itself.

This would be a real problem for England, I thought, since she might often be faced with the question of needing to reduce her imports relative to her exports. He entirely agreed and said he thought that much the more direct and preferable method.

Ruml [Beardsley Ruml (1894–1960), American statistician and economist, adviser to President Hoover and director of the Laura Spelman Rockefeller Memorial Fund, was a director of the NY Fed] asked whether under his scheme there could be also a control of exports of merchandise, and Keynes replied that he didn't see why not if that were really necessary. All this interested me very much, and I should have a section of my paper on it. The general thesis would be that many people had been vastly over-simplifying the problem and talking about exchange stability as though it were to be the grand cure-all, doing away with exchange control, bilateral trade, etc. But what we have to have, I feel is some sort of compromise, not only as between stable and variable exchange, but even as between free and controlled exchange. I am not sure also whether the compromise will not have to include some compromise between bilateral and multilateral trade, but without going into that, it seems clear to me that exchange control should not be dismissed as though it were clearly always undesirable, and clearly always linked with bilateral trade arrangements, etc.; it may be one of the necessary ways of maintaining exchange stability in the interest of multilateral trade.

In other words what I think I want to do more than anything else is not so much to discuss these particular plans but to discuss the nature of the problem and the kinds and methods of adjustment which we ought to explore. The chief danger today is in over-simplification of the problem, one crowd leaning heavily toward a simple picture of stable currencies, free exchange, multilateral trade, without really appreciating the limitations imposed upon such arrangements by the complexities of the modern world and the differences of viewpoints among the nations, and the other crowd going equally too far in the opposite direction and putting their faith sometimes in flexible exchanges, sometimes in controlled exchanges and bilateral arrangements. What I am trying to say is that the truth is not as simple as any of these but involves some compromise among them all.

ODD NOTE
Why don't we just take the bull by the horns and extend lend-lease. That is the way things are done in this country. Our biggest decisions are done casually. If we allow ourselves to dig in and have to save face, then we can't have any agreement. We can say war doesn't end when the shooting stops, but it will be projected for a couple of years, and therefore we must carry on under lend-lease (article VII provision) which we are all for if we can bring it about. But there are unfortunate restrictions in lend-lease: England couldn't get lend-lease aid if she had an export balance.

Appendix 8.2   AEA Presidential Addresses in the Interwar Years (1918–39)

1918 (published 1919)
Author: Irving Fisher
Title: *Economists in Public Service*
Pages: 5–21
Institution: Yale University
Key Subjects: American economic conditions; economic advisory; economic policy; economic psychology; history of economic thought; labor relations; methodology; taxation; war and economics.
Economists Cited: Willford I. King; Helen Marot; Vilfredo Pareto; Carleton Parker; Eugenio Rignano; William Graham Sumner; Frank William Taussig; Ordway Tead; Robert B. Wolf.

1919 (published 1920)
Author: Henry B. Gardner
Title: *The Nature of Our Economic Problem*
Pages: 1–17
Institution: Brown University
Key Subjects: American economic conditions; economic policy; industrial policy; methodology; war and economics.
Economists Cited: Arthur Bowley; Wilford I. King; Adam Smith.

1920 (published 1921)
Author Herbert J. Davenport
Title: *The Post-war Outlook*
Pages: 1–15
Institution: Cornell University
Key Subjects: Democracy; economic institutions; economic policy; economics and politics; public debt; socialism; taxation; war and economics.
Economists Cited: None.

1921 (published 1922)
Author Jacob H. Hollander
Title: *The Economist's Spiral*
Pages: 1–20
Institution: Johns Hopkins University
Key Subjects: American economic conditions; American economic thought; banking system; classical economics; economic policy;

federal reserve system; history of economic thought; labor relations; price fixing; Ricardian socialists; stationary state; taxation; war and economics.
Economists Cited: Walter Bagehot; Jeremy Bentham; E. L. Bogart; Étienne Boileau; Thomas Chalmers; David Hume; John R. McCulloch; Thomas Robert Malthus; Harriet Martineau; James Mill; John Stuart Mill; Arthur Cecil Pigou; David Ricardo; Jean Baptiste Say; Nassau Senior; Adam Smith; James Steuart; Frank Taussig; Thomas Tooke.

1922 (published 1923)
Author Henry R. Seager
Title: *Company Unions vs Trade Unions*
Pages: 1–13
Institution: Columbia University
Key Subjects: American economic conditions; American trade unionism; trusts and cartels.
Economists Cited: None.

1923 (published 1924)
Author: Carl C. Plehn
Title: *The Concept of Income, as Recurrent, Consumable Receipts*
Pages: 1–12
Institution: University of California
Key Subjects: Capital and income; consumption; history of economic thought; methodology.
Economists Cited: Frank Fetter; Irving Fisher; Felix Flügel; Karl Knies; Alfred Marshall; Henry L. Moore; François Quesnay; Henry Seager; Edwin R.A. Seligman; Sidney Sherwood.

1924 (published 1925)
Author: Wesley C. Mitchell
Title: *Quantitative Analysis in Economic Theory*
Pages: 1–12
Institution: Columbia University
Key Subjects: Economic psychology; history of economic thought; methodology; research institutions; statistical method.
Economists Cited: John E. Cairnes; Lawrence K. Frank; William S. Jevons; John Maynard Keynes; Alfred Marshall; John Stuart Mill; Fred C. Mills; Henry L. Moore; David Ricardo; Adam Smith; Rexford G. Tugwell; Thorstein Veblen.

1925 (published 1926)
Author: Allyn A. Young
Title: *Economics and War*
Pages: 1–13
Institution: Harvard University
Key Subjects: American economic conditions; American economic history; European economic history; war and economics.
Economists Cited: Karl Marx; Adam Smith.

1926 (published 1927)
Author: Edwin K. Kemmerer
Title: *Economic Advisory Work for Governments*
Pages: 1–12
Institution: Princeton University
Key Subjects: Economic advisory; economic development; fiscal policy; gold standard; international monetary policy.
Economists Cited: Jeremy Jenks.

1927 (published 1928)
Author: T. S. Adams
Title: *Ideals and Idealism in Taxation*
Pages: 1–8
Institution: Yale University
Key Subjects: American fiscal policy; taxation.
Economists Cited: Henry George; John Stuart Mill; David Ricardo; William Graham Sumner; Adolph Wagner.

1928 (published 1929)
Author: Fred M. Taylor
Title: *The Guidance of Production in a Socialist State*
Pages: 1–8
Institution: University of Michigan
Key Subjects: Socialism; socialist calculation debate.
Economists Cited: None.

1929 (published 1930)
Author: Edwin F. Gay
Title: *Historical Records*
Pages: 1–8
Institution: Harvard University

Key Subjects: Economic history; economics and statistics; methodology; research institutions.
Economists Cited: William Beveridge; Bruno Hildebrand; Wilhelm Roscher; Gustav Schmoller.

1930 (published 1931)
Author: Mathew B. Hammond
Title: *Economic Conflict as a Regulating Force in International Affairs*
Pages: 1–9
Institution: Ohio State University
Key Subjects: American economic conditions; international relations; war and economics.
Economists Cited: Adam Smith.

1931 (published 1932)
Author: E.L. Bogart
Title: *Pushing Back the Frontiers*
Pages: 1–9
Institution: University of Illinois
Key Subjects: American economic conditions; American economic history.
Economists Cited: None.

1932 (published 1933)
Author: George E. Barnett
Title: *American Trade Unionism and Social Insurance*
Pages: 1–15
Institution: Johns Hopkins University
Key Subjects: American economic history; American trade unionism; labor relations; welfare state.
Economists Cited: None.

1933 (published 1934)
Author: Abbott Payson Usher
Title: *A Liberal Theory of Constructive Statecraft*
Pages: 1–10
Institution: Harvard University
Key Subjects: Economic policy; history of economic thought; trusts and cartels.
Economists Cited: Jeremy Bentham; John Stuart Mill; Sidney and Beatrice Webb.

1934 (published 1935)
Author: Harry A. Millis
Title: *The Union in Industry: Some Observations on the Theory of Collective Bargaining*
Pages: 1–13
Institution: University of Chicago
Key Subjects: American trade unionism; collective bargaining; labor relations; New Deal; theory of wages.
Economists Cited: John E. Cairnes; John R. Hicks; William H. Hutt; William G. Smart; Beatrice Webb; Sidney Webb.

1935 (published 1936)
Author: John Maurice Clark
Title: *Past Accomplishment and Present Prospects of American Economics*
Pages: 1–11
Institution: Columbia University
Key Subjects: Economic advisory; history of American economic thought; methodology.
Economists Cited: Henry C. Adams; John Bates Clark; John R. Commons; Charles F. Dunbar; Theodore S. Ely; Thomas Cliffe Leslie; Alfred Marshall; John Stuart Mill; Wesley C. Mitchell; Simon Newcomb; Simon Patten; William G. Sumner; Thorstein Veblen; Francis A. Walker; David A. Wells; Stuart Wood.

1936 (published 1937)
Author: Alvin Johnson
Title: *The Economist in a World of Transition*
Pages: 1–3
Institution: New School for Social Research
Key Subjects: American economic condition; economic advisory.
Economists Cited: None

1937 (published 1938)
Author: Oliver M.W. Sprague
Title: *The Recovery Problem in the United States*
Pages: 1–7.
Institution: Harvard University
Key Subjects: American economic conditions; investment; New Deal; price fixing.
Economists Cited: Karl Marx.

1938 (published 1939)
Author: Alvin Hansen
Title: *Economic Progress and Declining Population Growth*
Pages: 1–15
Institution: Harvard University
Key Subjects: American economic conditions; economic growth; history of economic thought; population; stagnation; technological progress.
Economists Cited: Gustav Cassel; Paul Douglas; Ralph Hawtrey; John Maynard Keynes; Simon Kuznets; Thomas R. Malthus; David Ricardo; Dennis Robertson; Joseph A. Schumpeter; Adam Smith; Carl Snyder; Joseph J. Spengler; Arthur Spiethoff; Mikhail Tugan-Baranowsky; Knut Wicksell.

1939 (published 1940)
Author: Jacob Viner
Title: *The Short View and the Long in Economic Policy*
Pages: 1–15
Institution: University of Chicago
Key Subjects: American economic conditions; economic policy; economist advisory; history of economic thought; price fixing.
Economists Cited: John Maynard Keynes; Adam Smith.

Notes

We would like to thank Marcello De Cecco, Eric Helleiner, David Laidler, Robert Leeson, Perry Mehrling, Robert Mundell, and Paul Volcker for their helpful comments on a previous draft of this chapter. The usual disclaimer applies. This chapter greatly benefits from the use of Williams's archival material, and we would like to express our gratitude to Rosemary A. Lazenby (Federal Reserve Bank of New York, Archives Section) for her assistance and for granting permission to quote from Williams's papers. One document is also entirely reproduced in Appendix 8.1

Collections of Williams's papers can be found at the Archives of the Federal Reserve Bank of New York and at the Harvard University Archives. What follows is a brief description of their contents. The materials at the Federal Reserve were accumulated during Williams's tenure as an economic adviser there from 1933 to 1964 and include one series (J.H. Williams Estate Papers) that was accessioned after his death in 1980. In his role as an adviser to FRBNY officers, Williams provided advice via written memoranda, reviewed papers created by other at the Fed, presented speeches, and sat on various economic advisory committees. The bulk of the Williams material dates from 1935 to 1954 and is organized into six series:

Series 1: Federal Reserve Bank of NY Policy Development, 1934–1954
Series 2: Articles, Speeches, Statements, Addresses, 1932–1954
Series 3: Correspondence, 1936–1967

Series 4: Bank Officers, 1933–1956
Series 5: Economic Committees, 1932–1954
Series 6: J.H. Williams Estate Papers, 1935–1982

The Harvard collection is less extensive and comprises three containers, alphabetically arranged, of miscellaneous correspondence, memoranda, minutes, manuscripts and reports, 1929–1971 on monetary policy, the Council on Foreign Relations, international economics and the balance of payments, oil import policy. It also contains material from Harvard courses taught by Williams and documents relating to Professor Williams in the records of the Graduate School of Public Administration and possibly in the records of the Department of Economics.

1. See, among others, Fisher (1919), Mitchell (1925), Fetter (1925) and Kemmerer (1927). Appendix 8.2 contains full references to the AEA Presidential Addresses together with key subjects and main economists cited.
2. For other general references, see Dorfman (1949–1957), Stein (1969), Davis (1971), Coats (1992, 1998), Asso (1994), Barber (1998), Morgan and Rutherford (1998), Rutherford (1998) and Bernstein (2001).
3. For Williams's biography see Duesenberry et al. (1983).
4. Between 1932 and 1934 Williams also acted as US delegate at the World Economic Conference and participated in a Department of State mission to investigate Latin American exchange problems.
5. We are particularly indebted to Marcello De Cecco who has often recalled the importance of Williams's ideas in his work. His 1976 article on US domestic and international financial markets since 1945, has a rather strong *incipit*: 'This is an essay in the anti-Ricardian tradition of J.H. Williams' (De Cecco, 1976, p. 381).
6. In 1919, Williams, Charles Bullock, and Rufus Tucker contributed a pioneering and descriptive study of the history of the US balance of trade from 1789 to the end of the First World War (Bullock et al., 1919). In the following years Williams published regular updates of this work.
7. Archives of The Federal Reserve Bank of New York, Williams Papers.
8. See, for a different view, Tavlas (2003 [1997]).
9. On several other issues Meltzer finds that Williams's writings deserve particular attention. His critical essays on the first wave of proto-Keynesian models 'anticipated major controversies about the effects of government spending, deficits and debt in the 1960s and 1970s' (Meltzer, 2003, p. 610).
10. Clarke (1977). As Meltzer (2003, pp. 540 and 545) notes, the importance of the Tripartite Agreement was 'more symbolic than substantive ... as a political measure the agreement had greater merit'.
11. The standard reference, where most of these pieces are collected, remains Williams (1949).
12. One could add that the relative decline of power of the New York Fed was even more pronounced. See, again, Meltzer (2003).
13. As stated in an interview with William Diebold Jr, research secretary for the Economic and Financial Group, quoted by Ikenberry (1992, p. 301). See also Shoup (1975) and, on the EFG, Nerozzi (Chapter 3 above).

14. See, among others, Horsefield (1969), Ikenberry (1992), Skidelsky (2001), and Meltzer (2003). Recently Bordo and Schwartz (2001) have wondered – counterfactually – what would have happened to the international monetary system had the key currency approach been preferred to White's International Stabilization Plan.

15. Perhaps this group produced on these topics the most impressive collection of PhD dissertations in the history of economic thought. The best known, besides Williams (1920a), were Graham (1921–22, 1923), Viner (1924), Angell (1926), and White (1933).

16. 'As a graduate student nothing interested me more than the writings of the heretics' (Williams, 1948, p. 3).

17. It may be noted that while Williams observed that Cliffe Leslie's major weakness was that he did not develop a rival system, he also criticized Keynes's *General Theory* for sharing Ricardo's bias towards a universal application of a body of principles to all times and countries.

18. On the basis of his early writings on the inductive verification of the balance of payments adjustment, Flanders (1989) concluded that Williams could be labelled as a late classical economist because he focused on specific cases of disturbances to the classical mechanism and introduced some dynamic element in the classical picture. On the classical economists and capital movements, see Asso (2002).

19. Among others, Williams quoted Bagehot and Cliffe Leslie as anticipators of his views.

20. Williams's analysis of the effects of an exogenous real shock on trade flows prefigured the income or absorption approach to the balance of payments, in contrast to the prevailing acceptance of the price elasticity approach (Williams, 1920b).

21. Britain's capacity to exploit this virtuous circle helped to explain why, for a long time, '[it] has been able to concentrate capital and labor on a small amount of land' (Williams, 1929, p. 34).

22. In a letter to one of the authors, David Laidler recalls both Lauchlin Currie and Paul Samuelson commenting to him on Williams's work in ways that suggested that their high personal regard for him was tempered by a certain impatience with his lack of analytic precision.

23. See Fishlow (1989) for an application of Williams's ideas on this point.

24. Williams's contributions on this point are emphasized by Mundell (1997).

25. J.H. Williams, 'Our Meeting with Lord Keynes, October 20, 1943,' The Federal Reserve Bank of New York, Williams Papers. The whole document is reproduced in Appendix 8.1 at the end of this chapter. Hereinafter, we refer to it as 'Appendix 8.1.'

26. See Bloomfield (1950) where interesting similarities are drawn between Williams, Paul Einzig, and Ralph Hawtrey. Arthur Bloomfield worked with Williams at the New York Fed.

27. J.H. Williams, 'Gold Policy. Memo to Secretary Morgenthau,' 14 January 1935, The Federal Reserve Bank of New York, Williams Papers.

28. J.H. Williams, 'A Program for Banking Reform' (undated but 1935), Archives of The Federal Reserve Bank of New York, Williams Papers.

29. Ibid.

30. The reason for this comparison was that 'England with a central bank, and Canada without a central bank, entirely escaped bank failures.'
31. J.H. Williams, 'A program for banking reform.'
32. Williams strongly supported the use of open market operations and in 1932 played a key role in drafting the cable to President Hoover urging him to support vigorous open market operations combined with public works (Williams, 1932b). In a letter to one of the authors, David Laidler notes that in the early 1930s some of the ideas of the so-called Chicago tradition had flourished among a small group of Harvard economists – Williams included. On the debate about the 'uniqueness' or 'pervasiveness' of the Chicago tradition, see also Laidler (2003 [1993]), Laidler and Sandilands (2003 [2002]), and, more generally, the essays included in Leeson (2003b). Leeson (2003a) attempts to provide a solution to this dispute.
33. Williams to Rasminsky, 12 August 1943, Archives of The Federal Reserve Bank of New York, Williams Papers.
34. White's scheme was also to be preferred because the US was granted more veto powers. See J.H. Williams, Letter to the Board of Governors, 15 July 1943, Archives of The Federal Reserve Bank of New York, Williams Papers. Three months later, in the midst of the Washington negotiations, he reaffirmed that the clearing union plan contained the 'dangerous promise that countries by right of membership have a credit line for a substantial amount of US$.' J.H. Williams, 'International currency stabilization. Statement presented to the Board,' 7 October 1943, Archives of The Federal Reserve Bank of New York, Williams Papers.
35. These comments were included in an unpublished version of Williams's first article on currency stabilization (Williams, 1943). This version had only an internal circulation and can be seen in the Archives of The Federal Reserve Bank of New York, Williams Papers.
36. Meltzer (2003, p. 624) has observed that 'his arguments lost some of the persuasive power when the United States agreed to the British loan but he was right about the difficulties Britain would have in the post-war world.'
37. J.H. Williams, 'International Currency Stabilization,' 21 December 1944. Archives of The Federal Reserve Bank of New York, Williams Papers. See also J.H. Williams, 'Notes on a Meeting with Treasury Experts,' 10 September 1943, Archives of The Federal Reserve Bank of New York, Williams Papers.
38. On these issues, see J.H. Williams, 'Memorandum on a Meeting of the Board of Directors,' 17 August 1944, The Federal Reserve Bank of New York, Williams Papers and Williams (1944b).
39. Meltzer (2003, p. 619) also thought that 'although Sproul and Williams did not express their distaste for an international organization, they must have seen the plan as a further weakening of New York's influence on international economic policy.'
40. J.H. Williams, 'Statement at the Meeting of the Board,' 6 June 1944, Archives of The Federal Reserve Bank of New York, Williams Papers. See also Meltzer (2003, p. 619).
41. This point is discussed in Williams (1943, 1944a), and was explicitly raised in several internal memoranda: see J.H. Williams, 'International Currency Stabilization,' 21 December 1944, The Federal Reserve Bank of New York, Williams Papers.

42. Williams to Rasminsky, 12 August 1943, The Federal Reserve Bank of New York, Williams Papers. See also similar remarks in J.H. Williams, 'Letter to the Board of Governors,' 15 July 1943, The Federal Reserve Bank of New York, Williams Papers.
43. See various essays in Williams (1949) and particularly Williams (1944b, p. 115fn).
44. J.H. Williams, 'Statement at the Meeting of the Board,' 6 June 1944, The Federal Reserve Bank of New York, Williams Papers.
45. Ibid.
46. Williams to Sproul, 7 April 1944, The Federal Reserve Bank of New York, Williams Papers.
47. Keynes to Lord Catto, 22.2.44, T/160/1287, as quoted by Pressnell (1986, p. 154).
48. J. H. Williams, 'Statement at the Meeting of the Board,' 6 June 1944, The Federal Reserve Bank of New York, Williams Papers.
49. Ibid.
50. Adoption of Williams's plan also called for a large US loan to meet the transitional needs of the other key country, a thoroughgoing solution to the problem of the sterling balances.
51. Williams to Rasminsky, 12 August 1943, The Federal Reserve Bank of New York, Williams Papers.
52. J.H. Williams, 'International Currency Stabilization. Statement Presented to Committee on Foreign Relations of the Federal Reserve Board,' 24 September 1943, The Federal Reserve Bank of New York, Williams Papers.
53. Williams's Statement at the Meeting of the Board, September 1943, The Federal Reserve Bank of New York, Williams Papers.
54. Harrod to Robert Roosa, 16 May 1949, The Federal Reserve Bank of New York, Williams Papers.
55. Redvers Opie (1957) recalls a 'dramatic meeting' with Montagu Norman at the Bank of England in summer 1943 in which the governor warned that 'to support either the Keynes or the White plan was tantamount to selling Britain down the river.' On Hawtrey and the Bank of England, see also Skidelsky (2001, p. 213).
56. Harrod to Roosa, 16 May 1949, The Federal Reserve Bank of New York, Williams Papers. Emphasis in the original. Harrod really meant to write 'chose jugée,' that is, by 1943 things were already set against the adoption of Williams's plan.
57. On this issue the literature is large. See, among others, Fraser (1945), Van Dormael (1978), Garritsen de Vries (1996), and Meltzer (2003).
58. Keynes told Williams that the American delegation had made very generous concessions on these points and that 'a good deal of progress was made on this visit' (Appendix 8.1).
59. For a general reference, see Horsefield (1969), Van Dormael (1978), Gardner (1980), and Pressnell (1986).
60. J.H. Williams, 'Meeting with Treasury Experts,' September 1943, The Federal Reserve Bank of New York, Williams Papers.
61. Alvin Hansen and Dennis Robertson agreed on this point (see Hansen, 1944, p. 30). They dismissed Williams's plan since it implied the danger of formation of a currency bloc and could promote the splitting up of the world

into economic blocs which involved discrimination in trade and currency matters.

62. On these themes, see also Bernstein (1944).
63. J.H. Williams, 'Notes on a Meeting with Treasury experts,' 10 September 1943, The Federal Reserve Bank of New York, Williams Papers. The Bank of Canada official, Louis Rasminsky, shared White's fears and expressed his belief that the important core of truth in the key currency approach would not be lost in the fund arrangement. See his July and August 1943 correspondence with Williams in Archives of The Federal Reserve Bank of New York, Williams Papers.
64. J.H. Williams, 'Notes on a Meeting with Treasury Experts,' 10 September 1943, The Federal Reserve Bank of New York, Williams Papers.
65. In December 1943 Keynes wrote a letter to White in which he proposed a joint appeal for devising a separate program of transitional finance. See Gardner (1980, p. 117).
66. J.H. Williams, 'Notes on a Meeting with Treasury Experts,' 10 September 1943, The Federal Reserve Bank of New York, Williams Papers.
67. Ibid.
68. J.H. Williams, 'Memorandum on a Meeting of the Board of Directors,' 17 August 1944, The Federal Reserve Bank of New York, Williams Papers. (Keynes was also present.)
69. Ibid.
70. Ibid.
71. Quite likely, Keynes referred to Meade's proposal for an objective test of exchange rate variations which the LSE economist had brought to the attention of the committee on trade policy. See, on this point, Howson and Moggridge (1990) and Horsefield (1969).
72. J.H. Williams, 'Memorandum on a Meeting of the Board of Directors,' 17 August 1944, The Federal Reserve Bank of New York, Williams Papers. (Keynes was also present.)
73. Ibid. See also Appendix 8.1.
74. See again Williams's recollections of his discussion with Keynes in J.H. Williams, 'Memorandum on a Meeting of the Board of Directors,' 17 August 1944, The Federal Reserve Bank of New York, Williams Papers and Williams (1944b).

References

American Bankers Association, 1945, *Practical International Financial Organization through Amendments to Bretton Woods Proposal*.

Angell, J.W., 1926, *The Theory of International Prices. History, Criticism and Restatement*, Cambridge, MA: Harvard University Press.

Asso, P.F., 1994, 'The Economist as Preacher: the Correspondence between Irving Fisher and Benito Mussolini and Other Letters on the Fisher Plan,' in *Research in the History of Economic Thought and Methodology. Archival Supplement*, ed. W. Samuels, vol. 4, London: JAI Press.

———, 2002, 'The Home Bias Approach in the History of Economic Thought: Issues on Financial Globalization from Adam Smith to John Maynard Keynes,' in M. De Cecco and J. Lorentzen (eds), *Markets and Authorities: Global Finance and Human Choice. Essays in Memory of Susan Strange*, Cheltenham, UK and Northampton, MA, USA: Edward Elgar.

Barber, W.J., 1985, *From New Era to New Deal. Herbert Hoover, the Economists and American Economic Policy, 1921–1933*, Cambridge: Cambridge University Press.

———, 1998, 'Remarks on "America-ness" in American Economic Thought,' in Rutherford 1998, pp. 18–20.

Beckhart, B.H., 1944, 'The Bretton Woods Proposal for an International Monetary Fund,' *Political Science Quarterly*, 49(4) (December): 489–528.

Bernstein, E.M., 1944, 'A Practical International Monetary Policy,' *American Economic Review*, 34(4) (December): 771–84.

———, 1968, 'The International Monetary Fund,' *International Organization*, 22(1) (Winter): 131–51.

Bernstein, M.A., 2001, *A Perilous Progress: Economists and Public Purpose in Twentieth Century America*, Princeton, NJ: Princeton University Press.

Bloomfield, A.I., 1950, *Capital Imports and the American Balance of Payments, 1934–1939: a Study in Abnormal International Capital Transfers*, New York: Augustus M. Kelley Publishers.

Bogen, J.I., 1944, 'The View of Jules I. Bogen,' in *International Financial Stabilization: a Symposium*, New York: Irving Trust Company, pp. 3–17.

Bordo, M. and A.J. Schwartz, 2001, 'From the Exchange Stabilization Fund to the International Monetary Fund,' National Bureau of Economic Research, WP 8100, January.

Borneuf, A.E., 1944, 'Professor Williams and the Fund,' *American Economic Review*, 34(4) (December): 840–7.

Brown, W.A., 1945, 'The Repurchase Provisions of the Proposed International Monetary Fund,' *American Economic Review*, 35(1) (March): 111–20.

Bullock, C.J., R.S. Tucker and J.H. Williams, 1919, 'The History of our Foreign Trade Balance from 1789 to 1914,' *Review of Economic Statistics*, 1(3) (July): 215–66.

Clarke, S.V.O., 1977, 'Exchange Rate Stabilization in the Mid-1930s: Negotiating the Tripartite Agreement,' Princeton Studies in International Finance, No. 41, Princeton University, Department of Economics.

———, 1987, 'John H. Williams,' *The New Palgrave: a Dictionary of Economics*, ed. J. Eatwell, M. Milgate, and P. Newman, 4 Vols, London: Macmillan.

Coats, A.W., 1992, 'Economics in the United States, 1920–1970,' in *On the History of Economic Thought: British and American Economic Essays*, Vol. 1, London: Routledge, pp. 407–455.

———, 1998, 'What is American about American Economics,' in Rutherford 1998, pp. 9–17.

Cohen, B., 1998, *The Geography of Money*, Ithaca and London: Cornell University Press.

Davis, R.J., 1971, *The New Economics and the Old Economists*, Ames: Iowa State University.

De Cecco, M., 1976, 'International Financial Markets and US Domestic Policy since 1945,' *International Affairs*, 52(3) (July): 381–99.

de Vries, M. Garritsen, 1996, 'The Bretton Woods Conference and the Birth of the International Monetary Fund,' in O. Kirshner (ed.), *The Bretton Woods–GATT system: Retrospect and Prospect after Fifty Years*, New York: Sharpe.

Dorfman, J., 1947–59, *The American Mind in Economic Civilization*, 5 Vols, New York: Viking.

Duesenberry, J.S., J.V. Lintner, and E.S. Mason, 1983, 'John Henry Williams, 1887–1980,' *Harvard University Gazette*, 78(20) (January): 1–5.

Fetter, F., 1925, 'The Economist and the Public,' *American Economic Review. Papers and Proceedings*, 15 (March): 13–26.

Fisher, I., 1919, 'Economists in the Public Service,' *American Economic Review. Papers and Proceedings*, 9 (March): 5–21.

Fishlow, A., 1989, 'Conditionality and Willingness to Pay: Some Parallels from the 1890s,' in B. Eichengreen and P.H. Lindert (eds), *The International Debt Crisis in Historical Perspective*, Cambridge, MA: The MIT Press.

Flanders, M.J., 1989, *International Monetary Economics: Between the Classical and the New Classical*, Cambridge: Cambridge University Press.

Fraser, L., 1945, 'Testimony on the Bretton Woods Agreements Act,' The First National Bank of New York.

Gardner, R.N., 1980, *Sterling–Dollar Diplomacy in Current Perspective*, New York: Columbia University Press.

Graham, F.D., 1921–22, 'International Trade under Depreciated Paper: the United States, 1862–79,' *Quarterly Journal of Economics*, 26 (February): 220–73.

———, 1923, 'The Theory of International Values Re-examined,' *Quarterly Journal of Economics*, 27 (November): 54–86.

Hansen, A., 1944, 'The Views of Alvin Hansen,' in *International Financial Stabilization: a Symposium*, New York: Irving Trust Co., pp. 19–35.

Hirschman, A.O., 1945, *National Power and the Structure of Trade*, Berkeley, CA: University of California Press.

Horsefield, J.K., 1969, *The International Monetary Fund, 1945–1965*, 3 Vols, Washington: International Monetary Fund.

Howson, S. and D. Moggridge (eds), 1990, *The Wartime Diaries of Lionel Robbins and James Meade, 1943–1945*, London: Macmillan.

Ikenberry, G.J., 1992, 'A World Economy Restored: Expert Consensus and the Anglo–American Post-war Settlement,' *International Organization*, 46(1) (Winter): 289–321.

Kemmerer, E., 1927, 'Economic Advisory Work for Governments,' *American Economic Review. Papers and Proceedings*, 17 (March): 1–12.

Keynes, J.M., 1980, *The Collected Writings of John Maynard Keynes. Vol. XXV. Activities 1940–1944. Shaping the Post-War World: the Clearing Union*, ed. D. Moggridge, London: Macmillan.

Kindleberger, C.P., 1989, 'How Ideas Spread among Economists: Examples from International Economics,' in D.C. Colander and A.W. Coats (eds), *The Spread of Economic Ideas*, Cambridge: Cambridge University Press, pp. 43–59.

Laidler, D., 2003 [1993], 'Hawtrey, Harvard and the Origins of the Chicago Tradition,' *Journal of Political Economy*, 101(6) (December): 1068–103; reprinted in Leeson (2003b), vol. 2, pp. 135–72.

——— and R. Sandilands, 2003 [2002], 'An Early Harvard Memorandum on Anti-Depression Policies: an Introductory Note,' *History of Political Economy*, 34(3): 515–32; reprinted in Leeson (2003b), vol. 2, pp. 251–70.

Leeson, R., 2003a, 'From Keynes to Friedman via Mints: Resolving the Dispute over the Quantity Theory Oral Tradition,' in Leeson (2003b), vol. 2, pp. 483–525.

—— (ed.) (2003b), *Keynes, Chicago and Friedman*, London: Pickering & Chatto, 2 vols.

Liu, H.C.K., 2002, 'The Keynes Plan,' October, mimeo..

Meltzer, A., 2003, *A History of the Federal Reserve. Vol. 1, 1913–1951*, Chicago and London: University of Chicago Press.

Mikesell, R.F., 1945, 'The Key Currency Proposal,' *Quarterly Journal of Economics*, 59(4) (August): 563–76.

Mitchell, W.C., 1925, 'Quantitative Analysis in Economic Theory,' *American Economic Review*, 15(1) (March): 1–12.

Morgan, M. and M. Rutherford (eds), 1998, *From Interwar Pluralism to Postwar Neoclassicism*, Durham, NC: Duke University Press.

Mundell, R.A., 1961, 'A Theory of Optimum Currency Areas,' *American Economic Review*, 51(4) (September): 657–65.

——, 1997, 'Optimum Currency Areas,' http://www.columbia.edu/~ram15/eOCATAviv4.html (accessed 23 March 2009).

Opie, R., 1957, 'Anglo-American Economic Relations in War-Time,' *Oxford Economic Papers*, 9(2) (June): 115–51.

Pressnell, L.S., 1986, *External Economic Policy Since the War, Vol. 1: The Post-War Financial Settlement*, London: Her Majesty's Stationery Office.

Rowland, B.M., 1976, 'Preparing the American Ascendancy: the Transfer of Economic Power from Britain to the United States, 1933–1944,' in B.M. Rowland (ed.), *Balance of Payments or Hegemony: the Interwar Monetary System*, New York: New York University Press.

Ruggie, J.G., 1982, 'International Regimes, Transactions and Change: Embedded Liberalism in the Postwar Economic Order,' *International Organization*, 36(2) (Spring): 379–415.

Rutherford, M. (ed.), 1998, *The Economic Mind in America: Essays in the History of American Economics*, London and New York: Routledge.

Shoup, L.H., 1975, 'The Council of Foreign Relations and United States War Aims during World War II,' in *The Incumbent Sociologist*, pp. 9–52.

Skidelsky, R., 2001, *John Maynard Keynes, Vol. 3, Fighting for Freedom, 1937–1946*, New York: Penguin.

Stein, H., 1969, *The Fiscal Revolution in America*, Chicago: University of Chicago Press.

Tavlas, G.S., 2003[1997], 'Chicago, Harvard and the Doctrinal Foundations of Monetary Economics,' *Journal of Political Economy*, 105(1) (February): 153–77, reprinted in Leeson (2003b), vol. 2, pp. 173–99.

Van Dormael, A., 1978, *Bretton Woods: Birth of a Monetary System*, New York: Holmes & Meier Publishers.

Viner, J., 1924, *Canada's Balance of International Indebtedness, 1900–1913*, Cambridge, MA: Harvard University Press.

White, H.D., 1933, *The French International Accounts, 1880–1913*, Cambridge, MA: Harvard University Press.

Williams, J.H., 1920a, *Argentine International Trade under Inconvertible Paper Money, 1880–1900*, Cambridge, MA: Harvard University Press.

——, 1920b, 'Germany's Reparation Payments – Discussion,' *American Economic Review. Papers and Proceedings*, Supplement, 10(1) (March): 50–7.

——, 1928, 'Opportunities for Research in International Relations – Discussion,' Social Science Research Council, Hanover Conference, mimeo.

——, 1929, 'The Theory of International Trade Reconsidered,' *Economic Journal*, 39(154) (June): 195–209; reprinted in Williams (1949), chapter 2.

——, 1931, 'The Monetary Doctrines of J.M. Keynes,' *Quarterly Journal of Economics*, 45(4) (August): 547–87; reprinted in Williams (1953a), chapter 11.

——, 1932a, 'The Crisis of the Gold Standard,' *Foreign Affairs*, January; reprinted in Williams (1949), chapter 16.

——, 1932b, 'Monetary Stability and the Gold Standard,' in Q. Wright (ed.), *Gold and Monetary Stabilization*, Harris Foundation Lectures, Chicago: University of Chicago Press; reprinted in Williams (1949), chapter 17.

——, 1934, 'The World's Monetary Dilemma: Internal *versus* External Stability,' *Proceedings of the Academy of Political Science*, XVI(1) (April): 62–8; reprinted in Williams (1949), chapter 18.

——, 1936, 'The Banking Act of 1935,' *American Economic Review, Papers and Proceedings*, March; reprinted in Williams (1949), chapter 15.

——, 1937, 'The Adequacy of Existing Currency Mechanisms under Varying Circumstances,' *American Economic Review, Papers and Proceedings*, 27(1) (March): 151–68; reprinted, under a different title, in Williams (1949), chapter 19.

——, 1943, 'Currency Stabilization: the Keynes and White Plans,' *Foreign Affairs*, July; reprinted in Williams (1949), chapter 8.

——, 1944a, 'The Post-war Monetary Plans,' *American Economic Review*, Supplement, *Papers and Proceedings*, 34(1) (March): 372–84; reprinted in Williams (1949), chapter 10.

——, 1944b, 'After Bretton Woods,' *Foreign Affairs*, October; reprinted in Williams (1949), chapter 6.

——, 1945, 'Free Enterprise and Full Employment,' in *Financing American Prosperity. A Symposium by Six Economists*, New York: Twentieth Century Fund; reprinted in Williams (1953a), chapter 10.

——, 1948, 'An Appraisal of Keynesian Economics,' *American Economic Review*, Supplement, *Papers and Proceedings*, 38 (May): 273–98; reprinted in Williams (1949), chapter 1 and Williams (1953a), chapter 3.

——, 1949, *Postwar Monetary Plans and Other Essays*, Oxford: Blackwell.

——, 1951, 'International Trade Theory and Policy. Some Current Issues,' *American Economic Review*, Supplement, 41 (May); reprinted in Williams (1953a), chapter 2.

——, 1952a, 'An Economist's Confessions,' *American Economic Review*, 42(1) (March): 1–23; reprinted in Williams (1953a), chapter 1.

——, 1952b, 'End of the Marshall Plan,' *Foreign Affairs*, July; reprinted in Williams (1953a), chapter 9.

——, 1953a, *Economic Stability in a Changing World*, New York: Oxford University Press.

——, 1953b, *Trade not Aid: a Program for World Stability*, Cambridge, MA: Harvard University Press.

9
Shaping Monetary Constitutions for Developing Countries: Some Archival Evidence on the Bloomfield Missions to South Korea (1949–50)

Michele Alacevich and Pier Francesco Asso

9.1 Introduction

American economists have a long tradition of being 'economists in public service.' If we take a cursory look at the presidential addresses to the American Economic Association for the first three decades of the twentieth century (see Appendix 8.2), such subjects as the role of economists as policy advisers and public educators, or as influential consultants for foreign governments, public institutions and think-tanks were often given prominent consideration. A recent monograph (Bernstein, 2001) has provided a comprehensive overview of the strong relationship between 'Economists and public purpose in twentieth-century America', inspiring a lively debate on its nature and on the part played by some of its protagonists (Backhouse et al., 2005).

Irving Fisher was probably the first American economist to draw the attention of his colleagues to the growing needs of such professional requirements. Fisher entirely devoted his 1918 AEA presidential address to the design of the aims and qualities of the 'economist in public service', and to suggesting a detailed list of priorities for the post-war agenda. In the same context, he emphatically reminded his audience that economists ought to take direct responsibility for the shaping of a new economic order based on the principles of democracy and cooperation on a global scale. According to Fisher, 'our present opportunity is one which, if now missed, may never come again ... It is given to us as to no previous generation of economists to share in fixing the foundations for a new economic organization and one which shall harmonize with

243

the principles of democracy ... As economists in public service ... we are pledged not to serve simply our local community, our own country, or our own time, but to serve rather all humanity throughout the world and throughout future generations' (Fisher, 1919, pp. 20–1).

Following Fisher's manifesto, Edwin Kemmerer – the renowned Princeton 'money doctor' – used the same tribune to distinctively outline the prototype figure of the 'international economic adviser.' According to Kemmerer (1927), in the drastically changed post-war scenario, which also saw the US become the largest creditor country in the world, there were optimistic expectations for a massive recruitment of American economists. In fact foreign governments inevitably associated US intellectual expertise with the favorable execution of aid programs and stabilization loans. The hiring of American economists on the part of foreign countries and institutions was also associated with possible processes of technology transfers and a degree of preferential access to the American capital market. This latter aspect, Kemmerer recognized, 'undoubtedly has had much weight in the appointment of most American advisory commissions ... A country that appoints American financial advisers and follows their advise in reorganizing its finances, along what American investors consider to be the most successful modern lines, increases its chances of appealing to the American investor and of obtaining from him capital on favorable terms' (Kemmerer, 1927, p. 4). Thus, among the possible specializations that Kemmerer suggested his colleagues pursue there featured – as almost a natural priority – 'the subject of currency reforms [that] usually involves the re-establishment of the gold standard' (Kemmerer, 1927, p. 4).

As a matter of fact, and not surprisingly, the priorities of the US international economic advisers changed through the following decades. While currency reforms remained a central issue both in the 1920s and in the 1950s, the way of executing them underwent a major transformation. In this respect, an important example not thoroughly analyzed in the literature are the relations between the Federal Reserve and the governments of several less developed countries. In the first volume of Allan Meltzer's (2003) monumental and authoritative *History of the Federal Reserve* very little attention is paid to the role of Federal Reserve economists as professional advisers to foreign governments, central banks or other types of policy authorities and public agencies. From the mid-1940s on, in fact, a number of missions were organized under the auspices of the Federal Reserve Board to advise foreign countries on reshaping their monetary constitutions. Robert Triffin was the vanguard of this new era of economic advice, heading the first official mission to Paraguay

(Triffin, 1946). In particular, the 'Triffin mission' tried to establish some new milestones for post-war policy advice and form a new consensus for future missions: it decidedly moved away from the monetary automatisms and financial orthodoxy typical of the Kemmerer approach, which had characterized US monetary advice in the decades between the two world wars, and privileged an institutional framework in which central banks would have an active role in the promotion of domestic economic development (Eichengreen, 1989; Seidel, 1972; Helleiner, 2003).

Arthur I. Bloomfield, in those years an economist at the Fed in various positions, had an important part in the new course inaugurated by Triffin. He was responsible for the 1949–50 mission to Korea which aimed at establishing the country's new central bank as well as providing a thorough reform of the banking system. Besides its wide impact on the Korean economy and institutional setting, analysis of the Bloomfield mission enables a more thorough comprehension of the Fed's advisory approach – even to the extent that in some relevant aspects it departed from the so-called 'Triffin tradition.'

An attempt to present the Bloomfield mission in relation to the wider scenario of the Fed's role in the shaping of monetary institutions in post-war less-developed countries has been the object of another paper to which we refer the interested reader (Alacevich and Asso, 2009). The present chapter is more specifically focused on Bloomfield's activities as 'an economist in public service.' In its very simple structure, the chapter aims to address the following issues: after a brief reconstruction of Bloomfield's intellectual biography (Section 9.2), we try to illustrate his most original scientific contributions to the interpretation and the understanding of the international monetary system, from the heyday of the classical gold standard to the interwar collapse and subsequent reconstruction (Section 9.3). We believe that Bloomfield's intellectual characteristics – his strong drive for economic history and the history of economic thought – had a prominent influence on his policy activities. In Section 9.4, drawing from his archival papers,[1] we will try to show how Bloomfield managed to influence the writing of the new legislation that instituted profound changes to the South Korean banking system. A brief conclusion ends the chapter.

9.2   Arthur I. Bloomfield: a biographical sketch

Like John H. Williams and many other of his contemporaries, Arthur I. Bloomfield was a man of two careers: the first part of his professional life (1941–58) was entirely spent as a research economist at the Federal Reserve Bank of New York, while in the second part (1958–85) he was tenured as full (then emeritus) professor of economics at the University of Pennsylvania.[2]

A native of Montreal, Canada, born in 1914, Bloomfield received his education at McGill University (MA in economics and political science in 1936) and at the University of Chicago (PhD in economics in 1941). Here, as a student of Jacob Viner and Frank Knight, Bloomfield soon showed great talent for original research in contemporary economic history and international economics. His PhD dissertation was a successful attempt to bind these two different approaches together: it dealt with the problems associated with abnormal capital movements in the 1930s and tried to empirically evaluate their impact on the US balance of payments and on financial markets. Published in 1950 by the University of Chicago Press, it soon became recognized as a classic study of the connections between the international economy and the evolution of domestic monetary policy.

As he confessed in his autobiographical essay, 'it was from Douglas and Viner that I learned the importance of knowing the real world and real-world problems before attempting to apply abstract economic theory to reality, especially when offering policy recommendations' (Bloomfield, 1994, p. 6).[3] From the outset, Bloomfield had perceived that capital movements were a neglected item in the analysis of international adjustments and the stabilization of economic activity around its full employment equilibrium. He also believed that, through the working of financial markets and private inter-bank transactions, capital movements and foreign investments exerted a powerful influence upon domestic monetary magnitudes, the process of credit creation and, ultimately, the fluctuations of the business cycle. From a policy viewpoint, since his early studies, Bloomfield had unquestionably adhered to the ideas of the growing number of advocates of exchange and capital controls for the post-war world (Bloomfield, 1946): despite its historical interests, his research provided new evidence on the opportunity to put the international transfer of funds under some forms of collective management, extending the rationale for direct controls to the technicalities of foreign exchange markets, stock market speculation, and the sterilization of gold movements. While preparing his thesis, he also acted as research assistant to Oskar Morgenstern at Princeton University, collecting and analyzing a large amount of international financial data for major industrial countries both before 1914 and during the eventful interwar decades.

While the problems of capital movements and international financial markets were to remain his lifelong field of specialization, under the guidance of Knight and Viner, the history of economic thought soon became another area of research which Bloomfield pursued throughout his academic life. As a PhD candidate at Chicago, in 1937 he wrote a thorough reconstruction on 'Thorstein Veblen and his Analysis of Business Enterprise' which was presented in Knight's renowned 305 Econ. Class. Anticipating future lines of research, Bloomfield's debut as a historian of economics is remarkable in at least three respects: first, it is one of the earliest attempts critically to reappraise the *theoretical* contributions of the so-called institutionalist school through an original and exhaustive analysis of the contemporary literature in the field; second, it contains a lucid description of the differences, both methodological and analytical, between Veblen's and Commons's theories of the modern business enterprise; third, it contains – to our knowledge – the first presentation of the similarities between Veblen's and Keynes's interpretations of the instability of capitalism. As to the latter point, it should be emphasized that, as early as spring 1937, Bloomfield anticipated some of the themes which were to be developed by Routledge Vining's (1939) first classic article on Keynes and Veblen.

After leaving the University of Chicago in 1941, Bloomfield joined the staff of the Federal Reserve Bank of New York as a research economist, where he stayed until 1958. In this position, Bloomfield combined scholarly research on recent economic history and international financial and banking problems with active service as a member of various committees and commissions, both in the United States and abroad. While on leave from the Fed, he accepted appointments as a consultant and adviser to various central banks and institutions. As a research economist Bloomfield wrote a vast number of memoranda and papers on a wide range of topics, from international banking and finance to domestic monetary policy. Working under the direct supervision of the influential NY Fed president, Allan Sproul, he produced in-house memoranda which were subsequently relevant for the Federal plan of fixing banks' reserve requirements in a uniform manner.[4] In 1947 Bloomfield became the chief economist of the Balance of Payments Division and then senior economist in 1953. During his stay at the New York Fed he also served on several governmental commissions, the most noteworthy being the Wilbur Commission to Indo-China and the Randall Commission on US Foreign Trade Policy (Ethier and Marston, 1985, pp. 1–2).

As Jack Guttentag and Richard Herring (1985, p. 19) observed in a paper prepared to celebrate his university retirement, Bloomfield's insights on international capital flows and the functioning of financial markets 'managed to influence the research of several generations of scholars and have affected the conduct of monetary policy, particularly in the several countries in which he has advised central banks.' In fact, between the mid-1940 and the end of the 1950s, Bloomfield was a member of several official missions to developing countries – mainly in East Asia. The nature of these trips varied as well as the agency under which Bloomfield operated as a consultant. Looking at the most important ones, in his advisory activities Bloomfield helped to establish central banks, advised on the reforms of financial markets, banking systems, and currency regimes, and provided an evaluation of the economic impact of foreign aid programs. His most frequent destinations were South Korea, Indochina, and Malaysia. Besides the Federal Reserve System, Bloomfield advised on behalf of the Economic Cooperation Administration, the United Nations Reconstruction Agency, the US Government, and the Ford Foundation.

As an academic economist – ever since his early education at the University of Chicago – his chief areas of research remained international economics, economic history, and the history of economic thought. From the early 1940s, he was a frequent contributor to major academic journals and later served as a member of the editorial board of the *Journal of Post-Keynesian Economics*. Author of many books on international economics and economic history, he also published – following a strong Vinerian tradition – a collection of *Essays in the History of International Economic Thought* (Bloomfield, 1994). Full professor of economics at the University of Pennsylvania, he was also visiting professor at the City University of New York, Columbia, Princeton, Johns Hopkins, and the University of Melbourne.

9.3   Arthur Bloomfield: a historian of economics at the Federal Reserve Bank of New York

Until the late 1950s, in the macroeconomic analysis of open economies, capital movements did not receive much attention as compared to commodity movements. Together with James Tobin, Charles Kindleberger, Harry Johnson, Leland Yaeger, and others, Arthur Bloomfield played a significant part in redressing the balance. In his historical studies (Bloomfield, 1942–43, 1950, 1959, 1963), Bloomfield showed how the nature and role of private short-term capital movements before 1914 had usually been downplayed by other economists, and their degree of sensitivity to interest rates and exchange rate variations highly exaggerated. In his more technical and applied studies (Bloomfield, 1940, 1944, 1946,

1954a, 1954b), Bloomfield convincingly demonstrated the importance of integrating capital movements into both theoretical and empirical analyses, moving decisively beyond their supposed financial and adjustment function. In this section we will briefly summarize Bloomfield's main contributions to these issues.

Both during his stay at the Fed and as a university professor Bloomfield wrote classic works on the history of the international monetary system and on the changing forms of international financial transactions. With some of his contributions to academic journals he also participated in early debates on the causes and consequences of foreign direct investments (Bloomfield, 1940, 1942–43, 1944, 1959, 1963). His most significant scientific achievements were in these fields, beginning with his critical evaluation of the existing literature on the real functioning of past international monetary regimes.

According to many interpreters (Cleveland, 1976; De Cecco, 1984; Flanders, 1989; Eichengreen, 1992), Bloomfield's research provided path-breaking insights in undermining the traditional theory of the classical gold standard. In particular, in two essays (1959 and 1963) Bloomfield questioned the historical accuracy of the neoclassical picture of the gold standard, demonstrating the emptiness of the widely-believed myth that the gold standard worked automatically and in accordance to the prescriptions of Hume's price-specie-flow mechanism. In so doing he also challenged the classical view that the dominant and overriding objective of monetary policy was the maintenance of gold parity in order to safeguard the nominal convertibility of the money supply. His critical evaluation of the pre-WWI international monetary system was also directed to understanding the real reasons for its apparent smoothness and stability. In his opinion, external stability had very weak connections with the neoclassical view of central banks following some pre-determined 'rules of the game' in a symmetrical and passive fashion. Thus – even when it coincided with international stability and an overall maintenance of external equilibrium – the age of the gold standard entailed more institutional discretion, more political asymmetries and a greater variety of policy objectives than the Cunliffe Report (1918) and subsequent textbook-like descriptions had implied. Together with Ragnar Nurkse (1961) and Robert Triffin (1964), Arthur Bloomfield significantly contributed to revising the interpretation of how the gold standard actually worked.

Using empirical data collected from central banks' official and archival sources, Bloomfield provided unambiguous evidence of the highly discretionary monetary policy put forward by national monetary authorities in the heyday of the gold standard. He also showed that before 1914 short-term international capital flows had often a benevolent nature and played an important role in keeping the international monetary system in equilibrium. Particularly at the European periphery, most central banks proved to be unable to attract gold through discount rate changes. As a consequence, monetary authorities began to build a double line of defense of the exchange rate parity, fostering the stability of the pound and the general confidence in Britain's capacity to effectively manage the system: the outer layer, as Bloomfield showed, consisted of foreign currencies denominated assets and short-term credits on the London money market, while the inner (and thinner) layer consisted of earmarked gold reserves. It also followed that by the end of the nineteenth century – as Bloomfield pointed out – trading in foreign securities had become an accustomed practice of both public and private investors, exerting more powerful (and often undesired) effects on domestic monetary aggregates than those resulting from commodity movements.

Therefore the automatic working of the gold standard was, according to Bloomfield (1959, p. 25), 'a misconception.' Not only did central banking authorities 'not consistently follow any simple or single rule or criterion of policy, or focus exclusively on considerations of convertibility, but they were constantly called upon to exercise, and did exercise, their judgement on such matters as whether or not to act in any given situation, and if so at what point of time to act, the kind and extent of action to take' (ibid.) Frequent violation of the so-called 'rules of the game' thus entailed an autonomous conduct of monetary policy and central banks were actively engaged in sterilization policies which implied offsetting the domestic impact of reserve and gold flows on credit markets and the relevant monetary magnitudes. Moreover, the achievement and maintenance of reasonable stability in the level of domestic economic activity and prices was widely accepted as an important objective of monetary policy while no convincing evidence existed that, in the exercise of this discretion, central banks were governed by strict rules of behavior over the money supply. On the contrary, as Harold van Cleveland put it, Arthur Bloomfield was the first interpreter to show that 'the rules of the game seem to have been a bit of ideology invented by latter generations of bankers and economists attempting to play down the political dimension of monetary policy' (Cleveland, 1976, p. 14).

In his works on the history of the gold standard, there were many other important insights which influenced his professional research in other directions. To put it briefly, Bloomfield was among the first interpreters who believed that the success of the gold standard largely depended on its political asymmetry and on the existence of a stable and powerful economy which operated as the 'core' of the system: for the last part of the nineteenth century, this could be easily identified with Great Britain and the Bank of England, which exercised a great deal of hegemonic control over monetary conditions throughout the gold standard era. Bloomfield effectively showed that in the 20 years before the First World War, upward and downward movements of discount rates were cyclically synchronized, with the Bank of England acting as the leader of the international money market. Again, also from this perspective, it followed that the stability of the external accounts was not the only relevant criterion for determining the rediscount rate. Not only did monetary policy have its own independent goals but most central banks were also commercial banks and were very much exposed to competition in the money markets.

Thus, the fact that the gold standard apparently worked so well also depended on the strength of the British monetary authorities and on the widespread confidence in the compensatory nature of private short-term capital movements. At times of strain, Britain's capacity to attract financial assets from overseas proved to be an important source of support to its official reserves. From Bloomfield's work, economists and economic historians began to realize how the system was effectively controlled and how this control served the purpose of keeping monetary conditions consistent with the fundamental commitment of exchange rate stability and convertibility in gold standard countries. Using the terminology of his mentor at the New York Fed, John H. Williams, Bloomfield described the gold standard as a 'key currency' system with France and the US as co-protagonists capable of exerting significant influence on Britain's monetary policy and on the overall stability of the international monetary system.[5] Together with Lindert (1969), Bloomfield also showed that London was not the only financial center of the system since other centers were needed to serve the requirements of the European periphery. Particularly France, with its large gold holdings, played an essential role in maintaining overall stability, as long as it came in support of the Bank of England effort to manage the system in times of strain.

Thus, another crucial factor for stability was, according to Bloomfield, the credibility of cooperation between central banks, an issue upon which subsequent interpreters have put a great deal of emphasis (Clarke, 1967; De Cecco, 1984; Eichengreen, 1992). In contrast to the prescriptions of the traditional model, monetary policy tended to move in parallel, and cyclical movements of the relevant fundamentals of economic activity tended to be synchronous. Again, all this was possible because the Bank of England played a coordinating role and was able to orchestrate, as Keynes had put it, world credit conditions. The Bank of England leverage was effective so long as it preserved its capacity to produce the 'key currency' of the system. In fact, another source of endogenous stability rested on the widespread use of the pound as the international medium used in commodity transactions and highly preferred by foreign investors.

Apart from the highly influential impact of his historical studies, Bloomfield made a number of other original contributions to international financial economics. Associated with his research activities as a central bank economist, Bloomfield published many works which dealt with the international ramifications of monetary policy and the different behavior and techniques of private investors in international financial markets.

Before Bloomfield's contributions, the analysis of income transfers was the main argument of many, if not most, studies of capital movements. With the rise of the Keynesian doctrine, the analysis of transfers came to be integrated in the income expenditure approach but still capital flows remained an exclusive part of the theory of balance of payments adjustment. In his more theoretical and applied studies, Bloomfield challenged the cogency of this approach, providing important insights for the elaboration of a new 'portfolio approach' to international financial transactions.

Although he realized that capital movements could under certain circumstances ease the financing and even the adjustment mechanism, Bloomfield's studies of the international monetary system challenged at the outset the concept that short-term capital movements always played a benevolent role. His research thus followed the neo-Keynesian literature on capital movements, placing a strong emphasis on the destabilizing, exogenous, abnormal nature of financial transactions and on the need for maintaining some forms of official controls. In this vein, Bloomfield provided a fine description of the perverse behavior and disruptive effects of interwar capital movements, analyzing the interactions between spot and forward markets, the techniques and pattern of exchange speculation, the sterilization of currency, and gold movements (Bloomfield, 1940, 1942–43, 1944, 1946). Even in the years of the Marshall plan, he believed that financial transfers risked the production of undesired dilemmas and disturbing effects of a dis-equilibrating nature. In fact, in his view, a significant part of the US official foreign aid program was doomed to finance hot money movements and bring about an increase in governmental control of the private economy. Expressing his views unofficially in academic journals, he was pessimistic about the prospects for the overall impact of the recovery program – particularly if private investors came to be suddenly integrated in a global financial market: by building up uncovered positions in the forward exchange market, or by means of incorrect invoicing and private compensation arrangements, he argued that most capital tended to flow back from the recipient economies to the US (Bloomfield, 1954a, 1954b).

Applying a Keynesian approach to the American economy, Bloomfield also tried to show that capital inflows were unable to generate pro-adjustment income variations, because of their incapacity to stimulate the necessary variations of aggregate investments or of the foreign trade multiplier. An increase of autonomous capital inflows was thus likely completely to miss 'the first step of the Keynesian process' (Flanders, 1989, pp. 211ff.) In contrast, unfettered capital movements had strong repercussions in the stock markets and on credit conditions, which ultimately determined their possibly stabilizing or destabilizing effects. Whenever financial transactions took the shape of increases in foreign holdings of domestic bank deposits – under the common character of a capital flight, or of speculation regarding expected changes of the exchange rate parity – there was absolutely no guarantee that a primary income disbursement would occur, as long as they remained idle in the hands of foreigners. Moreover, the banking system was also unlikely endogenously to expand the money supply on the basis of these increased reserves because of their highly volatile nature and of widespread fears of a reversal of the movement.

Bloomfield's approach to international economics again started from Keynesian premises: balance of payments equilibrium largely depended on income changes rather than on terms of trade variations and was influenced by autonomous policy decisions affecting the level of aggregate demand. Therefore, the chief factor tending to cause parallel fluctuations in the trade and long-term capital balances (and thereby in maintaining a rough equilibrium of the external accounts) was the general influence that aggregate demand played upon the external accounts.

In his doctoral dissertation Bloomfield decidedly set aside the analysis of the transfer mechanism and proceeded to develop an analysis of asset allocation. US capital inflows in the late 1930s were the results not of net transfers of income but of a sudden shift in investors' preferences on behalf of domestic assets. In this study Bloomfield observed that a significant proportion of the US capital inflow in the late 1930s involved increases in foreigners' holdings of dollar deposits at US banks rather than investment in outstanding securities. Because such capital flows led to corresponding increases in the banks' demand for high powered money they were less likely to generate changes in income and interest rates that worked towards a re-equilibrium of the balance of payments (Ethier and Marston, 1985).

Bloomfield's theory of capital movements has thus been considered to be fully consistent with the modern portfolio approach (Ethier and Marston, 1985). In two of his early articles (Bloomfield, 1940, 1944), he analyzed the greater relevance of the international movement of out-standing securities as a typical phenomenon of portfolio diversification, which involved private investors, central banks, and the activities of the exchange stabilization funds. Already the largest item in the American balance of payments with the exception of merchandise trade, Bloom-field showed how a large part of security transfers was the result of regular arbitrage operations which also had relevant implications for the international propagation of business cycles.

We now come to analyze Bloomfield's activities as an economic adviser. In particular, through the analysis of archival material related to his 1949–50 mission to Korea – his first assignment 'and perhaps for that reason the most memorable' (Bloomfield, 1994, p. 10) – we will try to shed light on his contribution to, and interpretation of, the Fed's post-war advisory initiatives toward developing countries.

9.4   Arthur Bloomfield and central banking in South Korea

When the Bloomfield mission landed in Korea for the first time in September 1949 in order to help the government in drafting and putting to work a modern central bank, the political and economic prospects of the country were not particularly bright.[6]

The Republic of Korea was born as an independent state in August 1948, after decades of Japanese occupation, separated from its north-ern territories – which had fallen under the Soviet sphere of influence – along the 38th parallel. As a result of this dramatic split, the already dif-ficult economic conditions of the country had further declined. What had been 'a basic complementarity' (Bloomfield and Jensen, 1951, p. 12) between the northern industrial and mining sector and the southern agricultural sector, when divided turned into an enduring condition of shortages of foodstuffs (principally in the north) and of raw mat-erials and intermediate goods (principally in the south). Moreover, the Korean economic scenario was rendered more gloomy by the persistence of poor macroeconomic indicators. Among them Korea's development was seriously constrained by very low aggregate savings and the lack of anything resembling a money market or a stock exchange market. Due to the prolonged Japanese occupation, the country also suffered from the absence of a really independent monetary authority.

All experts agreed that the main economic problem of that period was a mounting inflationary spiral. As to its fundamental causes, the two American advisers drew up a long list which included monetary, institutional and structural factors: 'Large-scale, central-bank financed, deficit spending by the Korean Government, chiefly reflecting heavy defense and security expenditures, subsidies to government-owned enterprises and public utilities operating on a deficit basis, inefficient budgetary accounting controls, and poor tax collections, coupled with an undue expansion of bank credit to government agencies operating outside the budget' (Bloomfield and Jensen, 1951, p. 21). A growing aggregate demand on one side, and an economic system unable to efficiently increase production on the other, pushed up prices (and wages as a consequence), while goods were being hoarded, and the propensity to save further diminished (Choi, 1997).

Notwithstanding the unstable political and economic situation of the country, the Act Establishing the Bank of Korea drafted by Bloomfield and Jensen proved to be very rich and articulated, and distinctly modern in its overall approach. The bulk of the act (Bloomfield and Jensen, 1951, Appendix 1) was devoted to the definition of the main governing bodies of the new institution – principally, the so-called 'Monetary Board' – and to the definition of their functions, instruments, and powers. A relevant fraction of the act was devoted to re-designing on a clearer basis the financial relations between the bank and the government. Some attention was also given to the question of total credit control – recognized as the primary function and responsibility of a modern central bank – and to the shaping of the monetary instruments at the disposal of the institution in order to effectively exercise that control over the banking system.

The principal aim of the act was that of establishing a 'genuine central bank' (Bloomfield and Jensen, 1951, p. 43), as opposed to the previous central monetary institution, the Bank of Chosun, which had always been vulnerable to political pressures and had never been able to exert efficient control over the supply of money and credit. Bloomfield and Jensen, thus, opted not for a reformation of the previous bank, but for the foundation of a completely new institution, more independent from governmental control. The central bank independence was built on the wide powers which were conferred to the Monetary Board. The Monetary

Board was the principal body of government of the institution and 'the sharpest break from previous Korean banking tradition,'[7] that is from the Bank of Chosun.[8]

Some fundamental aspects of the act emerge with great clarity from the analysis of Bloomfield's collection of private papers. In particular, in the correspondence with their colleagues in New York and with the local authorities in Seoul, the two American economists showed a strong sensitivity to the historical context in which they were operating, and to the juridical and institutional traditions with which they were confronted. In the meantime, adapting the Fed policy to South Korea, they gradually became convinced that a partial departure from the Triffin approach was necessary. We will now consider these issues separately.

First of all, the relevance of the historical context and of the country's traditions. Bloomfield and Jensen called attention to both issues at the very beginning of their final report:

> Our mission to South Korea was undertaken at a time of spiralling inflation, a marked state of flux and transition in the country's economy, and political uncertainties associated with the Communist menace from North of the 38th Parallel ... Certain sections of our banking statutes ... had to be drafted primarily from the viewpoint of the prevailing abnormal state of affairs, and were admittedly unsatisfactory or incomplete from a longer run point of view. Other sections of the statutes had to be drafted in unusually broad terms in order to provide as much room as possible for future flexibility.
>
> (Bloomfield and Jensen, 1951, p. 5)

Also, the 'deliberate looseness' of some of the provisions relating to foreign exchange was due to the very fluid and changing situation, and to the need not to hamper or compromise the ECA efforts in its 'daily grappling with the Koreans over the whole foreign exchange set-up.'[9]

As Bloomfield made clear in a letter to Henry Wallich – the Fed economist who was then in charge of the Latin American missions – the exact wording of their statute was a way to point out, 'somewhat discreetly perhaps,' that the current situation in Korea was 'entirely inappropriate for any real banking reform.' Bloomfield added: 'had Frank Tamagna come out here in September [1949] (as we did) instead of the previous Spring, he would not, I am sure, have recommended any Federal Reserve mission at all.'[10]

The proposals that Bloomfield and Jensen could present were thus strongly affected by the precarious conditions of the Korean political and economic situation: 'it was both difficult and unrealistic to look too far ahead in drafting our acts or to insert detailed provisions covering situations or conditions not likely to prevail for some time, if at all.'[11]

Bloomfield insisted on the same elements a couple of years later in a letter to Lee Ho Sang, the chief of secretariat of the newly-established Korean central bank. On that occasion, Bloomfield reaffirmed that the statute had had to be structured in a flexible and adaptable way in order to cope with the political and financial uncertainties of the country. This was particularly true for what concerned the spectrum and technical characteristics of central bank operations: 'it had clearly been impossible ... to lay down detailed instructions and rules regarding all possible affairs and activities of the Bank. Broad powers were consequently left in the hands of the Monetary Board to decide upon various matters that were not deemed of sufficient importance to require special provisions.'[12]

Political considerations were also at the basis of their choice that most powers ought to be concentrated within the Monetary Board. A strong Monetary Board, in fact, was a compulsory option since, 'otherwise,' as Bloomfield wrote to Wallich, 'the objectionable influence of the Ministry of Finance (which is one of our primary objectives to eliminate) will intrude itself excessively.'[13] In the same line, Bloomfield and Jensen worked hard to take away from the government all supervisory powers over the new central bank monetary policy and accounts. In their original draft, in fact, the two American experts had provided that the bank should only be examined by a completely independent National Board of Audit. However, this safeguarding clause did not survive political scrutiny and the Korean parliament soon amended this article, adding to the National Board of Audit the Ministry of Finance, which Bloomfield and Jensen were trying to keep as far as possible from any intrusion in the bank's activity.[14]

While trying to keep the bank clear of political influence as far as possible, Bloomfield and Jensen were nonetheless aware that creating a new central bank completely independent from any political intrusion would not be feasible: the historical heritage of a central banking institution subservient to the political power was too strong and too close in time to be definitively overcome. As a result, the Monetary Board designed by Bloomfield presented a peculiar mix of 'advanced' and 'backward' characteristics. On the one hand it was undoubtedly strong, with huge decision-making and control powers: the formulation of strategies and objectives of monetary policy, for example, pertained totally to the board, while the governor had a merely operative role. On the other hand, however, the board inevitably remained exposed to government pressures, since four of its seven members were government appointees. As Bloomfield lucidly wrote in a letter to Wallich, 'our failure to write into the Act any stronger provisions regarding the bank's loans to the government was due ... to the sheer uselessness of attempting anything more at this time.'[15]

Notwithstanding the attempt made by Bloomfield and Jensen to draft an act that would take into account the historical heritage of the government's influence over the operations of the central bank, the Korean Minister of Finance strongly opposed the new central bank legislation. This opposition reached the point that, soon after the beginning of operations, he favored the presentation to the Korean National Assembly of a bill amending the act drafted by Bloomfield and Jensen, whose main provision was the abolition of the Monetary Board. These political attacks did not provoke the end of the Monetary Board even though, between the end of 1951 and the beginning of 1952, both the governor and the deputy-governor of the Bank of Korea were forced to resign from their positions.[16]

Second, and apart from the current circumstances, Bloomfield also emphasized the influence of Korean cultural and juridical traditions in drafting the statute of the new central bank. In fact, even a brief acquaintance with these traditions had shown the inappropriateness of their original plan: it was simply impossible to transfer to Korea provisions that were common characteristics of the US legal and financial systems. In this perspective, Bloomfield observed that unforeseen obstacles were particularly pervasive, and underlined 'the difficulties of giving precise Korean connotations to even such simple words as "control", "management", etc.'[17] As a consequence, it was not possible to cover all the details regarding central bank operations, or to treat them unambiguously. The issue was not a minor one, and in fact it had been promptly noted by the ECA Mission to Korea, which had already pointed out that 'the draft law deviates from the pattern of American statutes inasmuch as it does not contain a list of "definitions".'[18]

Third, the two advisers were aware that they were operating in a somewhat exceptional situation. The uncertain political and historical conditions, and the burden of Korean traditions, strongly influenced by Japanese culture, rendered the Korean case strikingly different from the Latin American countries that had already been visited by other Fed economists. Hence, the so-called 'Triffin tradition' could not be blindly followed, and some deviations from it were necessary.

The partial departure from the Triffin tradition soon became apparent in at least two specific characteristics of the Bloomfield mission.

First – as already observed in relation with the powers of the Monetary Board – a much higher level of incompleteness or looseness of several articles in the act was unavoidable. In Bloomfield's words, 'the whole situation may blow up at any time,' therefore 'our desire [is] to write as simple an act as possible and one designed chiefly to meet the situation now existing and likely to prevail in the near future.'[19] As the decade wore on, Bloomfield was aware that the situation in which the mission had to operate was in rapid transformation, and thus deliberately drafted 'provisions in the acts, which ... permit of a considerable measure of freedom and adaptability to changing conditions.'[20]

Second, the two American experts showed a much more evident and conscious attitude toward 'conservative banking principles'[21] than the one adopted by the Latin American missions. This more conservative approach was deemed to be necessary in view both of the serious inflationary bent prevailing in the country at that time,[22] and of the discontinuity that was to be posed in relation to the previous monetary authority, the Bank of Chosun. As for this latter point, it must be considered that before the war the Bank of Chosun had had a very activist orientation in promoting industrialization and financing the growth of new national productions, in close connection with the government's desiderata. Bloomfield's attempt to make the central banking institution structurally more independent, and moreover not a vehicle for inflationary pressures, resulted in his orientation toward a pretty 'orthodox' banking approach. By contrast, the Fed missions in Latin America had faced the opposite situation, trying to transform very orthodox Kemmerer-style central banks into more activist institutions actively engaged in promoting industrialization and proto-Keynesian planning.[23]

While in this respect the Korean mission departed from the Triffin approach to central banking reform, it is also necessary to remark the common background which inspired both the Latin American and the Korean missions. In both cases, the aim was that of funding a new type of central bank, inspired by similar analyses of the role of monetary institutions: the rigid Kemmerer-style central bank, mainly characterized by passive regulatory functions, was no longer considered sufficient for the needs of countries that were eager to jump on the bandwagon of development and growth: both Triffin in Latin America, and Bloomfield in Korea, agreed to design monetary institutions which were actively committed to pursuing real growth objectives for their own countries.

The Korean situation imposed some 'stringent limitations'[24] to this strategy, and the policy priorities of the new central bank were in the first place those of controlling inflationary pressures. Yet, once the inflation was under control, a number of further measures would become possible: 'above all, the basis will be laid for an orderly, planned program of economic rehabilitation and reconstruction.'[25] Bloomfield remarked this point in an academic paper which addressed the issue of how to reform central banking in developing countries: 'The majority of central banks in underdeveloped countries have in actual practice adopted a variety of measures designed more actively to promote the over-all development of their economies. Some of these measures are admittedly outside the traditional scope of central banking, but central banking in these countries should not necessarily be evaluated in terms of the standards and criteria applied in the more developed ones' (Bloomfield, 1957, p. 197).

Thus, while it is useful to underline the different directions taken by monetary and banking advisers in Latin America and in Korea – from orthodoxy to unorthodoxy in the former, and from unorthodoxy to orthodoxy in the latter – it must also be recognized that their starting points were very different. Both missions were in fact converging toward a new model of central bank reforms, neither prone to political interference, nor indifferent to the process of economic growth or to the historical contingencies which characterized specific contexts. As Frank Tamagna put it, Bloomfield's design of the Korean central bank 'would make it an effective instrument of national economic policy toward the immediate objective of stabilization, and the longer-range aim of self-sustained development' (Tamagna, 1952, p. 86).

Inflation remained a major problem for the Korean economy until the 1980s, when single-digit values were eventually reached. In 1957 a financial stabilization program was launched through which credit ceilings and other restrictive instruments were set for each single sector of production. Political instability caused the suspension of the program, but the implementation of the first five-year program, and its consequences on the internal rate of inflation and the balance of payments, pushed the Korean government to institute its revival. In 1965, a stand-by agreement with the IMF permitted Korea to reverse the persistent deficits of the balance of payments. More significant paradigm changes – with pre-announced inflation targeting and open market operations – took place under the revised Bank of Korea Act that came into effect in April 1998 (Park, 2002).

9.5   Conclusions

This chapter deals with the efforts made by the Fed economist Arthur Bloomfield to apply the economic lessons of the 1930s to the post-war reform of the monetary constitutions of developing countries. In particular, we have examined Bloomfield's intellectual biography and shown how he acquired an early interest in economic history and international economics. Attacking traditional views in praise of the automatic working of the gold standard, Bloomfield emphasized the role played by nineteenth-century central banks in guaranteeing stability and growth. Moreover, his critical account of the gold standard literature, helped him to develop a deep-rooted skepticism toward the dogmatic recipes which American advisers had been trying to sell to peripheral countries in the interwar era. From his studies Bloomfield also gained a profound knowledge of international capital markets that, in his view, strengthened the need for a national monetary authority, leaning against the wind provoked by the vagaries of short-term capital movements. The basic features of the act establishing a new Bank of Korea were conceived in the wake of the new Triffin approach, which had been elaborated during the Second World War, even though the act departed in a number of ways from the model of central banking that Triffin himself had drafted for some Latin American countries.

Analysis of the Bloomfield papers has made it possible to document the various forces that influenced the early post-war banking reform in South Korea. Bloomfield and Jensen attempted to draft a central monetary institution that could cope with the complex tasks of stabilization and reconstruction in a developing country, and at the same time paid due consideration to the historical, juridical and political conditions of the country. The American mission also agreed that to attempt a too strict separation between the bank and the government would be useless and naive, and as a consequence many points were deliberately left unexplained. This, in its turn, meant that they ultimately decided to write an act that left some gaps and ambiguities and perhaps some excessive margins of flexibility. The very definition of 'price inflation' was left somewhat vague, as Bloomfield recalled to Wallich. Rather, the American mission opted for the generic formula of 'abnormal price movements.'[26]

However, what was more fundamental, was that the institution be aware of the nature and the purposes of the different monetary instruments at its disposal, and that a rigorous use of them be made. It was decided that a greater number of objectives ought to be assigned to the new central bank, while the indication of their priorities and of the instruments to be used for their achievement was left to the full discretion of the central banker.[27]

The Act Establishing the Bank of Korea must thus be considered a statute 'in the making,' and Bloomfield and Jensen were perfectly conscious of this fact. The rapidly changing economic, political and institutional conditions of the country made a final reform impossible. When asked to comment on the more ambiguous aspects of his draft, Bloomfield stated clearly that: 'when financial stability has been firmly achieved in this country, certain provisions could properly be redrafted in the light of the new financial framework then existing.'[28]

Shaping monetary institutions in developing countries seemed to Bloomfield a medium-term task; not useless, but not definitive. Defending Jensen's and his work from some open criticisms 'written ... at ten thousand miles from "the scene of battle",' Bloomfield synthesized the nature of their mission thus: 'Jensen and I would be the last people in the world to suggest that our central banking Act represents an ideal piece of legislation in all respects. But we were not dealing with an ideal situation. As far as I am aware, it was the most abnormal situation in which anyone, certainly a representative of the [Federal Reserve] System, ever attempted to carry through a central banking reform.'[29]

Notes

Research in the Bloomfield manuscript papers was sustained by a grant conceded by the Economics Department together with the Rare Books, Manuscript, and Special Collection Library of the Duke University, Durham, NC, USA. The authors acknowledge their gratitude to the staff at the Rare Books, Manuscript, and Special Collection Library for their kind help during the collection of archival documents. The authors thank Ms Dorothy Bloomfield for her permission to use archival materials from the Arthur Bloomfield papers. The authors also wish to thank Robert Dimand, Pedro Garcia Duarte, Robert Helleiner, Robert Leeson, Steve Meardon, and Perry Mehrling, who read a first draft of the present chapter providing useful comments. The usual disclaimer applies.

1. Arthur I. Bloomfield's papers are held at the Rare Book, Manuscript, and Special Collections Library at Duke University, NC, USA. The collection covers the entire career of Bloomfield, as an economist at the Federal Reserve Bank of New York (1941–58), as an economic adviser to several overseas government, and as a scholar and professor on international finance, central banking, the gold standard, the economic development of the UK and the British Commonwealth countries, and the history of economic thought (1931–95). Following the many interests of Bloomfield, the collection is comprised of six main series: 'Correspondence,' 'Federal Reserve,' 'Gold Standard,' 'History of Economic Thought,' 'Research,' and 'Miscellaneous.' Documents regarding Bloomfield's overseas assignments as an economic adviser (Korea, Indochina, Malaysia, Zaire, British West Indies) are held in the 'Research Files Series,' and

more precisely in Boxes 6 and 7. Related material can also be found in the 'Correspondence Series.'

2. Bloomfield wrote an autobiographical essay which served as the introductory chapter to Bloomfield (1994).

3. In preparing his dissertation, Bloomfield (1950, p. x) also acknowledged his intellectual debts to Lloyd Mints, Frank Graham, and Oskar Lange.

4. Bloomfield papers, Duke University, Rare Book, Manuscript, and Special Collections Library (henceforth AIBP), Boxes 2 and 3.

5. On Williams and the key currency approach, see Asso and Fiorito (Chapter 8, above).

6. The responsibility of the mission was shared with John P. Jensen, assistant chief of the Fed Auditing Division, who was a specialist in bank supervision and examination. Jensen's work was conceived to be one of investigating the balance sheet positions of the Korean banks, but in fact he participated in almost all aspects of the mission. Bloomfield considered his performance 'altogether excellent,' as he reported in a letter to Mr Dillistin, 'Appraisal of Mr. Jensen's work in Korea,' 1 June 1950, AIBP. Bloomfield left the country in March 1950, while Jensen remained to see the new South Korean Central Bank – the Bank of Korea – open for business on 12 June. Other missions to Korea followed in 1951 and 1956, and to Indochina in 1953 and 1954. While at the University of Pennsylvania, Bloomfield was a member of missions to Malaysia, Zaire and the West Indies. See Bloomfield (1994, pp. 14ff.)

7. Arthur I. Bloomfield, 'A Report on Monetary Policy and Banking in Korea,' Seoul, Korea, 30 November 1956, p. 57, AIBP.

8. For an analysis of the role and functions of the Monetary Board, and its relations with the Korean government on one side and the bank's top officers – for example, the governor – on the other, see Alacevich and Asso (2009).

9. Arthur Bloomfield to Henry Wallich, Seoul, 8 March 1950, AIBP.

10. Arthur Bloomfield to Henry Wallich, Seoul, 8 March 1950, AIBP. Frank Tamagna was another Fed economist who, at the time of this letter, was in charge of the Far East, and had recommended the mission after a visit to Korea just after the end of the Second World War.

11. Arthur Bloomfield to Henry Wallich, Seoul, 8 March 1950, AIBP.

12. Arthur I. Bloomfield to Mr Lee Ho Sang, 28 February 1952, AIBP.

13. Arthur Bloomfield to Henry Wallich, Seoul, 8 March 1950, AIBP.

14. In 1952 Bloomfield criticized this amendment, stating that 'the Ministry of Finance should not have the power to examine the Bank of Korea, since that function can be adequately performed by the National Board of Audit alone; dual examination authority can lead only to confusion and unnecessary duplication,' Arthur I. Bloomfield to Mr Lee Ho Sang, 28 February 1952, AIBP.

15. Arthur Bloomfield to Henry Wallich, Seoul, 8 March 1950, AIBP

16. A.I. Bloomfield to Colonel Wm E. Carraway, 'The Controversy Between the Ministry of Finance and the Bank of Korea,' 15 December 1951, AIBP. Referring to the dismissal of the bank's deputy governor, Bloomfield commented: 'it is the latest, and to me the most revolting, in a long series of maneuvers by the Ministry of Finance to "move into" the Bank of Korea in violation of the spirit and the letter of the Bank of Korea Act; the technique employed has consisted, among others, of forcing the dismissal of officials who have opposed

the Ministry on banking matters and of engineering the appointment of former Ministry officials in their places,' A.I. Bloomfield to Colonel Wm. E. Carraway, 'Dismissal of Deputy Governor Chang,' 20 February 1952, AIBP. Bloomfield commented on this episode in several documents addressed to the United Nations mission to Korea (United Nations Civil Assistance Command, Korea – UNCACK): A.I. Bloomfield to Colonel William E. Carraway, 'The New Governor of the Bank of Korea,' 19 December 1951, AIBP; A.I. Bloomfield to Col. Wm E. Carraway, 'Miscellaneous Notes on Banking,' 23 January 1952, AIBP. During the controversy, Bloomfield was also the target of a direct attack: on 30 December 1951 the Korean newspaper *Sang Ko Il Bo* tried to discredit Bloomfield, attributing to him some remarks particularly critical toward both the Ministry of Finance and the UN mission, remarks which he was alleged to have made before some Korean businessmen, A.I. Bloomfield to Brigadier General W. E. Crist, 'The *Sang Ko Il Bo* Story,' 3 January 1952, AIBP; Yong Soon Chun to Dr Bloomfield, 2 January 1952, AIBP .

17.   Arthur Bloomfield to Henry Wallich, Seoul, 8 March 1950, AIBP.
18.   ECA Mission to Korea, Legal Section, Memorandum to Mr Bloomfield and Mr Jensen, 'Draft Act Establishing the Bank of Korea,' 30 January 1950, AIBP.
19.   Arthur Bloomfield to Henry Wallich, Seoul, 8 March 1950, AIBP.
20.   Arthur I. Bloomfield to Mr Lee Ho Sang, 28 February 1952, AIBP.
21.   A.I. Bloomfield to Colonel Wm E. Carraway, 'The Controversy Between the Ministry of Finance and the Bank of Korea,' 15 December 1951, AIBP.
22.   A.I. Bloomfield, 'An Appraisal of the Position and Prospects of the South Korean Economy at the End of 1951,' attached to A.I. Bloomfield to Col. Wm E. Carraway, 4 January 1952, AIBP.
23.   We are grateful to Eric Helleiner who called our attention to this point.
24.   A.I. Bloomfield to Colonel Wm E. Carraway, 'The Controversy Between the Ministry of Finance and the Bank of Korea,' 15 December 1951, AIBP.
25.   A.I. Bloomfield, 'An Appraisal of the Position and Prospects of the South Korean Economy at the End of 1951,' attached to A.I. Bloomfield to Col. Wm E. Carraway, 4 January 1952, AIBP.
26.   Arthur Bloomfield to Henry Wallich, Seoul, 8 March 1950, AIBP.
27.   For example, when Bloomfield was asked to clarify his interpretation of the provision which enabled the bank to 'grant advances, in periods of grave emergency when monetary and banking stability is threatened' (Act Establishing the Bank of Korea, Art. 69-c), he pointed out that that article had been conceived to avoid 'a run on banks,' that is, it was referred to the functions of lender of last resource of the central bank, and could not be applied to the current situation: 'the "emergency" situation described in this article does *not* apply to the type of condition prevailing *today*. Neither the current facts of serious inflation nor of reconstruction needs justify the application of this article.' Compared to the interwar years the situation had radically changed after the invasion and Bloomfield admonished the monetary authorities that 'on the contrary, the existence of inflation makes it mandatory for the Bank of Korea ... to restrict its loans to banking institutions to a minimum,' Arthur I. Bloomfield to Mr Lee Ho Sang, 28 February 1952, AIBP.
28.   Arthur I. Bloomfield to Mr Lee Ho Sang, 28 February 1952, AIBP.
29.   A.I. Bloomfield to Mr. Moore, 'Korean Central Bank Legislation', Federal Reserve Bank of New York – Office Correspondence, 20 April 1950, AIBP.

References

Alacevich, M. and P.F. Asso, 2009, 'Money Doctoring after World War II: Arthur I. Bloomfield and the Federal Reserve Missions to South Korea,' *History of Political Economy*, 41(2) (Summer): 249–70.

Backhouse, R., B. Coats, J.B. Davis, H. Hagemann, and M.E. Sent, 2005, 'Perspectives on Michael A. Bernstein's *A Perilous Progress: Economists and Public Purpose in Twentieth-Century America*,' *European Journal of the History of Economic Thought*, 12(1): 127–46.

Bernstein, M.A., 2001, *A Perilous Progress: Economists and Public Purpose in Twentieth-Century America*, Princeton, NJ: Princeton University Press.

Bloomfield, A.I., 1940, 'The Significance of Outstanding Securities in the International Movement of Capital,' *Canadian Journal of Economics and Political Science*, 6(4) (November): 495–524.

———, 1942–43, 'The Mechanism of Adjustment of the American Balance of Payments: 1919–1929,' *Quarterly Journal of Economics*, LVII(3) (May): 333–77.

———, 1944, 'Operations of the American Exchange Stabilization Fund,' *Review of Economic Statistics*, 26(2) (May): 69–87.

———, 1946, 'Post-war Control of International Capital Movements,' *American Economic Review*, XXXVI(2) Supplement (May): 687–709.

———, 1950, *Capital Imports and the American Balance of Payments, 1934–1939*, Chicago: University of Chicago Press.

———, 1954a, 'Speculative and Flight Movements of Capital in Post-war International Finance,' Princeton Studies in International Finance, No. 3, Princeton University.

———, 1954b, 'Three Studies on United States Foreign Economic Relations,' *Review of Economics and Statistics*, 36 (February): 109–12.

———, 1957, 'Some Problems of Central Banking in Underdeveloped Countries,' *Journal of Finance*, 12(2): 190–204.

———, 1959, 'Monetary Policy under the International Gold Standard: 1880–1914,' New York, Federal Reserve Bank of New York.

———, 1963, *Short-term Capital Movements under the Pre-1914 Gold Standard*, Princeton, NJ: Princeton University Press.

———, 1994, *Essays in the History of International Economic Thought*, Aldershot, UK and Brookfield, USA: Edward Elgar.

——— and J.P. Jensen, 1951, 'Banking Reform in South Korea,' New York, Federal Reserve Bank of New York.

Choi, Y.B., 1997, 'The Americanization of Economics in Korea,' in A.W. Coats (ed.), *The Post-1945 Internationalization of Economics*, Annual Supplement to vol. 28, *History of Political Economy*, Durham and London: Duke University Press, pp. 97–122.

Clarke, S.V.O., 1967, 'Central Bank Cooperation: 1924–31,' New York, Federal Reserve Bank of New York.

Cleveland, H. van B., 1976, 'The International Monetary System in the Interwar Period,' in B.M. Rowland (ed.), *Balance of Power or Hegemony: the Interwar Monetary System*, New York: New York University Press.

Cunliffe Report, 1918, *First Interim Report of the Committee on Currency and Foreign Exchanges after the War*, Cmnd 9182, London: HMSO.

De Cecco, M., 1984, *The International Gold Standard: Money and Empire*, 2nd edn, New York: St Martin's Press.

Eichengreen, B., 1989[1994], 'House Calls of the Money Doctor: the Kemmerer Missions to Latin America, 1917–1931,' in Guillermo Calvo et al. (eds), *Debt, Stabilization, and Development: Essays in Memory of Carlos Díaz-Alejandro*, Oxford, Blackwell; reprinted in Paul W. Drake (ed.), 1994, *Money Doctors, Foreign Debts, and Economic Reforms in Latin America from the 1980s to the Present*, Wilmington, DE: Scholarly Resources, pp. 110–32.

———, 1992, *Golden Fetters: the Gold Standard and the Great Depression, 1919–1939*, New York and Oxford: Oxford University Press.

Ethier, W.J. and R.C. Marston, 1985, 'Introduction,' in *International Financial Markets and Capital Movements: a Symposium in Honour of Arthur I. Bloomfield*, Princeton Essays in International Finance, N. 157: 1–6.

Fisher, I., 1919, 'Economists in Public Service,' *American Economic Review*, Supplement, 9 (March): 5–21.

Flanders, M.J., 1989, *International Monetary Economics, 1870–1960: Between the Classical and the New Classical*, Cambridge: Cambridge University Press.

Guttentag, J. and R. Herring, 1985, 'Funding Risk in the International Inter-bank Market,' in *International Financial Markets and Capital Movements: a Symposium in Honour of Arthur I. Bloomfield*, Princeton Essays in International Finance, N. 157: 19-32.

Helleiner, E., 2003, 'The Southern Side of "Embedded Liberalism": America's Unorthodox Money Doctoring during the Early Post-1945 Years,' in Marc Flandreau (ed.), *Money Doctors: the Experience of International Financial Advising 1850–2000*, London and New York: Routledge, pp. 249–75.

Kemmerer, E., 1927, 'Economic Advisory Work for Governments,' *American Economic Review*, Supplement, 17 (March): 1–12.

Lindert, P.H., 1969, *Key Currencies and Gold, 1900–1913*, Princeton Studies in International Finance, N. 24.

Meltzer, A.H., 2003, *A History of the Federal Reserve, vol. 1: 1913–1951*, Chicago: University of Chicago Press.

Nurkse, R., 1961, *Equilibrium and Growth in the World Economy: Economic Essays by Ragnar Nurkse*, ed. G. Haberler and R.M. Stern, Cambridge, MA: Harvard University Press.

Park, J.H. (ed.), 2002, *Monetary Policy in Korea*, Seoul: Bank of Korea.

Seidel, R.N., 1972, 'American Reformers Abroad: the Kemmerer Missions in South America, 1923–1931,' *Journal of Economic History*, 32(1): 520–45; reprinted in Paul W. Drake (ed.), 1994, *Money Doctors, Foreign Debts, and Economic Reforms in Latin America from the 1980s to the Present*, Wilmington, DE: Scholarly Resources, pp. 86–109.

Tamagna, F.M., 1952, 'Review of *Banking Reform in South Korea*', *Journal of Political Economy*, 60(1): 86–7.

Triffin, R., 1946, 'Monetary and Banking Reform in Paraguay,' Washington, DC, Board of Governors of the Federal Reserve System.

———, 1964, *The Evolution of the International Monetary System: Historical Reappraisal and Future Perspectives*, Princeton Studies in International Finance, N. 12.

Vining, R., 1939, 'Suggestions of Keynes in the Writings of Veblen,' *Journal of Political Economy*, 47(5) (October): 692–704.

Name Index

Aaronson, Susan   55, 64
Acheson, Dean   41, 55
Adams, Henry C.   230, 232
Adams, Thomas S.   177
Alacevich, Michele   5, 126, 130, 131, 245, 263
Aldrich, Winthrop W.   211
Alsop, Joseph W.   110
Angell, James W.   112, 138, 141, 142, 177, 235
Arrow, Kenneth   128
Asher, Robert E.   63, 64
Asso, Pier Francesco   4, 5, 58, 234, 235, 245, 263
Axtell, Robert   101

Backhouse, Roger   243
Bagehot, Walter   186, 229, 235
Baily, Martin N.   131
Baldwin, Stanley   164
Ball, George W.   54, 55, 57
Barber, William J.   55, 64, 137, 177, 182, 234
Barco, President Virgilio   110, 128
Barnett, George E.   231
Baumol, William   128
Beach, W. Edwards   152, 176, 177
Beckhart, B.H.   209
Bell, Daniel W.   21
Bentham, Jeremy   229, 231
Berle, Adolph   14, 22, 41, 70
Bernstein, Edward M.   19, 209, 217, 238
Bernstein, Michael A.   181, 209, 234, 243
Beveridge, William   139, 147, 164, 173, 177, 231
Bewley, Kenneth   56
Bidwell, Percy W.   28, 33, 56, 57, 64, 65, 67
Binmore, Ken   100
Black, Stanley W.   19

Blitch, Charles P.   129, 131, 134, 137, 138, 139, 142, 143, 145, 154, 155, 157, 159, 160, 161, 164, 166, 167, 171, 176, 177
Bloomfield, Arthur I.   1, 2, 5, 55, 64, 128, 235, 245–64
Bloomfield, Dorothy   262
Blum, John Morton   20, 21
Blum, Léon   13
Bober, M.M.   148, 149, 176
Bogart, E.L.   229, 231
Bogen, J.J.   209
Böhm-Bawerk, Eugen von   140
Boileau, Etienne   229
Bordo, Michael   15, 20, 21, 54, 61, 64–6, 235
Borneuf, A.E.   209
Boughton, James M.   2, 10, 16, 19, 131, 132
Bowley, Arthur L.   172, 228
Bowman, Isaiah   57
Bronfenbrenner, Martin   128
Brown, William A.   209
Brownlow, Louis   120
Bullock, Charles J.   107, 137, 144, 152, 162, 178, 234
Burbank, Harold   107, 137, 152, 153, 178
Burns, Arthur   4, 95
Burns, Evelyn   148
Bush, G.W.   4

Cairnes, John E.   229, 232
Callcott, Wilfrid H.   55, 65
Calomaris, Charles W.   75, 89, 130
Cánfora, Elba   128
Cannan, Edwin   107, 135, 147, 173, 174
Carlson, Valdemar   137, 138, 140, 177
Carraway, William E.   263, 264
Carver, T.N.   107, 137, 162
Cassel, Gustav   158, 176

Catchings, Waddill   73, 85, 168
Catto, Lord   206, 237
Cesarano, Filippo   54, 59, 65
Chalmers, Thomas   229
Chamberlin, Edward H.   134, 137,
     141, 145, 156, 159, 176, 177
Chandra, Ramesh   126, 132, 134,
     141, 177
Chang, Jung   124, 132
Chazeau, Melvin de   138, 139, 147,
     149, 152, 154, 176
Chennault, General Claire   123
Chiang Kai-shek   122, 123
Chickering, Jesse   128
Choi, Young Back   255
Churchill, Winston S.   125
Clark, Colin   137, 143, 171, 172, 176
Clark, John Bates   170, 232
Clark, John Maurice   112, 232
Clarke, Stephen V.O.   11, 182, 251
Cleveland, Harold van B.   249, 250
Clower, Robert W.   128
Coats, A.W. 'Bob'   234
Cohen, Benjamin J.   28, 33, 34, 41,
     61, 66, 182, 183
Cole, Arthur H.   138, 145, 147, 152
Cole, George D.H.   56, 171
Cole, Margaret   171
Collado, Emilio   21, 63
Commons, John R.   232, 247
Corden, Max   128
Cournot, A.   159
Craig, Bruce   19
Crist, William E.   264
Crowther, Geoffrey   56, 224
Crum, W.L.   137
Currie, Lauchlin   1, 2, 3, 4, 8, 28,
     35–37, 58, 59, 63, 67, 70, 73–4, 85,
     86, 89, 90, 105–33, 134, 137–41,
     146–54, 176, 177, 197, 235

Dalton, Hugh   107
Davenport, Henry B.   228
Davidson, Paul   128
Davis, Norman H.   54, 57
Davis, Ronnie J.   234
De Cecco, Marcello   52, 56, 61, 65,
     182, 233, 234, 249, 251

de Vries, Margaret Garritsen   237
DeBeers, J.S.   21, 22
Diamond, Douglas   130
Diebold, William   28, 57, 234
Dillistin, William H.   263
Dimand, Robert   262
Dobson, Alan P.   55, 65
Domar, Evsey   94, 128
Domhoff, William G.   27, 42, 54, 58,
     61, 65
Dorfman, Joseph   187, 234
Dornbusch, Rudiger   105
Douglas, Paul   92, 246
Drummond, Ian M.   54, 65
Duarte, Pedro G.   262
Duesenberry, James S.   80, 234
Dulles, Allen   125
Dulles, Eleanor L.   138, 139, 155,
     164, 177
Dulles, John Foster   138, 165
Dunbar, Charles F.   232
Duncan, G.A.   172

Eccles, Marriner S.   1, 3, 4, 69–90,
     105, 110, 112, 114, 117, 118, 119,
     128, 129, 132, 205, 210
Eckes, Alfred   41, 42, 49, 58, 61, 63–5
Edgeworth, Francis Y.   135, 175
Edie, Lionel   149, 167
Eichengreen, Barry   54, 59, 64–6,
     245, 249, 251
Ellis, Howard S.   156, 138
Ely, Richard T.   157, 177
Ely, Theodore S.   232
Ethier, Wilfred J.   247, 254
Ellsworth, P.T.   2, 8, 111, 129, 132

Fairbank, John   110
Feis, Herbert   41, 55, 57
Fetter, Frank W.   128, 138, 139, 157,
     158, 229, 234
Fiorito, Luca   4, 58, 263
Fisher, Irving   129, 137, 138, 158,
     159, 181, 228, 229, 234, 243, 244
Fishlow, Albert   182, 235
Flanders, June M.   8, 54, 182, 235,
     249, 253
Flanders, Randolph   28

Fluegel, Felix   229
Foley, Duncan   101
Ford, Henry   144
Foster, W.T.   73, 85, 168
Foxwell, H.   163
Frank, Lawrence K.   229
Frank, Robert   101
Fraser, L.   211, 237
Freidel, Frank   125, 132
Friedman, Milton   2, 4, 80, 86, 89,
   92, 107, 109, 110, 114, 130, 132,
   133, 184

Galbraith, John Kenneth   77, 80, 85,
   89, 90, 114, 119, 132
Gardner, Henry B.   228
Gardner, Richard N.   48, 49, 51, 52,
   55–8, 62–5, 182, 237, 238
Gardner, Walter   41, 220
Gay, Edwin F.   152, 153, 159, 162,
   163, 230
George, Henry   230
Georgescu-Roegen, Nicholas   128
Gintis, Herb   100
Goldenweiser, Emanuel A.   41, 87,
   220
Goodrich, Carter   57
Goodhue, Everett W.   154
Goodwin, Craufurd D.   54, 65
Goodwin, Richard   110
Gorman, W.M.   128
Gorsky, Anatoly   124
Graham, Frank T.   235, 263
Gregory, Theodore E.   135, 176, 178
Guttentag, Jack   247

Haas, George C.   7, 12, 20–2
Haberler, Gottfried   7, 107, 108
Halifax, Edward F.L.W., Lord   57
Halliday, Jon   124, 132
Hamilton, Earl J.   128, 138, 139,
   159
Hammond, Matthew B.   231
Hansen, Alvin H.   1, 3, 24, 25, 27–9,
   31, 34–42, 45–61, 63–5, 67, 73, 85,
   87, 88, 105, 119, 121, 132, 185, 233,
   237
Harding, Warren G.   144

Harris, John R.   109
Harris, Seymour S.   80, 108, 137, 138,
   160
Harrod, Roy   18, 19, 56, 66, 92, 102,
   210, 237
Hawkins, Harry   57, 64
Hawtrey, Ralph G.   107, 132, 168,
   176, 210, 233, 235, 237
Heath, Milton   137, 145
Helleiner, Eric   233, 245, 262, 264
Henderson, Hubert D.   31
Henderson, Leon   116, 117
Henning, C. Randall   22
Herring, Richard   247
Hickerson, John D.   57
Hicks, John R.   4, 98, 232
Hildebrand, Bruno   231
Hildreth, Clifford   128
Hirschman, Albert O.   109, 110, 130,
   191
Hitler, Adolf   26
Ho Sang, Lee   257, 263, 264
Hollander, Jacob   228
Hoover, Herbert   108, 112, 182, 236
Hopkins, Harry   116, 121
Horsefield, J. Keith   9, 17, 18, 22, 41,
   57, 60–2, 66, 210, 214, 235, 237,
   238
Howey, Richard S.   138, 161
Howson, Susan   212, 238
Hull, Cordell   31, 51, 55–7, 64, 131
Hume, David   183, 194, 229
Humphrey, Thomas   114
Hutt, William   232

Ikenberry, John G.   54, 66, 182, 234,
   235

James, Harold   54, 66
Janeway, Elliot   122
Jenks, Jeremy   230
Jensen, John P.   254–8, 261–4
Jevons, William S.   149, 153, 169,
   229
Johnson, Alvin   162, 178, 232
Johnson, Harry   248
Johnson, Lyndon B.   2, 4, 95
Jones, Byrd   110, 114, 131

Jones, George T.   144, 148, 152, 176
Jones, Homer   128

Kahn, Richard   93–4
Kaldor, Nicholas   132, 134, 137–8,
   139, 141, 160, 163, 178
Kalecki, Michael   94
Kemmerer, Edwin   138, 158, 181,
   230, 234, 244, 245, 259
Kesselring, Marshal Albert   106, 124,
   125
Keynes, John Maynard   6, 10, 12, 16,
   18, 19, 31, 34, 36, 39, 42–7, 50, 53,
   60–3, 66, 67, 73–4, 78, 83–6, 88, 89,
   90, 109, 118, 119, 121, 122, 132,
   134, 158, 164, 168, 175, 176, 184,
   185, 186, 193, 194, 198, 201, 204,
   205, 206, 207, 209, 210, 212–18,
   220, 223–7, 229, 233–7, 247, 252
Keyserling, Leon   88
Kindleberger, Charles P.   58, 65, 80,
   109, 132, 185, 248
King, Wilford I.   228
Klausinger, Hansjoerg   130
Knies, Karl   229
Knight, Frank H.   92, 134, 137, 138,
   156, 160, 176, 246, 247
Knight, Melvin M.   138, 164, 176,
   178
Kobyakov, Julius   131
Kreps, Juanita Morris   128
Krock, Arthur   120
Krost, Martin   115, 132
Kuznets, Simon   233
Kydland, Finn E.   20

Laidler, David   8, 66, 107, 111,
   129, 130, 132, 183, 233, 235,
   236
Lange, Oskar   263
Lake, David A.   56, 66
Laski, Harold   107, 170–1, 177, 178
Lasser, William   61, 66
Lazenby, Rosemary A.   233
Leeson, Robert   4, 55, 60, 66, 84, 88,
   89, 132, 133, 233, 236, 262
Leijonhufvud, Axel   128
Leslie, Thomas Cliffe   186, 232, 235

Lewis, H. Gregg   128
Lindert, Peter   251
Liu, H.C.K.   184
Lleras, President Alberto   126
Lubin, Harold   116, 117

MacArthur, Douglas   3
Macaulay, Thomas B.   150
MacCulloch, John R.   229
Machlup, Fritz   112, 130
Maddox, William P.   57
Mair, Jessie   139
Malthus, Thomas R.   229, 233
Mankiw, Gregory   4, 97, 99
Mao Zedong   123–4, 132
Marget, Arthur   152, 176
Marot, Helen   228
Marshall, Alfred   27, 136. 137, 148,
   153, 164, 168, 169, 175, 229, 232
Marston, Richard C.   247, 254
Martin, William McChesney   3, 4
Martineau, Harriet   229
Marx, Karl   169, 230, 232
Mason, Edward S.   63, 64, 137, 145,
   170, 176, 178
Mazur, Paul   117
McCabe, Thomas   3
McCarthy, Joseph   106
McCloskey, Deirdre   100
McGregor, D.H.   171
Meade, James   34, 212, 238
Means, Gardiner C.   137, 138, 154,
   176
Meardon, Steve   262
Mehrling, Perry G.   55, 66, 131, 133,
   134, 135, 138, 176, 177, 178, 233,
   262
Meltzer, Allan   69, 73, 75–7, 79–80,
   82, 85, 86, 89, 183, 185, 207, 210,
   211, 234, 235, 236, 237, 244
Menger, Carl   128
Menger, Karl   128
Merriam, Charles   119
Metzler, Lloyd   86, 128
Mikesell, R.F.   209
Mill, James   229
Mill, John Stuart   27, 168, 229, 230,
   231, 232

Miller, John P.   32, 152
Millis, Harry A.   232
Mills, Fred C.   229
Minter, William   54, 67
Mints, Lloyd W.   263
Mitchell, Wesley C.   112, 136, 169, 178, 181, 229, 232
Modigliani, Franco   86, 128
Moggridge, Donald   19, 66, 212, 238
Moore, Henry L.   229, 264
Morgan, Mary   181, 234
Morgenstern, Oskar   92, 128, 136, 173, 175, 178, 246
Morgenthau, Henry Jr   4, 8, 13, 15, 17, 18, 20–2, 28, 41, 42, 47, 51, 54, 75–6, 87, 116, 117, 118, 130, 183, 197, 199, 210, 211, 212, 219, 235
Moulton, Harold G.   65
Mundell, Robert A.   183, 233, 235

Nathan, Robert   114
Nearing, Scott   148
Nerozzi, Sebastiano   3, 234
Newcomb, Simon   232
Newman, William J.   54, 66
Nietzsche, Friedrich   150
Nixon, Richard M.   2, 4, 125
Norman, Montagu   214, 215, 222, 237
North, Douglass C.   128
Notter, Harley   41, 55, 57, 66
Nurkse, Ragnar   249

Ohlin, Bertil   7, 137, 166, 176, 178
Oliphant, Herman   21
Okun, Arthur   1, 4, 95–9
Opie, Redvers   54, 56–8, 63, 66, 210, 237

Pareto, Vilfredo   228
Park, J.H.   260
Parker, Carleton   228
Pastrana, Misael   110, 126
Pasvolsky, Leo   27, 33, 41, 54, 55, 57, 63–5
Patinkin, Don   110, 114, 128, 133
Patten, Simon   232

Peltzman, Sam   130
Penrose, Edith F.   64, 66
Perlman, Mark   128
Phillips, J. Ronnie   130, 133
Pigou, Arthur C.   137, 164, 229
Plehn, Carl C.   229
Prebisch, Raúl   109, 110
Pressnell, Leslie S.   55–8, 62, 66, 212, 237

Quesnay, François   229

Rasminsky, Louis   56, 201, 207, 236, 237, 238
Ratchford, Benjamin   128
Rees, Albert   128
Rees, David   19, 21, 61, 66
Reith, John Lord   56
Ricardo, David   168, 187, 229, 230, 233, 235
Riddle, J.H.   211
Riefler, Winfield W.   28, 55
Rignano, Eugenio   228,
Robbins, Lionel C.   31, 47, 55, 61, 63, 63, 66, 138, 139, 162, 178
Robertson, Dennis H.   42, 56, 62, 93, 220, 233, 237
Robinson, Joan   93–4
Rogers, James Harvey   155
Romer, P.M.   134, 178
Roosa, Robert V.   210, 237
Roosevelt, F.D.   3, 25, 32, 52, 54–7, 61, 69–73, 75, 77, 84, 85, 105, 106, 108, 112, 113, 116, 118–25, 129, 132, 183, 196, 212
Roosevelt, James   117
Roscher, Wilhelm   231
Rowland, Benjamin M.   56, 66, 182
Ruggie, John G.   211
Ruml, Beardsley   227
Rutherford, Malcolm   181, 234

Salant, Walter   130
Salant, William   130, 110, 113, 114, 115
Salter, Arthur Sir   56
Samuelson, Paul A.   74, 87, 95, 105–6, 114–15, 119, 129, 136, 137, 176, 235

Sandilands, Roger J. 4, 8, 67, 73, 74, 84, 85, 86, 87, 90, 105, 109–14, 116, 119, 124, 126, 127, 129–33, 134, 135, 138, 141, 176–8, 236
Santoro, Carlo Maria 54, 55, 67
Say, Jean Baptiste 229
Schmöller, Gustav 159, 231
Schulze-Gaevernitz, Gerhart von 148
Schumpeter, Joseph A. 107, 108, 110, 129, 135, 145, 176, 178, 186, 233
Schwartz, Anna 2, 15, 21, 89, 107, 110, 114, 132, 235
Scitovsky, Tibor 128
Seager, Henry R. 229
Seidle, R.N. 245
Seligman, Edwin A.G. 151, 162, 163, 178, 229
Senior, Nassau 229
Sheehan, Michael J. 54, 67
Shepherd, Geoffrey 138, 166
Sherwood, Sidney 229
Shields, Murray 65, 67, 68
Shoup, Laurence H. 41, 54–7, 67, 234
Shubik, Martin 128
Simons, Henry 92
Sirc, Susan 173, 178
Skidelsky, Robert 10, 18, 19, 45, 62, 67, 78, 90, 93, 235, 237
Smart, William G. 232
Smith, Adam 168, 170, 228, 229, 230, 231, 233
Smith, Vernon 128
Snyder, Carl 233
Soon Chun, Yong 264
Southard, Frank O. 21, 22
Spengler, Joseph J. 233
Spiethoff, Arthur 233
Sprague, Oliver M.W. 232
Sproul, Allan 36, 58, 59, 80, 207, 210, 237, 247
Spykman, Nicholas J. 54, 55, 67
Staley, Eugene 49, 57, 59, 63
Stalin, Joseph 125
Steels, Jean 154, 179
Stein, Herbert 69, 87, 90, 115, 133
Steindl, Frank 109, 110, 114, 129, 133

Steuart, James 229
Stinebower, Leroy 57
Stolper, Wolfgang F. 128
Sumner, William G. 228, 230, 232
Sweezy, Alan 111, 113, 114

Tamagna, Frank 256, 260, 263
Tarshis, Lorie 80, 119
Taussig, Frank W. 2, 7, 17, 57, 107, 111, 135, 137, 138, 140, 142, 145, 147, 148, 149, 150, 151, 153, 156, 167, 176, 178, 181, 183, 184, 186, 228, 229
Tavlas, George S. 234
Tawney, Richard H. 107
Taylor, Fred M. 230
Taylor, Myron C. 55, 57
Taylor, Overton H. 138, 167, 176
Tead, Ordway 228
Telser, Lester 110, 114, 129, 133
Thirlwall, Anthony P. 134, 179
Tobin, James 55, 57, 95, 248
Todaro, Michael P. 109, 110
Tooke, Thomas 229
Triffin, Robert 7, 244, 245, 249, 256, 258, 259, 261
Truman, Harry S. 3, 7, 51, 88
Tucker, Rufus S. 234
Tugan-Baranowsky, Mikhail 233
Tugwell, Rexford G. 70, 71, 84, 90, 167, 229
Turner, Henry Jackson 157

Upgreen, Arthur R. 57
Usher, Abbot P. 153, 176, 231

Van Dormael, A. 185, 237
Veblen, Thorstein 162, 169, 229, 232, 247
Vernengo, M. 3
Viner, Jacob 1, 2, 3, 7, 20, 24, 25, 27–29, 31, 33, 35–64, 66, 67, 110, 111, 112, 113, 130, 148, 149, 151, 181, 183, 185, 186, 197, 233, 235, 246, 247
Vining, Routledge 247
Volcker, Paul 233

Wagner, Adolph 230
Wakatabe, Masazumi 130
Wala, Michael 54, 67
Walker, Francis A. 232
Walker, Gilbert 138, 143, 171
Wallace, Neil 130
Walley, David 22
Wallich, Henry 256–8, 261, 263, 264
Watkins, G.P. 176
Watkins, M.W. 176
Webb, Beatrice 231, 232
Webb, Sidney 231, 232
Weintraub, Sidney 94, 102, 128
Welles, Sumner 14, 27, 55, 57, 131, 133
Wells, David A. 232
Whitaker, Arthur P. 55, 68
White, Anne Terry 8
White, Harry Dexter 1, 2, 4, 5, 6–23, 34, 36, 39–43, 47, 53, 58, 61–4, 66, 107, 108, 111, 112, 125, 129, 131, 132, 137, 138, 147–50, 152–3, 176, 179, 183, 184, 185, 186, 201, 204, 205, 208, 210–15, 219, 220, 221, 223, 236, 237
White, Nathan 19
Wicksell, Knut 166, 233
Williams, John H. 28, 36, 58, 62, 68, 107, 119, 137, 146, 151, 157, 158, 176, 181–220, 233–8, 245, 251, 263
Willis, Henry Parker 112, 181
Winant, John G. 57
Wolfe, Robert B. 228
Wood, Stuart 232
Working, Holbrook 176

Yeager, Leland B. 248
Young, Allyn A. 1, 2, 4, 107, 112, 119, 121, 127, 129, 130, 131, 132, 133, 230
Young, Evan 165
Young, John P. 63
Young, Peyton 10
Yule, G. Udny 157

Subject Index

Advisory Committee on Post-War
 Foreign Policy 57
American Bankers Association 182,
 211
American Economic Association 1,
 27, 114, 144, 174, 180, 243
American Keynesians 27, 98, 252,
 253, 259
American Statistical Association 144,
 174
Anglo-American Economic
 Cooperation 29–34
Arthur I. Bloomfield papers 261, 262
Atlantic Charter 30, 55
Austrian School 108, 112, 169, 175

balance of payments equilibrium 31,
 35, 39, 45, 51, 56, 58, 191, 192,
 194, 195, 246, 253, 254
balance of payments theory 182,
 191, 193, 194, 252
balance of power system 26, 54
balanced budgets 108, 115, 116,
 117, 130
Bank of Canada 201, 204
Bank of Chosun 255, 256, 259
Bank of England 13, 21, 217, 251,
 252
Bank of Korea 5, 245, 254–64
Banking Act (1935) 82, 86, 114, 198,
 199
Bentham's psychological hedonism
 169
Bloomfield mission 245, 248,
 254–64
branch banking 149, 154
Brazil 15, 21
Bretton Woods conference 2, 6, 9,
 18, 50–2, 61–2, 124, 184, 185,
 205, 209, 211, 218
Bretton Woods system 1, 124, 201
British Association section F 174

British Commonwealth 28–30
British empiricism 169
British Supply Council of North
 America 56
Brookings Institution 96, 110, 111,
 151

Cambridge cash-balance approach,
 and oral tradition 175, 136, 168
Cambridge economics 93–4
Canada 148, 246
capital movements 16–18, 38, 40,
 48–9, 112, 187, 190, 192, 193,
 194, 195, 196, 204, 217, 246–54,
 261
central bank cooperation 60, 196,
 208, 251
central banking in developing
 countries 245, 254–64
central banks 69, 80, 82, 84, 88, 114,
 194, 197, 217, 249–51, 261
Chicago economists 27, 55, 86, 92,
 112, 114, 184, 246, 247
Chicago plan for monetary reform
 130, 133
Chicago School, University of
 Chicago 1, 2, 4, 86, 110, 174,
 176, 151, 246–8
Chicago tradition 132, 133, 129,
 178, 179, 183
Chile 15, 21
China 15, 106, 110, 111, 122–4, 126,
 128
'China hands' 123
classical school 168, 169, 186
Cold War 3, 124–5, 132
Colombia 105, 110, 111, 112, 126,
 130, 131
Colombian Savings and Loan Institute
 127
Columbia University, Butler Library
 162

commodity corporation   35, 57, 58
comparative advantages   186, 188
conditionality   45–6, 185, 205, 215,
   216, 217, 219
convertibility   207, 249–51
cost controversy   164
Council of Economic Advisers   1, 2,
   3, 81, 88, 95, 131
Council on Foreign Relations   24–37,
   30, 54–5, 185, 234
Council of Italian-American Affairs
   130
countercyclical policy   35, 40, 49, 63,
   95, 97
credit creation   152, 198, 199, 246
Cuba   13, 14
'Curried Keynesianism'   116

deficit spending   76, 255, 257, 258
de-rating Bill   164
dollar shortage   202, 203
Duke University special collections
   library   91, 111, 128, 173, 262

economic advisers   181, 243–5, 247,
   248, 254–64
The Economist   89
Employment Act (1946)   79, 88, 89,
   131
employment strategies   110
Encyclopedia of the Social Sciences
   162, 178
European Payments Union
European Recovery Program *see*
   Marshall Plan
exchange control   30, 31, 37, 195,
   196, 202, 204, 206, 211, 212, 216,
   217, 246, 256
exchange rate, exchange rate systems
   (fixed, flexible)   9, 36, 46, 130,
   193, 196, 201, 202, 204, 207, 208,
   209, 211, 212, 213, 216, 217, 248,
   250, 251, 253
Exchange Stabilization Fund (US)
   14, 15, 16, 21, 254

Federal Bureau of Investigation (FBI)
   reading room   19

Federal Reserve Bank of New York   2,
   4, 58, 80, 82, 161, 182, 183, 184,
   185, 197, 211, 212, 245–8, 256,
   259, 262, 263
Federal Reserve Bank of New York,
   Archive Section   220, 233
Federal Reserve Board   1, 3, 58, 61,
   107, 110, 111, 114, 119, 129, 183,
   184, 197, 198, 199, 200, 201, 202,
   204, 205, 206, 207, 210, 244
Federal Reserve economists   28, 41,
   36, 58, 59, 182, 183, 209, 244,
   245, 247, 249, 251, 256, 258,
   259–63
Firestone Tire Company   15
fiscal policy   35–6, 40, 53, 63, 70, 74,
   77, 83, 86, 97–8, 107, 114, 119
Flying Tigers   123
Foreign Economic Administration
   (FEA)   106, 124
Foreign Affairs   19, 184, 206, 212
France   13, 17
Freshman Brain Trust   85, 111, 113
full employment   29–35, 51, 58, 79,
   81, 82, 83, 84, 88, 121–2, 246

General Agreement on Tariffs and
   Trade (GATT)   26, 34
German historical school   169, 177
German hyperinflation   158, 168,
   176
Gold Reserve Act (US)   14
gold standard   11, 15, 17, 20, 26,
   38–40, 60, 87, 107, 112, 113, 130,
   186, 189, 190, 192, 193, 195, 196,
   203, 244, 245, 249, 251, 261, 262
Government Reorganization Act
   (1939)   119
Grand Area   28–9.
Great Depression   8, 69–75, 83, 86,
   87, 89, 90, 107, 108, 111, 113,
   129, 137, 197, 198, 200
Grolier encyclopedia   135, 176

Harris Foundation   112
Harry Dexter White papers in
   Princeton University   8, 11,
   20, 129

Harvard economists　10, 27, 106,
　111, 137, 176, 181
Harvard tradition　136, 141, 175
Harvard University Archives　167,
　234
Harvard University and Baker Library
　162, 163
Harvard University Fiscal Policy
　Seminar　2, 119
Havana conference (1940)　14
Henry Morgenthau papers　20, 54
Hot Springs Food Conference　56, 61
Hoover Institution　111, 128
House Committee on Un-American
　Activities (HUAC)　2, 125

IMF *see* International Monetary Fund
IMF conditionality *see* conditionality
imperial preference system *see* Ottawa
　Agreements
impossible trilemma　204
increasing returns　134, 144, 152,
　171, 172
inflationary finance　107, 255, 256,
　259, 260
institutional economics, and
　institutionalism and American
　institutionalists　95, 169
Inter-American Bank　14
International Bank for Reconstruction
　and Development (IBRD)　35, 38,
　41, 46–53
　see also World Bank
International Clearing Union *see*
　Keynes's plan
International Development Agency
　35, 46, 49, 52
International Finance Corporation
　52
international investments　40, 50,
　250
International Labor Office (ILO)　110
international liquidity　38, 40, 43,
　46, 59, 218
International Monetary Fund (IMF)
　1, 6, 7, 9–10, 16–18, 20, 35, 38,
　41–6, 202, 203, 204, 205, 206,
　207, 211, 213, 215, 216, 217, 218,
　219, 260

international monetary system　185,
　192, 193, 194, 205, 208, 245,
　249–52
international reconstruction finance
　corporation　31, 59
international trade adjustments　149,
　246
international trade agency　33, 35
international trade theory　149, 153,
　186, 187, 188, 189, 190, 191,
　192

Jacob Viner papers　54, 110
Japan　28–9, 4, 122, 123, 131, 254,
　255, 258

key currency plan/approach　35–46,
　183, 184, 185, 188, 192,193, 196,
　200–19, 251, 252, 263
Keynes's *General Theory*　74, 85, 92,
　105, 115, 119
Keynes's plan　15, 16, 35–46, 185,
　201, 202, 203, 204, 205, 208
Keynes's *Treatise on Money*　92, 198,
　204,
Keynesian revolution　83, 114
Keynesians　1, 4, 94, 127
Korea　3, 4, 5, 243, 245, 248, 254–64

Latin America　28, 256, 258–61
Lawrence College (Wisconsin)　7
League of Nations　1, 201, 202, 206,
　208, 213
Lend-Lease Act　4, 31–2, 123, 210
Liberia　15
loan negotiations　45, 51, 106
London School of Economics (LSE)
　107, 150
Luis Angel Arango library, Bogotá
　128

marginalists　169
Marriner S. Eccles papers, University
　of Utah　71, 72, 73, 74, 77, 78,
　79, 81, 82, 84, 85, 86, 97, 88, 89,
　110, 128
Marshall Plan　252
McCarthy era　106

Mexico 7, 13, 14
Monetary Board of the Bank of Korea
    255–9, 263
monetary policy 40, 53, 69, 70–7,
    79, 80, 81, 83, 84, 86, 87, 89, 111,
    112, 114, 129, 134, 197, 198, 199,
    200, 204, 217, 218, 244–52, 255,
    257, 259–63
monopolistic competition 134, 135
multilateral trade 10, 28, 29–33, 48,
    53, 202
multilateralism 11–14, 25, 29, 37–8,
    51–4, 184, 201, 202, 207, 212, 213
Mutual Aid Agreement 32, 57, 210

National Archives (US) 8, 21, 110,
    121, 129
National Security Agency 124
natural law 170–1
New Deal and New Dealers 36, 52,
    53, 73, 74, 77, 78, 82, 83, 84, 87,
    90, 105, 106, 110, 111, 115, 116,
    118, 119, 121, 122, 206
New Keynesians 97
New York Post 116
New York Times 112, 114, 130

Okun Gap 1–2
Okun's Law 95–6
open market operations 76, 112,
    200, 260
optimum currency areas 183, 208,
    209
Ottawa Agreements 30–2, 51

Paris peace conference (1919) 160,
    165
physiocrats 168, 170
Plan of the Four Strategies 126
portfolio approach 252, 254
post-war planning 25–8, 33, 41
price-specie-flow mechanism 149,
    183
Princeton University Library 54,
    110, 111, 129
prohibition 108, 129, 162
pump-priming 168

quantity theory 108, 129, 168,
    197

Real Bills Doctrine 70, 73, 75, 86,
    107, 108, 198
rent and quasi-rent 153, 164
reserve requirements, excess reserves
    and 100 percent reserve plan 75,
    76, 109, 114–15, 198, 247
Ricardian vice 186
rules of the game 60, 194
rural-urban migration 110
Rockefeller Foundation 27, 55, 176
Roosevelt administration 25–8, 70,
    72, 84, 113, 118, 124, 183, 212,
    216, 217
Roosevelt Presidential Library, Hyde
    Park, NY 54
Royal Institute for International
    Affairs 30

scarce currency clause 62, 212
Seeley G. Mudd Manuscript Library,
    Princeton University 8, 11, 20,
    54, 110
silver 14, 21
social security taxes 76, 118
Soviets, Soviet Union and Soviet
    intelligence 124–5, 131
stabilization policy 29–39, 183, 244,
    246, 260, 261
Stanford University 7, 111, 128, 162,
    173, 174
State Department 15, 24–8, 32–4, 41,
    50–2, 54–7, 63–4, 210
Sterling area 213, 215
Sterling balances 10, 30, 51, 201
Suez crisis 16
Sussex School 110
Switzerland and Swiss banks 106,
    124, 125

Temporary National Economic
    Committee (TNEC) 121, 119
transfer problem 187, 252–4
Triffin approach to monetary reform
    244, 245, 256, 258, 259, 261

Tripartite Agreement (1936) 11, 183, 196, 207
Truman administration 88

unemployment statistics 120
United Nations 125, 207
United Nations Habitat conference (1976) 127
United States Congress 42, 48, 50, 62, 64
United States Treasury 3, 6, 7, 10, 13, 17, 39, 41–2, 45, 48, 51, 64, 111, 113, 114, 184, 209, 210, 212, 217

velocity of circulation 149
'Venona' project 125, 126

wartime cooperation 124
Washington economists 125, 133
Washington monetary talks 211, 212, 213, 215, 219
Washington Post 130
Wells prize 7, 108, 157
Western Hemisphere 28–30, 55
White plan 9, 15, 37–46, 185, 201, 202, 203, 204, 205, 208,
Williams papers 220, 233–4
World Bank 19, 46–50, 126, 130, 202, 207, 208, 210
World Economic Conference (London 1933) 11, 174
World War II 26–8, 128, 201, 261, 263